MUNICIPAL MANAGEMENT SERIES

Public Relations in
Local Government

THE MUNICIPAL MANAGEMENT SERIES

EDITOR

William H. Gilbert

Metropolitan Washington
Council of Governments

Public Relations in
Local Government

Published for the
Institute for Training in Municipal Administration
by the
International City Management Association

MUNICIPAL MANAGEMENT SERIES

David S. Arnold
EDITOR

Managing the Modern City

Principles and Practice of Urban Planning

Management Policies in Local Government Finance

Local Government Personnel Administration

Municipal Police Administration

Municipal Fire Administration

Urban Public Works Administration

Community Health Services

Effective Supervisory Practices

Public Relations in Local Government

Policy Analysis in Local Government

Developing the Municipal Organization

Managing Municipal Leisure Services

Small Cities Management Training Program

Library of Congress Cataloging in Publication Data

Main entry under title:

Public relations in local government.

   (Municipal management series)
   Bibliography: p.
   Includes index.
   1. Public relations—Local government.
I. Gilbert, William H., 1931–   II. Institute for
Training in Municipal Administration. III. Series.
JS89.P8   659.2′9′352   75–29400
ISBN 0–87326–012–0

Printed in the United States of America

Foreword

The rationale for the publication by the International City Management Association of this book, *Public Relations in Local Government,* is well expressed in the direct and practical opening words of its first chapter:

If you are in government, you are in public relations. You may not know it or you may not like it, but it is a fact, and to ignore that fact is to live at your own peril. This book is intended to help you recognize the public relations element in all the things your local government or regional organization does and to help you make certain your responsibilities are met in a way which will bring credit to you and your agency while advancing your programs for the common good.

As the above statement—written by an experienced practitioner—suggests, public relations is indeed a critical area of local government life. As the quotation also suggests, it may not perhaps receive the recognition accorded to other, more traditional, areas of local government management; the proficiency of the modern manager must depend in part, however, on an understanding and efficient use of public relations. It is only fitting, therefore, that the International City Management Association—which aims at increasing the proficiency of municipal administrators and strengthening the quality of local government through professional management—should be publishing this book as part of its Municipal Management Series.

This book provides a thorough treatment of public relations as applied to local government. It will serve the needs of all those involved in local government administration, but particularly of city and county managers, department heads, and officials of regional organizations. The book will also be of practical use to students and teachers in the field of public administration and in schools of journalism; to mayors, councilmen, and councilwomen; to media representatives and all those members of the public relations profession whose work brings them into contact with local government; and, indeed, to all concerned citizens who are interested in the developing field of public opinion, public attitudes, and public information—and in the managerial response to such factors.

Public Relations in Local Government replaces *Municipal Public Relations,* which first appeared in the Municipal Management Series in 1966. The editor for the present book is William H. Gilbert, Director of Public Affairs, Metropolitan Washington Council of Governments. Mr. Gilbert has drawn upon nearly thirty years of experience as a reporter and author, and as an official both in local government and for a prominent metropolitan organization. He has built on the admirable foundation laid down by the editor of *Municipal Public Relations,* Desmond L. Anderson, then Associate Dean of the School of Public Administration, University of Southern California. The result is an effective contemporary text that properly considers public relations to be an integral, rather than a peripheral, component of management practice in local government.

Three general comments may be usefully made about the overall structure and thrust of this book. First, the managerial perspective is emphasized throughout. That is, theory, research, and analysis are given due attention—but only insofar as they help enlarge the practicing manager's perceptions of his or her day-to-day operations in the public relations field. Wherever possible, therefore, the authors have taken pains to interject realistic, practical examples into their discussions; to clarify the terminology and theoretical constructs that are an essential part of such disciplines as sociology and psychology; and, generally, to strike an appropriate balance between theory and practical application.

Second, the authors have been selected on the basis of their expertise in the particular areas covered by their chapters and have been given appropriate latitude to discuss their subjects. We believe that the resulting lively blend of perspectives enhances the overall utility of the book. Some authors have concentrated on more practical applications, others have considered some of the basic policy questions involved: taken as a whole, however, the book provides an in-depth, managerial approach to local government public relations that, we believe, is not available elsewhere.

Third, this book, like others in the Municipal Management Series, has been prepared for the Institute for Training in Municipal Administration. The institute offers in-service training specifically designed for local government officials whose jobs are to plan, direct, and coordinate the work of others. The institute has been sponsored since 1934 by the International City Management Association.

We are grateful to the large number of local government professionals and other experts in the field who have made suggestions concerning the shape and content of this book. We would like to make particular acknowledgment of the work of the editor, William H. Gilbert, whose own professionalism significantly enhanced and expedited all aspects of the editorial work on the book, and of the assistance rendered by Ray Hiebert, Dean, College of Journalism, University of Maryland, in making an extensive review of the book. We would like to acknowledge also the assistance of the news staff of WMAL–TV, Washington, D.C., in providing technical information about their operation, and the bibliographic assistance material given by the Research Information Center of the Public Relations Society of America.

David S. Arnold, Director, Publications Center, ICMA, and Editor of the Municipal Management Series, and Richard Herbert, senior editor, Publications Center, worked closely with Mr. Gilbert during the editorial development of this book. The final editing throughout was done by Emily Evershed, who also prepared the Index.

MARK E. KEANE
Executive Director

International City
Management Association

Washington, D.C.
August 1975

Preface

This is a book about a relatively new function—public relations—and the growing prominence of that function in local government.

The *need* for public relations in local government—to generate public understanding of and support for what you are doing—has always been there. The *responsibility* for public relations—to inform the citizens of your community of what is going on and why—has always been there. But the *function* of public relations has not always been there. That is one of the reasons for this book.

Public relations has been practiced successfully for generations by the private corporations of this nation: by P. T. Barnum, by the automobile industry, even by pro football. Only since World War II has it emerged as a recognized part of the programs of our governments—local, state, and national.

In less than twenty years the practice of public relations has been a key factor in the election of three presidents and in putting a man on the moon. Today, in countless communities, no doubt in yours as well, public relations is serving the needs and desires of numerous citizens.

This book is intended to describe the responsibilities of and the opportunities for public relations in local government. It is intended for those on the job—officials in city halls and county courthouses around the nation, staff members of councils of governments and other regional organizations. It seeks to educate them on the public relations dimensions of their jobs and of their governments and to offer specific suggestions on how to conduct that aspect of their jobs—and how not to.

The book is also intended for college students, to increase their awareness of the need for good public relations in local government and to prepare them for laying the groundwork for public relations in government programs when they enter the public service field in a local government or a regional organization.

Municipal Public Relations, the predecessor to this book, was, in 1966, an initial effort on the part of the International City Management Association to bring a broad concept of public relations and communication into city halls. This volume takes the interest in real-life operations not only to cities but to counties and councils of governments as well. It also covers the changes in attitudes and demands that have been facing local governments since the 1966 book was published. Today, local governments are being made to recognize and emphasize the role of individual citizens in government proposals and programs through the process of citizen participation, a term virtually unheard of in 1966. Police officials are playing under a markedly different set of ground rules. The same is true of school systems. These pages try to take these changes into account in an up-to-date assessment of both the climate of America's local communities and the position of the public relations practice in these local governments.

This book examines public relations from every important aspect: the city or county council; government employees, including police; reporters and other members of the news media; and the broad spectrum of different publics within a community.

Part One sets the perspective, with chapters dealing with public relations in society and in the administrative process, and research and the public relations process.

Part Two covers program involvement, with chapters on the city or county council as a focal point of interests, on the multitudinous publics in a community, and on serving the public as members of a local government's staff. Additional chapters in Part Two describe the employee–citizen team as a cooperative venture; community group relations; and police public relations.

Part Three is devoted to informational reporting, with chapters covering the role of reporters and the mass media, special reports and events, and publications planning, development, and production.

In Part Four the subject of integrating the whole into an effective public relations program is discussed through the presentation of proposals on organizing and training for public relations.

This book would not have been possible without the quick, cooperative, and capable work of the individual chapter authors, who are mentioned elsewhere in these pages. Special thanks are also due these members of the staff of the International City Management Association: David S. Arnold, Director, Publications Center, International City Management Association; Richard Herbert, senior editor; and Emily Evershed, editor.

I am indebted to Walter A. Scheiber, Executive Director of the Metropolitan Washington Council of Governments, for his support and for allowing me the flexibility of schedule essential in an undertaking of this magnitude. Special mention is also due my wife, Lillian, and our son, David, for their interest, understanding and enthusiasm.

WILLIAM H. GILBERT
Director of Public Affairs

Metropolitan Washington
Council of Governments

August 1975

Table of Contents

Tables

Public Relations in Local Government

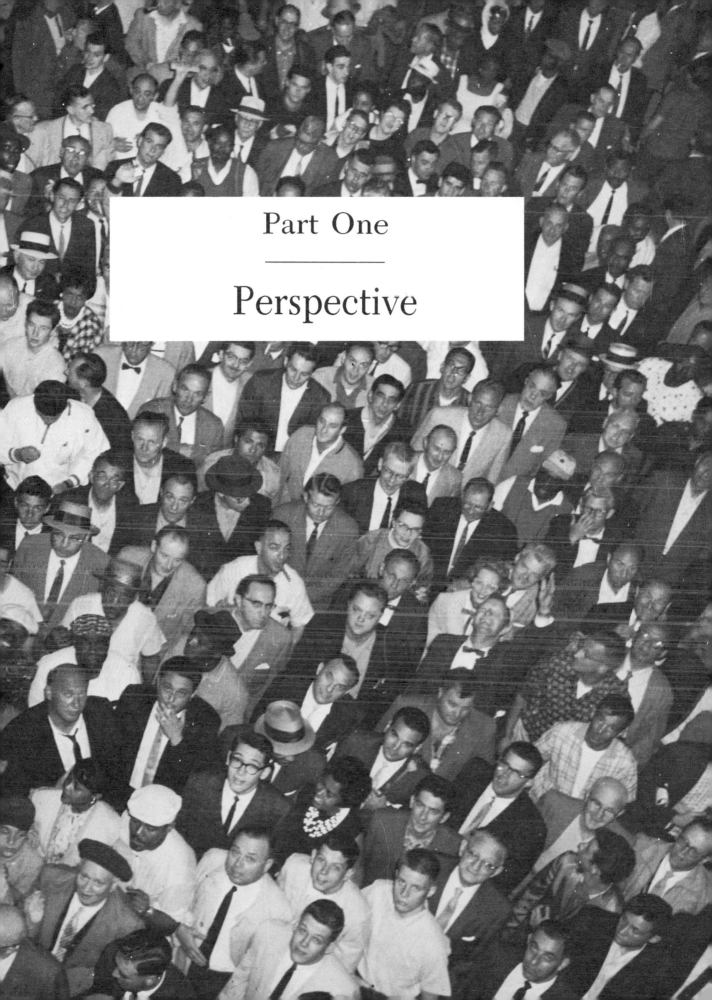

Part One

Perspective

1

Public Relations in Society

I f you are in government, you are in public relations. You may not know it or you may not like it, but it is a fact, and to ignore that fact is to live at your own peril. This book is intended to help you recognize the public relations element in all the things your local government or regional organization does and to help you make certain your responsibilities are met in a way which will bring credit to you and your agency while advancing your programs for the common good.

This opening chapter is intended as a broad overview of public relations—as it pertains to our society today and in its relationship within the administrative process. The chapter first gives the historical background of public relations—particularly in the United States —and covers the rise of press-agentry and of public exploitation, and the reform era which followed the latter. A general discussion of public relations in the various levels of government follows.

Next, the chapter deals with the distinction between public relations in business and public relations in government.

The chapter continues with an analysis of public relations and the administrative process, in the course of which management connotations are discussed and the administrative base is defined. A section on public opinion and communication follows, with discussions of: the significance of public opinion; the publics themselves; information and communication; and, importantly, the administrative responsibility for public relations. A discussion of ethics and public relations is then followed by a summary and some brief conclusions.

The Historical Perspective

In the Beginning

Awareness of the power of popular approval and support dates from antiquity. Much of what historians know of ancient Egypt, for example, has come from literature and works of art that were intended to publicize and gain public favor for the current pharaoh. The early Romans paid tribute to the forces of public opinion with the expression *vox populi, vox Dei*—"The voice of the people is the voice of God."

During the American Revolution, men like Thomas Jefferson, Samuel Adams, Thomas Paine, and Benjamin Franklin wrote pamphlets, contributed articles to the press, made speeches, and instigated word-of-mouth campaigns to stir up public support for what at the outset was not always a popular cause. The Declaration of Independence itself states that it was composed "out of a decent respect for the opinions of mankind." The eloquence of Alexander Hamilton, John Jay, and James Madison, exhibited through the *Federalist* papers and activities associated therewith urging the ratification of the Constitution, was one of the most notable examples of influencing public opinion in the history of statecraft.

While history provides abundant examples of attempts to influence public opinion (there are numerous and diverse antecedents of modern public relations), recognition of the concept of planned public relations is of fairly recent origin.

Two seemingly unrelated developments during the nineteenth century were among the more significant of the antecedents of modern public relations practices: (1) the creation of press-agentry, and (2) the "public-be-damned" attitude of business tycoons of that era.

THE GENESIS OF PRESS-AGENTRY

America was in the process of explosive expansion toward the undeveloped West. Fortunes were being built in banking, railroads, mining, and steel. Newspapers flourished in virtually every community as the principal, and frequently the only, medium of mass communication.

Circus owner P. T. Barnum early took heed of the growing power of the press and soon learned to use it for the promotion of his own interests. He bought many advertisements, but it was his unusual talent for obtaining free newspaper space for publicity stories which brought most of his customers to the circus box office. Thus he became the first press agent,

and achieved notable success through promotion of the midget General Tom Thumb; of Jenny Lind, "the Swedish Nightingale"; and of many others.

Professing to believe that "there's a sucker born every minute," Barnum did not hesitate to embroider the facts or, in numerous cases, to resort to pure fakery and staged events to gain a notoriety which paid off so well that he was able to leave an estate of $4 million when he died in 1891.

Press-agentry spread swiftly throughout most branches of show business, into advertising (where it flourished in the advertising of patent medicines, as in Figure 1–1), and into political campaigning. It has remained an integral part of those fields to this day.

Meanwhile, the stage was set for the next advance toward the present concept of public relations.

FIGURE 1–1. *Flamboyant advertising was an important aspect of the early days of public relations in the United States. The techniques of patent medicine salesmen were soon paralleled in political campaigns. (Source: reproduced from the collection of the Library of Congress.)*

AND THE "PUBLIC BE DAMNED"

In the years immediately following the Civil War, the nation experienced a period of unprecedented growth and expansion. It was a time of rugged individualism which saw the rapid rise of business monopolies and a great concentration of wealth in the hands of a few. It was the era of the "Robber Barons," who rode roughshod over all opposition in building new industrial empires.

Typical of the attitude of the time was the statement attributed to William Henry Vanderbilt, son of railroad magnate Cornelius Vanderbilt. Asked by reporters about the public interest in a proposed rail schedule change, the younger Vanderbilt is alleged to have said, "The public be damned. . . . I don't take any stock in this silly nonsense about working for anybody's good but our own because we are not. When we make a move it is because it is in our interest to do so."

REACTION AND REFORM

By 1900 there was a mounting wave of public outcry against the ruthless tactics and cynical practices of men like Vanderbilt. Theodore Roosevelt and Robert M. La Follette soon became the leaders of a popular antibusiness revolt among elected politicians, while the "muckrakers"—Lincoln Steffens, Upton Sinclair, Ida M. Tarbell, and others—turned their literary guns on business with books and articles describing illegal practices, overcharges, and other forms of corruption throughout the business world.

Faced with imminent danger from governmental action, business leaders turned to the press agents for help. For some years there was a publicity battle between the muckrakers on the one hand, bent on exposing the foulness of the large corporation, and the press agents on the other, applying huge quantities of whitewash in an attempt to belie the charges. Business almost invariably lost out in the final accounting to the public because the whitewash, in far too many cases, failed to obscure the record of facts from public view.

Establishment of the profession of city management was inspired in part by the muckrakers, who attacked not only big business but

graft, corruption, and inefficiency in municipal government as well. In 1904 Lincoln Steffens published *The Shame of the Cities,* a vitriolic exposé of malpractices in local government. This and other similar works undoubtedly aroused and crystallized the public demand for improvement in local affairs which in subsequent years resulted in widespread adoption of the council-manager system.

In 1906 one of the press agents, Ivy Ledbetter Lee, startled the business world by proposing an unprecedented approach. The public, he said, should not be ignored in the grand manner of the Robber Barons. Neither should it be tricked and misled in the manner common to the press agent. *The public should be informed. It should be given the truth.*

Lee had been a young reporter on the *New York Evening Journal* and the *New York Times.* He had worked as a publicity man with the Democratic National Committee and in a mayoralty campaign in New York City. In 1904 he had opened a press bureau with George F. Parker, a newsman who had served as press agent for Grover Cleveland, but they met with only meager success.

Employed by the Pennsylvania Railroad and by the anthracite coal industry to put his new system into effect, Lee issued a statement to newspaper editors that illustrated his concept of public relations.

This is not a secret press bureau. All our work is done in the open. We aim to supply news. This is not an advertising agency; if you think any of our material ought properly to go to your business office, do not use it. Our matter is accurate. Further details on any subject treated will be supplied promptly and any editor will be assisted most cheerfully in verifying directly any statement of fact. . . . In brief, our plan is, frankly and openly, on behalf of business concerns and public institutions, to supply to the press and public of the United States prompt and accurate information concerning subjects which it is of value and interest to the public to know about.[1]

Indicative of the application of the new approach was the reversal of the Pennsylvania Railroad's previous policy of news suppression when a wreck occurred in 1906. Lee carried reporters to the scene of the accident at company expense.

Lee was among the vanguard of press agents who discovered that careful presentation of the facts, rather than a patchwork of deceptive phrases, would win the confidence and the columns of the editors. His new approach, boldly advocated, won him both immediate financial success and recognition as "the father of public relations."

Although Lee's solution to the problems of harassed businessmen of the period did establish certain postulates which served as a framework for development of the new art of public relations, it should not be inferred that, with a single stroke, he transformed press-agentry into public relations. During the following decades the concepts and techniques of public relations developed at a remarkably slow pace. It was not until the forties that the rate was appreciably accelerated.

It must be borne in mind that, until the advent of the muckrakers, private business had been considered *private,* and little interest had been accorded public opinion. The "public-be-damned" attitude was a logical extension of this viewpoint and was not to disappear quickly.

SOMETHING MORE THAN HAPHAZARD

There were those in government, however, who had some appreciation for and understanding of public opinion. Political leaders and candidates became aware that their success or failure depended directly on the mood of the voting populace. They developed reasonably effective means of attracting votes for their party and themselves. In the earlier years, political campaigns were considered and organized as specialized, short-term affairs, a whirlwind of activity which reached an apex on election day and collapsed nobly or ignobly with the close of the polls. While this phenomenon still prevails, political public relations has become much more sophisticated and extensive. Commercial public relations firms conduct the major political campaigns today and serve both major national parties as permanent public relations departments. The first full-time permanent publicity bureau was organized within the Democratic party in 1929. Both parties now regularly advise their candidates to retain individual public relations counselors,

and successful officeholders often name public relations people and publicity experts as their administrative assistants.[2]

In corporate enterprise, increasing reliance on public relations resulted from a variety of factors, such as resentment and suspicion of business for its adverse practices and monopolistic and ruthless suppression of competition, and the anticipation of government ownership and operation of certain sectors of the economy highly vested with the public interest. Accordingly, those interests which turned first and most frequently to the newspapermen and journalists for their publicity *expertise* were the railroads, the electrical utilities, the oil and gas industry, and the steel and insurance companies.

This trend was highly accelerated following, first, the Great Depression with its social reform and accompanying criticism of business tycoons as economic royalists and second, the peculiar circumstances of World War II which demanded spectacular accomplishments of American business and industry. With these developments there has been an appreciable change from defensive and occasional propaganda campaigns to continuous publicity and public relations programs.

Today there is virtually no private enterprise which does not engage in some publicity and other public relations activities and hardly any business or industry of any consequence which does not have a formalized public relations program and personnel.

Paralleling these developments in private enterprise have been the publicity imperatives of government. There has always been a need for government publicity, if for no other reason than to inform citizens of the services available and the manner in which they may be used. With the developing complexity of government there was a corresponding increase in publicity. This function was assigned to someone irrespective of title and principal functions performed, whether statistician, administrative assistant, or clerk.

Administrative agencies of government disseminate substantial amounts of information. Various governmental officials compile and prepare such data to inform the public of services available from government and of duties required of citizens by governmental regulations.

By 1913 the United States Civil Service Commission was bold enough to announce an examination for a "Publicity Expert" whose "affiliation with newspaper publishers and writers is extensive enough to secure the publication of items prepared by him." Although this caused a congressional furor, the functions continued to be performed, and in 1917 President Wilson appointed George Creel head of the Committee on Public Information. The Creel committee operated as a large-scale propaganda agency during the war as it channeled information both outward to other countries and inward to citizens at home.

With newfound vigor bred of social change, the alphabet agencies (Figure 1-2) of FDR's New Deal, beginning with the Blue Eagle of the NRA (National Recovery Administration), precipitated a flood tide of publicists into the channels of government. The flow was accelerated during and following World War II with the establishment of such agencies as the Office of War Information (OWI) and the present United States Information Agency (USIA), which operates as an information channel for American diplomacy.

Such activity has had its effect upon Congress, which has sought, sometimes unsuccessfully, to curb especially those programs designed to influence public opinion and legislative action. These efforts have been initiated in part by congressional fear and jealousy of the growing power of the bureaucracy. An interesting coincidence of dates is seen when it is noted that in 1913 Congress forbade the

FIGURE 1-2. *The alphabet agencies of the New Deal brought a flood tide of publicists into the channels of government. (Source: reproduced from the collection of the Library of Congress.)*

hiring of "publicity experts" by government departments and followed this up in 1919 by prohibiting expenditures for influencing Congress. This prohibition was repeated in 1939 by a petulant Congress annoyed with the New Deal administration. Despite such prohibitions, administrative agencies not only play an important part in the legislative process but are engaged extensively in public relations activities.

Commonplace today are government news releases, press conferences, reports, information bulletins and other governmental publications, Post Office posters, and also various public services such as television announcements. Even the earlier congressional and citizen hostility which led to the shift from the title PRO (Public Relations Officer) to PIO (Public Information Officer) has gradually diminished—although some agencies now use public affairs office as a more accepted term for their public relations activities.

Similar developments have occurred in state and local governments although at a significantly slower pace. Through the land grant university system, established and promoted by national legislation and state enabling legislation, a vast network of public relations ambassadors has been in existence for nearly a century, blending the interests of federal, state, and local levels of government. Although several states on their own accord had already instituted agricultural advisers within their states, the Smith-Lever Act of 1914 established the basis of a federal system of such advisers, involving cooperative effort and financing by national, state, and local levels of government.

Resembling itinerant teachers initially, the county agricultural and home demonstration agents have been active for many years in every state in the union. While these agents are not the typical public relations functionary, they have proved to be a significant and useful prototype nonetheless.

Of the more traditional variety of public relations activity, Wright and Christian observed as far back as 1949 that nearly every state in the nation had established a state-supported public relations program to attract both tourists and industries.[3]

At the regional level, councils of governments and other regional councils across the nation in the 1970s have established extensive public relations programs to develop public understanding of and support for the efforts being made jointly by cities and counties in one region toward the solutions of that region's area-wide problems.[4]

Some of the most systematic efforts to promote effective public relations at the local level have been those of the International City Management Association (ICMA), which adopted a Code of Ethics for managers in 1924 and proposed a more extensive system of codes and creeds for all municipal officials and employees in 1962. The ICMA Code of Ethics was substantially revised in 1972.[5] Many of the ICMA training manuals (the Municipal Management Series, or Green Books) have chapters on public relations; as early as 1940 ICMA published a monograph by Elton Woolpert on *Municipal Public Relations*. Although a survey by ICMA in 1962 showed that the overwhelming majority of municipalities had no formal public relations programs, many individual managers have since pioneered effective public relations techniques, and some enthusiasts would maintain that a few municipal reports are among the most distinctive and best produced by human effort.

Distinctions between Business and Government

Whatever the similarities in the applications and uses of publicity and public relations in government and business, there are certain distinctions which relate to purpose and organization, ethics and morals, and public scrutiny.

PURPOSE AND ORGANIZATION

Private business exists to make a profit by selling goods and services to the public, whereas government exists to serve the people on a nonprofit basis. Therefore, business public relations programs are oriented to the *sales and profit* motive, while government public relations must evolve from a *service* viewpoint.

The corporate enterprise is a legal entity established under and required to comply with a somewhat limited number of lawful procedures. On the other hand, all governmental levels in American democratic society are circumscribed and limited. For example, the local government is a legal entity rigidly prescribed by law, restricted to limited and specified powers and to formally established procedure and method, and, in general, rigorously bound up in legalistic red tape in all of its principal activities. These safeguards and restrictions imposed by society make the government vulnerable because the public may and often does develop an impression of slowness—and an impression that this slowness stems from inefficiency rather than from legal circumscription.

Obviously, the effect on the citizen of such seeming dalliance is negative and constitutes a serious problem in public relations. This may be better viewed as a public relations challenge, however. Ordinary citizens regularly see their local government in a restrictive role—taking their money for taxes, giving them traffic tickets, requiring them to secure building permits, making them maintain their property in a given way. It is no wonder that the ordinary citizen is occasionally upset with "city hall."

On the other hand, local government does a great deal that is not restrictive. How much do citizens know of the successful recreation program, the improved street drainage system, the reduced fire insurance rates? The public official is responsible for informing citizens of all local governmental activity of consequence. Clearly, the majority of local government programs are positive and nonrestrictive. The private corporation, on the other hand, need not be concerned over whatever restrictive qualities its product may have. There usually are none.

ETHICAL AND MORAL DISTINCTIONS

Higher standards are required of government, and are often reflected in the behavior pattern the public expects of government employees. Should a business executive be arrested for drunkenness, he would probably escape with a small fine and a razzing from fellow employees. Should a city manager face a similar charge, he would be almost certain of losing his position. Such is the double standard of expected behavior distinguishing the public servant from the businessman.

Another aspect of the double standard is reflected in the fact that the citizenry not only accepts but expects the practice of publicity and advertisement on the part of business, but regards government public information activities as wasteful of the taxpayers' money and essentially propagandistic.

Another aspect of morality in government derives from the fact that government is monopolistic while private enterprise is expected to meet competition. The city council and city manager must attempt to provide good services at reasonable cost merely because it is their responsibility to do so. There is no direct competition to the city in most of its services and therefore no means of comparing either quality or price of the service. The citizen must take what the city provides. This pessimistic note should be modified, however, by the realization that there is in fact quality comparison from jurisdiction to jurisdiction: if the local officials do not measure up to quality standards of performance and service elsewhere they should not be retained in office.

In business, the competitive factor serves to force each firm to improve products and to reduce prices to attract customers who do have a choice. Relative absence of the competitive factor makes it incumbent on public officials to maintain a high sense of public duty.

PUBLIC SCRUTINY

Although all private enterprise is affected to some degree by public interest considerations, the business world conducts its affairs in an atmosphere of comparative calm and privacy. The world of government appears to belong to another universe. The late Paul Appleby, noted scholar and public official, had these observations in 1945, which still apply in the mid-1970s:

Government administration differs from all other administrative work to a degree not even faintly realized outside, by virtue of its public nature, the way in which it is subject to public scrutiny and public outcry. An administrator coming into government is struck at once, and continually thereafter, by the press and public interest in every detail of his life, personality, and conduct. This interest often runs to details of administrative action that in private business would never be of concern other than inside the organization.[6]

In local government administration, meetings at which decisions of any consequence will be made are ordinarily announced in advance and held in public. They are attended by the public and covered by the press. Numerous states have legislation, such as the Brown Act in California, which either prohibits or severely restricts the holding of any nonpublic meeting attended by a majority of the council members. The intent is to avert the making of private "deals" by unscrupulous council members. Such legislation is discussed in greater detail later in this chapter.

While there are other distinctions between business and government having a public relations impact, it is clear that the philosophy and techniques of public relations are conditioned particularly by the distinctions discussed above. Emphasizing these differences is essential because of the tendency to identify public relations with business and thus with a salesmanship approach. Perhaps the principal reason is that commercial public relations has been the dominant force in developing the public relations profession.

Public Relations and the Administrative Process

Public relations is a composite of relationships, both personal and institutional. It is both the reflection and the substance of public opinion. It includes all of the contacts within and extending outside an agency—personal or impersonal, direct or indirect, specific or general. The frequency, variety, and inclusiveness of such contacts indicate the pervasiveness of public relations throughout society. The handshake of the mayor, the voice of the telephone operator, the job done by the street sweeper, the conduct of the police officer—all establish relationships with the public, relationships which contribute positively or negatively to the sum total of public opinion about a local government. Every governmental jurisdiction, every agency within a municipality, every individual, obviously conducts public relations. Such relations may be consistently good and resultant public opinion high, or they may be poor or otherwise with a corresponding public attitude. Wherever humankind is, public relations exists as a matter of fact, irrespective of what is done or not done and regardless of quality. In this sense, public relations is pervasive.

In a sense, too, all public relations is personal; thus, *an agency's public relations status is a composite of relationships for all persons in the agency.*

The Management Connotations

Although public relations involvement in the administrative process has been obvious, appropriate distinctions have not always been clear. Wright and Christian, while recognizing that public relations is primarily good management, directed from the top but involving every person within or connected with an organization, claimed that "modern public relations is a *planned program* of *policies* and *conduct* that will build *public confidence* and increase *public understanding.*"[7] Nearly thirty years later, this still applies.

Among the efforts to develop a theoretical and professional base for public relations was a search for a proper definition of the term conducted by the editors of *Public Relations News,* Glenn and Denny Griswold. Some 2,000 replies were received, which variously characterized public relations as "a science; a system; an art; a process; a function; a relationship; a humanizing genius; a term; a business; a profession; a method; an activity; a program; a policy; a pattern of behavior; a moral force."[8]

Synthesizing the many definitions with their own insight, editors Glenn and Denny Griswold developed a definition in 1947 which still applies in the later 1970s: "Public relations is the management function which evaluates public attitudes, identifies the policies and procedures of an individual or organization with the public interest, and executes a program of action to earn public understanding and acceptance."[9]

Although many other definitions were contrived, the Griswold definition became essentially standard and was repeated in many texts.[10] It embraces a concern for policy determination which is overlooked in other definitions.

THE ADMINISTRATIVE BASE FOR PUBLIC RELATIONS

Although most public relations units in traditional organizations are primarily concerned with sampling attitudes and opinions and with certain facets of communications, here we assume a broader base. Public relations is both an influence upon and a consequence of program achievement. No one within an organization can be absolved of public relations responsibility. Attitude surveys and opinion sampling performed by the public relations staff have organizational and program significance far more pervasive than the usually conceived public relations needs. Publicity and communications are much more fundamental than "image building"; they lie at the heart of program achievement.

Relation of Public Opinion and Communication to Government

In a complex urban ecology which generates divergent human behavior and attitudes, no simple formulation of the nature and significance of public opinion and communication is possible. Few subjects have been more extensively analyzed and investigated than public opinion and communication, yet clarity and agreement have not been achieved.

Because public relations is conceived here as a means of program accomplishment, those views of public opinion and communication which hold promise of contributing to this end are included as reference points in the discussion that follows.

OPINION CONSIDERATIONS

That free governments derive their authority from the consent of the governed is a concept which has evolved over the centuries but which now has almost universal acceptance. But the citizen's historical resentment of arbitrary exercise of governmental authority is matched by his or her current bewilderment, stimulated by the rising complexity of public issues for which his or her experience has decreasing relevance.

Despite this apparent shift in the relative ability to deal with public issues, the power of public opinion provides the psychological environment in which public officials, agencies, and institutions prosper or perish. Under whatever system, it puts governments in and out of office, makes or breaks national heroes, and determines the success of public institutions and undertakings. Indeed, in 1974 it forced the first presidential resignation in American history. Public opinion, then, is a principal ingredient in social change.

No free government can survive easily without the willing support of many of its citizens. Such support derives from public opinion, of which all governments take cognizance. The late V. O. Key, Jr., eloquently set forth this thesis at the beginning of his last book:

Governments must concern themselves with the opinions of their citizens, if only to provide a basis for repression of disaffection. The persistent curiosity, and anxiety, of rulers about what their subjects say of them and of their actions are chronicled in the histories of secret police. Measures to satisfy such curiosity by soundings of opinion are often only an aspect of political persecution; they may also guide policies of persuasion calculated to convert discontent into cheerful acquiescence. And even in the least democratic regime opinion may influence the direction or tempo of substantive policy. Although a government may be erected on tyranny, to endure it needs the ungrudging support of substantial numbers of its people. If that support does not arise spontaneously, measures will be taken to stimulate it by tactical concessions to public opinion, by the management of opinion, or by both.[11]

In the American democratic society this concern for public opinion springs from the ideology upon which this government is based. Democratic doctrine assumes that a recognition of the wishes of the governed is a condition of governing rightly. Because of the universal political appeal of this concept, modern dictatorships took over much of the symbolism, ritual, and semantics of democratic ideology.[12]

Public opinion is a concert of individual opinion. The citizen's opinions, not unlike his or her behavior, are shaped and molded by the surrounding culture. Public opinion thus emerges out of a social situation in which human differences are articulated in reference to a particular matter or issue. They may result from an intellectual appraisal of factual data or from emotional reaction.

It was noted above that the process by which opinions are formed and altered has been subjected to considerable study. The variety of concepts have lacked unanimity. Inasmuch as the public relations model suggested here assumes a broad base of influence, it is undesirable to narrowly restrict the base of public opinion. Accordingly, Key's concept is paraphrased in the next two paragraphs.

The public opinion which government takes cognizance of includes both live issues and those based on the customs and mores of particular societies. Such opinion may be shared by few or many, may be the veriest whim, or may be settled conviction. It may be contingent opinion, or estimates of probable responses by citizens which condition governmental decisions. Views lightly held and transient opinions both have relevance. Sometimes a small segment of the society may hold a position so tenaciously that it may block or even direct public action. It may be that customs control particular governmental actions, but actions also may seek the modification of existing custom.

Governments may find it prudent to heed private opinions by action or inaction, by attempts to alter, divert, or pacify. Governments, however, may at times be so sensitive that opinion can be anticipated before action occurs, but opinion commonly gains its influence by being communicated. Such communication may occur directly between citizen and governmental functionary, but frequently it is done through specialized institutions such as political parties and pressure groups which shape, organize, and represent opinion to governments.[13]

THE PUBLICS—WHO ARE THEY?

It is clear that today we live in a pluralistic society consisting of people of diverse backgrounds and value systems. Each citizen may be affiliated with many and diverse groups in a society in which he or she develops and maintains multiple loyalties. As we organize ourselves into a variety of groups, there is no single transcendent group affiliation. We divide ourselves on various bases, such as social, recreational, political, religious, fraternal, civic or service, professional, and clientele bases. Consequently, governmental officials and employees find themselves dealing with a multiplicity of publics as well as individuals. The constituency of a city park and recreation department, for example, would include an extensive list of different groups who want to use, complain about, praise, and request the elimination, modification, or addition of facilities which are maintained by the department.

These constituency relationships are two-way in that they flow from and to both the jurisdiction and the constituents. Maintaining these relationships effectively requires concern for attitudes and actions of both parties. Not only must favorable public attitudes toward the government be cultivated, but also there must be fostered among public officials an attitude of goodwill and respect. Such good relations also form the foundation on which democratic government is constructed.

Through an increasing volume of behavioral research experts feel they are becoming more sophisticated in understanding both the general and the special publics. The general public, it is held, (1) is essentially passive in nature, (2) has only limited ability to comprehend complex data, and (3) is likely to reject data which is inconsonant with existing values and attitudes.

Accordingly, awareness of the nature of publics is necessary if communication is to be effective. If change in behavior and values is desirable, it should be planned through existing systems.

Certain distinctions are emerging between the general public and special publics. It appears that on only a few questions does the entire citizenry have an opinion. In reality, one issue may engage the attention of one sector of the population, while another arouses interests of a different sector, and a third question attracts still other special publics. On a particular issue, the interested public may consist of a well-structured, identifiable association, while on another question opinions may be diffused throughout the general public, which lacks any special organization. When the concern of a small special public prevails, it is presumed that it does so with the tacit consent of the general public.[14]

INFORMATION AND COMMUNICATION

Opinions and attitudes are influenced substantially by the nature of the communication system and the information available. The extent to which an effective communication system is established and maintained is both a measure of and an influence upon the effectiveness of the institution.

Individual Needs and Governmental Objectives. When the constituency of an institution includes all who live within particular jurisdictional boundaries—as with a municipality, county, or other local government—the communication network must interlace the institution with those groups in the community through which individual citizen contacts are made. The increasing mobility of citizens makes a steady flow of communication very difficult except when they join groups with a common interest bond. Despite this propensity to join groups, every person is an individual in his own right, and a key to effective communication therefore is identification of the institutional message with the aspirations and purposes of individuals.

The success and the stability of democratic governments ultimately are determined by the continuing approval of the citizenry which, in turn, is predicated on their interest and awareness. Paradoxically, citizen interest and awareness require communication from governmental sources, but traditionally citizens have been suspicious of efforts by governmental bodies to publicize themselves and the services available to the public.

Informed Citizenry and Governmental Goals. The highest conception of providing information to the public is that it enables the citizen to render intelligent judgments regarding the policies and activities of democratic government. American democracy is based on the premise that citizens are capable of self-government. In the formative years, the New England town

meeting afforded virtually every citizen of the community opportunities to know his or her town government. When issues arose, facts were available on which to base an opinion.

Today, except in a relatively small number of New England villages where the tradition has persisted, the town meeting has ceased to exist because of the changed nature of our complex society. Yet the governmental and social imperatives of shared information and common participation are greater today than in earlier times.

Always in the forefront of efforts to maintain open communication channels between governments and citizens have been the nation's news reporters and commentators. Their efforts in this century culminated in the adoption in 1957 by the American Society of Newspaper Editors (ASNE) of the following "Declaration of Principles":

Citizens must be able to gather information at home or abroad, except where military necessity plainly prevents; they must find it possible to publish or relate otherwise the information thus acquired without prior restraint or censorship by government . . . they should have freedom to distribute and disseminate without obstruction by government or by their fellow citizens. . . .

The members of the American Society of Newspaper Editors . . . are doubly-alarmed by measures that threaten the right to know, whether they involve restrictions on the movement of the press to sources of news and information at home or abroad, withholding information at local, state, or federal levels, or proposals to bring within the purview of the criminal statutes those who do not place security of the nation in jeopardy, but whose only offense is to disagree with government officials on what may be safely published.[15]

In accordance with the ASNE statement, which emphasizes the public's "right to know," states began to enact legislation such as California's Brown Act which prohibits executive or "secret" sessions of public legislative bodies except in certain personnel matters. By 1972 some forty-five states had legislation of some sort requiring that certain meetings be open for some matters.[16] Minnesota requires that most local meetings be open to the public. However, the law is unclear as to when and whether advance public notice is given.[17] The state laws of Washington, California, and Florida go furthest in proscribing closed council meetings.[18] Florida's open meeting legislation, or Sunshine Law (1967), has particularly broad coverage. It does not have the categories of exemption from open meetings that are found in other states, and virtually all the government bodies within the state are covered by the law.[19]

From the point of view of facilitating program achievement, perhaps it would be desirable to emphasize the complementary proposition of the public's "need to know." If citizens are to assume effectively their responsibilities for self-government, the discerning administrator will assure the availability of sufficient and adequate information.

While an informed citizenry is indispensable to democratic government, the critics of government, except for the fanatic fringe, are to be found primarily among people who are partly informed and partly misinformed. It is difficult to eliminate misconceptions once they have been assimilated and have taken the form of opinion. The antidote, of course, is systematic communication which provides a continuous flow of information to the public.

Complete and Accurate Information. Candid reporting repeatedly has engendered citizen appreciation and understanding of difficult governmental problems and situations. Often there is temptation to offer alibis, to reveal only partial truths, or to take refuge in the silence of "no comment" when a potentially embarrassing development occurs. Such evasiveness is strategically undesirable because it invites inquiry. There is nothing more challenging to a newspaper reporter than the intimation of a story being suppressed by governmental officials—with the Watergate scandal the classic example.

There is nothing more likely to precipitate a citizen revolt than a discovery that officials have been attempting to cover up. A simple error admitted openly and freely is usually forgotten quickly, whereas the same mistake subjected to the mystery of the cover-up process may become a major scandal. To minimize surreptitious rumor, complete information should be released at the earliest feasible moment to en-courage formation of opinions based on accurate data from the original source rather than the grapevine.

Ethically, of course, there is no justification for governmental deceit or distortion. The government, after all, is the citizen in an institutionalized sense—which should symbolize his or her highest aspirations of honor, justice, and fair play. The matter of ethics is discussed in greater detail later in this chapter.

While citizens and public officials alike require information to make decisions, to explain availability of services, and to evaluate performance, there are specific approaches to handling information. In the routine matter of giving information over the counter, the importance of using speech and hearing faculties simultaneously is indicated in the following quote:

In answer to a simple inquiry as to how many persons serve on the City Council, the answer "five" may or may not provide the information sought. But if we are to answer the same question by saying, "There are four members of the City Council, plus the Mayor who serves as Chairman, making five altogether," we then invite the questioner to clarify his inquiry and perhaps to obtain the information he really is seeking, such as the method of election of Council members, or the organization of the Council. . . .

Even in the simplest procedure by which we direct a visitor to the proper office, we can combine listening and questioning with our answers in such fashion as to prevent embarrassment and confusion. If a caller were to inquire as to where he could obtain a "permit," an adequate answer might be, "That would be in room four." But the additional moment required to answer, "Our *building* permits are issued by Mr. X in room four," could provide the caller with a specific person to seek in a busy office containing several people; furthermore, the additional information supplied in the longer answer could enable the caller to clarify his inquiry by saying that he had been dealing with Mr. A, rather than Mr. X; we in turn could reply that the caller was seeking a *business license* rather than a *building permit,* and that Mr. A could help him in room five.[20]

Regular Reporting. It is apparent that there is need for a continuous flow of information as it develops. In most state, county, and local governments public reporting is a legal requirement, particularly in fiscal matters. Public relations requirements of providing information to the public transcend this legal duty; they are imperatives both of common sense and of morality. Nor does the provision for making information public through such vehicles as the annual report fulfill the entire obligation of government. Information should be provided on events and activities as they occur.

Both legally required annual reports and public notices continue to be plagued by archaic, legalistic, and confusing specifications. How many public reports are readable and understandable? How many legal notices clearly indicate what the situation is? Requirements for insertion in newspapers of general circulation often are met by publication in weekly or legal papers of limited circulation.

Assessment of available resources and opportunities, coupled with ingenuity and innovation, will overcome what probably continues to be the most negative aspect of governmental public relations—namely, public reporting. Even financial problems associated with an effective public reporting system may be minimized by a little ingenuity.

In order to optimize opportunities of this sort, government officials must familiarize themselves with requirements of the information media in their areas and must develop programs which will achieve institutional objectives and also effectively utilize available media.

Whatever is undertaken to facilitate information flow and effective communication should be predicated on the prior understanding that communication is a mutual process between senders and receivers whereby information is transferred from its source to its destination where it is given meaning through reception and interpretation.

Administrative Responsibility

The primary purpose of administration is to achieve established organizational purposes and to assist in clarifying and delineating such purposes. Accordingly, all administrative functions should service or facilitate effective operation of the organization.

ADVISORY AND FACILITATIVE ROLE

It is the function of public relations to facilitate the effective rendition of services and to provide the public with adequate information on governmental services. Public relations is thus a means of defining and achieving program goals. Antilitter campaigns which have been administered successfully in some cities should be viewed as an administrative alternative to expending much larger sums of money for frequent policing of roadways by city crews. "Smokey Bear" campaigns provide information to increase citizen awareness that care by them is a much more desirable alternative than the tremendous costs incurred through depletion of natural resources and by the mounting of costly firefighting campaigns.

Contributing to program or goal achievement by providing information is itself a facilitative operation, as is the evaluation of programs by, for example, sampling community opinion regarding a municipal activity. These are, however, administrative operations which are commonly identified as public relations. Such operations may be handled entirely by line administrators themselves or they may be shared by the administrators with staff assistants who are often designated as public relations specialists. The extent to which this sharing occurs depends on a host of factors, such as the size and complexity of the jurisdiction, personal predilections of the administrator, availability of public funds, and controversial nature of the particular line function. However much these public relations operations are shared by the line administrator, he or she can never be absolved of responsibility for them.

While the public relations specialist does not have major responsibility for policy determination and administrative competency within an agency, he or she is concerned in a major way with public knowledge and understanding of city or county government activities. To the extent that these specialists have special knowledge about public reaction, or are skilled in certain techniques, they have obligations to the line officials in utilizing such knowledge and skills in advisory and facilitative ways which will make administrative performance more effective.

A caveat is in order at this point. Sometimes, in this advisory and facilitative role, public relations staffs overextend their role under the misconception that popular support can be built by a public relations program without much consideration for the substantive conditions involved. It is contrary to human nature, however, to accept information unless it conforms with individual experience, and any institution courts danger when it seeks to create a point of view which differs from realities. High-powered publicity cannot conceal ineptitude in government. Indeed, there are great hazards confronting any governmental administrator who attempts to hide his failures and organizational inabilities behind a façade of publicity. Effective public relations rests on a foundation of actual needs and effective service. This kind of support building is a substantive line function in which every member of an organization participates. It is not an isolated staff function.

Accomplishment of objectives, however, is no assurance that the agency will enjoy good public relations. Again, the competitive and pluralistic nature of modern society may produce a completely erroneous public image of the agency and its programs. As a competitor on the social market, the governmental institution must maintain community support if its activities are to continue and if its program objectives are to be accomplished. Some programs may not be attainable without publicity and attitude-building efforts. For example, without attempting in any way to alter the public's attitude toward the use of good books, a public librarian will publicize new additions to his or her stock and will report those branches which have the new books available for public distribution.

Beyond this type of activity, however, the local health officer, for example, may engage in overt public information and attitude-molding activities in order to convince people in disadvantaged neighborhoods that they should learn about personal health and the use of clinics and other health services. Health officers are not accomplishing their mission unless they engage in education of this sort and unless they con-

cern themselves affirmatively with altering prevailing public attitudes and values within their jurisdictions.

In still another way the facilitative and advisory role of public relations must be made clear. From the days of Ivy Lee's description of himself as a "physician to corporate bodies," public relations specialists have sought to overcome the stigma associated with the notion of a palliative or cure-all for an agency's ills. Public relations people have complained of this negative connotation, emphasizing that public relations is positive, too, and should be viewed as a preventive as well as a cure. From the task of soothing troubled feelings, they have moved vigorously to remedying the conditions involved which caused the troubled feelings. It should be borne in mind constantly that remedying malconditions is distinctly a management function and as such it obviously has public relations implications, but just as obviously it is not a separate or distinct public relations function.

It may be recalled from the discussion of the definitions of public relations that one of the problems of arriving at appropriate definitions has been the desire of public relations specialists to remove the unsavory stigma associated with the term. It bears emphasis that public relations will gain increased status and prestige as it becomes interwoven with the performance process of government to such an extent that government: (1) is sensitive to and capable of discerning needs of society; (2) renders excellent service; and (3) works positively to maintain open channels of influence so that a high level of morality may always have a chance to flourish—so that reason, the bulwark of justice, may always prevail.

The changed status cannot and should not be accomplished through a deliberate effort to demonstrate the value of public relations per se. Although they obviously have public relations implications, techniques for the development and continuance of democratic principles are fundamental to the democratic process itself and are not uniquely public relations contributions to the process. Public relations, as to the quality of relationships, is best when government is most effective. When government is ineffective, public relations as process through techniques will not change it; but modifying the governmental process so that it becomes democratically effective does change public relations as to the *quality* of relationships. Public relations narrowly construed cannot make bad government good, but public relations broadly construed is inextricably interwoven with the democratic process and is improved when the democratic machinery and its operation are improved.

MANAGERIAL LEADERSHIP AND PUBLIC RELATIONS

Both Politics and Administration. Public relations is inevitably bound up with managerial leadership, a responsibility which cannot be delegated.

Managers have a dual responsibility, namely to maintain good operating conditions within their jurisdictions and also to implement the legislative program adopted through the political process. They must be responsive to the changing objectives of government fashioned by politics. Yet the manager, no longer straitjacketed by the misconception of the politics/administration dichotomy, has a community leadership role to perform.

The professional manager no longer can leave to the politicians the arguments over values. His or her task is to see that there is enough tension among experts to produce a solution to each problem, one which considers every factor. The administrator's value system becomes involved; whether he or she likes it or not, he or she is catapulted into a leadership role.

Such a role involves not only the discovery of majority purpose but also development of community consensus. In this latter phase the leadership role is especially noticeable. Managers may suggest goals and indicate avenues of achievement hitherto unattainable in the minds of local citizenry and wielders of power. They may cater to opinions of clientele groups and other organized interests as well as legislators and the public at large. They will solicit goodwill and promote successful relations for the jurisdiction's and the manager's own welfare. If there is variance of opinion and judgment

managers have opportunity to teach and enlighten.

Thus, their educative function is especially significant. The extent to which, under any particular set of circumstances, managers carry out this function is dependent in considerable measure on many influences. But with responsible and professional managers there is an automatic control arising out of their own value system: their concern for the ethical as determined through wisdom. If they themselves cannot yield their point of view and if they cannot, through their teaching efforts, win the consent of the policy officials as institutionalized in their council, then, to maintain integrity, managers will resign rather than launch a crusade for their own point of view.

Both Conservator and Change Agent. The very nature of the role of the manager is such that he or she is responsible on the one hand for innovation and change, and on the other for conserving that which is desirable in the existing order against the wishes of those who seek change. The manager's role as change agent is brought into stark relief when viewed against public opinion which, once solidified, is stubbornly resistant to change. In the process of focusing on or aiding in the focus of opinion on public policy issues, participating in policy formulation, implementing a favorable program, and overcoming resistance to change in each phase of the continuing process, the manager is operating in part as a public relations official. Ability to accept changes for the sake of progress is an important phase of an effective public relations program.

Defending the organization to a client may be quite noble, but it probably causes an antagonistic client to become more aggressive. In fact, the very thing defended may be wrong. The city or county must stand ready, as a part of effective public relations, to change those procedures which citizen–clients dislike. The burden on the counter or contact employee becomes greater than we can realistically expect of him or her if the local government stands for good public relations despite unpopular procedures which could be changed. Bureaucratic red tape significantly influences the image of both the government and the manager. The manager's must be positively exerted to encourage procedural and organizational change where the organization is inconsonant with community needs.

But to say that these are political considerations is to beg the question. All public servants, in proportionately decreasing degrees, from the chief administrative officer to the humblest and least discretionary officer, will discover—if they are not already aware of it—that at times they must serve as a change agent and at other times as the pilloried defender of the status quo. This role is highlighted particularly at the local level of government because of the immediacy of interest with which governmental functions are vested at that level.

Primacy of Culture. Traditions, customs, mores, folkways, habits, all condition the environment in which these roles are enacted. The public employee who does not effectively adjust to the environment in which he or she plays a role fails to do so at his or her peril.[21] This is not to say that public officials must become so immersed in the culture of their jurisdiction that they become captives thereof and hence unable to function as change agents when it is appropriate to do so. Change is inevitable. And the public servant needs to know the community sufficiently well so that in each particular case he or she may determine which are the acceptable or least offensive ways of both innovating *and* defending the public policy.

Support through Participation. Working together for common purposes is the basis for group achievement. Personal involvement in the processes which lead to such achievement often develops both understanding and support, which are among the ingredients of effective public relations. Inasmuch as a major concern of public relations is support building, any expression of management leadership in the public relations context must take into consideration the leadership techniques for securing support. An important factor seems to be a sense of some participation in group decision making. The problem of participation has overall administrative implications, but it has particular significance in public relations.

In this era of great emphasis on citizen participation, it is essential, in order to serve over-all administrative purposes as well as to operate effectively in a public relations way, that the administrator find ways of involving people in a participating manner in the process of discovering solutions to problems. This entire question is covered in detail in Chapter 6.

EMPLOYEES AS PUBLIC RELATIONS AMBASSADORS

The officials and employees of a local government are its most effective public relations ambassadors. Like other facets of administrative responsibility, public relations is a cooperative undertaking in which every individual associated with the government has a part to play. This is especially true in view of the nature of local functions and the direct citizen–employee contacts involved.

All people associated with an enterprise, whether that enterprise be a city or a county, or the Kiwanis Club, are public relations representatives of such an enterprise and have a responsibility. They may be neither good representatives nor willing to accept the responsibility, but this does not alter the reality of the relationship.

Nearly every local employee, whether fire inspector, clerk, meter reader, recreation leader, water superintendent, refuse collector, or traffic patrol officer, normally has direct and frequent contact with at least some segment of the public. This fact magnifies the problem of control of the public relations image by the administrator, because he or she must rely on all such employees in the composite of their relationships with the public to project an effective view of the city.

Not only are employees' work relations with people important, but their innumerable indirect and off-the-job contacts are important as well. One dissatisfied employee can, by his or her deeds and words, do irreparable harm to the public view of the municipality. If such actions are multiplied by several complainers, the result can be devastating.

Much can be done through training programs, but training cannot substitute for a deep-seated loyalty and understanding of the institution by employees, which will be reflected in all their contacts with other people, private as well as public. Such loyalty cannot be inculcated solely through training programs; it must be inspired by the tone of conduct of the administration, through the development of a genuine attitude of support stemming from effective administration. These are differences between form and substance, between desire and behavior, between that which is sham and that which is genuine. Employees who are stimulated to make suggestions and recommendations will enhance the quality of administrative performance and public relations. Through the democratic exchange of information, ideas, motivations, and experiences, public relations may attain maximum effectiveness for local governments.

Preparing for and maintaining effective public relations is really a matter of increasing the social awareness of employees. City and county employees should not be taught to "be nice" to the public so that the government will gain a better public image. The training should rather be conducted so that employees understand typical citizen action and reaction and can more easily and effectively perform their services.

Where Is Responsibility Lodged?

Good public relations begins at the top and is a direct line responsibility, an integral and continuous part of management. The city manager and the county executive have an inescapable obligation to public relations, an obligation that is just as compelling as their responsibilities for sound public finance, effective personnel systems, and the like. They must instigate training for employees in all areas of public relations and must see that training programs are properly staffed, equipped, supported, and attended. It is the city manager or county executive's job to deal with the press on a knowledgeable basis and to develop good press relations for the entire community. It is their job, using all means available to them, to fashion improvement in the image of the community. They set the pace for the community, and if the public relations program is lagging, a matter of attitude is often involved. Too many officials consider the public relations function of management marginal at best. In this view, public

relations is a managerial responsibility to be attended to if there is time or if there are not more pressing matters at hand. There is a lack of appreciation of the fact that attention to public relations can make the whole task of governing a great deal easier and more pleasant.

As Wright and Christian have written:

Public relations begins at the top where policy is made. In business and industry public relations is a responsibility of management. In governmental and social organizations it is a function of administration. In military affairs it stems from command. If public relations is to achieve maximum effectiveness it must be directed by the responsible officials at the head of the institution or enterprise, and they must be conscious of its importance and power. . . .

The chief executive must always be the hub of the public relations wheel. From him must radiate the policies and decisions that will govern the institution's relations with the public.[22]

How, then, can public relations be administered systematically or in an orderly fashion?

First, it should be recalled that public relations is fundamental to and inseparable from the administrative process.

Second, it must be understood clearly that no one in the hierarchy, least of all the top administrator, can abandon responsibility for public relations or divest himself or herself of the representation function. Public relations, by its nature and relationships, is *nondelegable as to responsibility*.

Third, it should be noted that there are certain tasks and activities which can be separated out and performed by staff assistants. This separation and allocation of tasks, however, should not lead to a lack of continuing identification with the administrative process and organizational goals, regardless of the size of the jurisdiction.

The community survey used to gather data on citizen reactions has public relations importance. But its importance often transcends the entire administrative spectrum. A "public relations specialist," whether an assistant city manager or a technician, cannot have exclusive jurisdiction over or interest in such a survey. So it is with many other such activities.

It should be clear from this that many of the tasks which some writers and practitioners claim should be allocated to a public relations section or staff are of general administrative concern. They should be performed by all means, but within the general administrative context, not alone in the specialized setting of public relations.

In the small city, the city manager may necessarily perform most such tasks; in most communities they can be performed by an administrative assistant so designated without raising questions of political and social impropriety; in the medium-sized jurisdiction there may be one or more administrative assistants who perform some of the tasks, which may occupy either part or all of their time; in the metropolis there may be an entire section performing public relations duties, including media relations, preparation and distribution of annual and other reports, and other assignments. In such cases the designation "public affairs assistant" may be entirely proper. Such personnel should be organized within the hierarchy, however, under an assistant city manager or similarly designated person who has administrative responsibilities broader than those usually encompassed by the duties of a "public relations specialist."

Public Relations and Ethics

In a society operating under the democratic ethic, which recognizes the dignity and importance of the individual, this ethic has both public relations and management significance for the administrator. In terms of their relationships with all those associated with their jurisdiction or agency, chief administrators must regard themselves as in the service of all, dealing with each person fairly, honestly, and intelligently—recognizing and respecting the interests of each.

Upon this foundation—recognition of the dignity and importance of the individual—is erected a host of ethical considerations which transcend the public relations process in government. Here we shall examine briefly two principal aspects—ethical behavior in providing citizen services and ethical considerations in administrative communications.

Noting the mediating role among contend-ing individual desires within a public system, Stephen K. Bailey remarked:

Politics and hierarchy induce the public servant to search imaginatively for a public-will-to-be. In this search, the public servant is often a leader in the creation of a new public will, so he is in part accountable to what he in part creates. But in any case the basic morality of the system is in its forcing of unitary claims into the mill of pluralistic considerations.[23]

Delineating a particular responsibility of the public official in this representative role, however, Edmund Burke observed in 1774 that the citizen's

wishes ought to have great weight with him; their opinions high respect; their business unremitted attention. It is his duty to sacrifice his repose, his pleasures, his satisfactions to theirs—and above all, ever, and in all cases, to prefer their interest to his own.

But his unbiased opinion, his mature judgment, his enlightened conscience, he ought not to sacrifice to you, to any man, or to any set of men living. These he does not derive from your pleasure—nor from the law and the Constitution. They are a trust from Providence, for the abuse of which he is deeply answerable. *Your representative owes you,* not his industry only, but *his judgment;* and *he betrays,* instead of serving, *you if he sacrifices it to your opinion.*[24]

If Burke's public official owes to his constituents his mature judgment within a plural system of contending individual desires, then his judgment must be preconditioned by acceptable ethical standards. It is Bailey's contention that

personal ethics in the public service is compounded of mental attitudes and moral qualities. Both ingredients are essential. Virtue without understanding can be quite as disastrous as understanding without virtue.

The three essential mental attitudes are: (1) a recognition of the moral ambiguity of all men and of all public policies; (2) a recognition of the contextual forces which condition moral priorities in the public service; and (3) a recognition of the paradoxes of procedures.

The essential moral qualities of the ethical public servant are: (1) optimism; (2) courage; and (3) fairness tempered by charity.[25]

On the required mental attitudes, Bailey is of the opinion that awareness of the dilemmas and paradoxes inherent in all people and policies, in specific contexts, and in general administrative procedures leads to the development of other personal attributes which increase understanding and facilitate making ethical judgments.[26]

On moral qualities, optimism enables men to face ambiguity and paradox without becoming immobilized and to see possibilities for good in the uncertain, the ambiguous, and the inscrutable. Moral courage is not only the willingness to assume responsibility for decisions but more especially the willingness to take purposeful action and to make necessary decisions, the organizational significance of which transcends offense to personal friends. Justice tempered with charity "makes of compromise not a sinister barter but a recognition of the dignity of competing claimants" fortified by persuasive rather than coercive arts.[27]

Morality and ethics thus not only precondition but are constant influences upon administrative performance and behavior. At the local level, the behavior of those involved in the big city machines of Tweed, Crump, Shaw, and Tammany contravened acceptable standards of morality. Watergate is the classic case at any level. But these are the spectacular and the flagrant. Unethical conduct is involved in the misuse of public funds, personal favoritism, private gain, and administrative ineptitude. It is spawned in the agency-client relationships of federal and state regulatory agencies. The matter of conflict of interest relating to private holdings and public responsibility of the same public official is frequently headlined at all levels and in all branches of government. Where personal behavior of public officials deviates from acceptable standards of morality there is rising public clamor for statutory prohibition. Increasingly, legislators, administrators, and jurists are becoming circumscribed by law. In the mid-1970s over forty states passed laws regulating conflicts of interest, disclosure of assets, lobbying, and similar matters. California passed particularly comprehensive legislation in this area in 1973–74.[28] Some of this legislation is deliberately calculated to put the public official in the goldfish bowl. This serves as a restraining influence on impropriety while assisting the official to maintain high ethical standards of performance.

Impropriety and misconduct in public office are properly proscribed, but also reprehensible is the sometimes blatant, often clever, use of public relations techniques and communications media to minimize or conceal such offenses. Such abandonment of ethics in the use of public relations techniques can never be condoned. Perhaps an overly dramatic representation is Alan Harrington's caricature of the public relations man who

[makes] the mistake of all those who don't believe in anything: he thinks that through the artful employment of words and images he can fool the people all the time—*no matter what* the actual, physical state of affairs may be.

Imagine a clever but exceptionally corrupt PR man with a house of prostitution for a client. Why, this will soon turn out to be the noblest profession of them all! Here are those generous girls serving lonely men. Their lives are easier than the lot of the average housewife! He will produce statistics to show that as a group they have six tenths of one percent less heart trouble than housewives. He will release photos showing them happily playing volleyball in their off hours. He will arrange a press conference for one of the girls who has just returned from a world cruise. He will prove that the girls from his client's house make happier marriages than other women. He will saturate all media with these lying truths. But all the while, off-camera, broods the enduring truth, if you will, that no girl should have to go to bed with men she doesn't know. No matter how our PR man twists and turns and "presents facts," he cannot move out of the shadow of certain enduring truths, whether they be moral or economic.

All PR men are aware of the lurking presence of these truths, and are made nervous by them, doubly so because the majority are educated people with dim or corroded memories of classic principles.[29]

Even if all publicists are not jaded with deceit, the fact remains that arrangement and adjustment of facts to conceal, mislead, misrepresent, or confuse are all contrary to ethical public relations standards. The reprehensible administrator who is guilty of unethical administrative performance and behavior compounds his guilt by resorting to deceitful use of publicity. But the American free press, militant taxpayers' associations, and opposing political factions will not allow him peace. Even the less deceitful and those who seek to glorify the insignificant through publicity are vulnerable.

If these instances portray the negative aspects of morality in government and public relations, what, if any, are the positive alternatives to induce ethical standards of behavior?

Legislatures, employee associations, professional societies, and thoughtful individuals have been active for a long time in promoting high standards of conduct on the part of public officials. As early as 1924 the International City Managers' Association (ICMA) (now the International City Management Association) adopted a Code of Ethics, amended in 1938, 1952, 1969, and 1972, which has become the standard of conduct for all municipal administrative officers. In February 1962, ICMA disseminated widely a Suggested Code of Ethics and Creeds for Municipal Officials and Employees, including a suggested creed for city council members. These appear as Appendix A, together with a Suggested Creed for Administrative Officials and Employees.

Revealing their concern for ethical practices, the Public Relations Society of America adopted, in 1959, a sixteen-point Code of Professional Standards for the Practice of Public Relations. This was amended as a seventeen-point code in 1963. This amended code, together with "official interpretations" dating from 1966 and 1974, appears as Appendix B.

While it is recognized that desirable behavior cannot be legislated, new public concern born out of Watergate has created a period of public insistence on morality in government at every level. Adherence to ethical practices on the part of public officials is now mandatory for them—not only for moral reasons but for their very survival as well.

Conclusion

Public relations, good or bad, is a natural phenomenon. Wherever human beings are, it is with them every day, in every act, in every procedure. Effective public relations does not just happen. It is a positive, continuous activity in which everyone has an interest.

In this chapter we have looked back in time to the ancient origins of public relations. We have traced its history in the United States, in both private enterprise and government. Following this, we have outlined the distinctions between its practice in business and in government, covering the following subjects: purpose and organization; ethics and morality; and public scrutiny. Public relations and the administrative process has been the next area discussed in detail, with emphasis on management connotations and with a discussion of the administrative base. The importance of the relation of public opinion and communication to government has been covered in considerable detail, followed by an outlining of the administrative responsibility for public relations. The final question dealt with has been that of ethics and public relations.

Contrary to popular belief, public relations in local government is not of recent origin but is rooted in antiquity. It is partly because of attempts to impose new and unacceptable terms and to give it separate organizational status that it is considered "recent." These, among other factors, have brought about resistance to the concept of public relations. In this very resistance is a clue for gaining acceptance: organize it administratively throughout the hierarchy, using and developing techniques for *general administrative applicability,* not specifically for public relations alone.

Public relations is one of many important variables which affect the ability of an administrator to accomplish program objectives. It involves reciprocity between the agency (its personnel, its decisions, and its programs) and the attitudes and desires of persons and groups in the agency's external environment. It imposes on administrators the necessity for dealing with public relations as an inherent and continuing element in the managerial process. The administrator must be mindful of public relations considerations at every stage of the administrative process, from making the decision to the final point of its execution.

---

[1] Quoted in Sherman Morse, "An Awakening in Wall Street," AMERICAN MAGAZINE, September 1906, p. 460.

[2] For two descriptions of the role and extent of professional public relations in political parties and campaigns, see Joe McGinniss, THE SELLING OF THE PRESIDENT, 1968 (New York: Trident Press, 1969), and Richard M. Scammon

and Ben J. Wattenberg, THE REAL MAJORITY: HOW THE SILENT CENTER OF THE AMERICAN ELECTORATE CHOOSES ITS PRESIDENT (New York: Coward, McCann & Geoghegan, 1970).

[3] J. Handly Wright and Byron H. Christian, PUBLIC RELATIONS IN MANAGEMENT (New York: McGraw-Hill Book Company, 1949), p. 168.

[4] National Association of Regional Councils, REGIONAL COUNCIL COMMUNICATIONS (Washington, D.C.: National Association of Regional Councils, 1973), summary.

[5] International City Management Association, CITY MANAGEMENT CODE OF ETHICS (Washington, D.C.: International City Management Association, 1972). Available from ICMA.

[6] Paul H. Appleby, BIG DEMOCRACY (New York: Alfred A. Knopf, Inc., 1945), p. 7. Reprinted 1970. © Alfred A. Knopf, Inc.

[7] From Wright and Christian, PUBLIC RELATIONS IN MANAGEMENT, p. 3. Used with permission of McGraw-Hill Book Company.

[8] Denny Griswold, PUBLIC RELATIONS COMES OF AGE (Boston: Boston University School of Public Relations, 1947), p. 3.

[9] Ibid.

[10] See, for example, Gene Harlan and Alan Scott, CONTEMPORARY PUBLIC RELATIONS: PRINCIPLES AND CASES (Englewood Cliffs, N.J.: Prentice-Hall, Inc., 1955), p. 4.

[11] V. O. Key, Jr., PUBLIC OPINION AND AMERICAN DEMOCRACY (New York: Alfred A. Knopf, Inc., 1961), p. 3. © Alfred A. Knopf, Inc.

[12] Ibid., p. 4.

[13] Ibid., pp. 12–18.

[14] Ibid., pp. 10, 15.

[15] Robert U. Brown, "ASNE Spells Out Broad Scope of the People's Right To Know," Editor & Publisher, July 20, 1957, p. 9.

[16] Gerald McKay, "The Public's Right To Know," MINNESOTA MUNICIPALITIES, June 1972, p. 176.

[17] Ibid., p. 178.

[18] Ibid., p. 176.

[19] Anne Conway et al., "Florida's 'Government in the Sunshine' Law: A Summary Report" (Gainesville: University of Florida, Center for Governmental Responsibility, 1975), pp. 2–3. (Mimeographed.)

[20] City of La Habra, California, "Training in Public Relations and Communications," La Habra, January 1962, pp. 9–10. (Processed.)

[21] For a comprehensive sociological consideration of differing organizational environments, plus an interesting analytical model and typology, see Amitai Etzioni, A COMPARATIVE ANALYSIS OF COMPLEX ORGANIZATIONS (New York: Free Press of Glencoe, 1961). Available in paperback.

[22] From Wright and Christian, PUBLIC RELATIONS IN MANAGEMENT, pp. 42–43. Used with permission of McGraw-Hill Book Company.

[23] Stephen K. Bailey, "Ethics and the Public Service," PUBLIC ADMINISTRATION REVIEW 24 (December 1964): 235.

[24] Edmund Burke, WORKS, vol. 2 (Boston 1881), quoted in Glendon A. Schubert, Jr., "The Public Interest in Administrative Decision-Making," AMERICAN POLITICAL SCIENCE REVIEW 51 (June 1957): 346–68. Italics added.

[25] Bailey, "Ethics and the Public Service": 235–36. For an effective understanding of the "mental attitudes and moral qualities" essential to personal ethics in the public service, the entire article is recommended.

[26] Ibid: 236–40.

[27] Ibid: 240–43.

[28] Don Benninghoven, "Significant State Actions Affecting Municipal Government," in THE MUNICIPAL YEAR BOOK 1975 (Washington, D.C.: International City Management Association, 1975), pp. 3, 6.

[29] Alan Harrington, "The Self Deceivers," ESQUIRE, September 1959, p. 60.

2

Research and the Public Relations Process

THE ROLE OF RESEARCH in public relations is sometimes overlooked by those in local government management, yet it can be one of the most important components of the public relations process. The public relations office can provide unique and valuable service in the systematic collection and analysis of data concerning a municipality, its communications, and its publics.

Research, however, is a relatively new element of public relations. The old-time publicist or promoter would not have considered a scientific approach essential to his work. He plied his trade in a personal, subjective, intuitive, instinctive, and sometimes inspired manner. As they used to say at the dawn of the aviation industry, he flew "by the seat of his pants."

Today, however, the business of public communication is almost as complex as flying a modern jumbo jet, and its operation requires almost as much sophistication. There are varieties of media and different kinds of audiences. The effects of these variables on the impact of various messages can be subjected to objective analysis and measurement. In addition, public relationships between institutions and their various publics can be systematically diagnosed. The use of research in these areas allows management to predict accurately the responses of its publics to its policies.

The development of a research approach to public relations was urged by one of the profession's pioneers, Ivy Lee. Shortly before his

death in 1934, Lee told his staff: "The need for our services is the same as the need an Atlantic liner has for a pilot when it comes up the Bay . . . to safeguard the ship and the passengers from some unusual situation, some unexpected currents, some new condition that only the pilot, trained and familiar with it in his day-to-day work, can meet."[1] The public relations man, Lee said, must "bring an intelligent, detached, objective point of view, based on a multitude of experience and contacts, and a keen, up-to-date study of trends, of new forces, of new currents of opinion."[2] Public relations, Lee said, is really the "brain trust" of the institution it serves.[3]

Another public relations pioneer, Edward Bernays, described the need for objective data gathering and objective analysis to make public relations effective. He borrowed a term from the physical sciences to characterize public relations as the "engineering of consent."[4] In a democratic society, public consent can be earned if policies can be established that are acceptable to the public and if effective means of communication can be used to reach the public. Research can be just as important to this task as it is to the engineer who builds bridges, highways, and dams.

Public institutions, whether governmental, business, or nonprofit, must have the consent of the public to succeed. They must be publicly accountable for their policies and their actions. In a society with a free press and public access to information, the public will sooner or later insist on a full accounting. Continuous research must be done to provide the facts for such an accounting.

The public relations office should perhaps be called the "office of public responsiveness." It should have two branches: one to get response from the publics; the other to respond to the publics. One branch should perform the research function, the other the communication function. But they must work in concert, for they aid one another.

In a cost-conscious age the public relations function itself must be able to justify its expense. Here, again, research on the effectiveness of the public relations program will be increasingly important in a cost-effective analysis. Evaluation of the public relations program has many important benefits in addition to justification, and these will be brought out in this chapter.

One of the most important reasons for public relations research is to provide mechanisms to ensure feedback from the publics. Communication must be a two-way proposition, but mass communication in a mass society often precludes direct feedback from the audience. Continual research is the only means of assuring regular and meaningful response from those who receive the messages.

Research is important to many parts of the local government public relations process: it can help define goals, diagnose problems, identify publics, probe opinions, test programs, and evaluate results. It provides a way of going about the tasks of public relations systematically. A good public relations program should foster research in all of its aspects. And research really begins with the development of a research attitude and a research habit in all employees. Snap judgments and quick hunches should be questioned. Proposals and position papers should be as fully documented as possible, with data to support all conclusions and recommendations.

Such insistence on supporting data and full documentation need not stifle imagination and creativity in public relations. Here, as in politics, the brilliant idea, the sudden inspiration, the stroke of genius is often the spark needed to ignite the fire. But, once lighted, the fire

needs fuel to sustain it. And *facts* are the fuel for any political or administrative public relations program. Too often, in politics and public relations, the role of imagination and creativity is overplayed and programs fall apart for lack of facts. Research is the pathway to the facts needed to make the brilliant idea succeed.

In the discussion that follows, the three most important types of public relations research are defined: audience analysis; message analysis; and impact analysis. In other words, Who are the publics and what are their needs? How well are we getting our message across? and, How successfully have we done our job?

Then follows a broad outline of the research process: stating the problem; designing research; determining the sample; data gathering; analyzing, interpreting, and reporting the results.

The two chief methods of research—survey research and content analysis—are then discussed, the former in considerable detail. Some special suggestions regarding research, and remarks on mini-research versus maxi-research, are followed by a brief summary and a conclusion to the chapter.

Types of Research

It is possible to identify at least three types of research that are essential for effective public relations: audience analysis, message analysis, and impact analysis.

Audience Analysis

Research can help a local government in the analysis of its publics: who they are, what they need and want, what their attitudes are, what their images of their governments are, what flexibilities and rigidities exist in their opinions.

Survey research has become one of the most important types of public relations research; the survey of public opinion has become a separate profession and industry in America. George Gallup was the pioneer in this area, and the Gallup poll still is the most famous in its field: today, however, there are dozens of successful survey research firms.

Survey research can indicate what the public

approves, and it can do so over a period of time. Michael E. Schiltz, for example, examined large numbers of opinion surveys over a thirty-year period (1935–65) to determine public attitudes toward social security for the U.S. Social Security Administration. He found that "most Americans most of the time have supported . . . social insurance programs . . . at least as a means of responding to the needs of the poor."[5] Without such support government would be foolish to continue such programs.

Survey research can also point to what the public disapproves. In a well-known public survey for the U.S. Senate in 1973, the Louis Harris organization examined public confidence in American government in a detailed, 342-page report. The analysis ended with the conclusion that "the American people display much less confidence in their government than do their state and local leaders. But both the people and the leaders see a potential for effective, well-run government."[6] The study suggested many areas in which new government policies might win public confidence.

Survey research can point up the kinds of images that exist in the minds of various publics. In 1973 the Response Analysis Corporation undertook a national survey of attitudes toward food, farmers, and agriculture.[7] According to the results, nonfarm households had an image of farmers and their problems which was quite similar to that of farm households, especially on matters of costs, prices, conditions, and government control. But the nonfarmer's image of the agricultural use of pesticides was quite different from the farmer's. The study pointed up an area in which the cause of a bad image had to be dealt with, or in which a more effective communication plan had to be developed to explain a problem.

Such research can show where the public is misinformed and misguided. For example, in 1971 Louis Harris and Associates undertook a survey of public opinion on American attitudes toward alcohol and alcoholics for the National Institute on Alcohol Abuse and Alcoholism. They concluded that the public was aware of some of the basic facts on the subject and that there was much fear and apprehension of the danger of drink. "But there is also misapprehension and some confusion as to the causes and possible solutions to drinking problems, all of which indicates the need for an intensified campaign of public education."[8] The authors suggested using a coordinated approach involving the courts, the police, and social agencies, instead of depending solely on the judicial system, to clear the backlog and confusion in dealing with alcohol-related cases.

This type of research can also point out where the publics are uninformed, where they lack sufficient information to form valid opinions. Such a discovery can open up a most fertile field for those in public relations, for it is far easier to form a new opinion than change an old one. In 1970 the Harris organization undertook a study of public and community leader attitudes toward and understanding of the airlines for the Air Transport Association of America. The survey revealed "almost complete ignorance about the real elements of airline costs," about which "the public has not begun to be educated."[9] The study also uncovered a number of other facts about public attitudes toward airlines, such as the fact that airline safety was widely accepted. It thus provided a scale for decision making on the subject of which elements needed more aggressive communication and which did not.

MESSAGE ANALYSIS

Research can also focus on the messages that are sent out by government. Without some systematic audit of what is said, the original objectives may not be achieved.

It is possible, for example, to pretest a message to make sure it conveys the intended image or ideas. Before Standard Oil Company (N.J.) changed its name to Exxon Corporation it undertook several years of research, in many countries and with the aid of linguists, to find a word that carried a connotation of strength. It was important that the word be one that was not offensive in any language. Eventually "Exxon," a computer word, was chosen.

It is possible, as well, to post-test the message to find out what has been said. Content analysis can be used to determine the real transmission and the gaps in transmission which, over a period of time, can be lost in the day-to-day business of handling crises. In 1966 the director of a Washington educational association undertook a content analysis of twenty years of educational journals.[10] He found some surprising omissions: he discovered, for example, that educational associations had paid almost no attention to student affairs. Shortly thereafter student rebellion erupted, and the educational world was not prepared to deal with it. Such analysis can be used to point up areas of overemphasis and areas of neglect, thereby allowing for adjustments to meet the needs of the publics.

Message analysis can also be undertaken through readership studies to determine what the publics have actually received. Sometimes the message appears not to have been received at all, and at other times the message that is received is misunderstood. In 1967 the U.S. Public Health Service undertook a readership survey[11] of its employee magazine, a slick, expensive monthly called *PHS World*. The organization discovered, to its horror, that only 44 percent of Public Health Service employees regularly saw the magazine on which it was spending a quarter of a million dollars a year.

An employee of a Washington medical association undertook a readability study of medical journals in 1963[12] and discovered that few readers really understood most of the articles in the journals. Ironically, however, the research also revealed that it was this very lack of readability that enhanced the professional image of these journals in the minds of their medical readers.

Another sort of message analysis can be obtained from systematic audit of the mass media. Content analysis of the mass media can reveal what messages got into the public media, and how the messages might have been changed by the media's gatekeepers as the words went through the media processes. Survey research of the media gatekeepers themselves can reveal reporter and editor attitudes and can detail the reactions of these people to the kinds of messages sent to them.

For example, the National Lutheran Council completed a content analysis in 1965 of Lutheran news in the daily press.[13] The study revealed that less than 3 percent of all items in the newspapers concerning Lutherans came from the Lutheran church; that the word Lutheran was used in obituaries more than in any other kind of newspaper story; and that less than 1 percent of all items concerned Lutheran theology. Such analysis, then, clearly indicated the need for the National Lutheran Council to be more aggressive in getting meaningful religious news into the daily press.

A news media survey completed for the U.S. Department of Agriculture showed the attitudes of editors toward a particular press release.[14] A detailed questionnaire was sent to food editors concerning *Food and Home Notes*, a weekly release sent to 3,500 food editors. The survey helped to determine how, why, when, and where these editors were using the release, and changes were subsequently made to increase the effectiveness of the release.

IMPACT ANALYSIS

No doubt the most difficult, but certainly the most important, type of public relations research is the systematic study of how well the job was done. What impact did it have? To what extent did it inform, persuade, influence, or change public attitudes in the direction sought? This kind of research is usually more expensive and time-consuming, often involving experts, in-depth interviewing, or before-and-after studies in which evaluation takes place over a period of time so that trends and changes can be observed.

Experts or leaders can sometimes be brought together to provide meaningful evaluation of programs. A Washington association, for example, brought together two panels of influential readers to evaluate its quarterly journal. The members of these juries were given a set of questions about the journal in advance of the meeting to establish an agenda. Then the juries were convened for a three-hour tape-recorded session of free discussion. The tapes were transcribed, without identifying the speakers, and the transcriptions were summarized in a final report.[15] The results provided the association with an informed critique by its own members of the performance of its journal, and also gave the editors a wealth of constructive and imaginative suggestions for future development of the journal.

The in-depth interview can provide a useful method of probing attitude changes, because it can allow the interviewer to go beyond the surface opinion and to delve into when and why and how the opinion developed. After the U.S. Post Office became a semiprivate corporation, its internal communications program was revised in an attempt to cure growing personnel problems. Several years later the Postal Service sought to evaluate these efforts through in-depth personal interviews of a random sample of its middle managers around the country. The survey[16] revealed that while the service's internal communications media were accomplishing certain goals, such as building identification with management on the part of middle managers, there were also areas of failure which were leading to discontent. For example, the in-depth interviews uncovered a reservoir of resentment over the fact that communication channels were all one-way—from Washington to the local offices. It was then recommended that channels get feedback from the local level back to headquarters.

The most effective type of impact analysis is probably survey research repeated over a long period of time, so that policy changes can be clearly related to opinion changes and accurately audited. The Roper Research Associates, for example, have been performing this kind of analysis for the television industry on a regular basis since 1959.[17] Their study is designed to show the changing impact of television as compared with other media. In 1959 the Roper analysts found that 51 percent of their sample got most of their news from television, and 57 percent from newspapers. By 1971 the figures were 60 percent getting most of their news from television and 48 percent getting most of it from newspapers.[18]

All public relations research—not just impact analysis—ideally should be done on a continuing basis. The number of variables in audience and message are so great that the results of any one systematic investigation may have very lim-

ited application to any other situation. Research should not be an occasional or last resort but an ongoing and integral part of the process.

The Research Process

Although average working public administrators and public relations officers are not going to be experts on research, they will find it useful to know the basic considerations for conducting meaningful systematic study of any public relations problem. They will want to have the basic outline of steps in the research process firmly in mind, so that they can direct the experts and not be directed by them. In addition, they should know the pitfalls and the problem areas, what is acceptable, and what is shoddy.

The list that follows is designed to include the essential considerations for completing a research project. It is suggested that each of these steps be carefully thought out before the project is undertaken.

STATING THE PROBLEM

Research can only be directed at one specific problem at a time, and that problem has to be clearly defined with carefully stated limits. It would clearly be unwise to attempt to carry out a research effort for the stated purpose of "determining the most effective public information program," but by limiting the proposal one might make it quite possible "to determine the most effective medium of health information for the elderly citizens of Pinecrest."

In stating the problem it is important to describe its significance, to state the reasons for researching it, and to relate it to the final objectives and goals. It should be described in relation to some theoretical framework and to previous research (for example, What is already known about the health information habits of the elderly, and what theories can be referred to?)

Stating a hypothesis will help to clarify and define concepts and develop ways of testing validity. (Such a hypothesis, for example, might be that videotaped presentations are more effective than printed materials in transmitting health information to the elderly of Pinecrest.) The hypothesis is a proposition that can be tested and that suggests the design the research must take to be significant.

DESIGNING THE RESEARCH

Knowing the problem and stating the hypothesis, the researchers are ready to plan the project. Research design is a series of guideposts intended to keep a project going in the right direction. If the research is descriptive, the researchers must be concerned with the universe and the sample. If the research is experimental, they must be concerned with controlled groups and variables.

The research design should include a working guide, budget, and timetable for the project. The design should be practical. Researchers should not plan to take on more than they can handle—in time, money, or personnel. The design should describe the needs for the project and the steps necessary to bring it to conclusion. For a model guide to research costing, see Figure 2–1.

DETERMINING THE SAMPLE

Research is possible in public relations largely because of the laws of statistics. With a proper sample—though it may constitute a very small percentage of the total population under study—the results of the research can be projected on the total population with reasonable accuracy. It is not necessary to interview the head of every household in the city—an expensive and time-consuming task—if a representative sample of heads of households can be devised. The Gallup poll of national public opinion, for example, utilizes a base of about 1,500 interviews to represent more than 200,000,000 people.

At least three main types of sampling can be used, although others can be identified (Figure 2–2). *Random* sampling, which requires the least subjective judgments, is like shuffling cards and then picking them from the deck. Every card has an equal chance of being selected. A related and more convenient method is *systematic* sampling, which requires selecting a sample of n items from the universe of N items. At random, an item is picked from the first k items, and then every kth is chosen from this starting point (where k may be chosen to be N/n).[19]

The other two main types of sampling are *stratified*[20] and *judgmental*. In a stratified sample an effort is made to get the sample equivalently proportional to some known proportion in the universe. For example, if it is known that the elderly population in Pinecrest is 42 percent white female, 16 percent black female, 30 percent white male, and 12 percent black male the goal should be to get a sample stratified with exactly those percentages in each category.

A *judgmental* or *purposive* sample can be used when practical considerations (perhaps small size of the universe) preclude the use of a probability sample. The investigator uses his or her best judgment to determine what would be representative. Such sampling should be used only when the possible errors from bias would not be serious and when other types of sampling are impractical.

GATHERING THE DATA

Although it might seem like the major part of research, gathering the data should actually be the simplest, or at least the most routine, aspect of the project. The real work comes in stating the problem, designing the research, and selecting the sample.

In social science research the data are often gathered by nonresearch but *trained* lay persons. If the research has been properly designed the data gathered will not be affected by the person doing the gathering. The facts should be replicable no matter what individuals are involved.

Methods for gathering the data must be clearly laid out, whether in a questionnaire for survey research or in a schedule of items and categories for content analysis. The interviewers or itemizers should be thoroughly briefed on the project, should understand the goals and objectives, and should know the sponsoring agency.

ANALYZING THE RESULTS

To make the results meaningful the raw data must be analysed, and this usually requires the help of machines—calculators, sorters, and especially computers. Indeed, the development

Activity	Total	Week ending ___	Week ending ___	Week ending ___	___

1. Total
   a) Man-hours
   b) Cost ($)
   c) % of total completed					

2. Planning
   a) Man-hours
   b) Cost
   c) % completed					

3. Pilot study and pretests
   a) Man-hours
   b) Cost
   c) % completed					

4. Drawing sample
   a) Man-hours
   b) Cost
   c) % completed					

5. Preparing observational materials
   a) Man-hours
   b) Cost
   c) % completed					

6. Selection and training
   a) Man-hours
   b) Cost
   c) % completed					

7. Trial run
   a) Man-hours
   b) Cost
   c) % completed					

8. Revising plans
   a) Man-hours
   b) Cost
   c) % completed					

9. Collecting data
   a) Man-hours
   b) Cost
   c) % completed					

10. Processing data
   a) Man-hours
   b) Cost
   c) % completed					

11. Preparing final report
   a) Man-hours
   b) Cost
   c) % completed					

FIGURE 2–1. *Suggested guide to research costing.* (*Source: Russell K. Ackoff,* THE DESIGN OF SOCIAL RESEARCH, *Chicago: University of Chicago Press, 1953, p. 347. Copyright © 1953 by the University of Chicago Press; 6th printing, 1973.) This listing and its order are in no sense absolute.*

of computers has made contemporary social science research possible; without these monsters hundreds or thousands of man-hours could go into the necessary counting and computations. It is crucial that the project be designed with categories so that the raw data can be coded or classified according to some systematic method. The set of categories should be derived from a single classificatory principle; the categories within the set should be mutually exhaustive and mutually exclusive.

Obviously, the more specific the raw data the easier it will be to use a machine for tabulation and analysis. If questions are posed so that the answers can be readily categorized (yes or no answers, or multiple choice answers, for example) the data can be easily coded for sorting or computing. If the questions are open-ended, with long notes from in-depth interviews, the results will have to be digested and categorized separately before they can be analysed by machine.

There is a break-even point for machine tabulation. Generally speaking, if the number of items to be tabulated is under 500 it can be more efficient for a trained clerk to hand-tabulate the items.

As Kent Lloyd wrote in the predecessor volume to this book:

The purpose of statistical analysis by transferring raw data to tabular form is (1) to determine what is "typical" in the group through such measures of central tendency as the mean, median, and mode; (2) to indicate how widely individuals in the group vary in terms of range, quartile deviation, and standard deviation; (3) to show the relation of different variables in the data to one another—such as age, education, income, or occupation to [such variables as] attitudes toward government service; and (4) to describe the similarities and differences between two or more groups of individuals.[21]

INTERPRETING THE RESULTS

It is usually not enough to simply tabulate and analyse the results, showing averages, ranges, ratios, and relationships. That analysis must be interpreted. What does it all mean? How does it relate to other studies, to theory, to practice? How can the results be used? What are the limitations?

A problem in interpretation is the tendency to overgeneralize. It is important not to draw conclusions that stretch the facts beyond their limits. And it is important to keep the interpretation objective and free of the biases of the investigators, the public relations officers, and the public administrators.

REPORTING THE RESULTS

The results need to be reported in a meaningful way: if they are not, a lot of time, energy, and effort will have been wasted. Unless the results of the research are reported to the decision makers in such a way that they can integrate the conclusions into policy, there is little need for such research. Therefore, the report should be succinct, forceful, and direct, with as many graphs and charts and other visual representations as possible to dramatize key points and emphasize salient features.

Good public relations research can have the added benefit of providing promotional material for the program, because the results can be reported to the publics concerned as well as to the decision makers. Such reporting can demonstrate the concern of the decision makers for the attitudes, opinions, and reactions of the publics studied.

Methods of Research

One of the key decisions in the research design is the choice of a specific method. The method most often used in public relations is survey research, although content analysis can also be useful; both will be discussed here briefly.

SURVEY RESEARCH

Survey research is a relatively recent development in social science, but as a method of systematically probing public opinion and soliciting feedback it is growing rapidly in use and importance. Most people probably identify survey research with opinion polling, such as the Gallup poll and the kind of research undertaken by politicians or by advertising agencies for market research. But the use of surveys is growing in public administration as well. One city (Dayton, Ohio) has a full-time operation, the Dayton Public Opinion Center, which is continually examining its citizens for their attitudes and ideas.

Sampling Chart

Type of sampling	Brief description	Advantages	Disadvantages
A. Simple random	Assign to each population member a unique number; select sample items by use of random numbers	1. Requires minimum knowledge of population in advance 2. Free of possible classification errors 3. Easy to analyze data and compute errors	1. Does not make use of knowledge of population which researcher may have 2. Larger errors for same sample size than in stratified sampling
B. Systematic	Use natural ordering or order population; select random starting point between 1 and the nearest integer to the sampling ratio (N/n); select items at interval of nearest integer to sampling ratio	1. If population is ordered with respect to pertinent property, gives stratification effect, and hence reduces variability compared to A 2. Simplicity of drawing sample; easy to check	1. If sampling interval is related to a periodic ordering of the population, increased variability may be introduced 2. Estimates of error likely to be high where there is stratification effect
C. Multistage random	Use a form of random sampling in each of the sampling stages where there are at least two stages	1. Sampling lists, identification, and numbering required only for members of sampling units selected in sample 2. If sampling units are geographically defined, cuts down field costs (i.e., travel)	1. Errors likely to be larger than in A or B for same sample size 2. Errors increase as number of sampling units selected decreases
1. With probability proportionate to size	Select sampling units with probability proportionate to their size	1. Reduces variability	1. Lack of knowledge of size of each sampling unit before selection increases variability
D. Stratified 1. Proportionate	Select from every sampling unit at other than last stage a random sample proportionate to size of sampling unit	1. Assures representativeness with respect to property which forms basis of classifying units; therefore yields less variability than A or C 2. Decreases chance of failing to include members of population because of classification process 3. Characteristics of each stratum can be estimated, and hence comparisons can be made	1. Requires accurate information on proportion of population in each stratum, otherwise increases error 2. If stratified lists are not available, may be costly to prepare them; possibility of faulty classification and hence increase in variability
2. Optimum allocation	Same as 1 except sample is proportionate to variability within strata as well as their size	1. Less variability for same sample size than 1	1. Requires knowledge of variability of pertinent characteristic within strata
3. Disproportionate	Same as 1 except that size of sample is not proportionate to size of sampling unit but is dedicated by analytical considerations or convenience	1. More efficient than 1 for comparison of strata or where different errors are optimum for different strata	1. Less efficient than 1 for determining population characteristics; i.e., more variability for same sample size

FIGURE 2–2. *Types of sampling for use in surveys. (Source: Ackoff,* THE DESIGN OF SOCIAL RESEARCH, *pp. 124–25.)*

Type of sampling	Brief description	Advantages	Disadvantages
E. Cluster	Select sampling units by some form of random sampling; ultimate units are groups; select these at random and take a complete count of each	1. If clusters are geographically defined, yields lowest field costs 2. Requires listing only individuals in selected clusters 3. Characteristics of clusters as well as those of population can be estimated 4. Can be used for subsequent samples, since clusters, not individuals, are selected, and substitution of individuals may be permissible	1. Larger errors for comparable size than other probability samples 2. Requires ability to assign each member of population uniquely to a cluster; inability to do so may result in duplication or omission of individuals
F. Stratified cluster	Select clusters at random from every sampling unit	1. Reduces variability of plain cluster sampling	1. Disadvantages of stratified sampling added to those of cluster sampling 2. Since cluster properties may change, advantage of stratification may be reduced and make sample unusable for later research
G. Repetitive: multiple or sequential	Two or more samples of any of the above types are taken, using results from earlier samples to design later ones, or determine if they are necessary	1. Provides estimates of population characteristics which facilitate efficient planning of succeeding sample, therefore reduces error of final estimate 2. In the long run reduces number of observations required	1. Complicates administration of fieldwork 2. More computation and analysis required than in nonrepetitive sampling 3. Sequential sampling can only be used where a very small sample can approximate representativeness and where the number of observations can be increased conveniently at any stage of the research
H. Judgment	Select a subgroup of the population which, on the basis of available information, can be judged to be representative of the total population; take a complete count or subsample of this group	1. Reduces cost of preparing sample and fieldwork, since ultimate units can be selected so that they are close together	1. Variability and bias of estimates cannot be measured or controlled 2. Requires strong assumptions or considerable knowledge of population and subgroup selected
1. Quota	Classify population by pertinent properties; determine desired proportion of sample from each class; fix quotas for each observer	1. Same as above 2. Introduces some stratification effect	1. Introduces bias of observers' classification of subjects and nonrandom selection within classes

FIGURE 2–2. (continued.)

A particularly useful booklet on survey research is *Obtaining Citizen Feedback: The Application of Citizen Surveys to Local Governments,* by Kenneth Webb and Harry P. Hatry, published in 1973 by the Urban Institute. The authors made much use of the Dayton Public Opinion Center in writing the work.

Most survey research uses a questionnaire, with carefully worded and pretested questions administered to a carefully selected sample of the population to be studied. The steps in the survey process are similar to the steps in the research process described above. For a more specific outline of the steps, see Figure 2–3. At least three different modes of survey can be identified: personal interview; telephone interview; and mailed questionnaire. Each has its advantages and disadvantages, and these need to be examined in designing the research.

Personal Face-to-Face Interview. The personal interview is probably the best mode, although it is also the most expensive. A trained interviewer must administer the questionnaire to each individual in the sample. The rate of response is usually the highest of the three modes, because the interviewer is paid by the interview and can persist until a satisfactory response is obtained. The chances for misunderstanding are reduced, because the interviewer can explain the questions and use visual aids to inform and instruct.

Telephone Interview. This technique is on the increase as a useful mode of survey research, partly because it is less expensive than the face-to-face interview. Before the middle of this century, certainly, telephone interviews could not have yielded a valid sample of the total population, because telephone ownership was not sufficiently widespread—certainly not among those in the lower economic strata. Perhaps history's most famous polling blunder resulted from a failure to appreciate this sampling bias. In 1936 the *Literary Digest,* using a telephone survey, predicted that Alf Landon would win the presidential election in a year that saw FDR sweep every state but Maine and Vermont. The telephone poll badly biased the sample in favor of the Republicans.

Today, however, telephone ownership is sufficiently widespread to make its use in survey

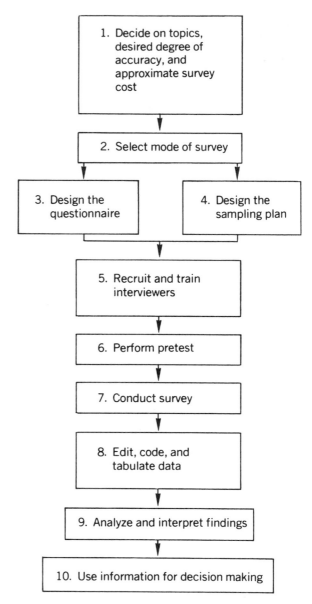

FIGURE 2–3. *Typical steps in the survey process. (Source: Kenneth Webb and Harry P. Hatry,* OBTAINING CITIZEN FEEDBACK: THE APPLICATION OF CITIZEN SURVEYS TO LOCAL GOVERNMENTS, *Washington, D.C.: The Urban Institute, 1973, p. 44. Copyright © 1973, The Urban Institute, Washington, D.C.)*

research practical. But it is still not without problems; a growing group has unlisted numbers, and there is still disproportionate lack of telephones in the inner city compared to the affluent suburbs. Finally, it is important to make certain that the telephone interviewers are as carefully trained as those who work face-to-face.

Mailed Questionnaire. This is probably the easiest and least expensive mode. It also has the advantage of providing more candid results because it can be completed in privacy and anonymity. The chief disadvantage is the low rate of return and the bias. Some social scientists feel that certain types of people are apt to return questionnaires and other types are not. If this is true, the results can be biased for certain characteristics.

Efforts can be made to reduce possible bias from nonrespondents by follow-up mailings, telegrams, phone calls, and even house visits. Mailed questionnaires require a literate universe, and one that is highly motivated to respond.

Special Problems. Certain survey research problems should be noted here. First of all, pretesting of questions and training of interviewers are essential. Researchers can ensure that the questions are not vague, misunderstood, and confusing only by trying them out on a small group in advance of the full-scale research. This trial run can save time and money and greatly increase the validity of the final results. Training sessions with the interviewers can also increase the effectiveness of the survey.

Second, one should not overlook the pitfalls in survey research. Webb and Hatry list a number that are important.[22] Beware of polls on complex issues about which the respondents lack information. Beware of question wording—what is said or not said can be misleading. Beware of sensitive issues and questions that tend to elicit silence or misleading answers. Beware of nonrepresentative results if inadequate procedures are used. Beware of the problems of invasion of privacy which concern some respondents.

CONTENT ANALYSIS

Content analysis is also a useful method of public relations research (see under Message Analysis, earlier in this chapter). First, it helps researchers audit their own messages. Such an audit can help determine whether objectives are being met and whether messages are readable, listenable, and digestible for the audiences. Second, it can help researchers examine outside messages, about themselves or about audiences in which they are interested—the mass media, in particular.

The data gathering work of content analysis is dull and laborious; it requires personnel with the perseverance of proofreaders, willing to devote careful attention to detail for long periods. The work is essentially the counting of items, but the items have to be carefully specified so that they will be counted in the right categories.

The real work of content analysis is in designing the research so that adequate categories are established for counting. The research designer has to clarify the units to be counted in each category. And both the units and the categories must be clearly defined so that all who do the counting will put the units into the same category. It is also important to establish some means of measuring intensity of content; the number of column inches of newsprint devoted to a subject can help establish intensity, and so can the placement (front page or inside page, top of front page or bottom of front page, etc.) or, in the case of broadcast, the time allocation (for example, prime time or fringe time). It is also possible to establish means of determining content direction—whether it is favorable or unfavorable, positive or negative, conservative or liberal, or neutral. But definitions must be particularly careful here.

Special Suggestions

Public relations research itself needs to be audited from time to time. It can be useful to have outside experts come in to examine the work, to make sure the sampling procedures are adequate, to check that biases are not hurting the objectivity and validity of the results, and to examine the overall design to ascertain that the right questions are being asked about the real problems. Such an audit can also help provide answers to criticisms regarding the findings.

Outside experts and consultants can and should be used as often as the budget allows in the design and analysis of local government public relations research. Polling firms can be helpful—and are also expensive. Local firms may have experts in particular subjects whose help can be used—statisticians, for example, or computer specialists. And local colleges and universities often have faculty members in the social sciences, communications, journalism, and public relations who can be brought in to help.

All research activity can be expensive (see Table 2–1). Webb and Hatry point out ways in which local governments might cut down some of the expense by using volunteers. But they note some disadvantages, including a higher percentage of dropouts and a greater lack of dependability than are found with paid data gatherers. They do not recommend volunteers for regular surveying.[23]

In special cases, however, volunteers can be very helpful. In Arlington, Virginia, as Webb and Hatry point out, the League of Women Voters provided the interviewers for a 1972 survey of citizen experiences and attitudes toward various aspects of the county's criminal justice system. Initially, twenty-four volunteered, but only fifteen completed their quota of interviews. A paid consultant was used to design the survey and train and supervise the interviewers, most of whom had had no prior experience. The results were quite good, with only 9 percent of the sample refusing to be interviewed.[24]

Mini-Research versus Maxi-Research

If the local government public relations office can establish a research attitude in its work,

TABLE 2–1. *Costs for four in person surveys at the Dayton Public Opinion Center, Dayton, Ohio. (Source: Webb and Hatry,* OBTAINING CITIZEN FEEDBACK, *p. 52.)*

Costs	Surveys			
	1 Sept. 1971	2 Oct. 1971	3 Nov. 1971	4 Feb. 1972
Data collection				
Pretest	$ 36	$ 48	$ 53	$ 46
Interviews and travel	2,720	2,981	2,254	1,936
Office help	140	488	310	195
Training costs	156	126	66	65
Field supervision	636	685	439	274
Printing	97	309	204	198
Data processing and tabulation				
Coding	552	1,028	441	416
Computer and keypunching	499	611	514	641
Total variable cost	$4,836	$6,276	$4,281	$3,771
Total interviews completed	696	803	697	805
Average interview time (minutes)	35	35	25	15
Variable costs per completed interview	$ 6.95	$ 7.82	$ 6.14	$ 4.69
Prorata share of fixed costs[1]	$ 6.70	$ 6.70	$ 6.70	$ 6.70
Total cost per interview (excluding start-up costs)	$13.65	$14.50	$12.80	$11.40

[1] Based on the assumption that fixed costs of about $40,000 per year should be spread over 8 surveys per year at an average of 750 interviews—or 6,000 total interviews per year. If fewer surveys are undertaken, this unit cost would rise.

there are many ways in which the professionals can keep their fingers on the pulse of opinion and can keep current with trends in events without engaging in major research efforts.

The day-to-day flow of communication can provide material for objective analysis without great expense. Outgoing communication—press releases, promotional materials, annual reports, and even public correspondence—can be categorized and filed by subject and theme, so that a running check can be kept on outgoing messages.

Incoming communication can also be categorized, tabulated, and filed on a daily or weekly basis. Clipping services and broadcast monitoring services are useful expenditures (but if they are used only to send items to the chief administrator to show how the public relations office got into the media, the expense may not be worth it). Clippings and broadcast reports can be categorized and analysed on a regular basis and charted for trends.

Correspondence, complaints, and telephone calls can also be recorded and categorized. Contacts with media representatives can also be noted. It is useful to have a form on which employees can note such contacts with the public and the press.

Several warnings are in order, however. First, one should not make the mistake of thinking that this mini-research can take the place of regular, full-scale research projects. Second, it is wise to remember that most public-initiated responses are negative. People write or phone in with complaints much more often than with compliments. Such response is apt to be negatively biased. Third, efforts to record contacts with the press have sometimes backfired, with

journalists claiming that this is an attempt to intimidate public officials or newsmen and that it violates the spirit of a free press. This situation, of course, can be easily avoided through adequate advance explanation.

Conclusion

This chapter has stressed the importance of research to the local government public relations process, has defined the three major types of public relations research (audience analysis, message analysis, and impact analysis), and has outlined the various steps in the research process, explaining how this process can best be used. The use of the two leading research methods—survey research and content analysis—has been outlined. Some special suggestions and some remarks on mini-research have concluded the substantive discussion.

If public relations is to serve its real purpose in public administration in our local governments, research must be a vital part of the process. It should begin with the development of a research attitude on the part of all public relations personnel. But it can and should go beyond that to the use of research experts for major studies on crucial issues at regular intervals.

Only with research can public message-sending achieve the feedback necessary for effective communication. Only with continual research can institutions remain in contact with and responsive to their publics. And only with research can the public relations activity be evaluated for an accounting of the effectiveness of the taxpayer's dollar.

[1] Ray Eldon Hiebert, COURTIER TO THE CROWD (Ames: Iowa State University Press, 1966), p. 315.

[2] Ibid.

[3] Ibid.

[4] Edward L. Bernays, "Emergence of the Public Relations Counsel: Principles and Recollections," HARVARD BUSINESS HISTORY REVIEW 45 (Autumn 1971): 297.

[5] Michael E. Schiltz, PUBLIC ATTITUDES TOWARD SOCIAL SECURITY, 1935–1965 (Washington, D.C.: U.S. Department of Health, Education, and Welfare, 1970), p. 181.

[6] U.S., Congress, Senate, Committee on Government Operations, CONFIDENCE AND CONCERN—CITIZENS VIEW AMERICAN GOVERNMENT: A SURVEY OF PUBLIC ATTITUDES,

survey undertaken by Louis Harris and Associates, Inc. (Washington, D.C.: Government Printing Office, 1973), p. 27.

[7] Response Analysis Corporation, WHAT THE PUBLIC SAYS ABOUT FOOD, FARMERS, AND AGRICULTURE (Princeton, N.J.: Response Analysis Corporation, 1973).

[8] Louis Harris and Associates, Inc., AMERICAN ATTITUDES TOWARD ALCOHOL AND ALCOHOLICS: A SURVEY OF PUBLIC OPINION (Washington, D.C.: U.S. National Institute of Mental Health, National Institute on Alcohol Abuse and Alcoholism, 1971), p. 202.

[9] Louis Harris and Associates, Inc., A STUDY OF PUBLIC AND COMMUNITY LEADER ATTITUDES AND UNDERSTANDING

OF THE AIRLINES (Washington, D.C.: Air Transport Association of America, 1970), p. 3 of separate summary.

[10] John W. Leslie, "The Growth and Development of the Educational Field as Manifest by a Content Analysis of Selected Professional Publications" (Master's thesis, American University, 1966). At the time he undertook this analysis, Mr. Leslie was director of the American College Public Relations Association, for whom the study was undertaken.

[11] Ray Eldon Hiebert, READERSHIP SURVEY OF THE PHS WORLD (Washington, D.C.: U.S. Public Health Service, 1967).

[12] Meadie Edgar Pace, "Readability in Medical Journals: A Study of Problems and Editorial Practices" (Master's thesis, American University, 1963). The study was undertaken for the American Psychiatric Association. Mr. Pace was employed by this association at the time the study was undertaken.

[13] Charles DeVries and Ray Eldon Hiebert, A SURVEY OF LUTHERAN ITEMS FOUND IN THIRTY-SIX DAILY NEWSPAPERS (New York: National Lutheran Council, 1965).

[14] Elizabeth Savigde Crosby, "A Newspaper Survey To Determine the Effectiveness of FOOD AND HOME NOTES, U.S.D.A." (Master's thesis, American University, 1964).

[15] Ray Eldon Hiebert, AN ANALYSIS OF A COLLEGE AND UNIVERSITY JOURNAL (Washington, D.C.: American College Public Relations Association, 1966).

[16] Ray Eldon Hiebert, A READERSHIP SURVEY OF THE POSTAL LEADER (Washington, D.C.: U.S. Postal Service, 1974).

[17] Burns W. Roper, PUBLIC ATTITUDES TOWARD TELEVISION AND OTHER MASS MEDIA, 1959–1971 (New York: Television Information Office, 1971).

[18] Because of multiple answers, the figures given here do not total to 100 percent.

[19] As an overall introduction to and handbook for sampling techniques, the following work is excellent: William G. Cochran, SAMPLING TECHNIQUES, 2nd ed. (New York: John Wiley & Sons, Inc., 1963); random sampling is discussed in Chapter 2 of the aforementioned book, and systematic sampling in Chapter 8.

[20] Ibid., Chapters 5 and 5A.

[21] Kent M. Lloyd, "Research and the Public Relations Process," in MUNICIPAL PUBLIC RELATIONS, ed. Desmond L. Anderson (Chicago: International City Managers' Association, 1966), p. 45.

[22] Kenneth Webb and Harry P. Hatry, OBTAINING CITIZEN FEEDBACK: THE APPLICATION OF CITIZEN SURVEYS TO LOCAL GOVERNMENTS (Washington, D.C.: The Urban Institute, 1973).

[23] Ibid.

[24] Ibid.

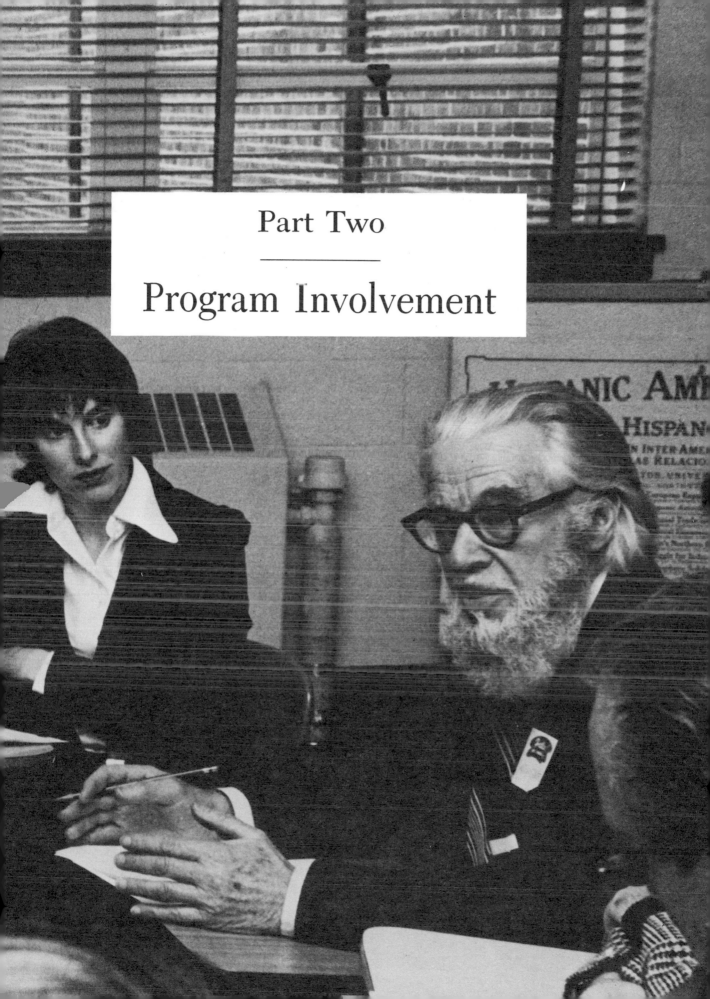

Part Two

Program Involvement

3

The Council: Focal Point
of Interests

THE LEGISLATIVE BODY—the city council, county board, or town selectmen—is and must be the focal point of a community's public relations. Certainly the council members, raised to prominence by the electorate, recognize the deep personal need for public understanding and acceptance, or they will not be council members for long. It is this role of the council as the *focal point of interests* that is the theme of this chapter.

While the chapters in Part One of this book dealt with public relations itself, this opening chapter of Part Two, and the five chapters that follow it, are concerned with the various aspects of the implementation of the public relations program.

In the present chapter, the attitude of citizens to their local government is detailed, followed by an example of the misunderstandings and problems in communications between local government and the public which points up the need for an efficient public relations operation. How should the council seek the public interest? And what, in fact, constitutes the public interest?

The public interest is, therefore, defined in its various aspects (as public consensus; as superior wisdom; as moral imperative; as personal values; as a synthesis of interests); a case study follows. The public's impact on the council is then explored in detail. Last, the council member's own role is discussed, with an outline of his or her responsibilities. A summary concludes the chapter.

From Both Ends of the Telescope—
and More

As the principal instrument in local government for translating myriad and divergent citizen interests and influences into governmental policy, the council, both as a body and as individuals, sets the tone for a government's public relations.

It is in the council that interests converge, both those emanating from within the government hierarchy and those from outside—from individual citizens and groups. Moreover, the convergence of such influences has high visibility because, under law and by its nature, the council transacts its business—makes its decisions—in full view of the public. Therefore, both schisms which exist within the community and differences among a local government's employees are often opened to full public view.

Furthermore, because an individual council member's tenure in office is dependent in considerable measure on the public relations of the local government as well as on his or her own public relations, the resolution of individual citizen grievances and other problems and needs by each council member, acting either unilaterally or in concert with one or more other council members, heightens the visibility of the council as the *focal point of interests*.

The electoral process by which council members ascend to public office provides the basis for the resolution of community interests, or the synthesizing of diverse points of view into governmental policy and programs. Some actual resolutions and syntheses occur during the political campaign. The synthesizing process, however, continues interminably. It occurs both formally and informally. Viewing the council as the legislative body, it is revealed by continuous legislative–executive relationships, legislative–employee relationships (ranging from department head to custodian, street sweeper, and file clerk), legislative–citizen relationships, and relationships of city council members with public officials outside the specific community. Some of these relationships are highlighted in this chapter.

Citizen Attitudes toward Local Government

One of the chief differences between government and private enterprise is that the "patrons" of government—that is, the citizens—are more more or less forced to lend at least their financial support to government operations.

While all persons are theoretically able to choose their occupations and places of residence, all are required to pay taxes, regardless of how they earn a living or where they live. And while they theoretically direct the use of their tax money by electing the policy-making officials of government, they obviously do not vote for each item of expense incurred by government.

Perhaps it is because of the attitudes that some people have about government, and the special attitudes that council members have about the public, that public relations is so important in local government. It is somewhat easier to list the attitudes of the public than it is to describe the attitudes of council members. We should bear in mind, however, the fact that in describing attitudes of the public we may also be describing council members' attitudes toward government—attitudes which they may have held before serving on the council, or attitudes which they may still hold.

A major concern expressed by the public toward government has to do with money. While taxes are here to stay, public acceptance of taxes is not guaranteed. It is thus not uncommon for dissatisfied citizens to feel that they are paying the salary of the public official whom they may be confronting at the moment.

Closely connected with the idea that the dissatisfied citizen pays the salaries of government employees—which is, of course, true to a certain extent—is the belief held by some that a majority of government officials are "political hacks feeding at the public trough," or that they are "politicians for profit." Or, we may look at it this way: the citizen who notices that a certain council member is using a city-owned automobile during the evening hours may assume that the official is using the vehicle for private purposes and is thus misusing the taxpayer's money. On the other hand, a citizen may admire or pity the official for having to leave his or her family in order to attend a meeting of importance to the community.

These different attitudes are rarely stated by citizens. We know that they exist, however, as a result of what we hear privately and what we ourselves may have at one time believed. The negative attitudes which the public may have toward government often are the principal basis for governmental concern with public relations. Fortunately, citizens also hold a variety of positive, constructive attitudes toward government.

Few communities provide opportunities for the development and maintenance of a public relations program that incorporates the best-known principles of communication and also permits experimentation with some of the less tried, but promising, techniques in this field.

Where do we find the "public" that cities, counties, school districts, and other local governments are trying to reach? In one sense, the task is simplified by the tendency of people to join with others of similar interests; this gives rise to a great number of groups which constitute a portion of what we call our "public." One person may join several groups, and one such group may actually represent a variety of interests and viewpoints. For a more thorough discussion of publics and group participation, see Chapters 4 and 7.

The council, then, has more than one public: there is a great variety of them. The members of the city council, for example, sitting as they do on the board of directors of the municipal corporation, represent not only their particular constituents but also the entire electorate. It is indeed a rude awakening for the new council member who finds his or her opinion on the public interest of a particular project violently opposed by major influential persons and groups, some of whom have worked long and hard to place the member in his or her new post.

The council member must have a high threshold of understanding and patience when the local chamber of commerce insists on lower taxes and at the same time decries competitive bidding and requests financial support. The point is that there are different publics for different purposes. The taxpaying resident business person with income property who has children in school, goes to church, and is a member of the leading service club is, in fact, a member of many publics, several of which consistently bring conflicting pressures to bear on council members.

From Policy to Operations

The people elect the city council. The council determines the policies of the city government. . . . In determining policy the councilman does his best to represent his constituents.[1]

The many influences upon council members make them acutely aware of the need for understanding and acceptance by the electorate. Nor are these pressures limited to matters of policy determination. Indeed, it would seem that no problem is too small, too unimportant, to be called to the attention of council members.

The city dweller whose rubbish is not picked up, the resident who gets a ticket for violating the overnight parking prohibition, the influential businessman whose nephew does not get a local government job, the person who lives along the street that is being rebuilt too slowly —all tell their council members and demand their rights as taxpayers. Council members must be ready and able to deal with each problem—policy, procedure, personnel, or operating detail—and give their constituents the rep-

resentation for which they were elected. An example is given below (involving a mayor rather than a council member) of a case that illustrates the communications problems legislators can face in their relations with the public.

RESOLVING AN "ARREST CASE"

Typically, the chief administrator of a local government is confronted with a wide range of problems, from minor complaints to major grievances.

This actual case, involving a mayor, occurred in a small California city. As the mayor recalls, it went something like this.

I am a realtor and many times people with civic problems come into my business office. One day two men came in, one of whom I recognized as a local minister. After sitting down, the other man, whom I did not know, burst out:

"We are good, law abiding citizens! We're respectable—and that Captain Dingle arrested her—like a common criminal. He forced his way into our home and said, 'Let's go, Skinner, I'm taking you in!' "

"Now, now," interposed the minister, "calm down, Mr. Skinner, we're here to get to the bottom of this. Let's not get excited! Please tell the mayor just exactly what happened."

"That's what I'm doing! He came in and started swearing and cursing and ordering her around. He said vile things, and I don't have to put up with that! Yes, I went to the chief of police and he didn't help at all—he said I should be glad she wasn't thrown into jail. You can't pick on us just because we live in a trailer park."

"Who is he?" I asked.

"Captain Dingle, that no-good badge happy captain," he replied. "He's the one who caused all the trouble. He told the trailer park manager that we were wanted by the police in four states—now she always looks at us funny when we come in."

"When did all this happen?" I asked.

"About three or four weeks ago. Without any warning he pushed the trailer door open, almost knocked her down—and said, 'Let's go, Mrs. Skinner, I have a warrant for your arrest!' "

"Are you sure that's exactly what the captain said?"

He almost shouted, "What difference does it make what he said? He swore, and called her dirty names, and he arrested her. We're good church people—we never had any trouble with the law! Why are they picking on us?—Just because we live in a trailer court, that's why."

"What did the captain say?"

"He said that she was under arrest—wanted by the police in Los Angeles. Why, we've never been in Los

Angeles. I'm going to the newspapers and tell them how my wife was treated just like a common criminal! We don't have to stand for it."

"What else did the captain say?"

"He said that she was a ———well, I won't repeat it, but he called her dirty names and was very abusive."

"Just exactly what did he call her? What did he say that was abusive?"

"Well—it wasn't exactly what he said, it was the way he said it!"

"He really didn't use any words that were dirty, or vile, or insulting?"

"No," he admitted, "but his manner upset her terribly. She was sobbing when I came home."

"You weren't there when the captain came?"

"No, but I came home right after he was there, and she was almost hysterical. We are good citizens, we would never do anything wrong. She was treated like a common criminal."

I asked, "In what way was his manner abusive?"

"Well," he replied, "he arrested her, and now her name will be smeared forever."

I asked, "How did the captain arrest her? Did he take her to the station? Did he handcuff her?"

"No," he answered with disgust, "he said she was under arrest and told her the L.A. police had a warrant for her."

"Then what did he do?"

"He went away, and left her, and when I came home, she was so upset she couldn't tell me what happened for a whole hour." He continued, "He had no right to upset her that way—to treat her like a common criminal."

"Mr. Skinner," the minister said softly, "let's leave the matter with the mayor, and when he has looked into it he will call us."

"Yes," I said, "I will call you. And thank you for telling me about this."

Later in the day, having finished a discussion with the police chief about vehicle preventive maintenance, I told him of Mr. Skinner and his wife, Margaret Skinner, who allegedly was arrested by Captain Dingle.

"I'll let you know about it," he said.

The following morning the chief sent over a memo with a teletype attached. The teletype message read as follows:

RE MARGARET SKINNER AKA MADGE SKINNER AKA VIRGINIA SKEEN AKA MARY SKEEN. WE HOLD LA SC B/W NO———CHARGING PERJURY AND VIOLATION OF PROB. SUBJ DESC AS FEM WHITE 26 YRS 5–2 108 LBS BRN AND HAZEL. HAVE INFO SUBJ IS NOW AT SPACE 31 HARVARD TRAILER PARK. PLS PICK UP AND ADVISE.

The memo, typed neatly on police department stationery, said: "Following receipt of attached warrant, Captain Dingle contacted suspect, and, after investigation, requested suspect to appear at station for fingerprint check. Captain satisfied suspect is not wanted fugitive, but print verification would be certain. Captain courteous, but firm, with suspect."

I put in a call to the minister and together we talked with the woman's husband. He still insisted that his wife had been arrested and that her good name had been ruined.

Finally, the minister accepted the job of counseling the man and his wife, who never did contact the newspapers, but I have often wondered what impression of police these people now have.

This case typifies the misunderstandings and communications problems which complicate the legislator's public relations.

Seeking the Public Interest

Council members, in the last analysis, have been elected to represent that nebulous concept—the public interest—as best they can. They are required, as the pressure point of community influences, to make continuous decisions relating to the public interest and to make complex value judgments on what in fact such an interest constitutes. But council members must first and foremost represent the public interest while maintaining a public image acceptable to their constituents.

THE ELUSIVE PUBLIC INTEREST

We should perhaps consider the term "public interest." It is easy enough to describe what the public interest is not. To say, "the public interest is what I say the public interest is," as stated by a certain mayor not too long ago, immediately evokes impassioned disagreement. The public interest cannot be described in such a cavalier fashion.

Boss Tweed of New York used to resent it when people would accuse his administration of graft and corruption and of favoring only a few at the expense of the public interest. "It's not so," Tweed would protest. "Everything I have done has been in the public interest." For an example he would cite a park he had just given to the people. The fact that the park was in the area of a swamp that Tweed had purchased and sold to the city for personal gain did not matter to him.

The public interest as a determinant of governmental action is probably the most cherished concept to be found in the annals of American politics. It is also the most vague and abstract.

When any community group announces a policy position, it seeks explicitly or implicitly to associate its stand with the public interest. In fact, nearly every active individual or group claims—sincerely, no doubt—to be acting in the name of the public interest.

Yet, in a pluralistic society such as ours, made up of so many conflicting, overlapping, and competing interests, it is virtually impossible for all factions to espouse commonly accepted goals. How can it happen, then, that all the forces can say they are acting in the public interest? Perhaps the confusion rests in the various ways the public interest is defined.

PUBLIC INTEREST AS PUBLIC CONSENSUS

For perhaps the greatest number of its supporters the public interest has come to mean *commonly held* interests or values which, if they are not universally accepted, are at least widely held. A decision is said to be in the public interest if it serves the ends of most of the public rather than just a limited sector. The key to this concept of the public interest, then, is its wide acceptance as a common interest. It qualifies as being public by virtue of its broad acceptance or commonness. As such, it is a consciously desired goal which individuals and groups are struggling to achieve.

Yet how wide must acceptance be for this definition of the public interest to be valid?

If a particular value were embraced by the great majority of the citizens it would be an accepted interest and almost completely noncontroversial. Consequently, there would be no need to debate or to secure public support. The public interest in these terms would be identifiable only with those matters with which governmental policy was largely unconcerned.

Some proponents of the public interest, however, argue that a standard of universality or consensus for the public interest is too demanding. We cannot hope to secure this on a realistic scale. But if we abandon the standard of either unanimity or consensus we are forced to defend the public interest as being an interest that is simply more widely held than other interests.

Frankly stated, then, we would determine the public interest through the act of counting noses. But if government were to resort to this on every issue that confronted it, the machinery of government inevitably would come to a halt. Furthermore, in evaluating an interest in terms of the number of people who subscribe to it, such important considerations as the intensity with which an interest is held would regrettably be overlooked.

PUBLIC INTEREST AS SUPERIOR WISDOM

Another concept of the public interest that commands considerable allegiance sees the public interest as *wise* or *superior* interest. In the day-to-day practice of American politics, the term public interest is most frequently equated with an interest that its supporters feel deserves a special priority because of its superior wisdom or desirability. Its validity as the public interest depends not on the range of its acceptance but on the superiority of its claim to rationality or wisdom.

A danger lurks here, however, for this definition of the public interest fails to qualify as being "public" at all. Once the knowledgeable leaders who possess this clairvoyance discover what would be wise for all people, the public interest can become quite paradoxically an interest that is unknown to the public that reputedly holds it. If we concede interests which the possessor neither knows nor recognizes, our understanding of the concept of interests will have to be thoroughly overhauled. Furthermore, the condescension and paternalism implicit in the suggestion that each man is not the best judge of his own interest bodes unhappily for democratic theory.

PUBLIC INTEREST AS MORAL IMPERATIVE

Perhaps a third definition of the public interest may prove more satisfactory. For many people who believe in the natural law or traditional American understanding of natural rights, the public interest as *moral imperative* makes a strong bid for acceptability. Life, liberty, property, equality, and justice are held to be inviolable standards that defy transfer or abridgment.

Having their sanction in higher morality they are values that all people are obligated to respect. The public interest, then, in this sense would be what Walter Lippmann said men would choose if they saw clearly, thought rationally, and acted disinterestedly and benevolently.

But there are problems inherent in this concept. For the public interest as moral imperative concludes in being neither public nor interest. Because of its divine origin, the standard would exist even if no one embraced it as an interest. What is more, there is implicit in this concept the peril that the majority will, in the name of a higher morality, attempt to impose the "truth" on all of society. The zealot, confident of having found the "true" public interest, may choose to impose a freedom that is no more than "doing what is right."

PUBLIC INTEREST AND PROJECTION OF PERSONAL VALUES

Another way in which the public interest is frequently discovered is through the process psychologists call "projection," which is simply a way of equating the public interest with one's own value system. People will usually do this when they feel that their views are surely held by a large number of persons in the general public without knowing in any precise way how many people, if any, actually *do* share them.

While there may be some merit in recognizing this projection as an interest, it is a bit untenable to accept this mirror-gazing as public. For if we are to admit that every person is representative of a public, we might as well discard any further thoughts of catering to the public interest. In view of the fact that no two people are exactly alike, the need to satisfy all of the publics in a community would reduce any effort of government in this direction to futility and defeat.

PUBLIC INTEREST AS THE SYNTHESIS OF VARIED INTERESTS

Fortunately, this is not a matter for continued concern. As it works out, the task of government is not to express an imaginary popular will but to effect adjustment among the various competing wills which at any given time are attempting to make their claims upon other groups in society by acting through or upon any of the institutions of government. Thus, the *public interest as a balance of interests* becomes another way of defining the concept we are analyzing.

To view legislative acts generally as being the product of a common or popular will is little more than a romantic fiction, for it ignores the facts. Individuals do not have opinions on *all* public affairs. They do not always know what is happening, why it is happening, or what ought to happen. It is ludicrous to insist that they should have an intelligent opinion worth expressing on every question that confronts a self-governing community. Unless they see an issue as threatening their interests directly or indirectly they are not motivated to take political action. However, when they are affected crucially by a matter before the legislature, you can expect them to join forces with like-minded persons in bringing pressure to bear.

These pressure groups, or interest groups, will make their preferences heard at some crucial stage in the policy process provided they are not manipulated into quiescence. They will write their council members, lobby before committees, drum up support for their cause among the electorate, and contribute money to advance their goals.

Most decisions on important questions of policy necessarily have to be made by officials—by officials who, while they may be elected by the people, are still independent in the sense that they must make choices of their own without being able to rely at every step for rule and guidance on specific orders formulated by the electorate.

Government by elected representatives ordinarily affords the opportunity to practically every interest in the community to find somewhere in the representative council a spokesman to voice its claims. But for the most part council members feel that their greatest responsibility is to produce an outcome that will represent a compromise of competing wills and a harmonizing of interests. Only in this way can they maintain a stable political climate and generate loyalty and support for the work they have accomplished.

PUBLIC INTEREST AND THE "MIDDLETON CASE"

A case that shows the benefit of the "public interest" as an effective compromise of competing wills is presented here.

The small city of Middleton, one of the multitude of incorporated towns which felt the initial impact of the post-war building boom, found itself knee-deep in a maze of earth-moving monsters which threatened to reduce the rolling and hillside terrain of this sleepy community to man-made mounds of fill dirt and cut shelves of sandy clay. This was the new concept of land development which was to engulf a vast portion of the state. Some of the established and larger cities were somewhat prepared to cope with the problem, but little Middleton, anxious to expand its boundaries, welcomed the subdivider and the earth mover, the cat and the sheepsfoot roller in an aura of naiveté.

Having no grading ordinance by which the moving earth could be contained, Middleton suddenly found itself facing a dilemma. Established residents awoke to find a mountain of earth sloping toward their rear yards, or gaped down unimaginable precipices, the crests of which began at property lines.

City hall phones rang frantically and the routing of all complaints followed a line of referral directly to the mayor. Mayor Atkins, a civil engineer by profession, handled the barrage with the oft-repeated explanation that all was legal and followed well-established principles of mechanics and sound engineering practices.

Whether filled slopes were compacted and formed to a maximum slope of one and one-half to one, or whether cut slopes were formed to a maximum of one to one was of no consequence to the irate residents. The sudden appearance of monstrous earth movers was interfering with a way of life. Some residents sold their property and moved away; others entertained lawsuits but were discouraged in their efforts by well-knowing attorneys. Some harbored feelings of resentment toward the city, but most feelings were assuaged by the healing element of time and the ingenuity of the residents themselves. Many once formidable hillsides were transformed into showplaces of landscaped beauty.

Mayor Atkins faced the problem repeatedly from one development to the next. As the pace increased, first two, then three, then four tract developments would mushroom into existence at the same time. He concluded that the plunder of the earth in the Middleton Valley must be controlled by other than conservative, minimum engineering standards.

The problem was compounded when the heaviest rains in a decade washed over and under many of the unvegetated and unestablished slopes. New homes stood in lakes of water, or water freely flowed under houses and had to be bailed out or pumped out. The resulting erosion was followed by a heated public reaction, in which the need for an adequate cut-and-fill ordinance was pointed out.

Mayor Atkins had foreseen this need and had already made frequent pleas to the city council for such control. However, past conservative policies in the city of Middleton, fostered by a conservative city manager, slowed down any movement toward such control. The status quo remained through a moderate building period until a sample ordinance was finally presented to the city council by the city manager.

In the meantime Mayor Atkins had been successful in persuading the city council to adopt the most recent editions of the widely accepted *Uniform Building Code, Uniform Plumbing Code,* and *National Electrical Code.* However, the need for a basic cut-and-fill ordinance still went unfulfilled. Atkins had carefully studied the ordinances of larger cities which, while not completely adequate, were further advanced and based on more cut-and-fill experience than other codes.

The ordinance first presented by the city manager incorporated big-city flavor into a little city's cup. Tentative tract maps prophesying ever-increasing building development plus continuing public criticism finally convinced the city council that the time had come to seriously consider the adoption of a cut-and-fill ordinance.

The proposal was greeted by real estate and building interests with arched eyebrows and minds unprepared for complete objectivity. In view of the widespread indignation of the citizenry, it was believed by the mayor that it would be a simple matter to push through his desired grading code. However, from the beginning of his effort until the ultimate adoption of the ordinance, the mayor learned that a subdivider's domain could not be readily controlled by local grading regulations in conservative Middleton —especially since subdivisions already were meeting all requirements of the state subdivision act. Having pierced the line of the city council and then having passed the ball to that line, Atkins then was faced with another delay in the passage of his ordinance.

During its first month of consideration, the city council gingerly tossed the proposal up and down, never allowing it to land, and at the same time never dropping the matter. It was then decided to set the first public hearing on the ordinance to take the pulse of public reaction.

The ordinance was patterned after the provisions of a nearby city's code regulating hillside grading. The general requirements consisted of the usually accepted engineering standards for cutting, filling, compaction, and control by licensed soil engineers. The unique portions of the code, however, would control heights and locations of slopes and would provide for detailed drainage facilities and specified slope planting requirements. The items which considered drainage and planting regulations were not objectionable, although, on the other hand, they were not relished by the land developer and the builder. It was, however, that section of the code that regulated slope heights and slope locations that incited a flood of protests. The council reacted like an unsuspecting child touching a hot stove.

Reducing the vertical height of a slope from forty feet to a series of terraced slopes, each not to exceed ten feet in vertical height, separated by four-foot-wide benches or terraces, was an example of what the ordinance would cost the subdivider in terms of usable building site area.

The current ordinance sections on slope locations merely required that property lines be established at the tops of slopes. The reasoning behind this regulation stemmed from a series of sour experiences of property owners who had had the misfortune of having to view the neglected faces of hillsides which belonged to property owners at the top. The old axiom "Out of sight, out of mind" never proved truer. The distasteful condition stimulated a rash of complaints by the lowlanders, and the city, although not obligated, was caught up in the business of requiring hillside improvements. To set the property line at the top of the hill would leave the slope as a part of the lower property. The bottomlander would then be responsible for and would have the view of his own slope. This requirement, although not costing the developer in land area, would have a slowing down effect in that grading crews would have to be more deliberate and accurate in forming their slopes.

The most violent protest emanated from John James & Son, Inc., Developers, who were putting the finishing touches on their first subdivision in Middleton. The proposed ordinance of course would not affect their current project, but tentative maps were being prepared for two more tracts totaling over 200 lots. The grading ordinance would deal a deathblow to their proposed project.

Lot sales for James & Son were being handled by Joe Mack, a local realtor and president of the Middleton Area Board of Realtors. The association of James and Mack threw the first punch in the name of the board of realtors, and the second punch arrived from James & Son's civil engineer, who objected on the basis that "state civil engineering practices were sufficient and adequate to satisfy all city grading needs." The city council felt the impact of both punches, not forgetting the lighter, but still tormenting, jabs from other interested groups.

The quick decision to table the proposed ordinance and refer it to the realty board and the chamber of commerce for study and comment was probably the only expedient thing to do. Whether by chance or design, this move by council brought forth some constructive suggestions and had the effect of backfiring on the special interest groups who at first visualized the "committees" as the burial ground of the ordinance.

The "chamber" committee, not qualified by experience or knowledge in this area, soon found themselves in abject disagreement. Upon the suggestion of the city manager, this committee quickly agreed to a "catch-all" provision which would allow the building official to exercise judgment or waive requirements in cases of "extreme hardship" or in cases of "small and unimportant work."

Mayor Atkins, in the meantime, was requested to discuss the matter with the realty board committee. The realtors, recognizing their community responsibility in this matter, looked at the ordinance objectively and agreed with Atkins's reasoning. Joe Mack, who was not a member of the committee, eventually found himself pitted against the entire remaining realty board, and his argument and appeals were rejected. The realty board committee, wishing to make some contribution to the cause, agreed to the same amendment as the chamber committee.

The ordinance regulating and controlling grading, filling, and excavating in the city of Middleton was adopted.

While the Middleton case study concerns itself with increasing the regulatory power of the local government, it is also a striking example of the balancing of interests in order to arrive at a solution adequately serving the public interest.

The Impact of the Public on the Council

We cannot explore the public's influences on council members without at least a short consideration of the public itself.

SENSING WHO THE PUBLIC IS

In 1785 Nicolas Chamfort, French writer, moralist, and supporter of the Revolution, wrote, "The public, the public—how many fools does it take to make a public?" Pope wrote that "the public is a fool," but Shakespeare had written earlier: "The public is the world."

A generation ago Professor William B. Munro described his "forgotten man" in local politics as someone who never appears before committees of the city council at public hearings, who never writes letters to newspapers, and who never reads the letters that other people write.

The chamber of commerce, the taxpayers' association, and the good government group do not count this "forgotten man" among their members. He has never signed a petition for or against anything. He isn't organized, can't be mobilized, and won't be hypnotized by the politicians. Because he makes no noise, we call him the silent voter; between elections his interests and desires are crowded out by his more vociferous fellow citizens. Yet when the polls are open, he is often the most influential factor in the whole electorate. When the ballots are counted, it frequently appears that he has turned the trick. Indeed, when upsets and surprises come on election day it is usually because somebody has failed to reckon with the potential sovereignty of the "forgotten man." With the ballot in his hand, he has become articulate, and as a rule he votes his resentment rather than his appreciation. He resents the fact that no one in the seats of the mighty has regarded his interests or paid heed to his unuttered opinions.

The "forgotten man" does not know much about the principles of political science and has never head of Aristotle, Locke, and Montesquieu. He would be stumped if you asked him about segregated budgets or police power condemnations, but somewhere on one of the city streets he owns a little home, or at least an equity in it. This ownership has taught him something about assessors and tax bills, about water rates and street paving assessments. Consequently, he does not accept the alibis which flow so freely from some elected officials about inevitably higher public expenditures and uncontrollable outlays. No one needs to tell him that the city administration is flawless, particularly if the garbage collectors come irregularly, if the sewer backs up in his cellar, or if he can't find a policeman when he needs one.

Moreover, he rides the buses or drives to and from work at peak hours, which makes him an expert on transportation, traffic congestion, and air pollution. He has as much right as any other person to form opinions on these matters —and he does so.

His attitudes, his voting habits, and his consistently decisive role in elections have been raised to new levels of recognition by coauthors Scammon and Wattenberg in *The Real Majority*.[2]

Professor Munro's "forgotten man" represents extremely important unuttered influences upon the local legislator—influences which cannot be ignored if council members are to do their jobs.

Interpreting the needs, desires, and wishes of the silent voter is not a simple task. It requires a sensitivity and perception of the "common interest" of a high order—indeed an uncommon behavior pattern. We have heard this ability expressed as "an ear to the ground," "sensing what's in the wind," and a "feel of the public pulse." The council member who fails to recognize the silent voter—the "forgotten man"—will not for long be unrecognized by the "forgotten man."

We might contrast the "forgotten man" with the other persons, groups, and organizations who directly cause the council member to be the focal point of community influences.

RESTRAINTS ON COUNCIL INDEPENDENCE

The direct and potent influences brought to bear on council members as a part of the decision-making process can be classified as personal, internal, and external.

Personal Influences. Personal influences are attitudes and opinions held by individual members. Hardly a council meeting will pass when at least one item on the agenda is not related to a preconceived idea held by a member. The council member who will not permit his or her children to sell candy door-to-door is asked to consider a request to allow a youth group to do so. The council member who owns a furniture store is asked to consider bids on office fixtures which he or she considers to be of inferior quality. The realtor on the council is asked to approve the purchase of property at a price he or she considers exorbitant. The pious Christian considers poolroom regulations or liquor licenses. The political conservative must act on urban renewal or a job training program for school dropouts.

Internal Influences. Internal influences are described as intracity organizational and include: council–manager relations; the influence of department heads, staff, and employees; and the limitations imposed by laws, codes, and ordinances.

The council–manager relationship involves the greatest amount of pressure on a council member, primarily because the manager can marshal the forces of research, logic, and managerial expertise. It is because this type of influence is so great and at times so overwhelming that we hear the term "rubber stamp council" when it appears that a city council follows the advice or recommendation of the manager to the apparent exclusion of other influences.

The consideration of the effect of the managerial influence on members of the council has become even more significant in view of the trend to regard a major part of the manager's job as involving policy formulation.[3]

Even if the manager's involvement in policy were not increasing, the legal framework of the executive–legislative relationship creates an atmosphere of broad influence for the manager. Even lacking a legal basis, the psychological impact of the manager's position, staff knowledge, professional expertise—all these provide tremendous influence on the council.

The legal limitations on council members, whether state laws, local codes, or simply policies set by precedent, also exert a restrictive influence, which on occasion may prevent council members from satisfying their constituents and their own ideas of good government.

Other influences of an internal nature are: the influences of technical staff, with special skills such as personnel, finance, or purchasing; pressure by employees and employee groups; and department heads who for one reason or another may have the sympathetic ear of a council member. (The threats or warnings of doom from the city attorney or the police chief are bound to have an influence upon even the most courageous and stalwart council member).

External Influences. The third general classification is external or "public" influences. Council members will be pressured by parents and pigeon-fanciers, lawyers and landowners, bankers and businessmen, realtors and residents, by all manner of reasonable and logical persons and groups, and by many who are not. All are members of the council member's constituency; all are advocating a cause.

The Role of the Council Member

To most residents and taxpayers, council members are the local government. They are responsible for its successes and are at fault in its failures. What, then, is required of the citizen who would venture into the maze of local government as a legislative representative?

No technical skill is required for a citizen to serve on a city council or county board. It may be assumed that in larger communities professional talents will be supplied by the staff and in smaller communities by the chief administrator or a consultant.

To be a council member requires that the candidate have integrity, good judgment, a substantial amount of "horse sense," and a devoted interest in the community and its future. In many areas members carry no partisan political label. They are in a position to exercise their best judgment and foresight and to do so fearlessly, for they are not dependent on this job for a livelihood.

It is generally considered desirable that the composition of the city council or county board represent a diversity of interests and occupations. In this manner, the council membership will be in a better position to reflect a cross section of local opinion.

Membership on a council or board is a high honor and an unusual opportunity for real public service. Every individual council member should understand the job as a whole and should consistently work and vote in a manner which will contribute toward the public good. Each individual council member and the council as a whole are concerned with the general public good. Where some local interest or some business interest is in conflict with the general public welfare, the latter should prevail.

Each council member should make a conscientious effort to be present at all meetings. Acceptance of the position includes an obligation to devote the necessary time to its work.

In addition to attending council meetings, it is necessary that each member do a certain amount of research, study, and inspection of proposals in advance.

Every member should shun anything which deviates from the path of honesty. Each member should make it clear that the council treats every citizen equally.

Council members must recognize that the desirable approach to any given problem is not always the popular choice. Frequently, their attitudes or decisions may differ from those of friends or of important local groups. At such times, they must remain steadfast and courageous. They should endeavor to justify their position in an effort to win the support of critics. But regardless of whether they are successful in such efforts, they must always retain the long-range outlook and insist on carrying out those programs and policies that will be for the ultimate benefit of the community.

Occasionally, council members may find themselves in a position where they have a personal interest in a matter up for consideration by the council. Clearly, there is only one answer to this sort of situation—to call attention to the situation and request that the chairman excuse them from participation while the matter is under consideration, and to disqualify themselves from voting.

Council members serve in a quasi-judicial as well as a legislative capacity, and, as such, it is preferable that they not discuss cases in any detail with applicant or protestant prior to consideration by the council as a whole. A council member can sometimes handle this delicate situation by advising the persons contacting them that all relevant matters should be submitted through proper applications and through established hearing procedures for consideration by the council.

Closed sessions of city councils, county boards, and other public agencies, at which the public and press are barred, are contrary to American tradition, and in many cases are against the law. They breed suspicion on the part of both press and public. There is no reason why matters relating to the general development and welfare of the community cannot be discussed in public. This has been discussed in Chapter 1.

It must be borne in mind that the council represents the public just as much as it does the local government as an abstract entity. Local citizens are not only members of several councilmanic publics, they are also individuals with different attitudes, prejudices, and opinions. Successful council members must understand voter behavior if they are to retain their positions of prestige and responsibility.

Summary

This chapter has dealt with the council as a focal point of various interests—particularly in its relationship to the public and the public interest. The citizen attitude toward the government has been discussed, followed by a section on problems of communication between government and citizen. Following this, the "public interest" has been carefully defined and analyzed, and an optimum attitude toward it has been stated. Next, the impact of the public on the council has been outlined. The final section has dealt with the role of council members and with their ultimate responsibility to the public that they serve.

[1] HANDBOOK FOR COUNCILMEN IN COUNCIL-MANAGER CITIES, 2nd ed. (Chicago: International City Managers' Association, 1964), pp. 1–2. Reissued by the National Municipal League, New York, 1973.

[2] Richard M. Scammon and Ben J. Wattenberg, THE REAL MAJORITY: HOW THE SILENT CENTER OF THE AMERICAN ELECTORATE CHOOSES ITS PRESIDENT (New York: Coward, McCann & Geoghegan, 1970).

[3] Clarence E. Ridley's monograph THE ROLE OF THE CITY MANAGER IN POLICY FORMULATION (Chicago: International City Managers' Association, 1958) gives the essence of a large volume of writing on this subject.

4

The Multitudinous Publics

IN A DEMOCRATIC SOCIETY, government exists to serve the people; hence public employees are—in a real sense—servants of the people. In ascertaining and achieving the purposes of government, therefore, public administrators will agree that they must be concerned with what citizens want from their government. This concern involves the complicated process of translating public opinion into public policy and then into administrative activity.

While much has been written about this continuum of opinion, through policy, to administration, knowledge on this subject is limited. Writings suggest a far more complicated process than merely identifying public opinions, shaping them into policy guides, and then initiating programs.

Little is known about what constitutes a "public" and its underlying influences; knowledge is scant as to how opinions of government personnel and community organization people mutually influence the decisions of public officials; only a superficial understanding exists of how public opinions are formed and circulated in the community; only in recent years has serious attention been given to transforming opinion into administrative programs.

Greater understanding of the opinion–policy–administration continuum will help the administrator and the public relations officer understand how governments can inform without propagandizing, change without paralyzing, and serve without dominating—goals of which they are, of course, well aware. Practitioners will agree that the major role of public officials is to translate public opinion into administrative action. This is, of course, no easy task. In this chapter, part of this continuum—the segment dealing with the "multitudinous publics"—is examined and a simple scheme is proposed through which local officials may analyze the publics in their cities and counties and initiate sound and effective opinion and information programs.

The chapter first takes up the subject of opinion and the publics. Opinion is placed in its context in the public relations process; a brief definition of opinion is given, the flows of influence and opinion are analyzed, and the relation of opinion to policy and administration is discussed.

Next, the publics are studied: What is a public? What are the various forms and types of publics? Communication, "the essence of the public relations process," is then treated in detail. How are attitudes shaped and how are ideas spread?

Finally, the chapter treats the matters of mobilizing the publics, linking them with groups in the community, and channeling opinion. A summary concludes the chapter.

Opinion and the Publics[1]

RELATION OF OPINION TO PUBLIC RELATIONS

The crux of public relations is, of course, the opinions of people. Programs are geared to conserve or protect favorable opinions, to crystallize active or latent opinions into favorable reaction, and to change or neutralize hostile opinions. Those engaged in public relations are constantly striving to initiate, lead, modify, or accelerate the opinions of people.

OPINION BRIEFLY DEFINED

Opinion may be defined as sets of beliefs, convictions, or views of individuals, groups, or organizations on certain matters or issues. In this definition, groups and organizations are treated as social entities possessing and expressing opinions just as an individual does. In the following discussion they will be referred to as "behavior units," exhibiting individual behavioral patterns similar to those of a person and functioning as individual contributors to the discussion processes.[2]

THE FLOWS OF INFLUENCE AND OPINION

Two techniques found useful in analyzing the opinion–policy–administration continuum are (1) the study of the flow of influence and (2) the study of the flow of opinion.[3] In the first the cause (that which influences) is examined to ascertain the effect (the opinion), while in the second the effect is examined to ascertain the cause.[4]

The Flow of Influence. Almost every aspect of the opinion–policy–administration continuum can be analyzed in terms of the direction in which influence is being exerted. Researchers are interested in the extent of the influence of mass media on their audiences. Students of small group behavior are interested in the extent to which one person influences the opinion of another person. The study of elite groups centers almost exclusively on those who possess influence, why they possess it, and how it is exercised. The focus is on the process by which one behavior unit influences the behavior of another unit. The difficulty in analyzing the flow of influence is that influence cannot be directly observed but it must be inferred from observable behavior.[5]

The Flow of Opinion. This appears to be a more useful concept for public relations work. Earlier it was stated that a set of beliefs, convictions, or views about any issue or matter constitutes opinion. Opinion is communicated directly from one behavior unit to another. Whatever form this act of communicating takes,

it can be observed, categorized, and measured to some degree. Behavior units can be identified and compared in their roles and performances.[6]

Unless opinion circulates between a government and a public, neither party may be influenced nor its behavior modified. However, this relationship should not be limited simply to a communication system which links a public to a government and vice versa. A flow is also involved which shapes and molds the behavior of both parties. Both flows, in one way or another, play a part in modifying behavior. Still, influence cannot be operative without prior transmission of opinion, whereas opinion can act independently of influence. The problem, then, is: How can parties involved in the flow of influence modify their behavior, unless the influence is conveyed to them in some manner?

In sum, influence (and thus modification of behavior) is a result of behavior unit interaction and can be manifested only when it is communicated in some fashion. Opinion, on the other hand, can and does circulate without corresponding modifications of behavior. Officials who reject opinion transmitted to them illustrate that influence and opinion need not flow concurrently. Such persons may cut off influence altogether and at the same time perpetuate the flow of opinion by reintroducing this rejected opinion into the channels of communication through a speech or newspaper article in which they explain their opposition to the submitted opinion.

An example might be: certain elements of the community inform a city manager that they want refuse collection three times a week instead of twice a week. The city manager rejects this attempt to influence his or her administrative behavior by delivering a speech before a leading civic organization in which he or she discusses in depth the policy and program of refuse collection in the city. The attempt to influence the manager failed because he or she was not interested in more frequent refuse collection, but the rejected opinion reentered the channels of communication.

Study of the flow of opinion centers on identification of particular opinions, their communication (by whom and to whom), and the nature and extent of their impact. The flow of opinion—the act of communication—sets the boundaries within which influence operates.

OPINION–POLICY–ADMINISTRATION RELATIONS

To gain understanding of complex social situations it is necessary to generalize patterns of social systems. The relation of opinion to policy and administration might best be seen as composed of several closely related yet discrete systems of social interaction.

A Concept of Social Systems.   The sociologist Talcott Parsons has formulated a complex academic concept of social systems, the essential elements of which may nevertheless be usefully applied to local government practice. Social action[7] is a starting point in what is known to social scientists as Parsonian theory, and social systems, it is held, develop spontaneously whenever the interaction pattern of two or more "actors" becomes stabilized and oriented toward specific goals. The basic element in the social system is role, and the social system, in Parsonian usage, is merely a network of such roles.[8]

This concept of social systems includes far more than formal organizations (local governments, religious denominations, trade associations, etc.). And the spontaneous development of social systems is not necessarily related to a legal framework of formal institutions.

A social system is not the same as a "society," at least for purposes of definition in the present discussion. A society is a more formal type of organization in an institutional or organizational sense. Common to any complex political society is a system of local governments. Each local government is continually working out sets of mutually compatible roles—that is, concrete social systems. These social systems operate within a complex framework (or matrix, to use the sociologist's term) of roles, values, and goals.[9] This environmental framework can be clarified by further definition.

A *role* is essentially the expectations that people have of others—particularly of others in their special positions in a social system as previously defined.

Values are more than attitudes and beliefs, because they involve what people think ought to prevail in their society. Values that are generally accepted in a society or a social system tend to become normative standards, that is, prescribed "oughts."[10]

System goals refers to what people are striving for in both concrete and abstract terms. A city government, for example, has quite specific system goals such as clean streets. A city also may be seeking a higher level goal of paving or repaving all streets within the corporate limits within five years. In abstract terms (and, of course, within the political process) the city is working toward a better urban environment: this process probably involves a set of system goals relating to housing, education, minority relations, and employment.

This, then, is the sociological framework within which a city, county, or other local government operates. Subject to the political process, each local government must work out a set of compatible roles—that is, a concrete social system within its environment of roles, normative standards, and system goals.

Pursuing this analysis further, it might also be held that each local government is in itself a complex of concrete social systems; these systems penetrate one another and function within a larger system of interdependence. Concrete social systems are embedded in a larger environmental framework. Each concrete social system, then, represents in part its own unique organization and in part the organization it draws from higher order and lower order systems.[11]

Processes of System Interaction.   The social systems involved in the opinion–policy–administration continuum are linked together by numerous forces and processes. For our purposes three significant processes are noted: (1) the decision-making process; (2) the opinion-submitting process; and (3) the opinion-making process. Each of these processes may exist independently of the others, but at the same time they are so linked that they form a whole. This is described below and is illustrated in Figure 4–1.

1. The decision-making process integrates public opinion in the formulation and the

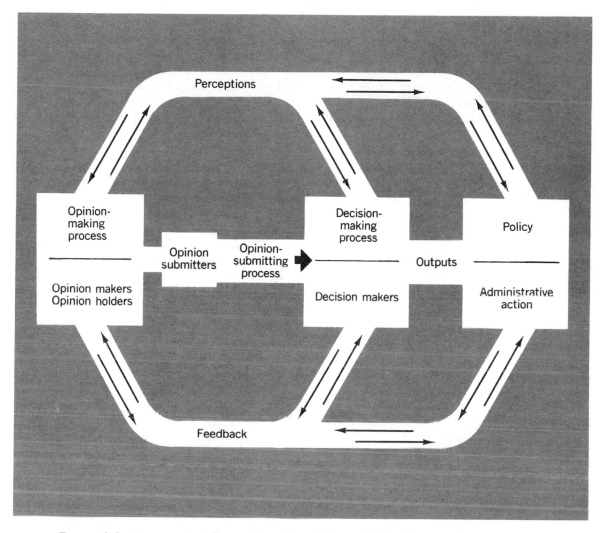

FIGURE 4–1. *Processes of social system interaction: decision making, opinion submitting, and opinion making.*

reformation of policy and its implementation. Participating behavior units are usually termed decision makers or policy makers.

2. The opinion-submitting process occurs whenever opinions are transmitted to decision makers by the publics or by institutionalized groups. Behavior units so involved are usually termed opinion submitters.

3. Opinion making pertains to the formation and circulation of issues throughout a community or within a public. This process involves the interaction of opinion holders and opinion makers.

In Summation. At this point some readers —including local government practitioners— may want to ask: "Why this involved discussion of something that is not important to me? I know what public opinion is. I am involved with it all the time."

Such a question has, of course, some validity when it springs from the practicing professional. It can perhaps be answered by emphasizing that the purpose of the discussion thus far has, in a sense, been to provide both a warning and an opportunity to local government administrators. Managers—as many of them will in fact recognize—are not aware of public opinion if they talk only with associates at Rotary Clubs and the like. School superintendents, to take another obvious example, may be in for quite a shock if they persuade the school board to adopt a policy on redistricting without consulting with teachers, school principals, and civil rights groups. There is, therefore, a case for emphasizing that those who act in local government should know the publics, and how opinion flows and continually interacts through social systems. In short: astute administrators know their communities and thus can anticipate problems.

A good understanding of opinion and the public, therefore, provides administrators with an opportunity to work both idealistically and realistically. By being as aware as possible of the social setting and the social systems within their jurisdictions, administrators can plan what is possible and begin to work for what is desirable. They are thus more than "caretakers" and administrators in what some might term the orthodox sense; they are also leaders in the dynamic sense: showing what can be done and persuading people to work toward larger community goals.

The Publics: Forms, Composition, and Structure

It is a common mistake to think of "the public" as one massive, monolithic assemblage that can be molded into some type of "mass opinion." The mass mind concept in our times is, in fact, faulty and should be divorced from our thinking.[12] In a sense, we may speak of something such as a "general public," but efforts to communicate persuasively with the "general public" are, as a whole, inefficient and often ineffective. The total public (general public) is complex and heterogeneous. Within it are found smaller publics which can be identified. The opinions of smaller publics can be ascertained and, in turn, influenced.

A CONCEPT OF A PUBLIC

The number of different publics is, theoretically, the number of distinct combinations of individuals within a given community. A public is only one form of social organization. Sociologists have identified other forms such as crowds, audiences, groups, and associations. These forms represent more institutionalized social structures than a public.[13]

A public may be defined as any loose association of individuals held together by common interests and objectives and by various means of communication. It is fairly transitory and unstructured. There are many publics; some are large in scope and membership, while others are narrow in purpose and claim relatively small numbers of people.

A public, as a loose association lacking formal institutionalization, should not be confused with more formal types of social organizations such as civic associations, fraternal orders, and political parties. These, like publics, are opinion groups, however, and decision makers are also interested in their attitudes, views, and convictions. (In distinguishing between publics and the institutionalized forms of associations, some illustrations may be helpful: veterans are a public, but the Veterans of Foreign Wars, the American Legion, and the Amvets are groups; physicians and surgeons are a public, but the American Medical Association is a group.)

Publics and institutional opinion groups can be regarded as being at the opposite ends of a continuum. As a public becomes more structured and formalized, it becomes an institutional opinion group. Somewhere along this continuum a public ceases to exist, but the exact point is difficult to ascertain.[14]

The important consideration is that there is a recognizable group of persons who are concerned with issues (i.e., people who have feelings and are willing to express themselves about a public matter). This is the "public" of "public opinion." This concept of a public was made famous by John Dewey.[15] Professor Dewey maintained that there are many publics, each consisting of individuals held together by a particular social action or idea. Each issue creates its own public. This public will normally not consist of the same individuals who make up any other particular public(s), although each individual will periodically be a member of several, if not many, other publics. For example, a person may be a church member, a golfer, an electrician, a parent, a rider of mass transit facilities, and a member of a local improvement association. Concomitantly, he or she can be a member of other publics, such as a business public, a temperance public, or a jazz music public. He or she can quickly shift attention as well as full participation from the issues of one public to those of another.

Members of a public need not be in person-to-person contact with one another. This leads to the characteristic termed "nonspatiability" by social scientists. Individuals who have never seen one another in person can experience a bond of common interest and unity. Such bonds have increased as mass communications have become more sophisticated.[16] Those publics existing on a person-to-person basis are known as "spatial publics."

FORMS AND COMPOSITION OF PUBLICS

The concept of a public given in this chapter, then, pertains to a grouping of individuals who are in relatively tenuous and unstructured relationship to each other and are united by a common interest and objective, and by communication. It has been noted that publics may be of two general forms: "spatial" and "nonspatial." In general terms, publics may be identified by their two primary characteristics as far as composition is concerned: place and interest. Figure 4–2 notes types of publics according to these two characteristics.

The discussion that follows describes the internal structure of a public—i.e., the opinion makers and the opinion holders.

STRUCTURE OF A PUBLIC

Opinion Makers and Opinion Holders. The structure of a public can be discussed in a variety of ways. Some of the structural features, such as spatiality, nonspatiality, and interest, have already been referred to. Here the basic structural relationship between opinion makers and opinion holders is discussed.

The inner circle of a public—the opinion makers—has been designated in different ways: the elite, the influentials, the opinion leaders, the issue makers, and so on. An effective public must consist of individuals or groups who successfully articulate and represent the beliefs, convictions, or views which hold together the loose association of individuals known as the public. (In this way, they have a strong influence on opinion.) These persons, to be successful, must work within a more institutionalized setting with access to communication channels and contact with decision makers.

Opinion holders usually make up the vast majority of a public. They cannot circulate views (opinions) to individuals and groups with whom they are not acquainted. They often disseminate opinions on a face-to-face basis but do not have ready access to channels of communication. Thus, we can distinguish the opinion makers from the opinion holders of a public by their access—or lack of it—to circuits of communication.

The implications in the relationship between the opinion makers and the opinion holders are numerous. The relationship is not necessarily static. In one set of circumstances some persons may be opinion holders and, in another, opinion makers. Shifts do occur, and frequently in a short space of time. Although the opinion makers frequently capture the limelight, the role of the opinion holders should not be overlooked. It is usually the opinion holders, or a particular element of them, who internalize the opinion.[17] Thus, they can become as influential as those who introduce opinions into the circulatory system.

Concentric Gradations of a Public. In the previous section a public was structured by the degree of access that members had to circuits of communication. This section separates a public into three gradations: the opinion makers, the attentive opinion holders, and the inattentive opinion holders.[18]

It may be helpful to use an analogy of concentric circles (see Figure 4–3) to show how members of the internal elements are constantly shifting their roles. If the circles in Figure 4–3 are visualized as being in constant spirals, it would indicate that a public is in an incessant state of motion, juggling its position of influence in relation to rival publics and constantly varying in magnitude of influence and number of members.

Place	National	Regional	Local
	Voters	New Englanders	Angelenos
	Citizens	Southerners	Brooklynites
	Adults	Middle Westerners	Texans
	Aliens	Far Westerners	

Examples of common interest publics	Race and nationality	Sex	Residence
	Black	Male	Urban
	Chinese	Female	Suburban
	Italian		Rural
	Indian	Income	
		High	Class
	Age	Low	Labor
	Children	Middle	White-collar
	Youth		Blue-collar
	Middle age	Profession	Managerial
	Senior citizen	Lawyers	
		Professors	Business and trade
	Religion	Surgeons	Stockholders
	Catholic		Employees
	Protestant	Economics	Customers
	Moslem	Consumers	Managers
	Jewish	Distributors	
	Buddhist	Producers	Educational status
		High tariffs	Students
	Occupation	Farm subsidies	Graduates
	Farmers	Free trade	Teachers
	Truck drivers		Educational administrators
	Salespersons	Social	
		Trial marriage	Government
	Politics	Planned parenthood	Voters
	Conservatives	Social welfare	Employees
	Liberals		
	Moderates		

FIGURE 4–2. *Types of publics by place and interest. (Source: Adapted from J. Handly Wright and Byron H. Christian,* PUBLIC RELATIONS IN MANAGEMENT, *New York: McGraw-Hill Book Company, 1949, p. 17.) Used with permission of McGraw-Hill Book Company.*

The outer limits of the concentric circles represent the inattentive opinion holders. They have neither the opportunity nor a strong inclination to become involved in the opinion-making process. Their access to circuits of communication is limited and their position is rather far removed from the epicenter of action (information-motivation). Thus, their information-motivation circuit is weak and frequently not clear. However, they constitute the great latent force of public opinion, one which occasionally can suddenly spring into action, playing an important, if not decisive, role in the influence process. This is why we should visual-ize a counter-spiral force which could be called feedback-reevaluation-assimilated opinion.[19] This indicates that the flow of opinion and influence is a two-way process and that the persons involved in the inner circle cannot avoid or overlook those farther removed, even though it may appear that the latter are relatively uninterested.

The attentive opinion holders are found toward the middle of the pattern of influence in a public. They are persons who are inclined to participate but who lack access or opportunity. As attentive members they are aware of the issues and informed about the activities in play.

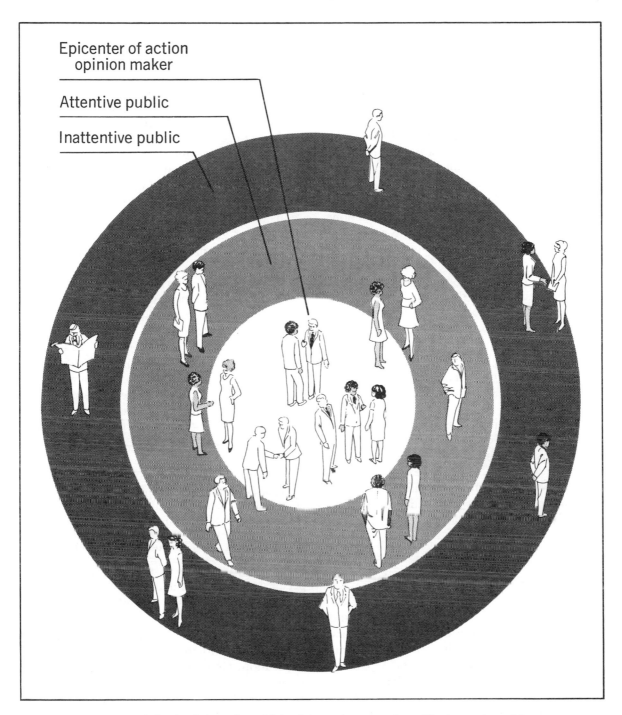

Epicenter of action
    opinion maker

Attentive public

Inattentive public

FIGURE 4–3. *Gradations of a public: opinion makers, attentive public, inattentive public.*

Frequently, they have a greater awareness of the totality of the implications than the opinion makers have.

Located at the epicenter of Figure 4–3 are the opinion makers. This element does not necessarily preempt the function of making opinion. However, they are the persons who strongly influence, as well as articulate and represent, the opinion of a public: they are engaged in the critical functions of opinion circulation, opinion formation, and opinion submitting. These functions often take place simultaneously, but the opinion makers do perform *several* functions in relation to their role, and in many cases they are more typically opinion assimilators and disseminators rather than opinion makers. In whichever capacity, they are found at the epicenter of action and so direct the input, magnitude, and extent of opinion (and as we have noted, in some cases, influence).

Communication: The Essence of the Public Relations Process

Effective communication is the essence of the public relations process. Since this important aspect is discussed elsewhere in this book, only brief attention will be given here to the subject. The primary concern is to examine leading factors that contribute to successful communication within the conceptual framework just developed.

SHAPING ATTITUDES:
THE ULTIMATE OBJECTIVE?

Undesirable as this may sound, the final objective of public relations is held by some to be the shaping of people's attitudes. It is not necessary to dwell any further on this controversial matter. The more important question is, Do we know anything about this process? The answer is affirmative, and a vast literature exists on the subject. To sift through this literature constructively would comprise a major undertaking.[20] In this section, then, some basic concepts concerning attitude formation and the dissemination of ideas will be outlined.

Some Basics Concerning Attitude Formation. The more interested people are in an issue the more likely they are to hold consistent positions on the matter. The more a person is emotionally involved in his or her beliefs, the more difficult it is to change the cognitions involved by information or argument. Once people commit themselves to a position this commitment becomes a major barrier to their change. People less interested in an issue hold weaker opinions and beliefs and thus are more likely to change their minds, but, concomitantly, the less interested take a longer time to reach a conclusion. A person functioning under pressure tends to accept the prevailing attitude of his or her favored group. The more pressure people feel, the less stable are their opinions during times of persuasion.

A person's behavior is influenced by many different groups; at any given moment, the group with the strongest influence will be most salient. Persons tend to see and hear communications that are favorable or congenial to their predispositions. The more interested people are in a given subject the more likely is their selective attention. People perceive messages or communications in accordance with their predispositions, desires, wishes, attitudes, needs, and expectations. As Chester I. Barnard observed long ago:

A person can and will accept a communication as authoritative only when four conditions simultaneously are obtained: (a) he can and does understand the communication; (b) at the time of his decision he believes that it is not inconsistent with the purpose of the organization; (c) at the time of his decision, he believes it to be compatible with his personal interest as a whole; and (d) he is able mentally and physically to comply with it.[21]

In sum, public relations officers must keep in mind three fundamentals for effective communication: (1) that the public for their communication consists of "peoples," and that these "peoples" live, work, and play with each other in the framework of social institutions and consequently each person is subject to many influences; (2) that people tend to read, watch, or listen to communication which presents points of view that they are predisposed to accept or to which they have a personal commitment; and (3) that the desired response or feedback from a public must be rewarding to it, otherwise nothing is likely to occur or what occurs will be negative.

Dissemination of Ideas. The process of gaining acceptance for an idea or point of view has intrigued students of communication for many years. It is a much more complicated matter than simply bombarding a public through the mass media. While the evidence for his complete hypothesis is very weak, Elmo Roper in his thirty years of opinion research does suggest that ideas penetrate the "whole" public very slowly and by a process similar to osmosis. Ideas, according to Roper, move out in concentric circles from Great Thinkers to Great Disciples to Great Disseminators to Lesser Disseminators to the Politically Active to the Politically Inert (see Figure 4–4).[22] This observation assumes that American society is stratified.[23] It emphasizes the importance of using opinion leaders in the public relations process, a matter discussed earlier.

The rate of flow in the transmission and acceptance of ideas is controlled by many factors. These include Walter Lippmann's famous Barriers to Communications,[24] as well as the "Regulators of Absorption Rate" developed by George Gallup (see Figure 4–4).[25]

The Diffusion Process.[26] The communication process in public relations requires influencing opinion among both sizable and distant groups. (A persuasive framework by means of which administrators can see this process is set forth in the example below, which was worked out by the U.S. Department of Agriculture [USDA]. While the USDA study dealt with an agricultural setting, the five stages shown below would appear to be generally applicable to local government.)

Studies of writings on the diffusion process

Lippmann's Barriers to Communications	Roper's Hypothesis	Gallup's Regulators of Absorption Rate of New Ideas
1. Artificial censorships	**Great thinkers** Adam Smith, Thomas Jefferson	1. Complexity of the idea
2. Limitations of social contact	**Great disciples** Robert Taft, Franklin D. Roosevelt	2. Factors of difference from accustomed patterns
3. Meager time available for paying attention to public affairs	**Great disseminators** Walter Lippmann, James Reston, Edward R. Murrow	3. Competition with prevailing ideas
4. Distortions because events must be compressed into short messages	**Lesser disseminators** Clergy, editors, etc.	4. Is idea susceptible to demonstration and proof?
5. Difficulty of making a small vocabulary express a big, complicated world	**Politically actives** 10 to 15 million citizens who take active interest in public affairs and provide local leadership	5. How strong are vested interests which will block proposed change?
6. Fear of facing those facts which seem to threaten established routine of people's lives	**Politically inert** 80 to 90 million citizens who seldom voice opinions but who vote, buy, decide	6. Does proposal meet a felt need? Frequency with which public is reminded of new idea.

FIGURE 4–4. *Theories on the dissemination of ideas. (Source: Scott M. Cutlip and Allen H. Center,* EFFECTIVE PUBLIC RELATIONS, *4th ed., Englewood Cliffs, N.J.: Prentice-Hall, Inc., 1971, p. 244.) Reprinted by permission of Prentice-Hall, Inc., Englewood Cliffs, N.J.*

suggest that acceptance goes through the following five stages (see also Figure 4–5):

1. *Awareness.* The individual learns of the existence of the idea or practice but has little knowledge about it.
2. *Interest.* The individual develops interest in the idea or practice, seeks more information, and considers its merits.
3. *Evaluation.* The individual makes mental application of the idea or practice and evaluates its merits for his or her own situation. He or she obtains more information and decides to try it.
4. *Trial.* The individual applies the idea or practice—usually on a small scale or in a minimum gain–loss situation. He or she is primarily interested in its application.
5. *Adoption.* If the idea or practice is successful, it is adopted.

Studies of the U.S. Department of Agriculture's efforts to disseminate innovations have concluded that new farm and home practices are communicated by these agencies in order of appearance in the diffusion process: (1) the mass media—radio, television, newspapers, magazines; (2) friends and neighbors—mostly other farmers; (3) agricultural agencies—extension agents, vocational educators, etc.; and (4) dealers and salesmen—surveyors of commercial products and equipment.[27]

Media and agencies of communication have varying impacts at each stage of the diffusion process. The mass media have their greatest impact in the *awareness* stage and then diminish in importance. In the *interest* stage the mass media play an important part, but farmers turn to friends and agricultural agencies for further information. In the *evaluation* stage friends and neighbors play the important role; In the *trial* stage agricultural agencies and friends and neighbors are both important factors. Dealers and salesmen are influential when commercial products are involved.

While studies reveal variations in the diffusion process, the outline given here can serve as a guide in a general way. Communicating a new idea or practice is a long and tedious undertaking. Studies indicate that the process can be managed to some extent and need not be entirely haphazard. Nevertheless, it must be borne in mind that *effective communication is expensive in time, understanding, and emotional control. The cost is nearly always greater than is normally estimated.*

Awareness	Interest	Evaluation	Trial	Adoption
Learns about a new idea or practice	Gets more information about it	Tries it out mentally	Uses or tries it a little	Accepts it for full-scale and continued use
1. Mass media: radio, television, newspapers, magazines	1. Mass media	1. Friends and neighbors	1. Friends and neighbors	Personal experience is the most important factor in continued use of an idea
2. Friends and neighbors, mostly other farmers	2. Friends and neighbors	2. Agricultural agencies	2. Agricultural agencies	1. Friends and neighbors
3. Agricultural agencies, extension, vo-ag, etc.	3. Agricultural agencies	3. Dealers and salesmen	3. Dealers and salesmen	2. Agricultural agencies
4. Dealers and salesmen	4. Dealers and salesmen	4. Mass media	4. Mass media	3. Mass media
				4. Dealers and salesmen

FIGURE 4–5. *Stages in the diffusion process.* (*Source:* Herbert F. Lionberger, ADOPTION OF NEW IDEAS AND PRACTICES, *Ames: Iowa State University Press, 1960, p. 32.*) *Reprinted by permission of Iowa State University Press.*

Mobilizing the Publics

MOBILIZING DOES NOT MEAN MANIPULATING

Much of public relations centers around the process of mobilizing the publics. This is the essential aspect of public relations, unfortunately, it has been the subject of much criticism. Public relations people have become known as "influence peddlers," "pressure boys," and "opinion manipulators"; this attitude has had unfortunate implications for the professional field. How can responsible government be achieved if the publics are not fully informed of governmental affairs and the public officials and administrators cognizant of public opinion? A city or county government has an obligation to keep its citizens well informed of its policies and activities and to treat them courteously at all times. When government officials abuse the public relations function, manipulating publics for selfish reasons, then they are rightly open to criticism.

The mechanisms of public relations have no moral character in themselves. They are merely instrumentalities which can be used for either bad or good purposes. Public officials should, of course, be fully aware of this fact and should employ full discretion in the course of their planning and implementation of public relations programs.

The purpose here is not to present a detailed discussion but to outline three activities fundamental to mobilizing the publics: (1) knowing the publics; (2) linking publics with institutionalized groupings, and (3) channeling opinion (see Figure 4–6).

KNOWING THE PUBLICS

The first responsibility in local government public relations is knowing one's public. Who are its members and what are their interests? What do they think, and why? How does a public reach its conclusions? It is important to remember that publics overlap; hence a person can belong to several publics (based on politics, beliefs, values, vocation, religion, membership in organizations, etc.).

As Chapter 2 points out, in recent years some fairly sophisticated techniques have been developed for identifying a public, for measuring its size, magnitude, and scope of influence, and for discovering what it thinks and why. A public servant should not become involved in a public relations program until he or she has the facts. These may be determined through the use of formal and informal surveys, questionnaires, interviews, opinion polls, and studies of voting patterns—or even by attending meetings and reading member publications.

Considerable insight may be gained by analyzing opinion leadership in the community: Whom do people look to for advice, guidance, and support? But gathering facts is not enough. Facts must be critically examined, evaluated, and reevaluated. Judgments must be made and decisions arrived at. In the final analysis, the public relations researcher must resort to a sort of sixth sense, but this sixth sense is not so much guessing as wisdom based on practice and experience.

LINKING PUBLICS WITH INSTITUTIONALIZED GROUPINGS

In the discussion earlier in this chapter of the "Concept of a Public" it was noted that publics and institutional opinion groups can be regarded as being at the opposite ends of a continuum. As a public becomes more structured and formalized it becomes an institutionalized opinion group. It is important to note that the more formalized and institutionalized groups dominate the flow of opinion and influence publics. Loosely formed associations of individuals are not effective in action until they are tied up with groups of a more formal and institutionalized nature. This contingency is one of the most important, yet most frequently overlooked, aspects of a public. On the other hand, more formal and institutionalized groups need the support of publics. Thus, a political party or an interest group, for example, may try to manipulate amorphous publics for a particular end.

In an open society, it is difficult to design a continuum for a public to the highest form of institutionalization that will be generally accepted. However, a general guide may be useful provided it is recognized as a superficial treatment of the subject.

Near the bottom of the continuum is the ele-

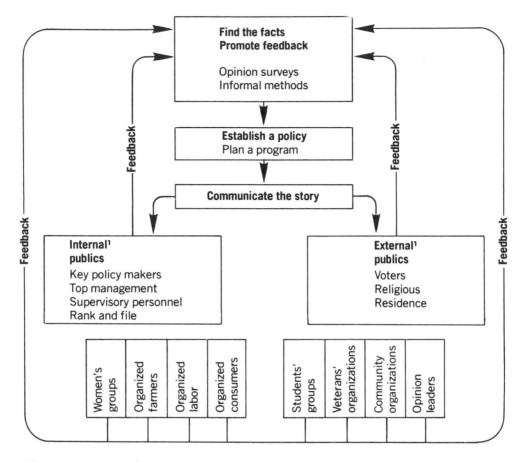

¹ For more complete details, see Figure 4–2.

FIGURE 4–6. *The public relations process.* (*Source: Adapted from Cutlip and Center,* EFFECTIVE PUBLIC RELATIONS, *p. 187.*) *Used with permission of Prentice-Hall, Inc.*

mentary grouping of a crowd. A crowd is a transitory and relatively unorganized grouping of individuals. In one case it may be dynamic, persistent, and somewhat organized, and in another situation it may be more passive (for example, an audience of some sort). A crowd, unlike a public, needs a definite locus in space, and its members are in physical contiguity to each other.

Near the top of the continuum are the primary groups; in these, the family, the churches, and the schools are frequently placed. Below these primary groups are a wide variety of institutionalized groups, such as political parties, interest groups, trade associations, labor unions, fraternal organizations, and business concerns, all of which strongly influence the flow of opinion.

While our continuum may be superficial, it is sufficiently detailed to indicate that a person concerned with public relations must deal constantly with attitudes, facts, and opinions from a wide number of collective groupings, and that, in the effort to influence people, the public relations official must think in terms of an almost infinite combination of forces. Behind all this is the delicate decision of which technique, approach, and circuit of communication to use. The public relations official must learn how to work with and not against the elements in play.

By skillful analysis of the issues, the people, the conditions, and the effects of the media of communication, he or she can direct a strong influence on public opinion.[28]

CHANNELING OPINION

After the facts are in and various evaluations and conclusions have been reached, there is the problem of channeling opinion. The circuits of communication in most communities are established and developed. The task of the public relations official is to locate these and decide on the means by which ideas and information will be fed in and circulated.

Channels of communication include personal, organizational, and mass media.

Personal media include those forms of communication used by individuals in direct contact with one another—face-to-face, by telephone, or by mail. Direct personal exchange is involved.

Organizational media are such impersonal instruments as house organs and memoranda, assemblies, and programs. These are utilized for communication with a differentiated public.

Mass media are those impersonal instruments of communication that are intended for, and made available to, anyone who is able to utilize them within the limits of their distribution. These media include periodicals (whether daily, weekly, monthly, quarterly, or some other time interval), and the electronic media, such as radio and television. While mass media, in contrast to organizational media, are often directed to specific categories of publics (geographic, economic, ethnic, racial, cultural), the communications are distributed essentially to undifferentiated audiences.[29]

Summary

In recent years a wealth of knowledge has been gathered concerning the "multitudinous publics," their forms, compositions, and structure, and their roles in making and conveying opinion and influence. This has resulted in better ways and means of mobilizing publics, both to achieve a more informed community and, in turn, to improve public service.

This chapter has covered the most significant aspects of the formation and communication of opinion and influence. First, opinion has been placed in context—with regard to the "public," to public relations, and to policy and administration. A theory basic to this chapter—that of the opinion–policy–administration continuum—has been outlined in detail. The publics have then been studied, with emphasis on the relationship between opinion makers and opinion holders. Communication, the shaping of attitudes, and the dissemination of ideas has been outlined next. The concluding subject has been the matter of mobilizing the various publics.

It should be emphasized once again that the study of public opinion is vital to success in public relations. It is particularly important that public relations officials be aware that they are dealing not with one but with many publics, each of which constitutes a specific problem and requires special study. Success in dealing with these publics requires acquiring a thorough knowledge of these "publics," effectively linking these publics with more institutionalized groupings, and successfully channeling opinion. The task is difficult, but the rewards in terms of effective and responsible government are high.

---

[1] Public opinion is also discussed in the section "Relation of Public Opinion and Communication to Government," in Chapter 1 of this book. The following are also useful: George Gordon, PERSUASION: THEORY AND PRACTICE OF MANIPULATIVE COMMUNICATION (New York: Hastings House, Publishers, 1971); and Bernard Berelson and Morris Janowitz, eds., READER IN PUBLIC OPINION AND COMMUNICATION (New York: The Free Press, 1966).

[2] Kenneth E. Boulding gives the following explanation of "behavior unit" in Chapter 1 of his CONFLICT AND DEFENSE: A GENERAL THEORY (New York: Harper Torchbooks, 1962). On pages 2 and 3 he states: "A behavior unit may be a person, a family, a species of animals or artifacts, a class of ideas, a theory, or a social organization such as a firm, a nation, a trade union, or a church." A mere aggregate of people is not necessarily a behavior unit. "The test . . . is whether it can be the subject in a sentence with a verb of action." The fundamental point is that opinion arises from the exchange of ideas about living issues (i.e., community matters on which individuals and groups take stands and express themselves). The term behavior unit is a convenient shorthand for the numerous group and individual behavior patterns in community settings.

[3] These two flows are discussed in more detail in James

N. Rosenau, PUBLIC OPINION AND FOREIGN POLICY (New York: Random House, 1961), see especially pp. 9–16. See also Karl W. Deutsch, THE NERVES OF GOVERNMENT: MODELS OF POLITICAL COMMUNICATION AND CONTROL (New York: The Free Press, 1963); Melvin L. DeFleur and Otto N. Larsen, THE FLOW OF INFORMATION: AN EXPERIMENT IN MASS COMMUNICATION (New York: Harper & Brothers, Publishers, 1958); Richard E. Charpin, MASS COMMUNICATIONS: A STATISTICAL ANALYSIS (East Lansing: Michigan State University Press, 1957).

[4] This difference is often confusing and has contributed much to differences in the thinking and writings of students in community politics and dynamics. This is explained in Chapter 7 of the present volume. For our purposes it is important to define carefully what is meant by influence. The ideas of Edward C. Banfield and James Q. Wilson are considered especially useful here. In their book CITY POLITICS (New York: Vintage Books, 1966), on page 101, they write: "We use authority to mean the *legal right* to act or to require others to act. We use influence to mean the *ability* to act, or to cause others to act, in accordance with one's intention. (Authority, then, may or may not give rise to influence; i.e., the legal right to require action may or may not suffice to evoke it.) We use power to mean influence the basis of which is something other than authority (e.g., the promise of favors and the threat of injuries)."

[5] Although this complicates the analysis, the usefulness of this concept in public relations activities still exists. The writings on persuasion show especial insight. See Gordon, PERSUASION, especially Chapter 8, "Political Persuasion," and Part Five, "Humanistic Persuasion." Scott M. Cutlip and Allen H. Center have provided several useful frameworks for working constructively with influence patterns. See their EFFECTIVE PUBLIC RELATIONS 4th ed. (Englewood Cliffs, N.J.: Prentice-Hall, Inc., 1971), especially Chapter 6, "Persuasion and Public Opinion."

[6] For further details see Bernard C. Hennessy, PUBLIC OPINION, 2nd ed. (Belmont, Calif.: Duxbury Press, 1971), and Leo Bogart, SILENT POLITICS: POLLS AND THE AWARENESS OF PUBLIC OPINION (New York: John Wiley & Sons, Inc., 1972).

[7] "Social action" is a rather precise term in Parsonian theory. It involves not only an "actor" (principal person) and a situation but also a psychological context of cause and effect and of standards or values. In psychological terms it is considerably more than a stimulus and an automatic response. It is rather the context—subconscious impulses, moral standards, attitudes, and beliefs—that provides a social setting.

[8] The general properties of any social system, in Parsonian theory, are: (1) two or more actors occupying differentiated statuses or positions and performing differentiated roles; (2) some organized pattern governing the relationships of members and describing their rights and obligations with respect to each other; (3) some set of common norms and values, together with shared cultural objects and symbols; (4) system boundary-maintaining tendencies (i.e., there tends to be more integrated organization among the components of the system while it is operating than there is between these components and elements outside of the system); and (5) a built-in tendency toward system stability or equilibrium. For more details see Edward C. Devereux, Jr., "Parsons's Sociological Theory," in THE SOCIAL THEORIES OF TALCOTT PARSONS, ed. Max Black (Englewood Cliffs, N.J.: Prentice-Hall, Inc., 1961), pp. 26–27.

[9] For a discussion along these lines, see Garth N. Jones, "Integration of Political Ethos and Local Government Systems," HUMAN ORGANIZATION 23 (Fall 1964): 210–22.

[10] A *value* is considered to be a statement of "good" or "bad," "right" or "wrong," something that is desired or thought to be desirable. Beliefs are of two types: (1) belief *in* something, such as a Supreme Being, and (2) belief *about* something, such as the earth being round. Within these two types of beliefs other implications are involved, such as beliefs subject to empirical proof. *Attitude* is a predisposition to evaluate some aspect of one's world in a favorable or unfavorable manner.

[11] For further details, see Garth N. Jones, PLANNED ORGANIZATIONAL CHANGE: A STUDY IN CHANGE DYNAMICS (New York: Praeger Publishers, Inc., 1969), especially Chapter 1.

[12] For two light but excellent articles debunking the "mass mind" that have retained their thrust, see Arthur Joyce Cary, "The Mass Mind: Our Favorite Folly," HARPER'S MAGAZINE, March 1952, pp. 25–27, and Peter Drucker, "The Myth of American Uniformity," HARPER'S, May 1952, pp. 70–77; see also the excellent discussion by Hennessy in his PUBLIC OPINION, Chapter 10, "Mass Communication and Public Opinion."

[13] For details beyond this discussion, see Chapter 7.

[14] Some formalization and structuralization, however, do not automatically place a public in an institutionalized classification.

[15] See John Dewey, THE PUBLIC AND ITS PROBLEMS (New York: Holt, Rinehart & Winston, Inc., 1927).

[16] See, for example, Wilbur Schramm, and Donald F. Roberts, eds., THE PROCESS AND EFFECTS OF MASS COMMUNICATIONS, rev. ed. (Urbana: University of Illinois Press, 1971).

[17] Internalizing the opinion is the process in which the public or a group finally feels that the issue is uniquely related to their position, if not solely part of their own collective thinking or efforts. This is discussed in Jones, PLANNED ORGANIZATIONAL CHANGE, especially pp. 115 ff.

[18] A wide variety of terms have been employed to describe these relationships. In discussing this matter in broader terms Elmo Roper designated six gradations moving outward from the inner circle in his "Who Tells the Story Teller?" SATURDAY REVIEW, July 31, 1954, pp. 25–26. This aspect is discussed later in this chapter.

[19] In this context the basic aspects of the feedback process involve: (1) the orderly collection of information about the functioning of a system; (2) the reporting of this information into the system; and (3) the use of the information for taking further social action.

[20] Those interested may find the following useful: C. I. Hovland, I. L. Janis, and H. H. Kelley, COMMUNICATION AND PERSUASION (New Haven, Conn.: Yale University Press, 1953); M. Fishbein, ed., READINGS IN ATTITUDE THEORY AND MEASUREMENT (New York: John Wiley & Sons, Inc., 1967); Harry C. Triandis, ATTITUDE AND ATTITUDE CHANGE (New York: John Wiley & Sons, Inc., 1971); Philip Zimbardo and Ebbe B. Ebbesen, INFLUENCING ATTITUDES AND CHANGING BEHAVIOR (Reading, Mass.: Addison-Wesley Publishing Co., 1970); E. Katz and P. F. Lazarsfeld, PERSONAL INFLUENCE (Glencoe, Ill.: The Free Press, 1955); C. A. Kiesler and S. B. Kiesler, CONFORMITY (Reading, Mass.: Addison-Wesley Publishing Co., 1969); Bernard Berelson and Gary A. Steiner, HUMAN BEHAVIOR, shorter edition (New York: Harcourt, Brace & World, Inc., 1967); and James D. Thompson and Donald R. Van Houten, THE

Behavioral Sciences: An Interpretation (Reading, Mass.: Addison-Wesley Publishing Co., 1970).

[21] Chester I. Barnard, Functions of the Executive (Cambridge, Mass.: Harvard University Press, 1938), p. 165.

[22] See Roper, "Who Tells the Story Teller?"

[23] For a fuller discussion, see Kurt B. Mayer and Walter Buckley, Class and Society, 3rd ed. (New York: Random House, 1970); and W. Lloyd Warner, Marchia Meeker, and Kenneth Eels, Social Class in America: The Evaluation of Status (New York: Harper & Row, Publishers, 1960).

[24] See particularly Lippmann's classic Public Opinion (New York: The Macmillan Company 1922; reissued in paperback, New York: The Free Press, 1965). A discussion of this topic is contained in Hennessy, Public Opinion.

[25] A discussion is found in Bogart, Silent Politics.

[26] The literature on the diffusion process is vast. A bibliographic reference is Garth N. Jones et al., Planning, Development and Change: A Bibliography on Development Administration (Honolulu: East–West Center, 1970).

[27] For further information, see Everett M. Rogers, Diffusion of Innovations (New York: The Free Press, 1962).

[28] Chapter 7 of the present volume discusses in detail various strategies and techniques for articulating publics and community groups with action programs.

[29] A more detailed discussion is found in Chapter 9 of the present volume.

5

Serving the Public

PROVIDING SERVICES to the public is the basic function and responsibility of local governments. Although the nature and scope of the services change somewhat from time to time and vary from community to community, the fundamental objective remains the same: to provide on a broad scale those services which help to meet the daily needs of the citizenry but which cannot be performed as efficiently or economically by individual citizens acting in their separate capacities. For example, it generally is economically impractical for individuals to attempt to furnish their own police and fire protection.

This was the rationale underlying the establishment of some of the earliest cities in history. The citizens realized that numerous services, particularly of the protective type, could be much more effectively performed by a central body supported by a majority of all the residents in the area.

Today the demand for services is greater than ever before and is increasing. The discussion that follows is concerned with the ways in which public relations can help local government meet these current increasing citizen needs for services. Starting with a brief summary of the reasons for the increase in demands for services, the chapter continues with a discussion of public relations and the concept of service. Serving the public through supplying information is the next topic discussed. The remainder of the chapter is concerned with government contacts with citizens: how service contacts mold opinion; direct and indirect contacts; and how services should be performed by various personnel (police, fire, public works, and other personnel). A brief summary concludes the chapter.

Citizen Interests and Wants

In the latter part of the twentieth century cities and counties have experienced an increase in public expectations regarding local government services. These demands on the part of the public relate not only to the quantity of services provided but to the quality of services as well.

The reasons for this heightened interest are numerous, but they are the result primarily of major changes in our cultural and institutional patterns. Among the leading factors have been: (1) the demographic transition of our society from one that was traditionally rural to one that is predominantly urban;[1] (2) the increase in the complexity of government policies, rules, and practices, and the difficulty that many citizens experience in attempting to comply with and understand such laws and procedures; (3) the tremendous increase in the mobility of the public and the resulting feeling of "rootlessness" on the part of millions of persons who do not reside in any one community for any great length of time; (4) the widening chasm in communications between the citizen and government and the difficulty in obtaining information or services, or even in making needs known to public officials; and (5) the increase in citizen demands without a corresponding understanding of the financial, legal, and political limitations faced by local governments in terms of providing services.

Public Relations and the Concept of Service

All local government employees from the top administrator downward are responsible for serving the citizens of the community. Although some of their responsibilities may be indirect (some personnel do not often have face-to-face contact with the public) their obligation to the public is always important. In a sense the public service responsibility of supervisors and managers is even greater than that of operating personnel, because the former group tends in fact to establish the public service climate of the organization through its own attitudes and its own actions toward the public.

Overall public opinion regarding local government is formed largely on the basis of public satisfaction with the quality and quantity of the services provided. Moreover, the way in which a service is performed can often be more important than the service itself as far as effect on the public is concerned. If citizens feel that they are being given considerate and fair treatment by a local government employee, they will have a better impression of the government. This holds true even when they are disappointed in their requests.

To establish good relations with the public, local government employees must not only be effective in performing their duties; they must carry them out in a manner that earns citizen approval and confidence. The citizen must not only be served well but must *feel* that he or she is receiving good service.

Service through Information

Unless citizens are aware of and understand public laws and regulations, they will be unable to carry out their civic responsibilities. At the same time, if citizens are uninformed about the benefits and services that are available they will not be able to use their rights and privileges.

That cities and counties are recognizing increasingly the need to keep the public informed regarding services and activities is apparent from the coverage of activities that appears annually in *The Municipal Year Book* and *The County Year Book*.[2]

THE MASS MEDIA

The basic problem in providing informational service to the public through the mass media, or even through correspondence, is that the communication is one-way. It is difficult for receivers of the information to clear up any misunderstanding if the information is not clear to them. It can be critical from a public relations standpoint if members of the public misinterpret information and perhaps act, or fail to act, to their personal detriment. Public reaction to such faulty informational services will be anything but favorable. Therefore, it is important that informational materials be clear and complete before they reach the public.

GREETINGS AND BROCHURES

While reports and events are described extensively in Chapter 10, some examples cited below illustrate ways of informing citizens of the kinds of services available.

A description of city services in Elgin, Illinois, has been prepared in the form of a pamphlet for general distribution to the public. It covers the city's financial activities, organization, boards and commissions, and service departments, and includes a list of phone numbers to call in order to obtain services.

Buchanan, Michigan, distributes "request-for-service" cards to the public through city departments and members of the city commission. The citizen fills out the card and sends it to the city manager's office or turns it over to any city employee. The cards are designed to make the request clearly understandable.

Fairfax County, Virginia, mails out thousands of copies of a four-page *Weekly Agenda,* in newsletter format, to individuals, organizations, and the news media.

Plymouth, Michigan, maintains a continuing public relations program to keep citizens informed on what the city is doing. New residents receive a letter from the mayor and city manager welcoming them to the city and outlining briefly the city services that are available. The letter includes the phone numbers for city hall and the fire department, and invites new residents to visit city hall, register for voting, and become acquainted with the administration.

Tucson, Arizona, has an active community relations program which, to aid and inform citizens, makes use of newspaper advertisements, television programs (including an "open line" program), and a twenty-four-hour answering service (see Figures 5–1 to 5–4).

Evanston, Illinois, has prepared postcard "Citizen Request Cards" so that citizens can mail in requests for service or information on any problem relating to city government. The cards have been distributed to city employees so that they can give them to citizens who make inquiries concerning other than their own departments.

Alexandria, Virginia, has issued a booklet giving historical background for the city together with a description of current city problems and services.

Rockville, Maryland, has issued a *Citizens Handbook* to provide information on city government and community services and facilities. It includes city offices, a city map, a street guide, and directories of parks and playgrounds, schools, and churches. Rockville also has issued a four-page folder to new residents to welcome them to the city. Information is given on governmental organization, elections, city government services, and recreation facilities; a directory of city officials is included.

EXPERIMENT!

Tonight at 6:30 p.m. the City of Tucson will begin an experiment in communications with YOU, its citizens.

The City's Community Relations Office in cooperation with Channel 4 gives you the chance to talk directly to the women and men who run your City government. Tonight's guest will be City Manager Joel Valdez.

Mr. Valdez will be as close and convenient as your telephone dial. He is the chief administrator of a 176 million dollar budget and 4263 employee organization, all provided by your tax dollars.

This is your chance to talk directly with him and hear what questions your neighbors have on their minds.

623-2555

MMMMopen line

For further information on other City information shows on television and radio, call Community Relations at 791-4401.

FIGURE 5–2. *Newspaper advertisement for a television open line conversation with a city manager, Tucson, Arizona. (Source: Courtesy of the Office of Community Relations, City of Tucson.)*

In terms of public relations, informational projects such as these can be invaluable to both citizens and governments from both a short- and a long-range point of view. In addition to acquainting citizens with local government services, they help engender and sustain public confidence.

Points of Service: Citizen Contacts

Most local government employees, in the course of their work, come into contact with

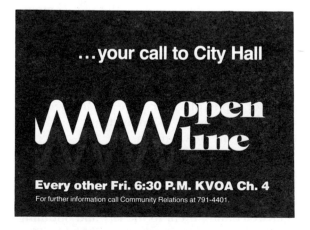

FIGURE 5–1. *Newspaper advertisement for a city hall open line on a television channel, Tucson, Arizona. (Source: Courtesy of the Office of Community Relations, City of Tucson.)*

**don't be
in the
dark about
your City
government**

**topic of
Tucson**

Tues. & Thurs.
7:00 P.M. KUAT Ch. 6

Sat. 12:30 P.M.
KGUN Ch. 9

For further information, call the
Community Relations Office, 791-4401.

members of the public either directly or in-directly. Many of these contacts are made daily. Employees meet citizens daily who come in to request information, apply for permits, or inquire about services. Daily contact with citizens outside government offices is common for police officers, firefighters, refuse collectors, meter readers, building inspectors, utility service personnel, and, at times, construction workers.

Although these daily contacts may be routine and part of the job to city or county personnel, they are always important to members of the public. Many people have some misgivings about going into government offices. Frequently, individuals must contact government agencies to perform tasks which they regard as onerous, such as paying a traffic fine or appearing in court, filling out involved forms, and being subjected to intensive questioning to obtain permits or licenses.

Citizens who contact officials for such purposes may be apprehensive and may fear the red tape involved. Because they are not familiar with the procedures, they may also fear that they may not qualify for a particular license or permit, or they may fear a fine or fee that they feel is unjustified or too high.

In other words, they may feel acutely that public officials, through their authority to impose such restrictions and penalties, may greatly restrict their personal activities, interfere with their plans or schedules, and perhaps create serious financial hardship.

SERVICE CONTACTS MOLD OPINION

In the long run the profusion of routine day-to-day contacts between government employees and citizens does much to influence the overall impression which members of the public have of the local government. Whether public opinion of the government is good or bad depends basically on whether citizens have been favorably or unfavorably impressed, or satisfied or dissatisfied.

FIGURE 5–3. *Newspaper advertisement for a local government television program, Tucson, Arizona. (Source: Courtesy of the Office of Community Relations, City of Tucson.)*

Can't get your damage
deposit back?
Is it turquoise or plastic?
Want contracts explained
in English?
Will that acre you're
buying grow anything
besides rocks?

These and other important
consumer questions, plus
how you can get **FREE**
professional help.

TONIGHT Topic of Tucson
Ch. 6 at 7 p.m.

topic of Tucson

City government is as close and
convenient as your T.V. dial.
For further information, call the
Community Relations Office, 791-4401.

FIGURE 5–4. *Newspaper advertisement for a local government television program designed to aid consumers, Tucson, Arizona. (Source: Courtesy of the Office of Community Relations, City of Tucson.)*

This emphasis on day-to-day contacts in no way negates the importance of public information programs and the utilization of mass media. The importance and value of the formal public information program have been stressed throughout this book. However, a single unsatisfactory personal contact with the local government on the part of a member of the public can change a good impression to a bad one. When individual contacts are multiplied hundreds and even thousands of times daily, it is apparent that the very act of providing daily routine services is critical in achieving and maintaining favorable public opinion.

DIRECT AND INDIRECT CONTACTS

While contacts between a local government and the public can be classified in various ways, a useful means of classifying them is to separate them into direct (or face-to-face) and indirect contacts. Direct contacts encompass all those occasions on which government representatives and citizens meet face-to-face, whether in city hall offices or in the field.

Indirect contacts occur, for example, in telephone conversation and through correspondence. Mass media, special reports, and photography are also avenues of indirect access to the public. These are primarily publicity resources and are considered in detail in Chapters 9, 10, and 11.

From the standpoint of effective communications, face-to-face contact is usually more effective, affording a better opportunity to achieve understanding. If the information offered or requested is not understood by either party, the *opportunity* is immediately available to furnish or obtain additional information. If the matter under consideration is of a technical or detailed nature, the face-to-face situation is especially helpful.

The face-to-face meeting, then, provides the most basic system of two-way communications. Although categorized as indirect, telephone contacts also provide two-way communication.

Despite its advantages two-way communication can contain potential difficulties which may lead to misunderstanding or, worse, to antagonism. These problems may be based in semantics or emotion or both. For example, the information being conveyed may be technical in nature (concerning, for example, meteorological data and the chemistry of smog). The client-citizen may be foreign born and unable to understand such technical language; or the client-citizen may feel uneasy in a government office and unable to think clearly or to recall pertinent information. Such problems emphasize the need for great care on the part of the government employee in communicating with citizens.

The Face-to-Face Information Service. The quality of the information service, which is the responsibility of the employee, is determined in part by:

1. The interest shown in citizens' problems: Do you give them complete attention? Do you listen to them? Do you ask questions to clarify their wants?
2. The quality of information given: Is your communication complete and accurate? Is it clear and concise?
3. The manner of speech: Is your grammar correct? Do you pronounce and enunciate properly? Are your words appropriate?
4. The personal attitude: Do you express cordial greetings? Are you polite and friendly?
5. The personal appearance: Are your dress and appearance appropriate? Do your facial expressions convey a helpful and courteous demeanor?

Various applications of these five determinants of information service quality are discussed below. It may be appropriate at this point, however, to summarize by quoting from a municipal public relations training manual:

Everyone has a different personality and must be handled or dealt with in a different way. In some regards, a person involved in public contact work must be like a chameleon [and] adapt himself to his environment.

A person who is slow and deliberate by nature might feel his problem isn't being given adequate consideration if it is too speedily handled. He will suspect carelessness and slipshod work.

Do not, of course, mimic any unfavorable characteristics your client or visitor might have, such as unpleasant manner, skeptical attitude or sarcasm. You might sum up the fundamental techniques in handling people in a few short points:
1. Respect the dignity of the individual.
2. Be a good and sincere listener.
3. Try honestly and sincerely to see the other fellow's point of view.
4. Ask questions instead of giving orders.
5. Speak kindly to and of others.
6. Smile—and mean it. Say "no" with a smile.

Remember that there are many different ways, good and bad, in which the visitor to a government office can be greeted and received. Among the factors entering into proper greeting and reception are:
1. A tidy office.
2. Acknowledging the presence of the caller promptly.

3. Adopting a "professional" manner in talking with the caller.
4. Not leaving the caller unattended without explaining where you are going and how long you might be gone.
5. Giving the caller a thorough hearing.

The importance of having the caller leave in a pleasant, satisfied frame of mind cannot be overemphasized. If he entered your office by mistake, adequate directions should be given to set him on his course. We should all bear in mind that these are respectable jobs we hold, but we are public servants. We cannot afford the luxury of a temper, discourteousness, and other forms of poor public relations.[3]

Correspondence. Special care should be taken in the composition of letters to be sent to local citizens. This is particularly true if a letter is concerned with technical or detailed matters which may be unfamiliar to the general public. A letter is used as a substitute for a direct or face-to-face contact, but letter writers should make an effort to create as favorable an impression as they would if they were speaking to the recipients personally.

One of the biggest problems in governmental correspondence is the tendency of public officials to use an excessive amount of legalistic or technical terminology. If the recipient is unfamiliar with such language he or she may only become frustrated and confused and blame the government for "all that red tape." This type of reaction is the exact opposite of the objective of correspondence—to communicate effectively with specific members of the public and to secure a desired response.

Certain basic concepts relative to effective correspondence with the public have been developed through years of experience in both public agencies and private industry. The following is a list of major criteria that may be used as a checklist in the preparation of correspondence:

1. See that the letter is friendly in tone and concise, clear, and accurate.
2. Get to the major point or issues early in the letter.
3. Use short sentences and paragraphs; restrict the length to the minimum that is adequate to convey the necessary information.
4. Avoid inexact, stilted, technical, and vague language.

5. Refer to the other person's letter if there was one and if it is related to the letter being prepared.
6. Be sure of the facts and information contained in the letter.
7. Be sure the letter is clean, with no smudges, sloppy corrections, or typographical errors.
8. Review the letter carefully before it is mailed to see that it meets these standards.

Although form letters or notices are often time-saving devices, care should be taken in their construction and discretion exercised in their use. Frequently, such correspondence may appear to be very impersonal to the recipient, especially if it is of the type where most or all of the body of the letter is preprinted with only the name and address typed in. This is most likely to create the impression in the mind of the individual that government personnel do not want to take time to write a personal letter and that this is just one more example of government red tape.

The decision to use a form letter depends on the individual case. It should not be used unless the information is completely adequate and sufficiently clear to answer the inquiry.

Telephone Contacts. Proper telephone usage improves communication between government and citizen and at the same time heightens citizen appreciation of governmental functions and personnel. When individual citizens can transact public business satisfactorily by telephone, without making special trips to government offices, they feel that efficient service is being given to them. Such contacts with the public are beneficial to government personnel also in that they replace other, more time-consuming, personal or mail contacts with the private citizen.

Communicating by telephone involves hazards as well as benefits in terms of public relations. The key to successful telephone usage is the *manner* in which the employee communicates with the person on the other end of the line.

Although the other party cannot see the government employee, the speech and tone of voice help form a picture in the mind of the citizen. As in all such contacts, the employee speaking *is the government* as far as the citizen is concerned.

The use of the telephone is so common in the day-to-day operations of local government that it tends to become routine procedure on the part of many of the personnel. If employees become careless in their attitude and manner on the telephone, a serious public relations problem may result.

A substantial amount of research has been conducted by both private industry and public agencies in the proper use of the telephone. The results of this research indicate that the following points should be recognized and practiced by persons who wish to use the telephone effectively:

1. A telephone should be answered promptly when it rings.
2. When answering a telephone, employees should identify themselves and their organization adequately so that the caller knows that he or she is or is not connected with the correct office. An example would be, "Planning Department, Ms. Jones speaking." Identification also applies when placing a phone call.
3. Talk directly into the telephone transmitter and speak clearly, distinctly, and naturally.
4. When a call needs to be transferred, this should be indicated to callers so that they will not become so deeply involved in explaining their problem or request that they will have to repeat much of it over again. This can be irritating to the caller and can waste the time of both parties. When transferring a call, secure sufficient information from callers to transfer the call to the proper party, so that callers do not feel that they are getting the "runaround."
5. Maintain a pleasant tone of voice throughout the conversation and use tact in talking with callers who may be emotionally upset. If a caller senses that the person to whom he or she is speaking is not arguing back, he or she will usually calm down within a short time.
6. Concentrate on what the caller is saying and talk only to the caller while you are on the telephone.

7. Talk only as long as necessary to furnish or to obtain sufficient information, but do not give the impression that an attempt is being made to get callers off the line before they finish what they have to say.
8. Keep pencil, paper, and a message pad by the telephone so that pertinent information can be written down immediately.
9. Persons should ordinarily place their own telephone calls; otherwise it may appear to the person receiving the call that the caller is not sufficiently interested or concerned.
10. Deliver all telephone messages promptly to prevent unnecessary delays in returning calls or embarrassment to the person for whom the call was intended.
11. End a telephone call as courteously as it was begun; a good final impression is important.

Reception Area Contacts. Another key contact between the government and the public is the reception area of public buildings and offices. Persons who come to a government office for the first time or are not familiar with the location of specific offices within a building will need directions. A half hour of wandering, lost, through the corridors of a vast, impersonal office building leaves the citizen with a bad impression.

Numerous devices can be used to guide people to appropriate offices. A directory of room numbers placed where it can easily be seen, or placards or signs giving directions to the most frequently used offices, can assist greatly. Perhaps most important of all is an information desk in the main entry area or lobby, with a receptionist in attendance throughout working hours. This person can direct visitors to the proper offices and can also save time for government employees by providing certain information directly. If misinformation or wrong directions are given, however, a bad impression will result. Special care should be taken in the selection of a receptionist, as this person may be the only local employee many citizens come into contact with.

Service Requests and Complaints. Every request for service and every complaint from the public is a potential public relations asset to a local

government, depending on how it is handled.

A complaint is a warning signal indicating that a problem exists in some aspect of services to the public. When a complaint or a request for service is received by a local government employee it should be given immediate attention and investigated thoroughly. The matter may be of a minor nature to the employee, but it will be extremely important to the citizen. If it is handled promptly and conscientiously, the action will be appreciated by the person making the request; if it is neglected or ignored, the result will be a poor impression of the government's concern.

Four basic steps are involved in processing complaints and service requests:

1. Welcome the complaint or request.
2. Assign specific responsibility for immediately determining the feasibility of providing the service, or of removing the cause of the complaint.
3. Provide a follow-up procedure to ensure that the matter has received proper attention.
4. In the case of a complaint, notify the person that it has been dealt with; in the case of a service request, be certain that the desired action has been taken, or, if it has not been feasible, that the person knows why.

It is important that the citizen always be notified promptly of the outcome of his or her request or complaint.

It is not possible, of course, to satisfy all service requests or reconcile all complaints in a completely satisfactory manner. Some complaints are unjustified and some requests are unreasonable. But it should be borne in mind that it is sometimes difficult for persons making the requests to understand this.

Those employees who handle complaints and requests must have a good understanding of human nature and must be able to meet the public well. They must understand that every person is different in background, experience, and personality and that each person must be handled as an individual. Even if the request is unreasonable, the employee should hear the other person out, remain objective and calm, and, if the request is impossible to grant, strive to make the person understand why.

Many local governments have developed special procedures for improving and streamlining the handling of complaints and service requests. The following are some examples.

Roanoke, Virginia, uses a postcard form which allows citizens who requested service or filed a complaint to comment on how well the request was carried out. When a complaint is received by the city it is referred to the appropriate department, which then sends someone to investigate and do whatever is possible on the spot. This person leaves a card at the home of the complainant. The card provides space for identifying data, the type of complaint, and several lines for comments. The card is stamped and self-addressed to the city manager's office. The response has been highly satisfactory. The returned cards have expressed satisfaction with the work done, and some have made additional suggestions for improvements.

In Ojai, California, when a service request is received from a citizen, the form is prepared in duplicate. The original copy is delivered to the department in which the service is provided. The employee who is designated to receive such requests determines the priority of the request and schedules a completion date. After the request is dealt with, the original copy is returned to the central file and the second copy is destroyed. For control purposes, the city manager reviews folders containing the completed requests and those which are pending.

Because it emphasizes the significance of complaints in effective municipal performance, the following is quoted from the public relations training manual for the city of La Habra, California:

We most often associate complaints with anger or irritation, and certainly many complaints which come to our attention are caused by ill feelings. But even the most embittered citizen is presumed to be seeking some sort of positive reaction to his complaint. We thus find it helpful to assume the attitude that complaints are requests for service and/or information. We differentiate these service requests from the more routine inquiries . . . because they represent a request for something which should have been provided in the normal operating pattern of government, or at least because the citizen honestly believes that his complaint is based on the failure of the city to provide some service to which he is entitled.

Thus, our most important attitude toward the complaint is that the complaint is genuine, that to the citizen his complaint is of vital importance. Indeed, our receipt of a complaint is of vital importance to us. Even if the solution to a particular complaint is beyond our responsibility, our willingness to listen and to at least suggest the source of solution can aid us in our job of informing the public. Cities vary as to the types of services they perform, and it is not uncommon for the citizen who feels he has been taken advantage of by some public or private agency to call upon his city government for help, and even to call upon the particular city agency whose title suggests a possible remedy for the problem.

Whether or not we believe that a complaint is valid, we cannot forget that to the complainant his problem is real and vital. While we encounter a variety of methods and types in the presentation of complaints, there are some citizens who find it particularly difficult to present their complaints rationally and in a form which we can readily understand. These people need our special attention and sympathy, as they often are the ones who feel that they have been deliberately mistreated when, in fact, there has been a breakdown in communications.

Our most important task, then, in receiving complaints is to fully understand their nature and specific facts. As in the case of inquiries, careful listening and thought-provoking speech are among our most useful techniques. . . .

Perhaps the only rule we need stress in this approach to public relations, other than those of courtesy and intelligence, is that we must, under all circumstances, listen carefully and completely to all complaints before replying. While we can tactfully prevent callers from inconsequential rambling, we cannot afford to obscure or confuse an honest complaint by argument or denial on our part.[4]

La Habra provides its employees with instructions on use of its service request form. These instructions appear as Appendix C of this book.

Personal and Physical Appearance. Members of the public judge a community not only by services but also by the appearance of the personnel, equipment, and facilities. As pointed out throughout this book, good public relations cannot be guaranteed by merely doing a good job; the public must be convinced that the service is good.

The personal appearance of employees who come into contact with the public is especially important and should conform to community standards.

The behavior and bearing of office personnel is an important factor in the formulation of public opinion. If persons coming into government offices see employees drinking coffee, reading magazines, or just "fooling around on the job," it will create a bad impression regardless of how they look otherwise. To prevent this, there should be a special room or area away from public view in which employees may relax on their coffee or lunch breaks; many jurisdictions provide such facilities.

The appearance of uniformed personnel is of particular importance, since the public is more apt to notice these employees. Uniforms which are soiled, unpressed, or in need of mending are quite conspicuous. The appearance of the uniform depends on the way it is worn as well as its condition. Police officers and other uniformed employees will create a much better impression if they are alert and conscious of their bearing than if they are untidy and careless in appearance.

The appearance of public buildings, equipment, and offices is also significant in the public's opinion of a government. Regardless of the design or age of a public building, its exterior appearance can remain favorable if it is kept in good condition and the grounds are cared for. The interiors of buildings and offices are also important. Just as many commercial establishments are judged by their interior conditions, so is a city or county judged by the inside of its buildings and offices. The public does not expect or desire to see government offices as elaborately furnished as business establishments, and if the walls, floors, and office equipment are maintained in a clean, neat condition the public will be favorably impressed. These same standards of appearance apply to other types of city equipment, such as motor vehicles, street maintenance equipment, construction machinery, street signs, etc.

Safety as a Factor in Public Relations. Sometimes overlooked is the role of good safety practices as a part of public relations, both inside and outside offices. Employees should be considerate of others in safety matters and should observe and report possible trouble areas or unsafe conditions.

Especially significant in the eyes of the public are the manners of public employees when driving motor vehicles—the source of some of the best and worst impressions on individual citizens. Observance of the normal rules of driving courtesy and of statutory vehicle safety are only minimum standards of safe vehicle operation. Public vehicles have distinctive markings and are easily recognized. Thus, the government is judged by the operator behind the wheel, whose basic standard when operating a nonemergency public vehicle should be to *always yield the right-of-way.*

PERFORMING THE SERVICES

During the course of a typical day in most communities, there may be hundreds and frequently thousands of contacts between employees and the public. Most of these contacts are of the type that might be called "service contacts," since they occur in connection with providing a service to the citizen in one form or another. These types of contacts usually involve a direct relationship between the government employee and the citizen, as is the case with many of the daily activities of police officers, firefighters, receptionists and counter clerks, and inspectional personnel.

Every government department needs to maintain good relations with the members of its respective publics, not only to achieve its program objectives more effectively but also to maintain public satisfaction with its services. Underlying these immediate departmental objectives, however, is a broader and more fundamental reason for high quality service contacts with the public. The public relations status of an organization is basically only as high as the amount of public respect attributed to its weakest unit. For example, if all the departments of a city enjoy favorable public relations except the police department, then it is likely that the overall public respect for the city will not be high.

Law Enforcement Contacts. The importance and variety of responsibilities of law enforcement personnel place them in an unusual position relative to public opinion. The very fact that so many of the police officer's public contacts are restrictive or disciplinary in the minds of the citizens gives him or her a key responsibility for developing public respect.

Law enforcement personnel will tell you it is

not easy to convince most citizens that they are "in the wrong" when they have violated the law. The reasons can be numerous. It may be a matter of personal pride, or the fear of possible fines, loss of privileges, or even imprisonment. Or it may be that the violator earnestly believes he or she is innocent. A fundamental reason for such an attitude often stems from the average American's traditional resistance to governmental rules, regulations, and restrictions.

There is no denying that the public relations responsibilities of law enforcement personnel are difficult. The basic question is, How can such personnel carry out their duties in an effective manner and yet satisfy, or at least not offend, the citizens involved? The key is the manner in which such enforcement actions are taken. This is discussed in detail in Chapter 8.

Fire Protection Contacts. Although fire protection personnel may not have as many direct contacts with members of the public as police officers do, their presence in all parts of the community and the special nature of their work are significant determinants of public opinion. Their duties consist basically of the protection of life and property of citizens from fires and many other types of emergency. The services offered the public are, in general, highly valued and appreciated.

While the effect on public opinion of the competency demonstrated by fire personnel in coping with fires and other emergency situations is of great importance, some aspects of the day-to-day operations may in the long run prove to be even more significant. A basic responsibility in fire prevention is inspections. The purpose is to guard against the unintentional creation or presence of fire hazards stemming from accumulation of waste materials, inferior wiring and other electrical and mechanical defects, and improper materials storage.

Two general types of inspection are handled by firefighters: inspection of commercial, industrial, and public buildings, and inspection of private residences.

In the former category fire personnel are usually authorized by state laws or local ordinances to inspect the interiors of commercial

establishments to determine whether the proprietors have complied with the laws and standards relative to fire safety. Even here, however, it is sometimes difficult to obtain the full cooperation of the persons operating such establishments. This is especially so if the person is in doubt as to whether his or her facilities and building meet the safety standards. In this situation a tactful, though firm, attitude will usually achieve more cooperation than a forceful approach. A basic purpose of such inspections is to convince the occupants that maintaining high fire safety standards will be to their benefit in the long run. Ordinarily, a sincere, objective approach is much more effective in achieving compliance than an authoritarian approach.

The inspection of private residences frequently is more of a problem than commercial building inspection. Ordinarily, fire personnel have no legal authority to enter the premises unless the residents give them permission to do so. Exceptions are where a definite fire hazard is known to exist, and even then a search warrant may be required.

It is common knowledge of fire personnel that many actual or potential fire hazards, such as defective wiring and ventilation, or accumulation of waste materials, exist in private residences and that if the opportunity were available to demonstrate and explain this to the residents in their homes many costly fires, injuries, and even deaths could be prevented.

The key to effective residential fire inspection is gaining entry by voluntary consent of the residents. If this can be done, then it usually is relatively easy to point out and discuss any fire hazards. A letter to residents often helps. Care should be taken by fire personnel even inside the home not to give the impression that they are "snooping around," and they should indicate by their attitude that they are there only to help the occupants make their home a safer and better place in which to live.

Gaining voluntary entrance is often a problem in the very homes where fire personnel know or suspect that a fire hazard exists. Usually this is because the occupant, or the occupant's landlord, realizes that he or she is not maintaining adequate safety standards and fears reprisals or possible repair expenses if he or she permits "government inspectors" in. This is a difficult problem to overcome, but if the fire personnel use a friendly, helpful approach in their initial encounter with the occupants, and take special care not to inject an authoritative tone in their voice, the person's resistance may be overcome.

Public Works Contacts Many of the physical facilities and services provided in a modern community are constructed and maintained through public works operations. The department responsible for public works and related activities has a special role to play in public relations. This is owing to two primary factors. First, the services and facilities which are provided are important for the convenience and comfort of the public. Second, the construction and maintenance of these facilities often create inconveniences and may even become nuisances for residents, and such conditions can lead to unfavorable public reactions.

Some of the more common activities and responsibilities which have public relations implications include construction and maintenance of streets and highways; checking plans, issuing permits, and inspecting new building construction; refuse collection and disposal; and maintenance and operation of street lighting systems and traffic signs.

All of these activities involve direct contacts between government personnel and members of the public at one time or another. Some involve more contacts than others, however, and some are more critical activities from a public relations standpoint, since they affect more people directly.

For example, a substantial amount of time and energy in a department of public works is spent in enforcing building and safety requirements for new buildings and other construction. This means checking building plans, issuing appropriate permits, and inspecting structures as they progress to make sure the specifications are drawn and the construction is performed in accordance with approved plans and building code requirements.

Citizens who are involved in construction which is subject to these regulations usually have established time schedules and may find

it not only annoying but expensive if they are unable to maintain their schedules because of delays caused by the local government. In the inspection of new construction, the inspection approvals are not limited to structural considerations but also must include plumbing, heating, ventilation, and refrigeration system approvals.

Inspection services is another area of operations where members of the public often tend to feel that they are being victimized by bureaucratic red tape and inefficiency. This is often the result of public ignorance of the law and a lack of insight as to the need for such standards. In order to prevent such negative attitudes, it is necessary for public officials responsible for inspection services to see that members of the public involved understand the reasons for and nature of the regulations and procedures involved.

Another phase of public works which has particular relevance to public relations is construction and maintenance of streets. Such projects can become irritating to the public, especially if the work is performed in residential areas. In view of the inconveniences involved, such as detours, "washboard" roads, accident hazards, and dust and dirt, it is little wonder that members of the public react as they sometimes do.

There are frequent personal contacts between local government personnel and citizens in street construction, particularly when work is going on in residential areas. Care should be taken to see that yards are not damaged or littered with dirt and debris, that driveway accesses are maintained, and that construction workers do not use private property or facilities such as water faucets without the consent of the owner.

One way to help prevent problems is to notify beforehand those persons who will be affected. The following examples present some effective methods for doing this.

Before street construction is begun in Montgomery County, Maryland, a letter is sent by the county construction engineer to all property owners along the streets to be worked on. The letter sets forth the construction schedule, the name of the contractor, the approximate timing for each major stage of development, the name and phone number of the county inspector assigned to the project, and related information. The letter concludes: "As homeowners ourselves, we can appreciate your feelings and will give them every consideration during our work."

Phoenix, Arizona, has utilized a public information program for residential street construction. The purpose is to provide residents with information on the formation of residential street improvement districts to be used as a basis for paving residential streets. The procedure includes the distribution of descriptive brochures and of booklets with detailed information on the formation of street improvement districts, the preparation of radio and television spot announcements, and the use of news releases and advertising.

Some officials now feel that if one group of employees who have the most effect upon the public's opinion of local government services had to be singled out, it would be those employees engaged in refuse collection and disposal. The ordinary duties of such personnel include the collection and disposal of garbage, rubbish, tree and garden trimmings, papers, cans, bottles, and ashes. These are, in fact, highly significant public relations activities. The fact that these employees are seen by residents several times each week, and that they often enter private yards to obtain the refuse, places them in more frequent contact with the public than almost any other employee group.

Many cities and counties, aware of the public relations involved in refuse collection, provide uniforms and train employees in proper ways of handling the refuse so as not to damage containers, etc. These personnel are also being given special training in the proper way to deal with the public, with emphasis on courtesy.

A special problem occurs when a change in collection procedures or schedules is needed. Glendale, California, conducted an extensive information campaign to help make a smooth transition. The new system required householders to provide uniform metal rubbish containers with tight-fitting lids; garbage had to be wrapped separately. An information leaflet was first distributed to 60,000 homes by house-to-

house delivery service, which was cheaper than bulk rate mail. A special version of the leaflet was printed for one area of the city where the collection day had been changed.

Two days after the leaflet was distributed news releases were run in three local newspapers repeating the information in the leaflet. The principal points in the changeover were also covered in the city hall newsletter, which goes to leading civic groups and key citizens in the area. Utility bills for the following month had a special printed insert to emphasize the importance of the changeover to the citizens. The sanitation supervisor and foremen visited numerous restaurants and other establishments to explain the change.

The results were excellent in terms of public cooperation. The key, again, was the use of effective communications to achieve public understanding and support.

Other Key Contact Points. Many other key points of contact between the local government and the public greatly affect public opinion. Examples of such key contact personnel include park and recreation personnel, especially in recent years when members of the public have had more leisure time and have spent more of it in public parks and in recreational activities. Other examples of personnel in contact with the public are city clerks and their staffs, and library personnel. Additional offices which are key contact points include human services offices, personnel recruiting offices, the chief administrator's office, and offices of department heads.

The success of these various public contacts depends ultimately on the ability of personnel to meet and deal effectively with the many individuals who come to the offices seeking information and help.

Summary

This chapter has dealt with public relations as it pertains to citizen services. Growing demands for services have been described; this has been followed by an analysis of the concept of service. An important part of any government public relations program—supplying information—has been discussed next. The remainder of the chapter has discussed, in considerable detail, the sensitive matter of government contacts with citizens. This last section stresses the need for various departments to handle these contacts (whether direct or indirect) tactfully and efficiently.

The present chapter has provided a background for employee–citizen contacts; Chapter 6 takes these contacts further in its discussion of the employee–citizen team.

---

[1] The population of American cities doubled between the beginning of the Civil War and 1900. By 1920 over half of the nation was living in cities. By 1970 about 73.5 percent of the population was urban.

[2] THE MUNICIPAL YEAR BOOK (Washington, D.C.: International City Management Association, annual); THE COUNTY YEAR BOOK (Washington, D.C.: National Association of Counties and International City Management Association, annual). Volume 1 of the latter publication appeared in 1975.

[3] City of Beverly Hills, California, PUBLIC RELATIONS TRAINING MANUAL, rev. ed. (Beverly Hills, Calif.: City of Beverly Hills, 1962.)

[4] City of La Habra, California, "Training in Public Relations and Communications," La Habra, 1962, pp. 11–12. (Mimeographed.)

6

The Employee–Citizen Team

Hⁿᵒᵂ ᶜᴬᴺ ᵀᴴᴱ ᴾᴿᴬᶜᵀᴵᶜᴱ of public relations aid communities in their efforts to achieve viability, vigor, and vision?

Conrad Joyner, professor of government and former deputy mayor of Tucson, Arizona, has called for communities to develop marketing expertise.

Years ago American business learned that successful marketing meant much more than advertising commercials. Public officials are now groping for answers to problems which most major corporations have virtually solved.

In essence, the secret to success in marketing is to provide the best possible goods and services, to let people know what these products mean to them, and to enlist individuals to sell other people on the value of goods and services.

Translated into the governmental sphere, this means that we must use every avenue available to communicate with the public and to involve them in the activities of their communities.[1]

The above comment provides the setting for this chapter's focus: the employee–citizen team. All too often, as professional observers have noted, administrators fail to realize that their employees are also citizens of the community and that they play significant roles in creating the image which government projects in the community. These employees share in community tasks and represent the government within their neighborhoods and organizations. Citizens, then, can be construed both as individuals who are and as individuals who are not employed in government. All support government through their tax efforts. All need to be informed. All need to be included in the governmental process.

This chapter, then, is concerned with ways and means of making the employee–citizen team a reality and an actively functioning aspect of community government. Gaining citizen confidence is the first subject discussed; to do this, a government should prove itself accessible and accountable, should make its purposes and activities clear to the public, and should manifest both consistency and integrity. Government employees are discussed next, from the points of view of (1) communications within the organization, (2) communication with the public, and (3) active participation in the community.

How is government–citizen participation actually achieved? A number of techniques are outlined: mini/mobile city halls; visiting governments; speak-out forums; and information/complaint services.

Considerable attention is given next to citizen committees, with definitions of the principal types. Following this, the relations of these committees to government councils is detailed. Finally, the practical use of meetings as means of communication is discussed. A summary concludes the chapter.

Gaining Confidence and Cooperation

If an effective employee–citizen team is to be developed and encouraged, certain factors should be considered. First, how are confidence and cooperation developed? Second, what are the employee's roles? Third, what is meant by the employee as a citizen-neighbor? Fourth, how are committees organized and what are their functions? And fifth, are meetings a true form of cooperation?

If a citizen–employee team is to be developed, a vital core a core of cooperation and confidence is necessary.

These two words—cooperation and confidence—could be the most overused words in government today. Their usage is debased, however, if residents experience lip service rather than action. It is not enough for local government to say it seeks the cooperation or confidence of a community. These attributes need to be earned through action. Chief administrators and public relations officers are usually fully aware of this.

Any discussion relating to fostering confidence and cooperation, then, should include the factors of accessibility, accountability, clarity, consistency, and integrity. Other factors may play supporting roles, but for the purposes and goals of this discussion these five factors are the most telling.

GOVERNMENTAL ACCESSIBILITY

It is important that government be accessible to those it serves. Therefore, the visible functions of government need to extend beyond the normal working day. Few residents are able to leave production lines to attend a planning board meeting, a finance committee meeting, or even a city council meeting.

Residents want to register complaints and often state that when they are ready to do business with the government the government is "shut down."

In one community an otherwise even campaign had only one salient feature to distinguish the candidates: the campaign plank that the government's business would be conducted on the people's time—when the people could attend meetings. The plank was a winning one. As their first step, the newly elected officials moved the board meetings from Monday afternoons to Monday evenings.

Communities experiencing pressures for citizen participation should consider evening and neighborhood meetings. The average citizen often refers to the "wait out" technique. Citizens feel that while government staffs can usually attend meetings held during the day, most

employed people might be successful only in getting off one afternoon to participate or oppose a certain action. They know it would be highly unlikely that they could be available for successive days should the matter in question continue.

It is not to be wondered at, then, that many citizens have lost interest because they could not gain access to the process. To many such citizens the irony is that, when they complain about an ordinance, they are told that complaining after an ordinance is adopted is too late, that they should have attended the public hearings if they had anything to say. A part of the so-called silent majority, then, may be silent because it has experienced this bureaucratic runaround.

One city recognized the uselessness of holding public hearings on a completed budget proposal. The time to hold the hearings, it was felt, was six months before the document was completed, when residents could have true input into the projects for the coming fiscal year. These meetings, then, were held in October on three successive nights. Leaders of organizations and individual citizens made presentations and requests. The format was informal. Interchange was positive. Every request was forwarded to the affected administrator. The administrator, in turn, indicated during budget preparation whether that request was submitted with his budget and if not, why not. This information was forwarded to the resident. Hearings on the completed budget document were held at different times during the week— mornings, afternoons, and evenings, because the community is a three-shift community, and the total community was invited to give review. This is the kind of approach that makes citizens feel that their interests are being considered and their participation is wanted.

Making the governmental process available to the public is one aspect of accessibility. Another aspect involves taking the government to the people on an individual basis. Government officials find that a useful technique is to serve as speakers to organizations. Many local governments have active speakers' bureaus. Other communities respond to requests for topical speakers. Such accessibility affords an interchange with small groups on the organization's home territory rather than at city hall.

In addition to providing speakers to organizations, governments today are actively soliciting placement of their officials on radio and television. Talk shows abound in most communities. These shows are generally warm and relaxed in atmosphere and allow the administrator to discuss various points of an issue before a wide audience.

Information/complaint telephone services are workhorses of goodwill for most communities if they are properly staffed. It is important that the staffs of these operations be thoroughly trained not only in the mechanics of government but also its policy. Larger communities have provided staff personnel for twenty-four-hour service, but more communities utilize an answering service during the hours when government offices are closed.

Personnel for such information/complaint services should be sensitive to the emotions of those who call. Is the person calling simply for information or has he or she already experienced the "telephone runaround"? A responsive staff member will sense when it is appropriate to let the person talk it out to get the caller's hidden agenda. Follow-through on complaints is crucial for those who call—not only about when the desired service was accomplished, but about how the service was accomplished.

Sometimes the caller is in the wrong but may not realize it. Callers may be in violation of local ordinances or may even be calling the wrong unit of government. Once again, tact and a willingness to work out solutions will maintain a friendship and understanding instead of fostering a hardening of attitudes toward government.

The first step toward cooperation and confidence, then, begins with accessibility—being available and making government available and convenient for the citizens.

GOVERNMENTAL ACCOUNTABILITY

Government must be accountable. Some administrators contend that accountability is a responsibility of elected officials. Fortunately, this breed is declining as the modern adminis-

trator has come to see that accountability is a continuous process for every operation in local government. Good news or bad news, setbacks or breakthroughs, frustrations or fulfillments should be reported to the public.

With this realization, chief administrators have realized also that the process of government must continue nevertheless, that programs must be monitored and plans developed. Managers have come to realize that much of their time could easily be eaten up in discussions with reporters or in responding to the public's requests for information. Because of this, administrators have created offices of public information and public relations.

The 1960s and 1970s have seen a change from a passive stance—responding to citizen requests for information—to an active one —anticipating citizen requests and preparing the proper information. Out of this has come such innovations as informational radio and television programs, government newspapers, mini city halls, and utility bill mailers.

Wise administrators have continued an open door policy to all the public, including members of the news media. But they have added the public information department to develop government's own channel of information to the public and to provide expanded information for the media.

A common complaint heard among local government personnel is that the media are interested chiefly in broad-based news. A regional television station, for instance, cannot devote its newscasts to only one community. If it did, it could lose much of its market. Consequently, many governments have developed their own strategies for seeing that information is given directly to the public by building up their own channels of communication.

It is important that these varied productions—be they in print or in the electronic media—be handled with both expertise and responsibility. They should be relevant to citizen concerns and should not shirk from citing government itself if government has failed in its programs. Take the following example, in which a government accepted the responsibility for a problem and indicated what residents could expect in the future:

Frustrated by the leaf collection process this fall? You're not alone. We in city government extend our apologies to all who had their leaves wait and wait and wait. While awaiting new and more efficient leafloaders, some of the older equipment broke down or was prematurely discarded. The new loaders came a month late. The worst rainy season since 1934 was another problem. The wet leaves made collection increasingly difficult to handle. We are working now for next fall. Our goal? Never to have another such nightmare as this year. Please accept our apologies. Thank you for your patience. Call City Manager's Office, 727-2123.[2]

These, then, are some of the concepts governments are using to maintain accountability with the public. Administrators realize, too, that if the message is to have value the wording must be clear and import understood by the reader/receiver.

GOVERNMENTAL CLARITY

Thus, we come to clarity. Much bureaucratic gobbledygook is frustrating to the average person. What makes fine sense to a director of finance or a planner may make little sense to most citizens. What the latter want to know is how much it will cost them, whether it will increase or decrease taxes, what they will get from all this talk, and whether they will be inconvenienced.

Governments should strive to interpret their actions to citizens in the words used by those citizens—whatever their backgrounds. (It does little good, for example, to provide a community newspaper in English for an area which reads Spanish.)

The following paragraph typifies what may be professionally intelligible but may prove incomprehensible to members of the public:

The PBS forwards Planning Packages to the appropriate Task Force, or if the Planning Package falls outside Task Force functional areas, directly to the Community Development Commission through the primary channel. The process also provides a two-way primary channel between the PBS and the MCD for interchanging information and pooling staff expertise. The PBS may receive Planning Packages referred through the secondary channel, review them and forward them to the appropriate Task Forces. The PBS may also refer project proposals or Planning Packages to the MCD or to the Neighborhood Councils for review through the secondary channel.

The process provides a two-way tertiary channel for feedback of evaluation information.

Those who cling to professional jargon fail to grasp the essence of clarity. Each profession has its jargon which excludes others from understanding. Some professionals mistakenly believe that "street language" can never accurately describe a specialized process. Sound governmental principles and good public relations practices hold that it is the community that is being addressed and not a selected small group of professionals.

GOVERNMENTAL CONSISTENCY

Administrators today understand the necessity for always being accessible, accountable, and clear. In each of these discussion areas, consistency has been implicit. A speakers' bureau, for example, cannot be developed merely for a bond referendum: it must function all year. And public hearings should not be held at the convenience of the citizens only when government wants an urban renewal project approved.

Government is a big business: it is a "people business," producing service. When community residents realize their desires are only solicited in times of governmental need, disenchantment begins. It is vital that government include the public from the inception to the completion in all its programs.

GOVERNMENTAL INTEGRITY

The last item in this discussion of the development of citizen cooperation with and confidence in government is the most crucial of all: integrity. Integrity is a hair shirt willingly worn. Much of modern society may take the easy way rather than the right way, but it is vital that government accept its responsibility for adhering to certain precepts, in particular honesty, dedication, conviction, full disclosure, and fair treatment.

Administrators face almost overwhelming obstacles when corruption, collusion, bribery, and/or pocket-lining are discovered during their administration. (State secrets are seldom secrets. Their nature is known through a community even before all the participants may know. Wise public relations practitioners are aware of this, whether they be city managers or directors of public relations offices.)

Successful administrators move quickly and publicly for a complete review, a complete accounting, and a correction so complete that it guarantees no further incidents. This kind of honesty helps produce a climate of cooperation and confidence—a climate conducive to active citizen participation.

Government Employees

In recent years government administrators have realized that, like their business counterparts, they must listen to and talk with their employees. In fact, they have discovered how much can be gained from communications with their employees, a process which involves significantly more than simply talking with them or listening to them.

A government employee is, to the citizen, the representative of government, wherever he or she may be. If the employee does not know why government is undertaking a program, the citizen will wonder whether government is willing to communicate effectively with the taxpayer.

Each of the employee's friends considers him or her a part of government. The way the employee regards his or her employer will reflect upon the governmental organization.

Is the employee paid a living wage? Does he or she have opportunities for advancement? Is the employee treated fairly? Does he or she receive sufficient fringe benefits? Does the employee feel that he or she is a part of a team?

INTERNAL COMMUNICATIONS

A recent discussion that the author had with a psychiatrist, a corporate consultant in interpersonal communications, and a director of corporate public relations revealed that the first axiom of communication is that organizations cannot communicate well with their external audiences if they cannot "put it together" internally.

A public posture of being responsive to the needs of the community and its social ills may seem hypocritical to the employee who cannot get any information about his or her pension.

Happy employees will produce positive public relations in the community; unhappy employees, on the other hand, will produce negative public relations.

Consider the size of local governments today. They range from a dozen employees to thousands of employees. Each of these employees speaks for the effectiveness of a government. After all, municipal employees shop, join clubs, vote, go to church, and live next door.

While local governments have long been concerned with their external public, they have only recently realized that one part of their public—the internal public—has often been overlooked.

Lynn A. Townsend, former president of Chrysler Corporation, in a speech to the International Council of Industrial Editors, said that a general approach to internal communication effectiveness would:

First, see to it that professional communication talent is put in place, and that preliminary research is done to determine specific communication strengths and weakness. Issue a written policy on internal communication which defines program purposes. Bring together the written, oral, and visual communication tools in a newly created communication department. Adopt specific plans and programs to encourage better upward, downward, and horizontal flow of information. See to it that the line and staff organizations work closely together in properly fulfilling their vital roles.

Make it known to all concerned that the formal communication program has the benefit of the support and personal participation of the chief executive. Encourage the communicators to do the selling job so important to winning the continuing support of all levels of management. And last, but certainly not least, measure communication progress—as carefully and objectively as possible.[3]

In his speech Townsend reports on the barriers to communication, particularly in a large organization. He cautions against those managers who feel corporation information is their personal province "as something to be parceled out to a favored few."[4]

One of the Townsend requirements in achieving productive internal communication is that substantially greater emphasis must be put on communication planning and measurement:

I am astonished at how often managers assume that communication can be effective on a haphazard basis. Managers agree that quality, or finance, or engineering, are functions which require planning and measurement. Why, then, should communication be left to chance—unplanned, unorganized, uncontrolled, unmeasured?[5]

He calls for top management to make the long-term investment in professional talent and communication programming:

It seems to me that many managers practice a double standard when it comes to communication. They wouldn't think of turning over the maintenance of a half-million-dollar machine to an unskilled person. They would certainly avoid entrusting the direction of a complicated engineering process to a person without an engineering background.

But these same managers will too often assign the internal communication function to an untrained individual. Good organizational communication requires skill with the techniques of communication, and depth experience in directing the flow of information.[6]

Townsend is describing an internal communication process which larger governments have already begun. Several local, state, and federal units of government have held communication surveys of their organizations to determine the effectiveness of and the problems of their internal communications—including both vertical and horizontal communications.

These organizations have discovered various side benefits from the surveys, such as finding out that certain procedures have upset their employees. One organization, for example, learned that its employees were upset by first learning of a policy decision which would affect them by reading about it in the newspapers. Such incidents are commonplace when little thought is given to the effect of policy changes upon employees.

Informed, satisfied employees will reflect a responsive government, one that plans ahead and communicates internally as well as externally.

EMPLOYEES AS COMMUNICATORS

Sometimes it is necessary to have formal communications training, not only for management

but for the entire staff. Who, for instance, has more frequent contact with citizens—the city manager or the refuse collector? Consider the housing inspector: he or she meets the public more frequently than the chief administrator does. Then there is the water billing office, which copes either effectively or ineffectively with perhaps thousands of residents each week. And what is the nature of the contact? Good communications training should be tailored to the needs of the employee.

The key to the effectiveness of employees' communication lies in their communication skills. It would be wise to pause a moment to differentiate between communication skills versus talking skills. All humans learn to talk, and often exhibit a passing speaking proficiency by the time they are two. Yet few of us will develop into skilled communicators without some training. Skilled communicators know how to listen and to talk, how to see that the idea within one person is the same idea being received and transmitted by another person. Skilled communicators develop their art through training, refinement, and perseverance. The citizen has a right to feel that his or her problems will be understood and will be transmitted correctly to the person in authority who will handle them.

This is why, from the morning refuse collector to the evening safety patrol, it is important that all local government employees at all levels have communications training. Communication is both a science and an art. Out of it comes an ability to transmit the proper message and decide whether that message should have a vertical or horizontal channel of communication.

CHANNELING INFORMATION

Today management is developing communications systems—channels of communication. Management is deciding in policy meetings who should transmit the information and how it should be transmitted.

One of the oldest channels of communication within the organization is the grapevine. This will probably exist to some extent whatever the state of communications within the organization. It will play a far larger role, however, when communications within the organization are inadequate. An active grapevine is a signal, then, for improving internal communications, for keeping employees fully informed through such means as sectional meetings, memorandum releases, and bulletin board notices.

Channels of communication may be personal (interviews, conference sessions, task forces, group sessions, or full meetings) or impersonal (illustrations, memoranda, bulletin board notices, newsletters, newspapers, and inserts in pay check envelopes). Their selection is limited by finances, personnel, time, and commitment. Governments severely hampered financially may move toward improving management organization or may use department head meetings to achieve successful horizontal and vertical communication.

Horizontal communication becomes more important as governments become more complex and departments become separated physically. Symptoms of horizontal communication problems are evident when long-term administrators remark that people just don't get together the way they used to. Studies have indicated that vertical communication tends to present fewer problems than horizontal communication does.

Weak or ineffective horizontal communication can result in parallel actions being undertaken by two or more operations within a local government, or in departments working unknowingly at cross-purposes. One author summarized today's communication needs as follows:

When we consider the nature of an organization and the growing trends of largeness, complexity, demand for greater efficiency, and so on, one conclusion is eminently clear: Today's organization requires communication performance at an unprecedented level of excellence. And chief among the demands made upon our organizations is the increasing necessity for an organizational climate compatible with the psychic needs of the organization's members.[7]

Government has a responsibility to provide a healthy communication setting for its employees, one that is consistently fed and professionally tended, and which has the active support of top management.

EMPLOYEES AS CITIZENS

Government has an opportunity to poll the public through its employees. The government organization provides a cross section of the community—from top management to the newest inner-office mail carrier. These employees reside within a variety of neighborhoods. Thus, the entire community is represented.

Management is beginning to consult these employees as sounding boards for possible future actions, or to determine community reaction to programs in progress.

Skill should be exercised in field interviews with employees. A successful technique is to use small groups of similar employees with a neutral supervisor as a discussion leader. Further, these interviews should be a routine matter, should be informal, and should not be held too frequently. Side benefits are also experienced. Employees will realize that management is interested in them, their neighborhoods, and their community.

Another communications program encourages all employees to report their neighborhood problems, such as poor street lighting, faulty sewer lines, or infrequent public safety patrols. Employees can be an important source for discerning needed community projects. If properly encouraged, employees can become ever more involved in the governmental process, and the entire community will stand to benefit.

EMPLOYEES AS PARTICIPANTS

A second way in which employees may serve in the public relations role in the community is as participants in the community's social, civic, religious, and volunteer organizations. Enlightened management today supports employee participation in these organizations, and is becoming a supportive partner in allowing staff to take time during the day for those civic meetings that support the entire community.

Government discovered in the sixties that it could not be a mere receiver of community activities—it had to be a participant as well. Consequently, younger division heads and other middle management personnel began appearing on civic boards and commissions along with senior department heads.

Civic organizations, and business and industry as well, liked what they discovered. They found men and women who were professional: knowledgeable of needs, clear in analysis, capable of planning, and thorough in administration.

Increased cooperation by employees with civic organizations and the private sector has, indeed, proved to be good public relations. Administrators, then, would do well to encourage their personnel to continue to participate in these organizations, and might support such participation through recognition and leave time.

In Summary

This section has dealt with a most valuable part of local government's public: its employees. A stable, contributing, and professional work force is the prerequisite of any operation and, particularly, of government.

The value of personnel who know both the past and the present is obvious when action must be taken. Fresh personnel will always spark an organization, but it is critical indeed that those who have served long in government retain a positive and vigorous outlook regarding their work.

A team effort results when informed employees are included in the communication process. Such employees are trained in all aspects of communication and can select the proper channels for their messages. They have learned to listen as well as to speak in communication. Their departments do not work at cross-purposes. Their administrators communicate with them.

Administrators who are able to communicate with their employees can learn much about the needs of the city's various neighborhoods. Business and industry can also learn much about government through the participation of government employees.

The result is that the external public finds a government that is stimulating, challenging, professional, and responsive to the needs of all of that public.

Government–Citizen Participation

The preceding discussion focused on employees as a major source of information about the community. Another larger source exists: the citizens themselves. Communities are vast repositories of citizen desires and frustrations. Governments have begun to realize that citizens need accessible channels to provide outlets for these desires and frustrations. The following discussion analyzes some alternatives used by local governments to allow individual citizens to become full partners in the process of government.

Those who have not attempted these approaches should be cautioned that it is often an American trait to ignore the crisis until it reaches the proverbial doorstep. Despite all efforts on the part of government, many citizens may still say they are uninformed or that government behaves like a closed corporation. Local governments should avoid pointing out the fact that the residential property tax probably pays less than a quarter of government's operations, or that the subject at hand has been on the front pages of the newspapers and in the first five minutes of every newscast for a month.

A few governments have sophisticated operations which include the entire scope of citizen input—decentralization of government, mobile city halls, traveling council meetings, permanent citizen participation structures. Others are involved in speak out forums, information/complaint telephone services, emergency reporting stations, aldermanic answering services, problem clip forms, and informal citizen training in the art of complaining.

A government seeking to improve the citizen input needs a willingness to listen, a desire to learn the facts, and a dedication to seeing that government serves its people effectively. An ability to listen is of paramount importance to any government providing these outlets to citizens.

Mini/Mobile City Hall

Consider the mini or mobile city hall. Unlike the true city hall with its staff of department heads and experts, these outposts are generally only one to a half-dozen people. They should be intimately informed of the governmental process plans. It is the chief administrator's responsibility to see that this staff is kept fully briefed and that new policy is routed to these outposts. For example, they should receive agendas of all meetings, as well as the background materials pertaining to those agendas.

It is important that the staffs be carefully chosen for these assignments and well trained, and that they possess an ability to get to the heart of a problem without taking sides. It would be wise to employ someone from the service area as a part of the mini city hall team, so that a "neighbor" is involved rather than "someone from city hall." It is vital to these operations that information given to the public be 100 percent accurate.

These staffs need specialized training in communications, sensitivity, report writing, public speaking, and municipal financing. They should make in-depth visits to all of the government's operations, so they can speak knowledgeably of those operations and the personnel who oversee them.

An often neglected aspect of their training is an analysis of the area the mini city hall is to serve. Social scientists can assemble social indicators into a meaningful presentation for the mini city hall staff. Thus, the staff will be aware of the problems with which the neighborhood must cope and will be understanding when problems are presented.

Major administrators and elected officials should visit these outposts on a regular schedule, so that neighborhood residents will know when they can speak directly with them.

If the mini city hall is a mobile van, its schedule should be publicized and its travel pattern should be consistent. For instance, if the pattern begins in a clockwise sweep around the community, this should be retained.

Various local governments have operated a full service government from these outposts. Information, complaint investigation, utility bills, parking tickets, taxes, dog licenses, rabies shots, voter registration, vaccinations, etc., have been provided at these governmental outposts.

VISITING GOVERNMENT

What if a community cannot afford a mobile van? Then governmental operations can be moved into the neighborhood on a personal, visiting basis.

Council meetings may be held in various neighborhoods on a regular schedule; this kind of activity, however, has met with mixed success. It should be remembered that the nature of these meetings will be of interest to the entire community rather than to just one neighborhood. Thus, attendance may actually decrease rather than increase because of change in location. Those who live outside the neighborhood may be unfamiliar with the area and so may hesitate to attend. Resource materials may not be available to the elected official during the meeting, but may be located back at city hall.

A tremendous amount of preparation is involved in developing governmental outposts or holding council meetings in a neighborhood. The public must be notified, and the service must be continued long enough to determine its effectiveness. A cue may be taken from business. Generally, new business operations are allowed from eighteen months to two years to "prove themselves." Yet often, in government, if a new service is not an overnight success it is quickly dropped. A length of time equal to the above is needed to establish these mini city halls within neighborhoods. Time must be allowed for residents to develop habit patterns of using these outposts of city government.

CITIZEN COUNCIL STRUCTURE

Another workable practice involves developing a citizen participation structure as an advisory arm of city government. The city may be divided into areas, citizen councils developed, and citizen participation coordinators employed to serve as liaison between the councils and the governmental structure. If the citizen participation structure is to be nonpolitical, the councils should cross political ward lines (if a ward structure is used for elective purposes). Such caution will avoid charges of using tax funds to support ward heel tactics. Greater success is likely when the neighborhood councils cross political lines and when more than one councilman represents the same area.

Those cities that have adopted such neighborhood councils have met with both frustration and success. What some regard as "the machinations of government" in any case appear confusing to the average citizen. It is difficult for him or her to accept the fact that from commitment to completion months and perhaps years may go by. It becomes more tiresome when several layers of government are involved. The reviews, the presentations, the public hearings can appear as so many roadblocks in the way of progress.

The neighborhood coordinator is the catalyst in this organization. This person should be able to accurately report the desires of the neighborhood to the city or county government. He or she should also possess an ability to translate the governmental process to the neighborhood.

SPEAK-OUT FORUM

Some communities have developed speak-out forums, in which the mayor, council members, chief administrator, or key staff members visit at a neighborhood facility such as a recreation center, school, or church.

While few major problems are uncovered in these forums, they do provide those who have never been to the city hall or county courthouse with an opportunity to meet their elected officials or administrators in a more informal setting than a council meeting. The style of these forums is informal and all complaints or suggestions are investigated.

Benefits can be greater than originally expected. In one speak-out forum a resident requested additional street lighting for her area. When city engineers went to the area they discovered that not only were additional street lights needed, but a railroad crossing sign was needed as well, as were brush reduction at intersections and removal of an illegal dump. Had it not been for the original request these problems probably would not have surfaced. The area was not densely populated and the citizen had never been to or called city hall.

For all these services, records should be kept of citizen complaints and their resolution. In time, the chief administrator will detect trends. (For example, if road patching requests become frequent from one area, it may indicate that resurfacing or a new patching material should be considered.) Increasing use of computer information systems is being made in this area.

Records on complaints should indicate the dates of reporting and the dates of clearance. If longer and longer periods of time develop between report and clearance, the city manager may reasonably question either the size or the efficiency of the work force.

The speak-out forum, then, in conjunction with this type of follow-up, gives the citizen an opportunity to serve as the eyes and ears of government.

INFORMATION/COMPLAINT SERVICE

An information/complaint telephone service is not intended to serve as a means of preventing citizens from directly calling other departments, managers, or elected officials. Rather, the service should serve as an extension of the government's efforts to reach the community.

All who answer telephones, and particularly those on the main switchboard and in the information/complaint service, should be trained in the handling of telephone complaints. The importance of a receptive attitude should be understood. Although no such person would cut a speaker off in mid-sentence, some individuals do become "transfer happy" on the telephone. Those who staff telephones should be trained to take the information, repeat the information to the caller for correctness, and indicate that immediate investigation will begin. They should avoid indicating that what the caller seeks will be done: the caller's request may not be within the province of the local government. Once the investigation is completed, the citizen should be called regarding disposition. If the disposition is not satisfactory, it is advisable to make arrangements for mediation. The process requires good telephone courtesy throughout. This subject has been discussed in greater detail in Chapter 5 of this book.

Another important aspect of citizen outreach

is the emergency telephone hot line. Many communities have telephones for this purpose at traffic signal intersections connected to their central public safety communications. Citizens should be encouraged to use these phones to report fires, crimes, and personal emergencies.

Some communities use a twenty-four-hour telephone answering service for the elected officials of the community. It is important that elected officials check back frequently if the service is to be effective.

COMPLAINT TRAINING

Lastly, an educational process may be undertaken to assist the public in complaining more effectively. Elsewhere, this book discusses the direct mail process used by many communities to give information on particular services and programs under way. It is important that the name of the supervising department and its telephone number be included in the mailer.

Some communities publish monthly or quarterly clipping forms on which residents may report specific problems. Generally, the response is significant the first time such a form is inserted into the daily newspaper. Once returned to city hall, the clippings are copied and sent to the appropriate department. They are kept on file until cleared, and a check is made with residents to determine that the problems have been resolved satisfactorily.

The field of handling citizen complaints is for those of stout heart, steely character, and a determined mind. If something is truly "not right," these staffs should stay with the citizen until wrongs are redressed. Such programs need the full support of the administrator, as well as his or her patience and tolerance. Positive administrative support in ferreting out and correcting these individual problems offers benefits in the long run. How much better it is to correct the problem of one individual rather than to wait until a mass protest develops with its resulting loss of public confidence.

Citizen Committees

The preceding discussion has been concerned, essentially, with citizen–government relations as they affect the individual. The discussion has led from analysis of communities, to internal and external activities of individuals, to participation by citizen groups—committees.

Committees and commissions are used for a number of different reasons. The complexity of government is such that governments have turned to citizen committees for additional manpower resources.

The role of these committees has increased in importance, and citizens have come to regard them as an active adjunct to government. The public will no longer accept tokenism appointments. The committee membership will reject a rubber-stamp role. The roles of the membership and the purposes of committees will come under scrutiny. The public will insist that these committees exist in order to facilitate current programs or to recommend future ones.

CHANGING CITIZEN ATTITUDES

Such a changing citizen attitude was forecast early in the seventies by Robert Aleshire, who wrote:

If cities are to deal with neighborhoods, a sharing of power born of negotiation, enforced by frequent usage, and preserved by careful respect must be developed. The form of power sharing need not be simply along traditional lines of division of responsibility and authority. A more behavioral and pluralistic approach is required. At the same time, the art form of negotiation and the relevance of the indicators to measure progress must be upgraded. Consensus planning and decision-making will be the new style of city leadership.

City governments must not assume that they have the God-given power to decide for people and the power to allow people to participate. All public power comes from the people. The city government is the tool through which people exercise their collective power. Building a sense of neighborhood requires that perspective of the origin of power.[8]

Some larger communities have experienced suspicion over the formation of a new committee. Minority groups have felt that their members have been placed on these committees not to serve, but to be "muzzled" or "brainwashed" by the local government. Even the so-called "safe" appointee has become an activist. Such experiences suggest that an analysis of its real purpose and role during the committee's genesis is very important.

In some instances such an examination may be painful, as it may call for relinquishing paternalistic authority. John Arnold has written:

The challenge for us is to rededicate ourselves to the process, to find new ways to involve the citizens, even to the relinquishment of decision-making power to nonprofessional individuals and political groups. The old citizen advisory committee concept doesn't cut it anymore. We need to begin thinking in terms of neighborhood operation of city services —or if not operation, perhaps control, with such a contractual relationship to the central government for the operation of services.[9]

It is important for administrators to see that the appointing agency does not shirk this analysis of the committee function. Time taken for this purpose could be important in preventing committee dissatisfaction later on. The councils should be aware that these committees see their role as interfacing with the elected council. Councils should take care not to be drawn into situations which force them to redefine a committee's authority. This might cause the community to feel that as long as the committee recommends actions of which the council approves, then the committee is being "mature and reasonable", but when the committee acts in defiance of the council it becomes a "naughty child."

Sharing of such power requires a sincere conviction that committee members can be as competent and concerned as those who are elected. Continuous abrogation of a committee's charge not only questions government's credibility, it condemns it.

PARTICIPATING CITIZENS

What kinds of people are found on these committees? What is the membership selection process for them? Do they have supporting staffs? What is the relationship with the central government? These are logical questions.

A study by David Slipy of citizen participation on the committees of three Minnesota communities revealed that over 68 percent of the persons serving had incomes exceeding $15,000 a year, that 84 percent were employed in either professional or managerial positions, and 68 percent had either completed college or had gone on to postgraduate work.[10]

In addition, the common thread which tied these individuals together was their involvement within their communities.

As well as belonging to an average of 6.1 community organizations, over 98 percent of those influentials devoted some time to community service, over 80 percent had served on at least one committee actively concerned with a specific community problem. Influentials in the three communities had over a 95 percent voting turnout in the last local election, and the typical influential could name at least three quarters of his city's officials.[11]

Not only were these individuals active in their government, they were also far less critical of government than those who had never served a service organization. Slipy indicates that the initial involvement is a key to citizen involvement, and once involved, residents will become active in more than one civic cause. That particular story can be told often. The Model Cities experiment produced a spate of elected officials. Many of them had had their first active exposure to city government by serving on a Model Cities task force or neighborhood commission.

If it is an American tradition "not to become involved," how does government get the nonparticipant into the ranks? In fact, they can be approached through their interests. If their interest is preservation of residential zoning, they may be reached through land use activity. If a citizen feels he or she does not have enough time for a continuing role, he or she could be considered for a special project committee such as a referendum.

Another problem regarding committee composition is that often minority groups and women are selected only for committees that deal with their problems. Women are often asked to serve on day care or beautification committees, and blacks are sought for committees concerned with the inner city. It is important to ensure an active place for minorities and women on all types of boards. Committee membership should reflect as broad an experience and background as possible.

"REACHING CONTRACT"

What are the responsibilities of council and committee during the formation stage? The first responsibility is to "reach contract" between the council and the committee membership. The assignment should be clarified and accepted by both parties. Modifications should be encouraged before the committee's work begins. The hard questions should be asked: Does the committee only review? Does it recommend? If areas of final authority exist with the committee, what are they? Do the committee's recommendations carry greater or lesser weight than a protest demonstration? How shall members be removed? How shall the council's appointments be removed if they prove ineffective?

Second, a communication channel between the council and the committee should be established which exceeds written minutes or reports. Many councils place one of the committee's members on its own major committees or schedule regular briefing meetings to the committee and the council.

Third, a time frame should be agreed upon and accepted by both parties; it should be subject to renegotiation. A deadline serves to maintain pace and instill a regard for achieving stated goals. Outside developments, however, may cause either a temporary standstill, an abandonment of the project, or a totally new time frame. This is often the case when local bodies are working on multigovernmental programs.

It is the responsibility of the governing body to prepare the committee for what might lie ahead. Such a preparation should reveal the council's support of the committee if it will be operating in an emotionally-tinged arena. The governing body should also be able to assure the new committee that it supports new public administration techniques:

The old public administration tends to view conflict as non- or counter-productive. If accommodation cannot be secured within normal hierarchical channels, the bargaining process is invoked and participants are expected to abide by rules which they may not have had a hand in making. New public administration accepts conflict and confrontation tactics as legitimate processes through which the incompatible objectives of opposing groups in a pluralistic society are brought to light. It operates on the assumption that the basic rules may be changed. Old public administration seeks accommodation to existing rules.[12]

The council, in summarizing its charge to the new committee, might indicate that it is looking for "fresh air, sound judgment, and objectivity in opposition."

COMMITTEE TYPES

What kinds of committees will be sharing power with the council? The names of these groups will probably change from community to community. The first five groups listed below are presented in ascending order of power sharing with the city council or county board.

The first is generally a neighborhood committee, which may be a protest, planning, or watchdog group. The second, the standing committee, is appointed for specified terms and has a specific action, such as park beautification, as its focus. The third, the interagency or intergovernmental committee, coordinates activities, suggests activities to be undertaken, or reviews the activities of one layer of government for another. The fourth, the board or commission, is formed to supervise programs or departments. It may set internal policy and supervise the staffs of its agencies. The fifth, the authority, is a semiautonomous group that directs programs or departments. Authorities have the greatest amount of shared power and may enter into contracts, solicit bids, and set rates or fees without the council's review. Such authorities keep the elected officials appraised of their actions. A sixth group, the task force, is formed to study or identify problems, and, generally, to recommend corrective action. It may be an adjunct of any of the above committees or it may be completely separate.

Membership on these committees is often dictated by the way in which the group has come into formation. Citizen committees that develop outside the realm of government are very often spontaneous in their formation.

Neighborhood Committees. Residents may realize that city hall is planning a highway to go through their neighborhood. Someone will become upset enough to invite his or her neighbors over to discuss the highway plan. Eventually, the group coalesces into the Citizens for Peaceful Neighborhoods. It will retain its identity until a final resolution is achieved. If a satisfactory resolution for the neighborhood is reached quickly, the group will dissipate just as quickly. But if the problem is significant and involves a lengthy period of time, the group may mature. It may realize that other such problems may develop for which it should "be prepared." Ultimately, it may even realize that rather than being against proposed projects, it could propose projects itself.

Such activity has happened and will continue to happen. A protest group can transform its original negative attitude into a positive force for future planning. During such a process, bylaws are developed, officers elected, and dues collected.

The attitude that government takes toward this organization in its infancy will color the group's attitude toward government in its mature role. Government should look on the initial protest group exactly as it looks on the long-standing commission. The protest group is also composed of citizens. Because government receives its power and strength from the people, it should realize that those who disagree may be more nearly correct in their stance than those who support all governmental activities.

Standing Committees. The second category of citizen groups, standing committees, are generally appointed by the chief officer of the parent group. A planning council may have standing committees, and its president appoints them. City councils and county boards also have standing committees. The mayor or the president of the council generally appoints, although in many communities the entire council or board nominates and elects.

Generally, the membership of these standing committees reflects the purpose of the group. Beautification committees, for instance, would include members of the garden council, landscape architects, and someone from the grounds division, ex officio. A standing committee may or may not have a continuing budget other than that for the committee's specific project.

Interagency and Intergovernmental Committees. Interagency and intergovernmental committees are quite another matter. The outline for membership to these committees is sketched out in the bylaws of the organization they serve. Usually, each affected agency will nominate its own representative for the agency it serves.

A committee on this level has significant responsibility, and an ability to be discerning regarding the community's needs is a prerequisite. Intergovernmental committees should have high frustration levels. Sometimes their work is opposed not by the local community or by regional groups, but by state or federal levels of government. For instance, a local health planning council opposed a major addition to one of the community's hospitals. The regional council of governments supported the council. Yet, abruptly, the state level approved the project and dismissed the local committee's position without explanation. Frustration mounted, as all those involved had been told that the local and regional position would "carry weight" in the capitol.

Boards, Commissions, and Authorities. It is at the fourth and fifth levels of shared power—the board, commission, or authority—that the community may experience an election process but not always. Usually, a more comprehensive nomination mechanism is developed and the mayor or council ultimately appoints. The composition of these shared power groups shows a greater number of professionals or specialists than that of almost any other committee structure. It is also on these levels that the area to be served demands citizen–recipient representation.

A staff is made available because these groups actually direct a program or agency. In most instances the staff answers to an executive director who may serve at the pleasure of the board, commission, or authority. Some communities state that these groups may recommend the hiring or firing of the executive director, but the council may confirm or deny the proposed action. These groups often develop their own agency budgets independently of city hall, provided they control their revenues. All activities, however, are subject to review by the council.

Of these three groups, the authority is most autonomous and in recent years has been under attack from citizens on the basis of aloofness to the desires of the public. Citizens have demanded recourse when they have objected to bus fares, library hours, or hospital rates. Because of some abuses of delegated power, authorities and their objectives are coming under closer scrutiny by city councils and county boards.

Governing bodies listen more closely to the community when vacancies occur on these authorities. Although the administrative staff may also suggest nominees, those politically elected will go to their constituents for nominees. Interest groups, too, are active in seeking placement for their members.

Recently in one community the neighborhood planning councils realized that not one "citizen" served on the planning board. All were either lawyers or affiliated with land development. Pressure was brought upon city hall. Included in the next appointments were some "citizens" holding membership in planning councils.

Task Forces. The membership of a task force is varied by its nature. In some instances the membership of an investigatory task force is fully appointed and announced only after the council has completed its slate. Often, a task force to study crime may be assembled quietly and announced dramatically. On the other hand, task forces serving the community, for example, bicentennial commissions, have their membership needs circulated publicly.

Depending on its assignment, the task force may or may not have supporting staff or financing. Task forces usually have a single-purpose assignment and a specified life span. Although its final recommendations may include a permanent structure, the task force is ultimately dissolved.

Charter Commissions. The seventies have seen increasing efforts toward governmental consolidation. Task forces called charter commissions have been formed. Their purpose and function are sufficiently different to merit separate discussion.

The members of a charter commission have a very different job from that of city councilmen, state legis-

lators, or those who serve on commissions of inquiry created to recommend solutions to specific problems. Their role is similar to that of a constitutional convention delegate. For a relatively short period of time they surrogate for the entire community in designing or redesigning the basic structure of local government.

A charter commission will provide the mechanism for problem solving. It will not solve problems. However, the institutional patterns and the procedures it presents will not be neutral—their design may anticipate a particular outcome. Charter commissioners are change agents and even though their task is to recommend systematic changes, they undoubtedly see substantive implications in such changes even if limited to traditional economy and efficiency values. Add the abstract values of responsibility, responsiveness, and representativeness and you need only ask the question—responsive to whom?[13]

SHARED POWER

A citizen committee has force in direct ratio to the amount of power delegated to it by the council. Sherry Arnstein makes a trenchant statement regarding citizen participation in relation to the committee structure. She parallels committee power with a typology on an eight-rung ladder, the lowest section of which is labeled nonparticipation. Its two lowest rungs include manipulation and therapy; the second section of the typology is tokenism, with three rungs: information, consultation, and placation. The last section of the typology is the degree of citizen power: the sixth rung is partnership, the seventh, delegated power, and the eighth, citizen control.[14]

The idea of citizen participation is a little like eating spinach; no one is against it in principle because it is good for you. Participation of the citizens in their government is, in theory, the cornerstone of democracy—a revered idea that is vigorously applauded by virtually everyone. The applause is reduced to polite handclaps, however, when this principle is advocated by the have-not blacks, Mexican-Americans, Puerto Ricans, Indians, Eskimos and white. And when the have-nots define participation as redistribution of power, the American consensus on the fundamental principle explodes into many shades of outright racial, ethnic, ideological and political opposition.[15]

Those communities that have made full citizen participation efforts, through existing committees, boards, or commissions, report the participants are changing. They no longer smilingly agree, but more often pointedly disagree. Citizens are persistent and that persistency becomes firmer when they become committee members. Minority groups who participated in the social programs of the sixties have experienced intensive activity through required citizen participation structures. No longer are they overwhelmed by the establishment, nor will they tolerate token gestures.

On or off committees, citizens today are not in awe of the governmental process. Elected officials cannot pull their election certificates around them and expect compliance from those serving on committees. Rather, these citizen groups are more likely to hammer out new goals, standards, and rules that are different from those parceled out by city hall in the formation stage. This trend has been established and will probably be expanded if the nation as a whole does not turn away from government.

Other two-way communication methods and decision-making mechanisms—such as neighborhood, city, and area-wide goal setting and planning activities—designed primarily to encourage the development of newly-organized units to participate in the pluralistic process, need to be developed and tested.

Confidence in the government will return when the people see the government once again as themselves, doing for themselves what they want done, in a way they prefer.[16]

Meetings as Communications

No discussion involving the employee–citizen team would be complete without reviewing meetings as a form of cooperation. Unfortunately, many meetings give testimony to the erroneous belief that all government needs is a committee meeting for its various problems. Too many meetings show hasty preparation, poor organization, little focus, and less accomplishment.

PURPOSE OF MEETINGS

Meetings are called to address problems and develop solutions, propose plans, develop strategy, or review applications. The preceding discussion has led up to those meetings through which citizens participate in government.

Meetings can involve only two people—a citizen and an employee. These meetings may be long or short, but have little formalized structure. The meetings of various committees, boards, commissions, or authorities are more formal and have an enlarged cast of players. Smaller committees will have a chairperson; larger committees may have subcommittee chairpersons and other officers as well. Community observers (either as neighborhood groups or as individuals), the news media, and governmental liaison may also attend.

PERSONNEL IN MEETINGS

As in all meetings, the chairperson often determines success. He or she should be aware of all possible alternatives the group may take. He or she should know the positions committee members may take and should remain objective in the face of audience opposition. Disruptive tactics aimed at discrediting the actions of the committee became frequent in the sixties and did not die out in the seventies. Opposing factions are also skilled in using the news media to their own advantage. Nonetheless, the chairperson must keep the meetings open to all members of the public and see that the meeting does not fail because of a stacked audience.

In difficult meetings the chairperson should be less prone to outline an "either this or that" action to the committee. Instead, he or she should indicate the vast range of positions the group might take. Most groups support or reject an action, refer it for further study, partition it, table it, or take no action at all. An understanding of these various alternatives supports the committee without backing it into a corner.

MECHANICS OF MEETINGS

The governmental employee's role is to be of professional assistance to the committee. He or she needs to advise the committee leadership of the mechanics of the meeting because these mechanics can affect the success of the meeting itself. The time and location are important. A meeting to outline neighborhood improvements would not attract a good attendance if it were scheduled for mid-morning, when most homeowners were at work. Attendance would also be sparse if that same meeting were held at city hall rather than in the neighborhood itself.

As government's liaison, the employee should assist the committee in agenda preparation and see that it is in the hands of the committee a day or two before the meeting. More time should be allowed on major matters for committee preview. The agendas should be complete, and supporting documents should be included. These documents need not be voluminous, but should be comprehensible and to the point.

The length of the agenda is another factor that may determine the success of a meeting. Few meetings accomplish much after two hours unless the group is a small, well-knit organization. An overwhelming number of agenda items precludes either thoughtful discussion or sound decisions. As the committee struggles through such an agenda it becomes resentful, feeling its only role is to say yes to the city council.

If additional spokesmen are necessary to the meeting, the employee should see that they are notified and that they reply in time. Finally, the employee should review parliamentary procedure with the entire committee. These rules were developed to facilitate meetings, but abuses have led many groups to shy away from them. The employee should encourage an informal, reasonable application of these rules so that the meeting results in progress rather than a parliamentary tango.

All those involved with any meeting should realize that listening and speaking are communication's partners. The temptation of an employee or chairperson to dictate what should be done must be resisted. Citizens must come to their own decisions when opportunities are presented. The employee should present all sides and aspects of a question.

Productive meetings are not achieved through happenstance. They are the product of open minds, thorough preparation, a sound agenda, and a fundamental concept that progress is a cooperative effort. A further discussion of meetings will be found in Chapter 7 of this book.

Summary

Employee–citizen participation in the governmental process is an aspect of government that is taking on increasing importance today. This chapter has outlined the ways in which good public relations can make this mutual participation an effectively functioning reality.

The discussion has taken the process through several stages, beginning with government's own responsibility to show its concern for the citizen and thereby win his or her confidence. Next, the importance of government's relations with its employees has been outlined, with particular emphasis on good communications within the organization and on encouragement of employees to participate in community activities. This is one means of making citizens aware of their government. Other means of bringing government to the citizen have also been outlined.

The next stage, the actual committee, is then described in its different forms and in its participatory relationship with the council. The final subject is the role of meetings in the citizen–government relationship.

With this chapter the emphasis, in Part Two of this book, has begun to shift from the public viewed as citizen to the public viewed as community. In Chapter 7 the emphasis will be on the community itself.

¹ Conrad Joyner, "Marketing City Services: Overlooked Opportunity," PUBLIC MANAGEMENT, February 1970, p. 9.
² Orville Powell, COMPASS (Winston-Salem: City of Winston-Salem), January–February, 1973, p. 1.
³ Lynn A. Townsend, "A Corporate President's View of the Internal Communication Function," in JOURNAL OF COMMUNICATION 15 (December 1965): 208–15.
⁴ Ibid.
⁵ Ibid.
⁶ Ibid.

7 William V. Haney, COMMUNICATION AND ORGANIZATIONAL BEHAVIOR: TEXT AND CASES (Homewood, Ill.: Richard D. Irwin, Inc., 1973), p. 13.

8 Robert A. Aleshire, "Organizing for Neighborhood Management: Drawing on the Federal Experience," PUBLIC MANAGEMENT, January 1971, p. 8.

9 John E. Arnold, "People Involvement: Participation To Restore Confidence," PUBLIC MANAGEMENT, September 1971, p. 11.

10 David Slipy, "Community Service: A Look at Who Does the Work," NATION'S CITIES, August 1973, p. 26. Reprinted with permission from NATION'S CITIES, the magazine of the National League of Cities © 1973.

11 Ibid.

12 Robert F. Wilcox, "Have Things Really Changed That Much?" PUBLIC MANAGEMENT, March 1971, p. 7.

13 William N. Cassella, Jr., "The Role of the Charter Commission," PUBLIC MANAGEMENT, July 1971, p. 19.

14 Sherry R. Arnstein, "Eight Rungs on the Ladder of Citizen Participation," in CITIZEN PARTICIPATION: EFFECTING COMMUNITY CHANGE, ed. Edgar S. Cahn and Barry A. Passett (New York: Praeger Publishers, Inc., 1971), p. 71.

15 Ibid.

16 Arnold, "People Involvement," p. 11.

7

Community Group Relations

COMMUNITY GROUPS and associations are playing increasingly important roles in government. These groups are initiating and supporting campaigns to stimulate greater citizen participation. They are identifying and presenting community issues, contributing to efforts for municipal reform and improvement, and providing innovative solutions to complex neighborhood problems. Representatives of community groups and associations serve on special citizen planning bodies, advisory committees, and various other agencies.

The involvement of community groups and associations is indispensable to meaningful local government. They help bridge the gap between governments and people in communities. They are effective influences for increased governmental service and economy and for greater political responsibility. They are prime vehicles through which democratic government functions.

Well-planned community relations programs are therefore essential to responsible government. Government administrators are becoming increasingly aware that they need a thorough appreciation of the importance of community groups and associations and of the ways and means by which they can incorporate them into city and county government. The plans and decisions that result from well-conceived community involvement will be as much products of citizens' ideas as they are of professional staff and elected and appointed officials. Because, if successful, such plans and decisions will be products of collaborative efforts in the community, it should follow that program implementation will be easier to effect and out-

comes will be more meaningful to the community as a whole.

Broad and purposeful community involvement is difficult to achieve. It requires patience and thoughtfulness on the part of staff members and public officials; openness, trust, and honesty on the part of all parties concerned; and a willingness on the part of those involved to listen to each other. Before meaningful participation can begin, means for public communication must exist—a problem that plagues public officials and interested citizens increasingly in this age of rapid social change and "credibility gaps." In recent years channels for public communication have often been so weak that citizens have had to "take to the streets" to make their messages heard. Increasingly, it is recognized that public officials will have to provide the means by which citizens can participate and be heard. This includes both the process and the information. New approaches are required, and, in fact, by the mid-1970s they were indeed emerging.

The primary goal of this chapter is to examine the recent developments in means of achieving citizen participation in government; this includes the identification of key factors and issues involved in working with citizen groups and organizations. The chapter is also concerned with articulating the activities of community groups and associations in constructive civic action programs.

The discussion begins by analyzing the nature of the local community through its social context and its groups and associations. The focal points of community interests are then described as follows: the ideal community; an informed citizenry; efficiency in government; legislative relations in the public interest; participation in local development; participation in government.

Next, the action process itself is outlined, along with various methods of effecting community action. The chapter closes with a brief summary and some general conclusions.

Nature of the Local Community

The local community has become a center of focus for both the practitioner and the student of local government management. The term "local community" is confusing and inconsistent: the tendency is to think of a community in geographic terms. But because of the rapid means of transportation and communication today, the community becomes for most purposes a functional rather than a geographical concept. The boundaries of communities do not necessarily coincide with the legal boundaries of governments. The community, in the minds of both practitioners and citizens, may be larger or smaller than a given city or county. A community differs in size, for example, with the services associated with it, such as water supply and public protection. The community signifies direct social relationships and grass roots government.

There is a growing interest in community life today as people have come to feel that they have lost much of it in the twentieth century wave of industrialization and urbanization. In recent years a prime concern has been for the urban center—its alleged ineffectiveness as a political or social unit and shortcomings in quality of life. In many urban communities there is said to be little sense of belonging, or feeling of identification, or intimate association. The current popularity of such words as "disorganization," "disintegration," "decline," "insecurity," "breakdown," and "instability" indicates the growing concern with community life as it is today in the urban and industrial setting.

The problems of contemporary community life, however, are not limited to urban centers. Of equal concern are the numerous small communities, many in rural settings, that have experienced over the last thirty years sizable losses in population. Loss of opportunity for those with intelligence and initiative tends to weaken and even destroy patterns of community life.

To come to grips with this mounting concern it is first necessary to determine carefully the meaning of the term "community." Although this may be an overgeneralization, a community might be defined as a place of interacting social institutions which produce in the residents an attitude and practice of interdependence, cooperation, collaboration, and unification. Some areas of relatively close proximity do not clearly exhibit these characteristics: this is especially true of large urban agglomerations. Other areas, even where the residents do not live in close proximity, do exhibit such characteristics: ranching areas in the West are an example.[1]

The above concept incorporates such sociological dimensions of a community as value systems, social stratification, interpersonal relationships, power structures, and ecological patterns. Public relations researchers might best center their primary interest on how people live together and meet their functional needs through community social institutions (including groups and associations and perceived patterns of behavior). The community might best be seen as a web of social structures, all closely interrelated. From these social structures a complex of positions or statuses has evolved which in turn prescribes various roles for individuals. Through performance of these roles the various institutions meet the functional needs and demands of the community.[2]

SOCIAL CONTEXT OF AMERICAN COMMUNITIES

American communities, broadly interpreted, have adopted technical abundance as a way of life. In such a framework, the values and basic patterns of human and institutional relationships become subject to constant and progressive reinterpretation. The effects of scientific progress and technological ingenuity are reflected in a wide variety of social phenomena, such as: the virtual elimination by machines of hand labor; the ability to plan to some predictable degree; economic and social growth and development; an increase in life span; an increased mobility of people, things, and ideas; wider educational opportunities; added leisure for vast segments of society; a lessening of the competitive struggle for simple survival; and shifts in the bases of prestige and status.

What does this abundance mean in terms of community life? Translated into higher living standards and greater general security, it can enable a community to discover and release its human resources in greater quantity and higher quality. A community can become a means, in part, of achieving the "good life" (a subject discussed later in this chapter). For the "good life" can be achieved only in small and meaningful social group relationships, and this can occur only in the environment of viable community life.[3]

This does not mean that social problems end with technical abundance. All that is meant is that the goal of technical abundance, although subject to criticism today, is a very real force in American local community life. In the United States this goal is in sight for most communities or has, in fact, been met. Growing technical abundance profoundly shapes and influences the entire social context in which Americans, including local government employees, live, and if any single word has exemplified this condition that word has been "progress."[4]

This "progress" takes place within a pluralistic society. Every community has a large number of competing influences that are usually organizationally based. Their alignment depends more on the problem at hand than on any other factors. Thus, the total society is open and is constantly adapting itself to new conditions.[5]

GROUPS AND ASSOCIATIONS: PRINCIPAL BUILDING BLOCKS OF THE COMMUNITY

Groups and associations are the principal building blocks of the community. They come into existence because certain people share values and interests. When individuals and groups wish to accomplish something they form an organization. In some cases the organization is rather simple in structure and purpose, while in others it is a complex, multipurpose affair involving institutional groupings of various sorts such as governments, business concerns, and churches.

Groups and associations on the local community level are employed frequently to accomplish either short- or long-range objectives. Sometimes they become an integral part of more formalized institutions. Sometimes they evolve as institutional entities in their own right. Because of their critical position, they may be regarded as the principal building blocks of the community. These blocks are reinforced and joined together into a working social whole, a community, by prevailing social forces and institutions. In this sense, groups and associations are viewed in static structural terms, whereas the prevalent social forces represent the dynamics of community life. This dichotomy is satisfactory only for analytical purposes. Both ingredients partake of structural as well as dynamic qualities.[6]

GROUPS AND ASSOCIATIONS: INDICATIONS OF MAGNITUDE AND COMPLEXITY

In an essay such as this chapter, space precludes a detailed coverage of the true extent of social groups and associations in the local community. A brief outline is all that is possible.

Community Associations. Studies reveal that American community life is highly organized. During World War II, for example, the U.S. Office of Civil Defense "could communicate any message of importance to every citizen of the country." This was accomplished through the use of 1,000 national organizations, which were selected from some 10,000 national associations.[7]

In the fifties, the extent to which Americans were organized into associations was described as follows:

The major fraternal orders . . . claim a total membership of about 20,000,000 persons. As of the late 1930's there were over 1,500 chapters of national college fraternities and 600 sorority chapters. The distinctive "service clubs" (Rotary, Kiwanis, Lions, Civitans, Optimists, etc.) cover the nation with some unit in practically every urban center.

Among special women's organizations, the National Federation of Women's Clubs includes 14,000 member organizations claiming 3 million individual members. There are giant veterans' organizations—the American Legion, Veterans of Foreign Wars, the

American Veterans Committee. In rural areas, there are about 11,000 agricultural co-operatives with well over 3 million members; the American Farm Bureau (about 1½ million members) has state bureaus in 47 states; the National Grange lists approximately 800,000 dues paying members; the 4-H Clubs enrolled in 1935 about 2 million youth.

As of 1945, there were 123 national organizations devoted in whole or in part to work on problems of inter-racial and inter-cultural relations.

As long ago as 1940, the CIO was composed of 42 national and international unions and organizing committees with 225 state, county and local union councils and 419 local industrial unions.

There are 1,500 national trade associations, 4,000 chambers of commerce, 70,000 labor unions—and 100,000 women's organizations. At the time of the AFL–CIO merger in 1955 it was estimated that more than 40,000,000 persons belonged to unions.

And so it goes. These, note, are in addition to the elaborate formal organizations represented by business enterprises, foundations, and many other forms of private associations.

There is an enormous proliferation of formally organized special interest associations of the most diverse kinds. Specialized associations have multiplied, whereas the parts played by traditional groupings based on proximity, diffused common values, and direct and inclusive personal relations have all diminished.[8]

Warner and Lunt's study of a "Yankee City" provides additional insights. In a city with a population of 17,000 they were able to identify 900 associations. These associations included almost 13,000 memberships held by fewer than 7,000 persons. A generalization could be made to the effect that nearly every adult member of the city belonged to one or more associations.[9]

Impressive as these statistics may be, it is equally disturbing that research findings indicate that, although local government is commonly viewed as being "closest to the people," the physical and psychological distance between city hall and neighborhood is often considerable. During the 1960s the inability of government, and especially municipal government, to respond adequately to demands for more and better public services was accompanied by a sense of powerlessness and frustration on the part of citizens. Many citizens, especially the poor and minority groups, felt that they were unable to gain access to the "system" and to influence, through bureaucracy, the ballot box, or any other democratic means, the

public decisions affecting their lives. In the wake of declining and uncertain services and persisting bureaucratic remoteness, they began to feel more and more alienated.

Today, sizable "pockets" of populations located in large metropolitan centers as well as in depressed rural areas still feel this alienation. Lacking access to responsible and viable community groups and associations, they are largely unorganized and thus "voiceless." Their social needs are often misunderstood and misinterpreted by public decision makers. Until these people are given the opportunity to speak, how can public officials and servants determine what are the best services for them?[10]

Clifford Graves, of the U.S. Department of Housing and Urban Development, identifies the principal problem in this area when he writes:

Until metropolitan institutions are relevant to the lives of citizens, there will be no meaningful metropolitan citizen participation. It is presumptuous of those of us who advocate metropolitan citizen participation to do so without first demonstrating relevance.

At least two essential conditions for relevance can easily be identified: concern for immediate issues, and the ability to deliver results. Most metropolitan agencies come off poorly on both accounts.[11]

Graves asks: If you lived in the inner city and were concerned about drug pushers at the high school and about deteriorating housing in your neighborhood, would you attend a public meeting of the "Metropolitan Coordinating Council of the Northeast Region" that was being held fifteen miles from your home? If you were a business executive recently transferred to the neighborhood and facing the likelihood of another move in several years would you attend a meeting to discuss redevelopment of the "Northeast Region?" A major challenge today, then, is to bring all kinds of people into the process of public decision making—giving them a chance to speak and a way in which to make meaningful contributions. This has proved a difficult task, partly because of "weak conceptualization in social science."[12] More will now be said about this problem.

Community Social Groups. Community associations are easily recognizable social entities.

However, there are various types of social groups which often are not so easy to identify.

We all belong to and participate in several kinds of social groups: families, friendship circles, political clubs, and work, educational, religious, neighborhood, and recreational groups. As is the case with many other aspects of human social behavior, this everyday sort of experience is difficult to define or describe in meaningful terms. Although a great deal of mental effort has gone into defining the characteristics of a social group, this may not be a very profitable activity. One writer is reputed to have said of elephants that he could not define one but would have no trouble recognizing one. In the same way, we all know roughly what we mean by a social group. Beyond this point, however, we often encounter difficulty.

The difficulty of developing an understandable working concept of a social group is not sufficient grounds for avoiding the problem. Social groups, elusive as they may be in conceptual terms, exist and play critical roles in community life. Those engaged in community relations appreciate the possibilities inherent in a useful social construct for incorporating social groups into a public relations program. This construct probably can best be considered within a framework of questions: What are the features of social groups? What should the level of analysis be? What are the functions of a social group?

All social groups have certain common features which sociological literature generally agrees are as follows:

1. The relations among the members are interdependent; each member's behavior influences the behavior of others
2. The members share an ideology—a set of values, beliefs, and attitudes—which regulates their mutual conduct
3. Social groups provide functions—internal in the sense of psychological satisfaction for members and external in the sense of relationships with broader social units
4. Social groups are usually functionally related to other groups and, taken together, form social organizations and institutions.[13]

These common features may be analyzed in several ways. Is it more profitable, in community relations work, to study the behavior of individuals in groups or the behavior of the groups themselves? Any public relations program takes this question into consideration. No neat answer is forthcoming. Since this chapter deals with social groups, however, the prime concern is with group behavior rather than individual behavior. It is important for those in community relations to remember that there is a significant difference in these two types of behavior. In short, the social group is a behavior unit.[14] It has its own unique characteristics and behavioral patterns, and operates within a set of norms prescribed by the group and by the society. Social group behavior and not individual behavior is typical, particularly so in urban societies marked by the following three big emerging bureaucracies: corporate enterprise, government, and private social associations. Those in community relations are going to function increasingly within the environment of big organization. What the nature and consequence of this emerging social order may be we can only speculate on. Progressive community relations will require that public relations people keep abreast of research and developments in this area.[15]

From the set of common features given above, one may sum up the general functions of a social group as psychological satisfaction for individual members and functional involvement with larger social organizations and institutions. The goals, or motives, provide a way of differentiating social groups.

Social groups conform to a set of norms which guide individual behavior (actions, thoughts, feelings) in social relationships. The main problem here is to distinguish between norms associated with a particular group and those that are a product of the sociocultural environment. In stable communities the norms of social groups are generally compatible with those of the larger social setting; but some social groups have norms incompatible with those of society at large (those of racketeers, for example).

In developing a community relations program it is important to study group awareness. How does a group of persons perceive of itself as a social unit? This is a formidable undertaking, but public relations research techniques provide some insights.[16]

In sum, while the characteristics of social groups may be difficult to identify exactly, it is well not to underestimate the roles and influences of these groups in community affairs. Social scientists have devoted much attention in recent years to social groups in all types of organizational settings. Those in public relations can make themselves fully aware of these findings and can evolve means by which to incorporate them into improved programs of community relations.

THE GROWING COMPLEX OF GROUPS AND ASSOCIATIONS

As has been stated, our growing industrial and urban society has already formulated the organizational way of life. Organizations of all kinds have evolved (and are still evolving) highly complex forms for attaining political, economic, and social goals. They are found on national, regional, state, and local levels. However, their interests converge primarily on the community level. The large national and regional as well as the smaller community organizations are devoted to the grass roots approach, and they employ a host of techniques and coordinating devices to reach deeply into local community life.

What are the social implications of this highly organizational way of life on the local community? How are community social groups built into the more highly organized and institutional forms of associations? What are the methods and ways by which the various groups and associations relate themselves to the local community?

One authority puts the answers to these and related questions in the following terms:

Local communities are highly open chains of interaction initiated at far removed centers. . . .
Multiplication of specialized associations, especially of the centralized, hierarchical types, leads to the development of numerous mediating, coordinating, or tangential organizations.

Items: co-ordinating committees; clearinghouse organizations; councils; multiplication of offices and associations charged with mediating and co-ordinating tasks; federated associations.
Both the total structure and the internal structures of large formal organizations are highly complex; in the latter numerous specialized statuses are arranged in intricate systems within systems; in the former, varied groups, communities, and associations are interrelated in extended networks, chains, and subsidiary social systems.[17]

One authority in public relations, Louis B. Lundborg, viewed, at mid-century, the complex of organized groups and associations with some alarm and with good reason. He observed that while conflicts and differences exist in the community, the community in itself is a blending of divergent interests, and within it are found interlocking and overlapping groups and associations. A resident of a community is typically a member of several social groups and associations. Through such individual relationships the social groups and associations become interlocked.

The interlocking directorates of big corporations that have been viewed with alarm by social and economic observers are nothing compared with the interlocking areas of influence within a community, and from one community to another.[18]

Successful local government management requires a thorough understanding of the nature of the community. The general characteristics of the American local community have been sketched out earlier in this chapter. Some reference points have been given to help those in local government management better understand the nature of their own communities. More such points are now necessary to bring into sharper focus the subject of working with community groups and associations. Those community relations projects and programs which typically fit within the domain of local government are included in the discussion that follows. For convenience of treatment, ideas relating to community relations have been arbitrarily grouped into types. These types can easily be viewed as focal points of community interests.

Focal Points of Community Interests

A good introduction to this subject might be a broad look at community interests—one that will encompass the elements of the ideal community.

ELEMENTS OF THE IDEAL COMMUNITY

In 1921 Edward C. Lindeman sketched out nine elements that the ideal community should provide for its residents. These elements, which are listed below, are just as applicable today as they were then.

1. *Order,* or security of life and property through the medium of efficient government.
2. *Economic well-being,* or security of income through an efficient system of productive industry.
3. *Physical well-being,* or health and sanitation through public health agencies.
4. *Constructive use of leisure time,* or recreation through organized and directed play.
5. *Ethical standards,* or a system of morality supported by the organized community.
6. *Intellectual diffusion,* or free education and public institutions within the reach of all.
7. *Free avenues of expression,* or means by which all the elements of the community may freely express themselves; free newspapers and public forums.
8. *Democratic forms of organization,* or community-wide organization through which the entire community may express its thoughts and see that its will is done.
9. *Spiritual motivation,* or religious association which may diffuse all forms of community organization, the religious or spiritual motive.[19]

Community Organizational Mazemanship. Local government performs the significant role in incorporating these elements into the community. To work effectively toward the goal of the ideal community, administrators, working within the political process, will want to become experts in what might be termed community organizational mazemanship—i.e., the skill of achieving the objectives of the ideal community through a maze of organizational (social groups and associations) complexities. They will need to be sensitive to the community as a politico-socio-economic organism and a complex community of human beings. Lindeman's nine elements of the ideal community have a wide-angled focus and thereby give a good perspective within which more narrowly focused community action programs can take place—in cooperation, of course, with the community residents themselves.

AN INFORMED CITIZENRY

Good government in the democratic sense requires an informed citizenry. City and county leaders have a responsibility to report faithfully and fully to their citizens about policies that have been adopted and why; about accomplishments, problems, difficulties, and failures; and about future plans. To aid them in the task of reporting, there are a number of community groups and associations with programs in governmental affairs. These community organizations recognize that citizen action cannot be effective if their members and the public do not understand the organization and function of local government, and are not informed about specific community problems and issues.

Some of these community organizations have as their main purpose the education of their members for leadership and participation in governmental affairs through lectures, discussions, conferences, and related educational techniques. Other organizations sponsor similar educational programs for the community. Some organizations have as their major objective the presentation of information necessary for citizens so that they can vote intelligently at special or general elections. Still others try to stimulate citizens to exercise their voting rights without any special or general elections, or without any special reference to problems or issues. Some organizations restrict their activities to matters of particular concern, such as education, health, and welfare.

While community relations programs that contribute to an informed citizenry are one of the primary concerns of progressive local government, no subject is probably as sensitive. Local officials can easily be attacked as "propagandizers" using the facilities of the community to maintain their own positions. Such an accusation can be avoided by developing close working relations with responsible community groups and associations.

The bases for such relations are well-conceived educational programs that serve to educate the youth as well as the adult population of the community in the matter of government programs and problems. Projects and means that can help a local government achieve sound public relations programs can be found throughout this book.

Two major aspects of a community relations information program are: (1) general information on local government affairs, and (2) information concerning special problems and issues. (Usually, there are a number of groups and associations that are interested in community relations projects which fit into either or both categories.) Following are examples of these major aspects of such programs.

General Information on Local Affairs. Every community has organizations that are interested in informing the public on general local affairs. To maintain good community relations, public officials will want to learn to work effectively with all of them and to keep the leadership of these organizations fully informed.

Since many of the leading community groups and associations have close working relationships with chambers of commerce, it is a common practice for governments to enter into contractual agreements with the local chamber for certain types of informational, promotional, and related activities. The program of the city of Inglewood, California, is typical, and has been in operation for many years. The city provides an annual grant to the chamber of commerce which is about 15 percent of the chamber's annual budget of some $125,000. In return, the chamber of commerce performs a number of services such as preparing monthly business reports, taking responsibility for retail and commercial promotions, disseminating publications and information, and giving general assistance to community groups and associations interested in municipal affairs. (The details of this are summarized annually in the official city report.)

Information concerning Special Problems and Issues. Research has continued to become a more important part of organizational life. Administrators today realize that the contemporary problems and issues cannot adequately be dealt with unless facts and proved solutions are available.

While much more research on local prob-

lems is necessary, the immediate job ahead seems to be more one of making the present research findings "operational" rather than of undertaking more research. Too many excellent research reports, at considerable cost in time and money, have ended up on the dusty shelves of libraries and agency archives. Too often, administrative memories are short and investigation is undertaken in a matter that has already been adequately researched.

In summary, research has already provided a large body of possible solutions to local problems. What is important now is that administrators learn how to find and put into use the available research findings: always assuming, of course, that the findings have potential practical utility. Research is expensive; today's administrators will want to learn how to economize on this matter. The best means is first to learn what community groups and associations have already done in research on the area's problems, and second to develop cooperative working relations with these organizations. In other words, in this area use of the library can be a good adjunct to a knowledge of community relations.[20]

GREATER EFFICIENCY AND ECONOMY IN LOCAL AFFAIRS

Many community groups and associations have as their sole objective greater efficiency and economy in local government, and nearly all of them have this objective as part of their total program.

Despite their constructive efforts, there is frequently a tendency for such groups to assume a negative attitude toward government spending, and local leadership must guard against efforts that jeopardize long-run efficiency and economy. (What constitutes the short- and the long-run public interest is a question open to debate. One thing is certain. Most people are not too interested in the long-run public interest. Who can be excited about the long run when the chances are that he or she will not be around?)

There are a number of means by which a community relations program can build a balanced and constructive approach to efficiency and economy in local government. A common approach is to work with community organizations in making a study of the efficiency of all departments. Another is to cooperate with "watchdog committees" in such matters as the evaluation of fiscal policy, or the interpretation of budget documents.

Services have been expanded in a number of communities by securing the support of volunteer associations in areas where there is inadequate financing. In other cases, the city or county has found it more economical to contribute to volunteer organizations than to undertake the responsibility for certain functions itself.

In many communities the morale and performance of government employees have been greatly enhanced by public acknowledgment, on the part of community organizations, of distinguished service of public employees. By the same token, community organizations have increased their civic contributions because government leaders have publicly acknowledged their services to the community.

LEGISLATIVE RELATIONS IN THE PUBLIC INTEREST

Some undesirable situations in local areas can probably be corrected only by legislation. Community groups and associations can be effective means by which legislation is enacted in the public interest. In working with these community organizations, government personnel will want to maintain a nonpartisan approach and avoid any accusations of favoritism.

In some cities or counties it is the practice to request the service committees of leading community organizations to prepare a program of legislative needs. It is customary to review proposed legislation (ordinances and codes) on particular functional areas of government with the interested community organizations, and to solicit their opinions and assistance.

The aid of the local bar association is frequently sought in many communities for types of assistance ranging from the review of the present legal base to the drafting of ordinances.

COMMUNITY RELATIONS IN LOCAL DEVELOPMENT

In a society dedicated to technical abundance based on a free and open economic and social system (pluralistic society), community organizations become particularly important. Programs for development depend on the needs of the community, and are generally of two types: (1) community planning and (2) economic development.[21]

Community Planning. Planning is a continuous process necessary for guiding and implementing the future development of the community. It is a process in which citizens, in cooperation with local government officials, determine the kind of community they want (this includes both immediate and long-range goals) in the context of their resources and capabilities. In many respects the most important part of community planning is the achievement of consensus on community objectives (better schools, industrial development, parks and open spaces, revitalization of the central business district, housing).

The local government, through its professional staff, is continually developing and revising plans in line with community goals through capital improvement programs, operating and service programs, the operating budget, and the capital budget. Often, such work is done in close cooperation with the superintendent of schools, administrators of neighboring governments, state highway department administrators, and others.

In recent years increasing attention has been given to social and economic planning in cooperation with the local chamber of commerce, the local human services council, and other significant groups concerned with public health, education, youth employment, juvenile delinquency, and related areas.

Community organizations can work with the government and other organizations in planning and development in several ways. First, such organizations can be helpful in outlining community objectives. They can be useful in surveying needs and resources as well as evaluating information.

Second, community organizations can work with other groups, both official and private, in delineating specific steps to be taken. Such steps could include the revision of a zoning ordinance, the drafting of subdivision regulations, the development of a housing code, special educational programs for preschoolers, and parking surveys of the business district.

Third, community organizations can undertake important, if not critical, roles in educating citizens on the content of planning programs and their effects on the community. They can help in running workshops and clinics intended for the study of community problems and to inform the public at large.

Economic Development. Although most communities devote considerable attention to problems of economic development, only a few have been able to deal positively with such problems. Effective community relations appears to be one of the prime vehicles for successful economic development. Some communities with limited resources and markets have been able to build flourishing local economies, while others more fortunate in resources have experienced a slow economic development.

Community organizations primarily concerned with economic development usually have such general objectives as: (1) improvement of physical facilities in order to attract business; (2) promotion of retail trade; (3) development of tourist trade; and (4) establishment of a sound and balanced industry. To achieve these objectives they employ a wide variety of approaches, consisting of publicly financed programs, privately financed programs, or a combination of the two.[22]

The role of chambers of commerce, discussed earlier in this chapter, is especially significant in economic development because of the very nature of its member businesses, which implement economic development and are affected by it.

CITIZEN PARTICIPATION IN GOVERNMENT

Basic to the discussion up to this point is the participation of citizens in local government.[23] To improve the responsiveness and effectiveness of services and to restore citizen support and confidence in local government, reformers have increasingly advocated decentralization of public service delivery and participation of citizens in planning and execution of local programs.[24]

Many operations of local government have been decentralized. Police stations, fire houses, schools, libraries, and playgrounds are examples of local facilities that have been organized on neighborhood bases. Many cities are divided into wards or precincts for administrative as well as electoral purposes. Since the late nineteenth century, settlement houses have provided social services to residents of geographically defined areas.

Citizen participation also is not new to local government. In addition to voting, holding office, and belonging to educational, religious, business, taxpayers', and other civic groups, citizens are involved in various public programs funded in part with federal dollars and administered by local agencies. These programs include public housing, urban renewal, comprehensive planning assistance, community action, health planning, and Model Cities.

The role of "local people," however, has usually been limited to offering information and advice to public officials. In some jurisdictions, target area residents have acted as partners or even as adversaries in decision making, particularly in the community action and Model Cities programs.[25]

Despite the recent efforts, centralization and citizen participation "mechanisms" to date have been unsuccessful in many communities in achieving quality services and opening two-way city hall–neighborhood communication channels. This has been especially true in the larger urban areas. As a result, reformers have called for various innovations in urban administration. Their new approaches reject many of the tenets of the municipal reform movement of the first half of the twentieth century—including centralization of authority under the chief executive, professionalism, efficiency, economy, nonpartisanship, and at-large elections—and substitute such values as devolution of power, citizen control, responsiveness, effectiveness, and neighborhood-based political responsibility.[26]

In 1967, for example, the U.S. Advisory Commission on Intergovernmental Relations recommended that large cities and counties be authorized to establish, on the petition of affected residents, neighborhood subunits of government with elected neighborhood councils. These would be responsible for providing supplemental services in neighborhood areas and would be granted taxing authority such as a small fractional millage on local property assessment, or a per capita tax. Neighborhood units could be dissolved unilaterally by the city or county governing authority if they became nonviable.[27]

The National Advisory Commission on Civil Disorders (Kerner Commission) recommended the establishment of effective grievance response mechanisms, neighborhood city halls, and multiservice centers as means of increasing the proximity and accountability of local government to the community.[28] Shortly thereafter, the National Commission on Urban Problems (Douglas Commission) recommended that municipalities over 250,000 in population establish neighborhood city halls to administer certain decentralized services (health and welfare, police, recreation, employment, and code inspection).[29]

In addition to these official commission recommendations, observers have advocated similar reforms designed to narrow the gap between city hall and the neighborhood. Common proposals deal with complaint handling machinery, little city halls and multiservice centers, neighborhood or community development corporations, and community control of such functions as education and police.[30]

In modifying bureaucratic decision making, personnel, and accountability practices, some of these measures tend to blur distinctions between decentralization as a "structural–professional" concept and citizen participation as a "nonstructural–nonprofessional" concept. Moreover, they point up the fact that centralization–decentralization and participation–nonparticipation cannot be considered as "either–or" propositions. Instead, at issue are questions concerning the devices and degrees of decentralization and participation in diverse communities. Hence, community school boards and consolidated school districts are not necessarily mutually exclusive ideas, nor are neighborhood government and metropolitan government.

Although a wide range of decentralization–participation devices can be identified, they can be classified under three progressively greater degrees of decentralization: (1) territorial, (2) administrative, and (3) political.

Territorial Decentralization. This involves steps taken by local officials to bring government physically closer to the people it serves, in order to facilitate the expression of resident needs and preferences during the formulation of public policies and to provide feedback channels through which citizens can indicate poor quality and unresponsive service delivery and can obtain remedial action. The pattern and frequency of the city hall–neighborhood interaction are determined on a territorial basis, and no delegation of substantive policy making or discretionary authority is made.

Examples of this approach are: holding meetings of the chief executive, legislative body, or various public agencies on a regular basis in neighborhood areas; setting up citizen complaint-handling machinery; and creating resident advisory committees. The dispersal of certain local facilities to geographically defined subareas of a city or county (such as police precincts, fire stations, and branch libraries) is a standard type of territorial decentralization; but since it often involves the field delivery of services rather than citizen–official interaction, this activity may not always fit the objective of enhanced citizen "voice."

Administrative Decentralization. This is a devolution of the administration of particular public services to neighborhood areas, with delegation of substantial decision-making authority, discretionary power, and program responsibility to subordinate officials. Actions taken here include the establishment of neighborhood councils or boards, appointment of neighborhood managers, and creation of little city halls and multiservice centers.

Political Decentralization. This involves efforts by local chief executives and legislators to redistribute political power and policy-making authority through the creation of new, autonomous subunit governments. These substructures would exercise substantial control over the delivery of certain services and would possess significant independence regarding fiscal, programmatic, and personnel matters. They would be directly accountable to a neighborhood constituency and secondarily responsible to the central political unit.

This type of decentralization could be achieved through adoption of the proposal of the Advisory Commission on Intergovernmental Relations for neighborhood subunits of government or neighborhood corporations, or the creation of community controlled school boards and similar functions.[31]

A survey conducted in 1971 on these three kinds of decentralization–participation approaches revealed generally slow progress.[32] A few cities and counties were making progress in decentralizing services and involving citizens in decision-making activities. Most of the progress was in the areas of territorial and administrative decentralization, with citizens playing an advisory and, to a lesser extent, a policy-making role. The degree of authority, responsibility, and discretion devolved to subordinate organizational levels or citizen groups varied widely in accordance with jurisdictional size, location, type, form of government, and other factors—such as the availability of federal Community Action or Model Cities funds. With regard to political centralization or community control, the survey findings revealed that little had been accomplished. Experience to the mid-1970s continues to indicate that it will take some time for reality to catch up with rhetoric.

Articulating Community Groups and Associations

While progress in incorporating community groups and associations into the decision-making process in this age of a "temporary society"[33] has encountered difficulties, American life is too dynamic, and the confidence in local action and progress too great, for community leaders to accept complacently the present state of community affairs and life. Recently a new concern has been shown for ways to reconstruct and incorporate social innovations within the community. Local officials have critical roles to perform in the process of preserving and rejuvenating the community. How they can articulate community groups and associations with action is the subject discussed immediately below. This will be treated under two major headings: (1) Alternative Methods of Articulating Community Action, and (2) Stages for Articulating Community Action.

ALTERNATIVE METHODS OF ARTICULATING COMMUNITY ACTION[34]

Among methods for articulating community action, the following appear especially useful; this discussion of them relies heavily on Lillian F. Dean, in an article in *Regional Council Communications.*

1. Citizen committees and forums
2. Surveys and questionnaires
3. Community meetings
4. Public hearings
5. Nominal group process
6. Charrette process.

Citizen Committees and Forums. Citizen committees have been described as "small groups of people which keep minutes and waste hours."[35] Unfortunately, this is too often the case—as it is with committees generally. Committees frequently are established with the expectation that this is the best approach for solving urgent problems. Members of citizen committees are often carefully chosen to avoid problems and controversy. Thus, when the committee meets, it struggles to figure out what it is supposed to be doing and carries on discussions in which no one knows exactly what has been accomplished. It is little wonder that decision makers and citizens become frustrated with the committee approach.

Many of the problems of working with committees can be solved by good staff work. Citizen committees can be effective means of solving problems, generating solutions, and involving citizens. The following are some guidelines for effective committee work:

1. The purpose of the committee should be defined in writing. This purpose should be reviewed with committee members and progress made toward achieving predetermined goals should be noted.
2. The decision-making authority of the committee should be defined carefully. Is the group advisory only? Does the committee have authority to write and publish its own reports and findings? Is the committee responsible for carrying out a program that has been approved?

3. The committee should be encouraged to develop its own action program. When members are involved in the committee work at an early stage, this will undoubtedly heighten their interest, commitment, and performance.

4. Committee membership should encompass a variety of skills, backgrounds, ages, and interests. One of the primary purposes of a committee is to bring a variety of perspectives to bear on a problem.

5. Resource persons and information should be made available to the committee. This will contribute to building a common base of understanding. During committee discussions, it is important to separate fact from opinion and identify underlying premises.

6. It is important to select a committee chairperson with leadership skills. In addition to knowing the subject at hand, the chairperson should understand how to "enable" others in the group to participate. A "rotating chairperson" may be a useful approach.

7. Meetings should be planned with a variety of formats: variations from group discussion include nominal groups, buzz groups, role playing, tours, movies, etc.

8. Sufficient time should be allowed for the committee to accomplish its work. Committee members need time to become acquainted with each other as well as with the problem(s). It is important to identify alternatives and develop recommendations. Deadlines are essential.

9. Appointing ad hoc instead of standing committees should be considered. This reduces staff work and provides a focus to the committee's work.[36]

A "citizen forum" is frequently used as a method of gaining citizen participation. While there are numerous ways of organizing a forum, the concept basically involves appointing a large number of citizens to a board (a forum) to act as advisers to a government body. Often a forum is divided into committees according to functional areas. Because a large number of citizens are usually involved, it may be possible to appoint members with a variety of backgrounds, who represent a number of interest groups. Experience shows that forums can be useful, but large amounts of staff time are necessary. Committees of the forums will operate in different ways and will achieve varying degrees of success. A potential danger is that a permanent structure will be built which does not encourage a continual "reaching out" to community groups and organizations.

Surveys and Questionnaires. Administrators and public relations officers will find surveys and questionnaires essential to provide the "feedback" required for responsible decision making. It should be noted, however, that surveys used to gather factual information such as age, place of employment, and years of education (i.e., census data) add little to the knowledge base of community participation. The important functions of a survey are to indicate the effect citizens have on public decision making and to provide this information to those who participated in the process.

There are many types of surveys such as personal interviews, mailed questionnaires, and telephone surveys. It is important that care be taken to choose a survey method that is effective in reaching different groups of people at a reasonable cost. For a true random sample response, personal interviews are usually the best approach, even though they are usually expensive. Care in designing and pretesting the questions is of the utmost importance. Too often, attitude questions have been asked for the purpose of confirming preconceived ideas. The assistance of specialists and the careful training of interviewers are important. Surveys provide opportunities for using volunteer assistance, and thus are effective means for securing citizen participation. Careful training and supervision of volunteer personnel, however, is essential. The subject of survey research is treated in detail in Chapter 2 of the present volume.

Community Meetings. Citizens who never attend formal meetings of governing bodies do attend community meetings when they are held close to their homes and in familiar surroundings.

For such a meeting, it is essential to present an issue that is important to the community. While issues can sometimes be "created" through effective publicity, there is no substitute for one that directly affects local citizens.

Some practical suggestions for planning community meetings are given immediately below.

1. Date, Time, and Place of Meeting. Administrators should work with local community residents in planning the date, time, and place of the meeting. A time and a date that do not conflict with other community events should be chosen and a "neutral" place where the citizen participants will feel comfortable should be selected. It is important to plan well ahead of the meeting to ensure that space, electrical outlet, seating, and related requirements are met.

2. Public Information. The public information about the meeting is of vital importance. All possible avenues should be used to reach as many people as possible, including newspaper advertisements, radio and television announcements, and letters. There should be follow-up, with as many personal contacts as possible, to explain the purpose of the meeting to citizens and to invite their attendance. All local officials should be personally contacted and should understand the purpose of the meeting. Local citizens are often willing to assist with public information efforts and usually have valuable insights concerning approaches for reaching the public.

3. Presentations. Presentations should be short. Typically, audience interest begins to wane after ten to twenty minutes. Simplified graphics that visually explain the key points should be used. The person making the presentation should remember that not everyone can easily read charts, maps, and similar materials. It is a good idea to pretest the presentation before a "friendly" group of citizens and encourage their feedback. It is a useful technique to build in opportunities for reaction and participation through small group workshops, question and answer periods, written questionnaires, and similar means.

4. Meeting Atmosphere. The atmosphere created by the meeting is important. Does the professional always appear as the "expert" and the "authority"? Are citizens restless and uncomfortable? Do the local hosts (both citizens and local officials) who greet people help create

a friendly atmosphere? A coffee break in the middle of the meeting can give the group a chance to stretch, relax, and informally discuss items. If the audience is emotional and "out to get you," the best course is to relax and listen. If a person is really unfair, people in the audience will probably come to the assistance of the speaker. It is important to be a good moderator, listening to what everyone has to say and letting people in the audience respond to citizen opinions whenever possible.

5. Seating Arrangements. Seating arrangements play a more significant role in the success of community meetings than is often realized. As two veterans of public service, Donald and Alice Stone, have put it:

If uncomfortable chairs weary the seat, then minds and persons wander from the meeting. Unscientific arrangement of chairs prevents effective communication and obscures decisions.[37]

Whenever possible, seating arrangements should be based on careful preassessment of the audience attending the meeting. Open confrontations can be avoided or minimized by proper seating arrangements. As Donald and Alice Stone observed, the simple shifting of chairs changed a desultory meeting in which there was little exchange into a highly productive occasion.[38]

6. Meeting Evaluation. It is essential to evaluate every meeting held—identifying strengths and weaknesses. Citizens who were in the audience should be invited to join in the evaluation. Maintaining records of meetings held and citizen participation methods used may become a very useful tool. Attendance lists from the meetings should be kept so that follow-up information or notices regarding further meetings can be sent. It is advisable to continue to inform citizens about activities and other opportunities for participation.

As with all citizen participation activities, it is essential that the sponsoring agency be completely honest regarding the purpose of the activity and the effect it will have on the community. It is important to listen.

7. Public Hearings. Public hearings, although usually required by law for certain activities, may be considered opportunities for

community involvement. They differ from community meetings in a number of ways: (1) they are often held in "official" locations such as the city hall; (2) their express purpose is to hear citizen opinion rather than provide information to the public; (3) official notice in newspapers is required.

The two critical areas in which public bodies can strengthen public hearings as a citizen participation approach are numbers 8 and 9, immediately below:

8. Public Notice. The letter of the law is usually met by small notices in newspapers. Such notices rarely provide background information on the issues to be discussed or the importance of the hearing. If the hearing is important, it is advisable to use all available channels of communication, including newspaper feature articles, radio announcements, special letters to government officials, and newsletter announcements. Some examples of such notices appear in Chapter 5 of the present volume.

9. Community Involvement. Often at public hearings a formal atmosphere discourages persons who do not have a formal presentation from speaking. It is important for the person presiding over the hearing to encourage those in attendance to give their opinions. Written questionnaires are sometimes means of obtaining ideas (written comments are often far more frank than spoken ones). It is important that all information presented by citizens be recorded and written into a summary at a later date, and that citizens present are apprised of other opportunities for expressing their views. A great deal is lost when public officials are not present to listen to citizen opinion.

There are limitations to public hearings as a method of citizen participation, however. Perhaps the most significant of these is the "structured" nature of the hearing. People speaking in favor of a proposal usually speak first and are followed by those opposing it. While questions may be asked for clarification, there are rarely opportunities for discussion. Also, hearings often follow after a major activity has already been initiated; thus, it is too late to make substantial changes in the proposals. Public hearings can never be a substitute for a variety of citizen participation opportunities throughout the decision-making process.

Nominal Group Process. This is a small group technique useful for generating creative ideas and selecting priorities. It may be used for identifying problems, solution components, and issues. It is not a substitute for careful research and in-depth study.

The technique developed from innovative research reveals that persons think most creatively while working in silence but in the presence of others. Basically, it structures the activity of the group so that progress is made toward the goals of the meeting and all persons have equal opportunities to present their ideas. It is a method well suited to committee meetings and conferences. Many variations of this technique are possible. The procedure for running a nominal group as developed by André Delbecq is representative.[39]

The nominal group technique is divided into six phases:

1. Nominal group activity
2. Round robin listing of ideas
3. Group discussion
4. First vote
5. Group discussion
6. Final vote.

Prior to the meeting, seating is arranged so that seven to eight persons may comfortably sit at each table and easily see flip charts. The question to be used for the nominal group should be carefully worded and should have been pretested before the meeting.

Phase 1: Nominal Group Activity. (1) The purpose of the nominal group is to learn and listen to the ideas of all persons present. The first and most important step is the "idea generating" nominal group. The nominal group consists of members writing their individual ideas on paper in silence but in the presence of others.

(2) Participants work in silence for approximately ten minutes. They are then asked to jot down any ideas that come to mind on the work sheet that has the question written on top. Research findings show that the most creative ideas are generated after the person's first reactions have been written down. Findings also show that this "nominal" generation of ideas

in the presence of others results in more and higher quality ideas than do traditional brainstorming techniques.[40]

(3) If persons begin to talk during the silent nominal group work session, they should be requested to remain silent so that others may finish their work.

Phase 2: Round Robin Listing of Ideas. (1) Following the nominal group work session, a recorder lists the ideas of the group on flip charts so that all may see them. People give ideas in a round robin fashion until all ideas are listed. Each person in turn briefly states one of his ideas without discussion.

(2) Although the recorder may be a group member, it is usually best to have a trained recorder who is not participating in the discussion.

(3) The recorder should pay attention to the exact words used by the person speaking in order to record onto the flip charts the suggestion of the group member.

(4) Members should be encouraged to suggest new ideas even if they do not have them written on paper. When a person's ideas have all been listed, he should pass the list on to the next person.

(5) Research findings show that the round robin listing facilitates the participation of each person yet focuses attention on the listed ideas rather than on "who said what."

Phase 3: Group Discussion. (1) When all ideas have been listed on flip charts, the recorder encourages the group to discuss the lists. This provides an opportunity to clarify confusing statements, discuss the merits of individual suggestions, and lobby for priorities.

(2) If the group chooses, it may be useful to read through the written list of ideas so that each is reviewed.

(3) Duplications of ideas should be eliminated, and attempts to combine ideas should be resisted, since the latter often dilutes the ideas being articulated.

Phase 4: First Vote. (1) Participants are asked to vote for the six items listed that they feel are most important. The following instructions often facilitate the vote:

(a) Select the six items you feel are most important and list them on file cards, one per card. Include both the number of the idea and the wording.

(b) Spread the six cards out in front of you. Now select the card that is most important and place it face down on the table; then place on top of that the card that is next most important, etc.

(c) Score each card from 0 to 100, with 100 being the most important. No two cards should receive the same score.

(2) Following the voting, the total points for each item should be listed on flip charts so that all may see. This method of voting has been demonstrated in research to reflect accurately the views of the group.

Phase 5: Group Discussion. During this second discussion period the group reviews the vote and how they feel about it. Again, persons feeling that certain ideas are very important should restate why they think this is so.

Phase 6: Final Vote. (1) A final vote is now taken, following the procedure as used in First Vote.

(2) If there are several tables working on the same question, each may wish to report to the entire group.

The nominal group technique may be modified to fit a variety of group situations and problems. Sometimes nominal group and round robin listing may be sufficient to meet group needs; at other times a careful priority vote may be needed. When a large group is present it is sometimes desirable to have a final vote on the top-priority items from each table. At other times individual tables may be assigned to different problems or issues.

The nominal group technique serves to stimulate creative thinking and provide the opportunity for all present to express their ideas. Participants usually feel that the meeting has been worthwhile and that their ideas have received fair consideration.

Charrette Process. A charrette is a process that brings together the full range of participants needed to solve a problem or develop a plan; and, through a series of intensive working sessions with deadlines, it produces a plan that has broad citizen and official support. The charrette process provides a new base of experience from which new attitudes and alliances can be formed, and provides a setting for the emergence of strong citizen leadership for plan implementation. Citizens are involved throughout the process as full partners.

The charrette process was conceived in 1967 in the Office of Construction Services of the U.S. Department of Health, Education, and Welfare in an effort to find ways in which decision making could be more relevant to the real needs of communities. The word charrette comes from nineteenth century Paris, where art students cramming for final exams would rush their drawings in hand-drawn carts called "charrettes." Hence the application of the term to a final, comprehensive, deadline-oriented effort.

A charrette may last from several days to several weeks, depending on the community's needs. Much advance preparation is necessary, however. The basis of this advance planning is the steering committee, which is formed specially for the charrette and includes representatives from the key organizations: citizens, officials, and agency representatives. The steering committee identifies who *must* be present if the charrette is to be successful, issues invitations and publicity, selects talent and leadership for the charrette conference, makes arrangements, develops background information, and the like. Several months are usually needed for this phase of the process.

The charrette conference itself is carefully monitored by an experienced "charrette manager," who watches carefully for development of ideas and solutions. The charrette itself is divided into several phases.

1. Generation of Ideas. Usually, a charrette will begin with a wide-open slate. Participants are asked to define goals, problems, and issues that need resolution. The full group is divided into issue-oriented smaller groups for more detailed examination of the problems. As new issues surface, they are added to the list. Sessions continue throughout the day, with different people participating at different times.

2. Identification of Solutions, and Analysis. During this second phase, bridges and linkage between functional groups are built up. At this point all available information and resource persons are drawn in; new alternatives are proposed and examined. Out of this work, carried out under deadlines, new creative solutions often emerge.

3. Proposal Development. Staff and resource people take key ideas and solutions identified in the charrette and refine the proposals in terms of working drawings, models, statistics, and maps. These are then presented to citizens for further reaction and modification.

4. Final Production. Citizen spokesmen make the final presentation to the "jury" of community officials, who are then given the opportunity to "officially" approve the project.

5. Implementation. Before the charrette closes, a team of citizens is selected to develop a strategy for implementing the plan, thereby providing for continuity and follow-through. Often, the new community leaders that have emerged from the charrette serve on the committee.

One of the keys to the success of the charrette is the constant flow of publicity that accompanies all phases. Citizens are informed in every possible way about the charrette and what is happening. Periodically, the results and progress to date are provided in an open community forum to which all are invited. At this time, the working people who would normally be unable to participate are given a chance to suggest changes.

Charrettes have been used for a variety of problems and projects, including community plans, new communities, bond issues, Model Cities, urban renewal, and highway right-of-way decisions. Charrettes are most effective when issues are defined, leadership is visible, and funds are available for the proposed project. However, successful charrettes have been carried out even when these factors were not always present.

STAGES FOR ARTICULATING
COMMUNITY ACTION

Community action may be viewed as progressing through several stages: (1) the initiating stage, (2) the mobilizing stage, and (3) the executing stage.[41] Within this total process there are numerous steps that do not necessarily group themselves into the neat sequential or chronological order of these three major stages. However, it is useful to generalize the total efforts within these three major stages, because they do provide convenient reference points in an overall action program.

The initiating stage is characterized by the recognition of a community problem or number of problems. A community problem is nonexistent until it is recognized and articulated by someone. Community action cannot take place unless the organized interests feel that there is a common problem. Once the problem has been articulated within the framework of values, beliefs, and attitudes shared by those who recognize it, the second stage, the mobilization of effort, takes place.

The executing stage occurs when there is organizational involvement for the solution of the community problem. The nature of the involvement will be conditioned by the culture of the community. Each of these three stages will now be examined in greater detail.

Initiating Social Action in the Community. Probably the most difficult part of community relations is initiating social action. Social inertia, like physical inertia, is a strong barrier against any kind of movement (change). Once the inertia has been displaced and change is under way, it takes only a small amount of energy to continue the process.

In the earlier section, Focal Points of Community Interests, a number of action projects were suggested as means of "influencing" people in order to achieve social action. When community life is not working the way certain people think it should, they do something about it. They talk to their friends, hold meetings, organize groups, and stir associations into action. They try to arouse public interest (and indignation), channel efforts of action-oriented community elements, and win support of the community publics.

Social change involves many elements and facets of the community, and any action group soon finds itself within a medley of contending voices. How to work in a constructive fashion with this medley is the next concern of this chapter.

Mobilizing Social Groups and Associations. From the beginning, it is important that any action group learn who is in favor of the program and who is against it, and, in the latter case, the kinds of opposition anticipated and from what quarters. The action group will need to organize support for its program and overcome opposition or inertia. This should be done in a constructive and systematic manner.

In the early stages of the process of initiating social action, a survey should be prepared of probable community organizational support and opposition. The information needed to make such a survey can be secured from several places and by several means. Printed records are one source. Newspaper stories and releases, annual reports and special reports, statements of purposes, and community studies or surveys all may give indications of an organization's potential for social action.

Often, current and specific information is directly available from the organizations, or from friends or acquaintances of the members of the organizations. Frequently, information is acquired by sending an observer to meetings of the organizations or by inviting representatives of the organizations to meet with the initiating action group. The information secured needs to be mapped out in an accurate manner.

Community life is not static. Support and opposition will change as the program develops. The "survey" (Figure 7–1) should be corrected from time to time according to the changed conditions of organizational potential.

Mobilizing Publics. An action group cannot reach the people of the community by depending only upon the more formal types of community social groups and associations. Some people do not belong to any organization, and others may belong to an organization which is not vitally concerned. However, all members of a community in varying degrees of intensity belong to publics in a community.[42] These publics are joined together through communication networks and thus are frequently in strong positions to influence the final outcome of community action projects.

Surveying the influence potentials of the publics is generally a more difficult job than making a comparable survey for community organizational potentials. Publics are tenuous and unstructured social entities and lack formal institutionalization. Their amorphous and tran-

Names of organizations	Estimated number of members	Probable relation to project	Support activities
	200 active 400 inactive	Active cooperation in project, including financial and moral support	Provide workers to distribute literature, interview, and raise funds
	200 estimate	Limited financial support	Furnish funds for publicity; certain printing facilities available
	400 active, inactive, no figure	Moral support	Could use organization's name as a cosponsor
	600 active	Neutral-positive bias	Will inform its members of project and permit distribution of information
	400 active	Neutral-negative bias	Probably difficult to have item placed on meeting agenda
	400–500 active	Opposed	Will take a strong position against the project

FIGURE 7–1. *Survey of community organization influence potentials.*

sitory nature makes it difficult to determine accurately an individual public's influence potential.

Over the years a variety of sophisticated techniques have been evolved by means of which the influence potentials of publics can be measured.[43] The findings of such surveys should be mapped out in a manner not unlike that suggested for community social groups and associations.

Executing Social Action in the Community. When social groups and publics have been mobilized, influential parties in the community will have taken their stands, important community decisions will have been made using the democratic political process, and organizational resources pledged. The task then is to keep the action goal clearly in mind and to utilize the available resources in a skillful as well as an economical manner.

The job of the public relations officer is now particularly critical to the success of the action program. Rumors, half-truths, screaming headlines, or mere misunderstandings can destroy a sorely needed new action program, force retrenchment of an old one, spoil the accumulated work of months or years, crucify re-

spected citizens, and crush well-established community associations.

Community leaders and organizations learn to endure such conditions and perform effectively under them for the sake of achieving their goals. Public opinion plays a dominant role in our society. Any enterprise must develop competence in dealing with the public.

Disagreement and controversy are unavoidable. The object is to use such differences in a constructive fashion. Opposition can be used in many ways to test and expedite an action program. Objections may point up weaknesses in a program. Probing questions may reveal undesirable consequences which the initiating group and its supporters were unable to see. Responsible opposition can serve the function of more clearly defining a problem.

Controversy in a constructive framework is essential for a viable society. Those involved in community relations programs learn to recognize this fact and also to accept it as fundamental.

Finally, a community relations program's best defense against attack will always be a reservoir of goodwill. It is essential that any group acknowledge this fact and spend considerable time deciding how to build a positive position in a community. Every community group and association, or combination of these, has a responsibility to bring regularly before the public its purposes, its backing, and its work and accomplishments.

General Conclusions

Any community relations program will have as its end product the building of a more desirable place in which to work and live, utilizing the political process to achieve this goal. Local government has the major responsibility for carrying out the policy decisions in this area. American society is organized into numerous social groups and associations with strong civic inclinations. Through constructive programs and leadership, the energies and resources of these community organizations can be channeled so as to building a more desirable community. However, any program is always a two-way proposition. Local government officials and employees play their part by participating in community life. They can involve themselves through participation in clubs, associations, and other private concerns in the community; they can provide sponsorship or leadership for youth groups and similar organizations, and can initiate and organize community betterment programs.

By the same token, all groups and associations should be encouraged to participate in and assume constructive roles in the affairs of the community. This will require that local government exercise ingenuity in devising techniques by means of which such organizations can become involved, directly or indirectly, in local affairs.

An excellent example of a successful government–community action program of this type is Goals for Dallas, begun in 1965, which is concerned with planning for the rapid growth that has taken place in Dallas in recent years. Dallas has wanted to ensure that the city's future would be shaped by its citizens and would not be left to chance.[44] By 1972, 27 percent of Dallas's goals were considered achieved, and progress had been made to a greater or lesser

degree on another 71 percent.[45] Community organizations have been among the most active participants in this program.

Some may be concerned that self-serving interests may gain influence within the government. This is always a danger under any circumstances. However, if community efforts are spent in building responsible citizenship toward the ends previously noted for the "ideal community," then this danger is minimized if not negated. In any event, our democratic system has served us well over the years, and in no area of public relations is this more evident than in community relations. Community organizations articulate many of the desires of the community and are in positions to assist in vital ways in carrying out the various community programs.

The job of the public official is to learn what these desires of the community may be and to integrate them in a constructive fashion within the framework of the community's resources. Community goals are articulated through the political process and formalized through the legislative process. The key task for the local government manager, therefore, is to administer policy decisions reached in this fashion. A coordinated and integrated program of civic improvement in which every individual and organization has an opportunity to participate should be the goal of every community: the local government manager clearly has much to contribute toward this end.

Summary

This chapter has discussed, in considerable detail, the relationship of community groups to the local government process and the various means through which good public relations can effect the best working partnership between groups and government.

First, the community itself has been analyzed; then, both associations and social groups have been given a definition. Progressing from the general to the particular, the discussion has outlined the focal points of community interests. These encompass (1) the ideal community, (2) citizen information, (3) legislation and the public, (4) participation in planning and development, (5) community participation in government.

The chapter then outlines a series of methods through which community action can be articulated. Next, the action process itself is discussed, in terms of the following stages: (1) initiation, (2) mobilization, (3) execution. The discussion closes with some general conclusions.

[1] See Charles R. Adrian, "The Community Setting," in SOCIAL SCIENCE AND COMMUNITY ACTION, ed. Charles R. Adrian (East Lansing: Michigan State University, 1960), pp. 1–4.

[2] For a short treatise on this subject, see Donald W. Olmstead, SOCIAL GROUPS: ROLES AND LEADERSHIP (East Lansing: Michigan State University, 1961).

[3] For an excellent treatment of this fundamental social fact, see the classic work by Robert A. Dahl and Charles E. Lindblom, POLITICS, ECONOMICS, AND WELFARE (New York: Harper & Brothers, Publishers, 1953), especially pp. 519–25.

[4] For a good treatment of American life and culture as it relates to state and local government, see: Charles R. Adrian, STATE AND LOCAL GOVERNMENT (New York: McGraw-Hill Book Company, 1950), especially Chapters 2 and 3; see also Roland I. Warren, THE COMMUNITY IN AMERICAN LIFE, 2nd ed. (Chicago: Rand McNally & Company, 1971), Chapter 3; and Maurice R. Stein, THE ECLIPSE OF COMMUNITY: AN INTERPRETATION OF AMERICAN STUDIES (Princeton, N.J.: Princeton University Press, 1960), especially the Epilogue. For excellent treatments of America's move into the postindustrial period, see Orion White, Jr., and Bruce L. Gates, "Statistical Theory and Equity in the Delivery of Social Services," PUBLIC ADMINISTRATION REVIEW 34 (January/February 1974): 43–51; and Herman Mertins, Jr., and Bertram M. Gross, eds., "Special Symposium: Changing Styles of Planning in Post-Industrial America," PUBLIC ADMINISTRATION REVIEW 31 (MAY/JUNE 1971), entire issue.

[5] Some scholars advance a contrary power elite concept. For a summary of the pluralist versus the power elite concept, see Charles R. Adrian and Charles Press, GOVERNING URBAN AMERICA, 4th ed. (New York: McGraw-Hill Book Company, 1972), pp. 98–111. Good studies on the theory under discussion in the text include: Nelson W. Polsby, COMMUNITY POWER AND POLITICAL THEORY (New Haven: Yale University Press, 1963); David Ricci, COMMUNITY POWER AND DEMOCRATIC THEORY: THE LOGIC OF POLITICAL ANALYSIS (New York: Random House, 1971); and Murray S. Stedman, Jr., URBAN POLITICS (Cambridge, Mass.: Winthrop Publishers, Inc., 1972), especially Chapter 8.

[6] The literature is voluminous on this subject: useful references are Terry N. Clark, ed., COMMUNITY STRUCTURE AND DECISION-MAKING: COMPARATIVE ANALYSIS (San Francisco: Chandler Publishing Co., 1968); Michael Aiken and Robert R. Alford, "Community Structure and Innovation: The Case of Public Housing," AMERICAN POLITICAL SCIENCE REVIEW 65 (September 1970): 843–64; Roland L. Warren, ed., PERSPECTIVES ON THE AMERICAN COMMUNITY (Chicago: Rand McNally & Company, 1966), Section Three. Newer thinking is found in David R. Godschalk, PARTICIPATION, PLANNING, AND EXCHANGE IN OLD AND NEW COMMUNITIES; A COLLABORATIVE PARADIGM (Chapel Hill: University of North Carolina Center for Urban and Regional Studies, 1971).

[7] Floyd Hunter, "Studying Associations and Organization Structures," in APPROACHES TO THE STUDY OF POLITICS, ed. Roland Young (Evanston, Ill.: Northwestern University Press, 1958), p. 351.

[8] Ibid., pp. 348–49. Cited from Robin M. Williams, Jr., AMERICAN SOCIETY: A SOCIOLOGICAL INTERPRETATION (New York: Alfred A. Knopf, Inc., 1951), pp. 468–69.

[9] William Lloyd Warner and Paul S. Lunt, THE SOCIAL LIFE OF A MODERN COMMUNITY (New Haven: Yale University Press, 1941), p. 303 ff. The importance of such organizations to the well-being of community life and affairs is underscored in the classic study by Edward C. Banfield and Laura Banfield, THE MORAL BASIS FOR BACKWARD SOCIETY (New York: The Free Press, 1958).

[10] One of the best examples in this area has been seen in national family planning programs, where it was found that people would accept family planning services when they were provided in a way compatible with social and cultural patterns. See, for example, Steve Polgar, ed., CULTURE AND POPULATION: A COLLECTION OF CURRENT STUDIES (Chapel Hill: University of North Carolina, Carolina Population Center, 1971), pp. 196 ff.

[11] Clifford W. Graves, "Citizen Participation in Metropolitan Planning," PUBLIC ADMINISTRATION REVIEW 32 (May/June, 1972): 199. This issue also contains an excellent symposium on "Neighborhood and Citizen Involvement."

[12] Ibid.: 198–99. For a provocative essay on this subject, see Sharon Perlman Krefety and Allan E. Goodman, "Participation for What or for Whom? Some Considerations for Research," JOURNAL OF COMPARATIVE ADMINISTRATION 5 (November 1973): 367–80.

[13] The literature on social groups is vast indeed. Two suggested references useful for those in public relations are Olmstead, SOCIAL GROUPS: ROLES AND LEADERSHIP, and Heinz Eulau, THE BEHAVIORAL PERSUASION IN POLITICS (New York: Random House, 1963), particularly Chapters 1 and 2. For a more scholarly approach, the following is recommended: Amitai Etzioni, THE ACTIVE SOCIETY: A THEORY OF SOCIETAL AND POLITICAL PROCESSES (New York: The Free Press, 1968), especially the Epilogue. For an excellent elementary treatment, see H. Randolph Bobbitt, Jr., and others, ORGANIZATIONAL BEHAVIOR, UNDERSTANDING, AND PREDICTION (Englewood Cliffs, N.J.: Prentice-Hall, Inc., 1974), Chapter 5.

[14] For a definition of behavior units see Chapter 4 of this book, and Kenneth E. Boulding, CONFLICT AND DEFENSE: A GENERAL THEORY (New York: Harper Torchbooks, 1962), pp. 7–18.

[15] A few suggested references are: Robert A. Dahl, WHO GOVERNS? DEMOCRACY AND POWER IN AN AMERICAN CITY (New Haven: Yale University Press, 1961); Polsby, COMMUNITY POWER AND POLITICAL THEORY; Webb S. Fiser, MASTERY OF THE METROPOLIS (Englewood Cliffs, N.J.: Prentice-Hall, Inc., 1962); and Bertram M. Gross, ORGANIZATIONS AND THEIR MANAGING (New York: The Free Press, 1964).

[16] Public relations research is discussed in detail in Chaptor 2 of the present volume.

[17] Williams, AMERICAN SOCIETY: A SOCIOLOGICAL INTERPRETATION, p. 463.

[18] Louis B. Lundborg, PUBLIC RELATIONS IN THE LOCAL COMMUNITY (New York: Harper & Brothers, Publishers, 1950), p. 36.

[19] Edward C. Lindeman, THE COMMUNITY: AN INTRODUCTION TO THE STUDY OF COMMUNITY LEADERSHIP AND ORGANIZATION (New York: Association Press, 1921), pp. 7-9. This quotation is also found in Ernest B. Harper and Arthur Bunham, eds., COMMUNITY ORGANIZATION IN ACTION (New York: Association Press, 1959), pp. 21-22.

[20] Chapter 2 of the present volume is valuable concerning the use of research in public relations. For an excellent guide to information retrieval systems, see Fred Hogge and Norman Wengert, SEARCHING THE SOCIAL SCIENCE LITERATURE ON WATER: A GUIDE TO SELECTED INFORMATION STORAGE AND RETRIEVAL SYSTEMS—PRELIMINARY VERSION, Completion Report Series, no. 37 (Fort Collins: Colorado State University Environmental Resources Center, 1972). Although slightly dated, the following is also useful: Paul Wasserman, INFORMATION FOR ADMINISTRATORS: A GUIDE TO PUBLICATIONS AND SERVICES FOR MANAGEMENT IN BUSINESS AND GOVERNMENT (Ithaca, N.Y.: Cornell University Press, 1956).

[21] For details beyond this discussion, see Hans B. C. Spiegel, ed., CITIZEN PARTICIPATION IN URBAN DEVELOPMENT, vol. 1: CONCEPTS AND ISSUES (Washington, D.C.: National Training Laboratories Institute for Applied Behavioral Science, 1968).

[22] For a comprehensive survey of local economic development, see Donald R. Gilmore, DEVELOPING THE LITTLE ECONOMIES (New York: Committee for Economic Development, 1959).

[23] For discussion beyond this section, see John H. Strange, ed., "Special Issue—Citizens Action in Model Cities and CAP Programs: Case Studies and Evaluation," PUBLIC ADMINISTRATION REVIEW 32 (September 1972), entire issue; Jones C. Davies, NEIGHBORHOOD GROUPS AND URBAN RENEWAL (New York: Columbia University Press, 1966); and C. George Benello and Dimitrios Roussoupoulos, eds., THE CASE FOR PARTICIPATORY DEMOCRACY (New York: Viking Press, 1971).

[24] See U.S., Advisory Commission on Intergovernmental Relations, THE NEW GRASS ROOTS GOVERNMENT? (Washington, D.C.: Government Printing Office, 1972). Much of the following discussion on decentralization is derived from this source.

[25] For more details, see Fred M. Cox and others, eds., STRATEGIES OF COMMUNITY ORGANIZATION (Itasca, Ill.: F. F. Publishers, 1970), especially Chapter 6 and 7.

[26] Insights of A. J. Cervantes, a successful insurance executive who served two terms as mayor of St. Louis, are especially revealing. He states that the "techniques that work in business often break down when they come up against political reality." Business methods can be applied by the government executive to the common housekeeping functions: computerizing records, regularizing contracts, systematizing inventories, bidding purchases, cultivating public relations, professionalizing budgets, etc. He goes on to write: "In politics and government, unlike business, intermediaries exist between the ultimate consumer (the citizen) and the provider of the services (the government). The intermediaries are the neighborhood political leaders, the neighborhood association leaders, the representatives of labor and business, and the representatives of many other groups. Without support of these groups, one cannot govern. . . ." A. J. Cervantes, "Memoirs of a Businessman–Mayor," BUSINESS WEEK, December 8, 1973, pp. 19-20.

[27] U.S., Advisory Commission on Intergovernmental Relations, FISCAL BALANCE IN THE AMERICAN FEDERAL SYSTEM, 2 vols. (Washington, D.C.: Government Printing Office, 1967), vol. 2, pp. 16-17.

[28] U.S., National Advisory Commission on Civil Disorders, REPORT OF THE NATIONAL ADVISORY COMMISSION ON CIVIL DISORDERS (Washington, D.C.: Government Printing Office, 1968), pp. 151-54.

[29] U.S., National Commission on Urban Problems, BUILDING THE AMERICAN CITY (Washington, D.C.: Government Printing Office, 1969), pp. 350-54.

[30] Among the many studies on the subject, see Alan A. Altshuler, COMMUNITY CONTROL: THE BLACK DEMAND FOR PARTICIPATION IN LARGE AMERICAN CITIES (New York: Pegasus, 1970); Milton Kotler, NEIGHBORHOOD GOVERNMENT: THE LOCAL FOUNDATIONS OF POLITICAL LIFE (New York: Bobbs-Merrill Co., Inc., 1969); and Hans B. C. Spiegel and Stephen D. Mittenthal, NEIGHBORHOOD POWER AND CONTROL: IMPLICATIONS FOR URBAN PLANNING (Washington, D.C.: U.S. Department of Housing and Urban Development, 1968).

[31] See George J. Washnis, NEIGHBORHOOD FACILITIES AND MUNICIPAL DECENTRALIZATION, 2 vols. (Washington, D.C.: Center for Governmental Studies, 1971); and Judith E. Grollman, THE DECENTRALIZATION OF MUNICIPAL SERVICES, Urban Data Service Reports, vol. 3 no. 2 (Washington, D.C.: International City Management Association, 1971).

[32] See U.S., Advisory Commission on Intergovernmental Relations, THE NEW GRASS ROOTS GOVERNMENTS? p. 21.

[33] The transitional or temporary nature of contemporary organizational life in the United States is a much discussed item. See, for illustrations, Warren G. Bennis, CHANGING ORGANIZATIONS (New York: McGraw-Hill Book Company, 1966), especially Part One; Warren G. Bennis and Philip E. Slater, THE TEMPORARY SOCIETY (New York: Harper & Row, Publishers, 1968); and Alvin Toffler, FUTURE SHOCK (New York: Random House, 1970). The following article pinpoints this problem for the public official. Frederick Mosher, "The Public Service in the Temporary Society," PUBLIC ADMINISTRATION REVIEW 31 (January/February 1971): 47-62.

[34] This section builds heavily on Lillian F. Dean, "Community Involvement," in REGIONAL COUNCIL COMMUNICATIONS: A GUIDE TO ISSUES AND TECHNIQUES (Washington, D.C.: National Association of Regional Councils, 1973), Chapter 5, pp. 22-33.

[35] Adult Education Association of the U.S.A., BETTER BOARDS AND COMMITTEES, Leadership Pamphlet no. 14 (Washington, D.C.: Adult Education Association of the U.S.A., 1957), p. 21.

[36] Dane County Regional Planning Commission, HANDBOOK FOR EFFECTIVE COMMITTEES (Madison, Wis.: Dane County Regional Planning Commission, 1972), entire pamphlet.

[37] Donald Stone and Alice Stone, "The Administration of Chairs," PUBLIC ADMINISTRATION REVIEW 34 (January/February 1974): 71.

[38] Ibid.: 76.

[39] This technique, which is given below, has been developed by André L. Delbecq, professor in the Graduate School of Business, University of Wisconsin, Madison. For a detailed discussion of the research on which it is based,

see Andrew Van de Ven and André L. Delbecq, "Nominal and Interacting Group Processes for Committee Decision-Making Effectiveness," JOURNAL OF THE ACADEMY OF MANAGEMENT 14 (June 1971): 203–12.

40 Donald W. Taylor, Paul C. Bemy, and Clifford H. Block. "Does Group Participation When Using Brainstorming Facilitate or Inhibit Creative Thinking?" ADMINISTRATIVE SCIENCE QUARTERLY 3 (June 1958): 23–47.

41 This section rests heavily on the writings of the author on the subject of planned organizational change. See the following three studies by the author: Garth N. Jones, "Preventive Medicine at Work: A Hypothetical Case of Managed Organizational Change," PHILIPPINE JOURNAL OF PUBLIC ADMINISTRATION 9 (July 1965): 241–58; "Change Behavior in Planned Organizational Change Process: Applications of Socio-Economic Exchange Theory," PHILIPPINE JOURNAL OF PUBLIC ADMINISTRATION 13 (October 1969): 1–23: and PLANNED ORGANIZATIONAL CHANGE: A STUDY IN CHANGE DYNAMICS (New York: Praeger Publishers, Inc., 1969). Three excellent pamphlets by Desmond M. Connor published by Development Press, Ottawa, Canada, are: DIAGNOSING COMMUNITY PROBLEMS, 1966; UNDERSTANDING YOUR COMMUNITY, 1968; and STRATEGIES FOR DEVELOPMENT, 1968.

42 For further details on publics, see Chapter 4 of the present volume.

43 Chapter 2 of the present volume covers this subject.

44 Gordon McDiarmid, V. N. MacDonald, and J. R. Nininger, GOALS FOR DALLAS: A CASE HISTORY, vols. "A" and "B" (Kingston, Ontario: Queen's University, 1974), vol. "A," p. 1.

45 Ibid., vol "B," p. 5.

8

Police Public Relations

THE NATIONAL ADVISORY COMMISSION on Criminal Justice Standards and Goals makes the following statement:

Every police agency should constantly seek to improve its ability to determine the needs and expectations of the public, to act upon those needs and expectations, and to inform the public of the resulting policies to improve the delivery of police services. . . . As the most visible symbol of the law, police must conduct themselves in a manner that inspires respect for the law. To be worthy of public trust, police authority must be exercised in a manner consistent with the highest principles of a free society.[1]

This chapter elaborates on the theme stated in the above quote. After an opening section in which the reasons for a police public relations program are detailed, the public relations process as it applies to the police function is discussed. Next, both internal and external police relations are treated in considerable detail, the latter with emphasis on: citizen encouragement; organized citizen groups; institutional associations; social service agencies; civic clubs; and other government agencies. The subject of media relations follows. Fair Trial, Free Press Codes are discussed, followed by sections on working with the media and on developing programs to counteract problems. Positive police–community approaches occupy the last part of the discussion. The chapter ends with a conclusion which stresses the role of change in police–community relations.

What are the reasons for a police public relations program, why is it needed, who performs the function, what is involved? This chapter tries to answer these questions.

The Purpose of Police Public Relations

Public relations is the major catalytic tool by which public support can be achieved. But public relations should represent the actual world; it should not present an "image" sought by either the police chief or that person's superiors.

Wilson and McLaren, in their book *Police Administration*, emphasize the following:

Public support is essential to effective police administration.

Public relations should be used to gain public support in order to secure the benefits of the support in terms of increased finances and backing to be used to do a better job.

The long term way to improve the police image is to provide effective, enthusiastic, fair, and just service in as professional a manner as possible. Communicated progress in these efforts should be deliberate and immediate.

A better police image does not come overnight nor is it enhanced by superficial community relations programs.

Police service improvement can be facilitated through dialogue with the community.

Fair and just treatment of all citizens should be a fundamental policy of every police department.[2]

As Chief Don R. Derning succinctly concluded, "The foundation of police public relations is built on public trust. . . . It must be earned with efficient police service . . . every act by an officer is important."[3]

Public relations is a special task. It is not a convenient shield for the truth. It is identifiable and it is a program. It should be assigned to an individual for implementation within the entire police department. The individual may be either the police chief or the second in command in smaller cities. In larger communities a separate public relations bureau is found within the department, and in still larger communities an individual is assigned to the police public relations function by the community's director of public relations.

Those who are assigned this public relations function should be assured that they will not be alone in the activity. While it is their responsibility to see that a public relations program is defined, developed, and implemented, they should also realize that they will not be the only person in the department engaged in public relations: it should be the responsibility of every person in the department to practice sound public relations under the direction of the public relations officer.

The Public Relations Process

The public relations process goes beyond a mere description of the police function. It is a four-step process that is management-oriented, measurable, and accountable. Those departments that in reality do not want to know their position within the community, or do not want to evaluate their actual effectiveness, shy away from the public relations process.

Any involvement of a serious nature with public relations includes these essentials: (1) commitment on the part of management; (2) competence in the public relations staff; (3) centralization of policy making; (4) communications from and to publics; and (5) coordination of all efforts toward defined goals.[4]

Such a statement clarifies the preceding discussion and underscores the importance of an assigned public relations function. As Cutlip and Center stress: everybody's job becomes nobody's job.[5]

Management, whether it has a one-year or a multiyear plan, should include the public relations function at the outset. Thus, the police public relations person can develop compatible, supportive programs characterized by a direct focus and measurable objectives.

Thus, too, if a police department makes the commitment to a workable public relations program, it will also be agreeing to accept the public relations process: (1) research–listening, (2) planning–decision making, (3) communication –action, and (4) evaluation.[6]

The first, research–listening, involves probing the opinions, attitudes, and reactions of persons concerned with the acts and policies of an organization, then evaluating the inflow. "What's our problem?"

The second involves bringing these attitudes, opinions, ideas and reactions to bear on the policies and programs of the organization.

It will enable the organization to chart a course in the interests of all concerned. "Here's what we can do."

The third involves explaining and dramatizing the chosen course to all those who may be affected and whose support is essential. "Here's what we did and why."

The last involves evaluating the results of the program and the effectiveness of techniques used. "How did we do?"

Each of these steps is as important as the others. Each one is vital to an effective program. Too often there is too little research, too little planning, and too much publicity. Emphasis on fact-finding and planning largely distinguishes public relations from straight publicity.[7]

Internal Police Relations

Public relations serves the police department both internally and externally. It requires a continuing program among the department's personnel. With the exception of refuse collection and disposal employees, these officers are the group with which the public has the most contact. If the public is to draw its conclusions from observing the police officer, then attention must be paid to those programs which develop in each officer a sense of self-worth.

Because the police function has often been considered something of a paramilitary function, communication has often tended to be downward, from the chief to the personnel on patrol. In problem departments, such is still the case. Morale is low, completion of duty functions are haphazard, and turnover is high.

Some departments have responded to these problems by instituting not only a downward communication system but also an upward one. A fully developed and well-considered internal

FIGURE 8–1. *Washington, D.C., police officers. (Source:* THE POLICE CHIEF, *March 1973, cover. Courtesy of the International Association of Chiefs of Police, Gaithersburg, Maryland.)*

communications process provides not only for vertical but for horizontal communications as well. Such a situation promotes respect and support for the police program. Every member knows what is going on and why. In a complete communications system, the foot patrol knows what the narcotics unit is facing, and vice versa. Each group comes to realize that no one function within law enforcement is more vital than the other. Each function is needed to achieve the goal and each complements the other.

A spirit of give-and-take results. Officers feel free to recommend either alternatives to the way in which the department operates or new programs upon which it can embark. Officers

are also made aware of the variety of assignments and opportunities available to them. They come to understand the rationale behind the officer reassignment and to seek advancement.

If the public relations professional works effectively with the departmental staff in furthering these communications activities, each officer will come to realize that he or she is valued, he or she is professional, and he or she has an opportunity to grow within the profession.

It is a good policy for a chief to see that the officers—from the patrol officer to the deputy chief—receive credit for the work they perform. In turn, the officers are more apt to consider their actions when they become accountable for them. They will realize that no one can "hide behind a badge."

CEREMONIAL RECOGNITION

Two other activities that can be directed by the public relations program are ceremonial recognition of officers and the holding of "ventilation sessions." When an officer truly performs in an outstanding manner the department may wish to consider public ceremonial occasions in which to honor the individual. Planning will indicate who among the various publics should be notified and invited to participate. Although most officers do not enter the field for public recognition, professionalism or a single action may warrant such an honor. Care should be taken, however, that commendations do not become so common or widespread as to dilute their purpose—the development of self-worth.

VENTILATION SESSIONS

The second activity, the holding of ventilation sessions, falls within that area of public relations that is concerned with preventing problems from arising. A small group of officers from diverse assignments meets to discuss the operation of the department, their roles within the department, and the programs now under way. Skilled handling prevents these meetings from degenerating into gripe sessions. The interaction of various levels and various divisions develops positive communication on the strengths and weaknesses of the department. It provides the in-depth follow-up to the written memorandum—perhaps the most ill-used medium of communication. Once again, credit for ideas or presentation of problems should be given to the individuals who brought the situation to light for action.

Such activities as total communication, assertion of self-worth, the development of leadership, and the recognition of actions will help achieve a positive and dynamic department in which fewer mistakes are made, the staff is "in the know," and the public comes into contact with officers who are truly professional.

While these functions are everyone's duty, they need to be considered and supervised by the public relations officer. Confidence and competence are crucial to many of these suggestions. It is important that police officers feel that their ideas will be valued. If their ideas contradict current policies, the officers should know that their ideas are just as acceptable as if they did not and that follow-up will be provided. The climate must be supportive. Police departments that become defensive over the suggestions made by a rookie officer are not fulfilling either their law enforcement or public relations functions properly.

COORDINATED FUNCTION

In other areas of internal public relations the responsible individual will work closely with the local government's public relations director to see that departmental activities are included in employee newsletters and other publications, and will suggest individuals who are willing to work with community groups or to speak with other agencies or organizations.

Other internal public relations activities discussed elsewhere in this book are also applicable to police public relations. Some of them are also mentioned here because of the critical role they play in providing the professional climate needed for the department's success.

External Police Relations

Just as all of a local government is involved with external public relations, so is the police department. Some external programs however, involve the police function in a somewhat different way and will be expanded here.

In this discussion, external public relations is applied both to citizens as individuals and citizens as identified groups (or institutional associations).

POLICE–COMMUNITY RELATIONS

A word about police–community relations is appropriate at this point. One of the important concerns in our society today is that police be fully sensitive to the needs of the various publics that they serve. It is important that training programs be geared to this concern. As one author has stated:

Experience indicates that through well-designed and implemented programs, police and community members can productively work together to reduce stereotypes and to obtain realistic and individualized pictures of each other. But if police–community relations programs are to be useful, certain basic elements must be built into them.

1. They must have the complete confidence and backing of the police chief. . . .
2. The programs must be long enough so that initial hostilities can be worked through between police and community residents and *specific productive work* done. . . .
3. Directors of programs must be carefully chosen and have an extensive background in the conduct of task-oriented groups.
4. Staff members must also be carefully chosen and well trained. . . . Staff must include community organizers, police officers, and group leaders, as well as support staff.
5. Programs must be task oriented, having as their prime focus not simply the ventilation of feeling, but the accomplishment of certain specific tasks. . . .
6. Funding must be sufficient to allow follow through on specific projects generated by the program.[8]

CITIZENS AS INDIVIDUALS

Citizen Encouragement. The individual police officer should be the most important source of citizen encouragement. Most citizens have few if any contacts with a police officer. The manner in which this officer presents himself or herself, or conducts an investigation, is long remembered by citizens and will probably determine their willingness to "get involved" with the police in the future. By presenting themselves properly, conducting police business in a professional manner, and, in general, displaying a high degree of concern for a citizen's problems or needs, police officers are cultivating support for themselves, the police department, and the community's government as a whole.

Efforts to familiarize the public with police programs and police operations are important tools used by most police departments to encourage communication between police officers and the public. As two authorities have put it, "The active interest and participation of individual citizens and groups are a resource so vital to the success of most police programs that deliberate efforts should be made to arouse, promote, and maintain public concern in departmental affairs."[9]

When police make the effort to go into schools, businesses, industry, and civic and citizen groups it encourages citizens to become involved. Citizens, after all, cannot be expected to support something they do not understand.

Official recognition is a more direct, but limited, form of citizen encouragement. This is accomplished primarily by three methods. If a citizen has performed a noteworthy action, his or her name can be mentioned on radio or television spots in which a police department releases police activity reports. A more official form of recognition is for the police department to mail a letter of appreciation to the citizen. The highest form of offical recognition is the awarding of the Citizen Commendation Certificate. There are cases where all three forms of recognition would be afforded a citizen for the performance of an exceptional deed.

Citizen Commendation Certificate. The Citizen Commendation Certificate is the highest and most official form of citizen recognition. It usually includes a ceremony in which the citizen, the police representative, and, sometimes, local officials are present. The certificate commends the citizen for extraordinary action and is signed by the highest ranking officer in the police department.

Organized Citizen Groups. Police officers not only interact with organized citizen groups but are many times part of them. Sometimes the police department itself helps organize such groups.

Groups such as neighborhood citizen councils meet periodically with police and other local officials at open meetings which are usually held in a school, church, or recreation center in the neighborhood. Any citizen from the neighborhood is welcome to ask questions, inform the police and city officials of problems or potential problems, or discuss some other matter concerning the neighborhood and its citizens.

These meetings are valuable for determining the mood and needs of the neighborhood. They also afford an opportunity for citizens, police, and local officials to see each other as individuals and develop a more positive working relationship.

An important element of citizen council meetings with police representatives is a follow-up by the police on requests, inquiries, or suggestions from participating citizens. It is important that the citizen know the results of the follow-up.

FIGURE 8–2. *Police officer in Winston-Salem community service unit provides assistance.* (*Source: Courtesy of the City of Winston-Salem, North Carolina.*)

USING A DATA BASE

The preceding sections have suggested ways in which the department can become actively involved with the citizen participation process. However, the police department does not always have to work directly with citizens to predict their needs. It can also turn to its data base to predict what citizens will need in the future.

An increasing number of police departments are attempting to use valid data to project citizen needs. This is not only in the form of crime statistics and police calls; it also includes citizen surveys and requests.

Crime statistics and the number of calls answered by police are important in determining where and when to assign personnel. The need for new programs or organizational changes can be indicated by these same statistics; however, these statistics do not necessarily mean that new programs or organizational changes will be accepted and supported by the community.

Citizen surveys which attempt to determine citizen satisfaction with existing police performance and service can be used to indicate the need for new programs or revamping of others. The rating given police performance and service may point out the need for new training or retraining of police officers.

If the need for a new program has been determined, a survey of the affected segment of the community should be made. The results should indicate whether the citizens desire this new program, whether they think it is workable, and whether it will meet with resistance. The size and timing of this new program should also be indicated by the survey.

INSTITUTIONAL ASSOCIATIONS

The individual citizen and his or her relationships with the police have been discussed above. Another segment of the citizenry, that of the institutions, also requires a well-defined external public relations program. Included in this segment are elected officials, business and industrial leaders, labor union leaders, schools, social service agencies, civic clubs, and other agencies within the local government.

Elected Officials. The one statement concerning politics which is probably made most often by police officers is that "the police should stay out of politics." This is an idealistic and almost impossible task. Nearly everything the police do in their external operation is political—not just their functions at political meetings and demonstrations, in labor–management disputes, and the like. The police are in fact involved in politics every time they come into contact with the public.[10]

For too many years the police have been a "closed fraternity." Police need to develop clear-cut guidelines and programs and then make an overt effort to communicate them to the public on a nonpartisan basis.[11] However, a police administrator has an obligation to his or her department to refrain completely from partisan politics.[12]

Sometimes a police administrator is faced with the problem of an individual council member attempting to influence or obtain favors from the department.[13] The police administrator is responsible to the council as a whole and should maintain a high degree of professionalism when dealing with individual council members.

Business and Industry. In order to maintain a working relationship with the business and industrial community, many police departments meet with representatives of the business and industry world—chambers of commerce, employers' associations, labor unions, and the like—on a regular basis. This is best accomplished on an open and informal basis.

One such means is an informal luncheon followed by an open discussion of those business and industrial problems which are police-related. These are give-and-take sessions in which both sides discuss problems and offer suggestions. To make these meetings effective, police officials should follow up these discussions. This can be done by contacting members of the business and industrial community on an individual basis. A spirit of cooperation is thus achieved and various problems concerning the police and business and industry can be solved. More important, the police and the business and industrial community come to understand each other better and know what each can and cannot expect of the other.

School Programs.   One of the best opportunities for good police–community relations is offered by taking various police programs into schools—from the kindergartens upward. Excellent programs of this kind include the Officer Friendly, drug education, crime prevention, and the police–school liaison programs. The last named has the greatest continuity and is the most comprehensive.

A police–school liaison program is initiated when an officer is assigned to a school to act as both a law enforcement officer and a resource person who can also be a counselor. He can listen to student problems, help coordinate efforts to reduce delinquent activities, and foster better understanding between the police and adolescents.[14]

School administrators and teachers also develop a give-and-take relationship with police officers through these programs. The exchange of information and the mutual goodwill that is created are well worth the cost of maintaining at least some of these programs.

Social Service Agencies.   Police officers are called upon for a wide range of services. Many times when an individual's problems or needs are magnified he or she turns first to the police. The problem may range from birth control to inadequate medical care for neighboring children. Whenever an officer gives the negative answer, "There isn't anything the police can do," it leaves a negative feeling toward the entire police department. One way to avoid this

FIGURE 8–3. *Traditional school patrol. (Source: Courtesy of the City of Winston-Salem, North Carolina.)*

is to refer the citizen to the appropriate social service agency, or to a unit such as a police community services unit that can in turn refer the individual to the appropriate agency.

When an officer refers or takes someone to a social service unit, there should be a follow-up to ensure that the citizen was properly cared for.

Civic Clubs. Civic clubs are among the stronger—if not the strongest—organized supporters of police and police departments in the United States. They sponsor such activities as Police Week and Crime Prevention Week.

Police departments have a variety of programs which they make available to these clubs. Some of the programs include police speakers who provide information and exhibits on drugs, home and business security, shoplifting, and self-defense for women (Figure 8–4). Many police officers are active members of various civic clubs.

Other Governmental Agencies. In recent years there has been a tendency for police departments to return to the "old town hall" concept.

FIGURE 8–4. *Storefront officers in Fort Worth making self-defense materials available.* (*Source: Courtesy of the City of Fort Worth, Texas.*)

Police departments are now increasing their interaction with other governmental agencies. At one time most police departments were more or less set apart from other governmental agencies and were almost a separate government of their own. The changing social climate and economy have necessitated a closer cooperation with these agencies.

The foregoing discussion has illustrated some specific police public relations concepts as they would relate to the department's external public—the citizens, either as private citizens or as members of an identified public body.

Relations with the Media

Another public of the police department is the media: newspapers, magazines, radio, and television. These four categories are envisioned when a discussion focuses on the media, but even these categories are changing. Public television, direct control governmental mailings, speakers' bureaus, and the government channel in cable television have thrust local government into a new role as producer of news and reporter of events.

The nature of the police function may bring it into conflict with the news media. It is the responsibility of the police public relations officer to determine what is to be done. It is important that the officer begin by knowing the local media.

First, the officer should survey the local media to determine their strengths and weaknesses. Is a station short of reporters? Is a newspaper assigning the police beat to neophytes? Do the community's reporters want advance warning of impending actions? Do they violate or do they hold in trust those confidences which serve both the media and the police?

Second, the officer should survey the police department and reconcile this response with what the media recount to the public relations officer.

Third, the public relations officer should determine the role that each news agency holds within the community. Some agencies appeal only to youthful audiences, others appeal to the "establishment," etc.

Fortunately, no unit of government may dictate to the news media when, what, or how governmental activity may be reported. This strength of democracy can sometimes increase the frustration level within police operations.

When is a document a public document? When should the media be informed of an impending narcotics raid? When should the media be told of discovered police harassment? Who should talk with the media? Must the media have "media passes" to perform their function within the community? These questions—all of them touching on vital First Amendment rights—are not easy to answer. Quite apart from the substantive legal questions involved, the matter, in practice, comes to be essentially one of trust—trust on the part of all parties involved; a respect for each other's profession. Such an acceptance leads to better reporting and better police attitudes.

Different procedures for working with the media exist for different police departments across the country. While no single "right" way exists, many "wrong" or self-defeating situations survive. If the procedure is a comfortable, stable, and productive process, it should probably be continued.

FAIR TRIAL, FREE PRESS CODES

If no operational framework exists, the public relations officer should conclude the preliminary survey by determining a procedure for coexistence. One method that has been used successfully has been the drawing together of representatives from law enforcement, the judiciary, bar associations, and the media to determine a procedure code, often called a Fair Trial, Free Press Code.

Out of these frank, no-holds-barred sessions an operating standard can emerge which contains a wide variety of possible activities. The result can be a definitive policy statement, developed locally by those involved, within which each party can operate freely.

Those who have experienced these sessions have come away with respect for one another. The adversary relationship has yielded to an understanding, an acceptance of future conflicts, and an anticipation of continuing association. When those conflicts arise, participants can "level" with each other, clear the air, and move forward.

Generally, these sessions will span three months. At first, participants may be on the defensive. Transition occurs when each recognizes the dilemma in which the other is often placed. Finally, the group advances to that point of realization in which the needs of the community are recognized. From this point of recognition, the sessions define roles, functions, and operating procedures. A plan or code is adopted which is held viable for as long as the majority of the participants are within the community.

Participants agree to acquaint their agency members with these policies and to oversee their administration within their own organizations. As times change, so will the needs of the member agencies. This will dictate revisions within the code.

Working with the Media

Chapter 9 of this book contains a thorough discussion of working with the media, and the need to understand and respect their production deadlines and special news needs. A trained police public relations person will quickly learn these needs and develop plans to meet them.

Public relations officers need to be acquainted with the regional and national media—in radio, television, daily newspapers, weekly news magazines, and the professional journals. They should develop a working relationship with the local media and, as best as they can, with the regional and national media.

Problems with the Media

Local governments today have become sophisticated users of information channels. They have developed their own newspapers which go directly into residents' homes. They have developed speakers' bureaus to enable them to reach any and all organizations. They have placed participants on talk shows, and they have their own radio programming. Larger communities are developing their own television studios to make use of the government channel reserved in cable television franchises.

Although public relations officers may work toward a positive relationship with the media and may develop their own communications channels, problems will still arise. Their seriousness and the damage they inflict will reflect the extent to which the public relations function is embraced by management.

Police departments develop action plans for disaster. Unfortunately, these action plans often omit the media or the public's desire to know what is going on. It is essential that public relations officers review these plans before the disaster to see if they are practical and if the needs of the public have been respected. If they have not, then public relations officers should have the authority to see that they are revised.

Any police public relations officer should ask himself or herself if the disaster plan is well known or fully accepted. What would his or her role be—and the roles of the other officers within the department? How would members of the news media operate during these times? Would information be available to them or would the "lid be clamped on"?

Another media problem can be "playing favorites." Some administrators "throw stories" toward one particular news organization—particularly if another has reported unfavorably on a police action. Such a reaction is childish and immature at best. It is at these specific times that appropriate action must be taken—either to correct the department if the report is true, or the news agency if it is untrue.

Another pitfall to avoid is remembering only those news agencies who assign reporters every day. The majority of American cities are of such a size that it is impossible for a community's media to cover all of government every day. The public relations officer should try to assist the news agency through news leads, or actual stories if they are desired. It is important not to overlook neighborhood papers in metropolitan areas.

Instead of dismissing the media because of these various problems, the public relations officer should examine the nature and cause of the problems thoroughly. Often, they may be as simple as a misunderstanding of terms.

When a problem seems to be a hopeless

cause, public relations officers would counsel a "write-off"—to free energy for those relationships in which a productive association can be developed or for the development of alternative communications channels.

Programs to Counteract Problems

Police public relations has defined action plans to counteract problems, seek assistance from other cities, and develop specialized departmental and other community information/service programs. These programs merit discussion in any chapter focusing on police activities.

Modern administrators know that it is not enough to respond to problems as they unfold. The successful administrator anticipates problems and develops programs to counteract them. Many police departments are actively engaged in this today. The programs range from informal meetings among police officers intended to anticipate and prevent internal problems, to programs intended to promote police sensitivity to and awareness of all of the publics that they serve—including minorities, ethnic groups, women, teenagers, the elderly, etc.

Conflict Resolution Teams

Some communities have developed conflict resolution teams. These teams are trained and equipped to deal with disturbances and disorders and to help eliminate their causes. The teams consist of experienced police officers, civilian specialists, and members of the community. They are not only useful in their communities, but are available also to advise other local and state agencies upon request.[15]

Sharing Knowledge

Many communities have mutual problems. It is not necessary for a city or county to develop many programs from start to finish on its own. Police departments in different communities are providing each other with the format they used in organizing a particular program, instructions on how it works, and what has been learned from the experience. In recent years the Law Enforcement Assistance Administration (LEAA) has required some cities receiving federal funds for similar programs to meet on a regular basis to discuss their progress and problems.

Research on programs of other cities provides an interchange of information, a promotion of goodwill, and a possible monetary savings for everyone involved.

Officer Friendly Program

Officer Friendly, Family Crises, Teen Drugs, and similar programs reach into the community and are preventive in contrast to reactive programs. They expose the police officer as an individual, promote better understanding between police and community, and help prevent problems which could eventually develop into police-related problems. The return in cooperation and goodwill is tremendous.

The Officer Friendly program sends officers into grade schools in three stages:

1. The officer who is given the title Officer Friendly goes into the classroom and talks with the young students. This is probably the children's first opportunity to talk with and ask questions of a police officer. This is the police officer's opportunity to make a good first impression for all law enforcement officers.
2. Officer Friendly teaches some safety rules (crossing streets, bicycle safety, who to call if they need help or information, etc.). This can be done with the aid of Officer Friendly booklets, which have been geared to the age level of the students.
3. He or she displays and demonstrates police equipment and police vehicles to the young students. In conclusion, the police officer awards Officer Friendly certificates and paper police badges to the students.

The Officer Friendly program was initiated in the Chicago Police Department in 1966.[16]

Family Crises Units

The Family Crises Unit is composed of officers who have received special training in psychology, sociology, and the use of available referral agencies. It deals mainly with noncriminal situations in which members of a family

FIGURE 8–5. *Officer and children in Fort Worth. (Source: Courtesy of the City of Fort Worth, Texas.)*

have problems which they cannot resolve by themselves. If the problems are unresolved after counseling with family members, the unit refers the family to an appropriate agency and, for best results, follows up on the case to determine if it can be of further assistance.

TEEN DRUGS

Teen Drugs and similar programs are essentially drug education programs. However, a counseling service made available to parents with children who use drugs can be of invaluable assistance. The programs are directed to all age levels beginning with fifth-graders and extending through adults. Major emphasis is placed on the junior high school level in hopes of making students aware of the dangers of drug abuse. The programs are conducted mainly through the use of movies and visual aids, including displays of confiscated drugs.

CRIME PREVENTION TRAILER

A Crime Prevention Trailer (a renovated mobile home) is an excellent, mobile, means of exhibiting displays and information concerning the work and services of the police department. The trailer can be made available to schools, fairs, shopping centers, or any gathering where safety is the theme.

An ideal trailer will contain examples of the work of the uniformed officer, a drug display, a display of confiscated weapons, an alarm system display, a communication display, a traffic diorama, and a mannequin police officer who, through the use of an intercom system and a hidden officer, talks with and answers questions of visitors. The trailer can be updated from time to time.[17]

POLICE DEPARTMENT TOUR

Tours of police departments should be presented to all ages, with special emphasis on junior and senior high school students. The number of people who are taken on a tour per time may range from one individual to a group of fifteen to twenty. Students are shown all phases of the police department, including the communications center, the records division, and the work of the uniformed patrol division. Through this, police departments hope the public will better understand what it is to be a police officer. In addition, the tour has a positive psychological effect on young people.

Sometimes the poor conditions of police facilities go unchanged because the public is unaware that these conditions exist. A secondary effect of tours is that sometimes they help create a public awareness which in turn accelerates improvements. Careful planning should go into these tours—not only of the program but also of publicity and scheduling.

POLICE ATHLETIC LEAGUES

Police Athletic Leagues are usually aimed at youths between the ages of eight and fifteen from low-income families. The police department supports these leagues both physically and financially. Many times the Police Athletic League program can be coordinated through the YMCA, and financial aid can be obtained from the business community and civic groups.

Some sports which can be included in a Police Athletic League are boxing, swimming, basketball, baseball, and football. Managers and coaches can be drawn from police personnel, both on and off duty.

Benefits do not end with the youth who are involved in Police Athletic Leagues. There is a spillover effect from the youth to adults.

Parents see many things through the eyes of their children, and through their youngsters, may discover that policemen are friendly, helpful persons who devote a relatively small part of their time to restrictive and punitive tasks.[18]

Many other programs have been used which have had long-term positive effects on many communities. Through the police administration network, and through regional administration centers and professional public relations organizations such as the Public Relations Society of America, police administrators and their public relations officers have a wealth of resources on which to draw.

Summary

The present chapter has outlined various aspects of police public relations programs. The purposes of such programs have been discussed in some detail; this has been followed by an analysis of public relations as it applies to the police function. Before a police department can relate constructively to the public, its internal relations should themselves be constructive. A discussion of both internal and external relations follows. Relations with the media is the next subject handled. After an outline of program development for the purpose of counteracting problems, the discussion terminates by presenting a series of positive police–community programs.

Change Is the Key

The key to the police profession is change. Change has opened the door to new areas of

FIGURE 8–6. *Officers on patrol duty in Winston-Salem.* (*Source: Courtesy of the City of Winston-Salem, North Carolina.*)

involvement, new program concepts, and new demands.

Today police are involved more than ever before with the communities they serve. Today's police department needs to have a new sensitivity to and awareness of its various publics. The term "public trust," used in the quotation at the beginning of this chapter, refers today to just these various publics.

The image of the police officer is changing as well, particularly as women are joining the force in increasing numbers. It is essential that police public relations officers today try to keep up with—and ahead of—these changes. Indeed, the truly professional police officer or police public relations specialist will view this change as an opportunity to grow and mature in the course of serving the public.

[1] Quoted in Don R. Derning, "The True Measures of Police/Public Relations," THE POLICE CHIEF, March 1973, p. 8. This quote was taken from a report of the National Advisory Commission on Criminal Justice Standards and Goals, reviewed at the first National Conference on Criminal Justice, Washington, D.C., 23–26 January 1973.

[2] Orlando W. Wilson and Roy C. McLaren, POLICE ADMINISTRATION, 3rd ed. (New York: McGraw-Hill Book Company, 1972), pp. 216–17. Used with permission of McGraw-Hill Book Company.

[3] Derning, "The True Measures of Police/Public Relations," p. 8.

4 Scott M. Cutlip and Allen H. Center, EFFECTIVE PUBLIC RELATIONS, 4th ed. (Englewood Cliffs, N.J., Prentice-Hall, Inc., 1971), p. 155. Reprinted by permission of Prentice-Hall, Inc., Englewood Cliffs, N.J.

5 Ibid., p. 157.

6 Ibid., p. 186.

7 Ibid, pp. 186–87.

8 Jesse G. Rubin, "Police Identity and the Police Role," in THE POLICE AND THE COMMUNITY, ed. Robert Steadman (Baltimore: The Johns Hopkins Press, 1972), pp. 48–49.

9 Wilson and McLaren, POLICE ADMINISTRATION, p. 232.

10 Thomas F. Adams, ed., CRIMINAL JUSTICE READINGS (Pacific Palisades, Calif.: Goodyear Publishing Co., Inc., 1972), p. 356.

11 Ibid., p. 358.

12 Wilson and McLaren, POLICE ADMINISTRATION, p. 27.

13 Ibid., p. 23.

14 Samuel Dixon and Robert C. Trojanowicz, CRIMINAL JUSTICE AND THE COMMUNITY (Englewood Cliffs, N.J.: Prentice-Hall, Inc., 1974), p. 301.

15 Ibid., p. 297.

16 Robert M. Platt, ed., THE CONCEPT OF POLICE–COMMUNITY RELATIONS (Kennedale, Tex.: The Criminal Justice Press, 1973), p. 66. Platt says: "The Sears Roebuck Foundation has copyrighted the name Officer Friendly. During its 1970 fiscal year, the Sears Roebuck Foundation grants made it possible for 113 full-time and 46 part-time Officer Friendlies to reach 1.3 million children in 35,000 classrooms of 2,660 schools" (p. 67).

17 Wilson and McLaren, POLICE ADMINISTRATION, p. 231.

18 Ibid., p. 431.

Part Three

Informational
Reporting

9

The Role of Reporters
and the Media

REPORTERS AND THE MEDIA, the subjects under discussion in this chapter, serve as an opening theme of Part Three of this book. Part One dealt with the public relations process itself; Part Two was concerned with programs and with government's responsibilities for them. Now the emphasis shifts to public information and the media.

This chapter opens with a discussion of journalism which includes a history of broadcast news and a definition of the role of the news reporter (whether newspaper, radio, or television) as conveyor of information to the public. How can the media and local government work together? This question and its various ramifications are treated in considerable detail. A discussion of the day-to-day mechanics of servicing the press and the broadcast media concludes the chapter.

Journalism: An Overview

Journalism in the United States today is undergoing more change—and is subject to more attack and criticism—than probably at any other time and place in history.

Today, journalism is not so much discovering the role that a free press plays in a democracy as it is finding acceptance from two hundred million Americans who have been deluged with more information concerning events than at any other period since the dawn of history.

Like most of our technology, journalism has undergone great change since World War II. Many good magazines have vanished, great newspapers have folded, television was born and has developed into an ever more popular news-disseminating device.

Space missions, assassinations, great sporting events—all of these have been brought live and in color into homes throughout the world.

From its early days, when announcers read from the newspapers of the day, television news has grown into a journalistic giant with live cameras, direct transmissions, trained journalists, and an entire new concept of presenting the news. Journalism schools, which used to turn out only print-trained reporters and editors, now emphasize communication arts, with heavy broadcast training. With the rate of growth over the past decade, it seems safe to assume that the end of television's technology and development is nowhere in sight.

It seems safe to assume, also, that the faster television grows the more powerful it becomes, and the more the citizens of a nation rely on it, the more governments will make an attempt to control it.

Television is probably the single most important force in mass communications today. It can, by means of its ability to carry live images into every nook and cranny of a nation, elect presidents, expose dishonesty, and bring either great joy or great hardship, depending on how it is used.

Television and radio are the sole means of communication in the United States that are totally controlled by the people of the nation, in the sense that, because the airwaves used by broadcasting are owned by the public, the public must therefore be served by both media. Newspapers do not, of course, have this restriction placed on them.

By the same token, this public ownership of the air also brings federal licensing to bear upon the thousands of stations, large and small, that cover the nation. Every three years each station must present its record of service to the Federal Communications Commission to prove that it is worthy of having that license renewed for another three years.

In recent years groups have been organized to challenge these license renewals. In some cases the motivation for such challenges has been profit, harassment, anger. In some cases there has been an honest belief that some stations haven't been doing the job in the manner promised when the license was applied for three years previously.

BROADCAST NEWS: THE BACKGROUND

A history of broadcasting is not required reading, but it is important for an understanding of how both television and radio have evolved into the communications forces that they are today.

In the early years, radio stations were sidebar investments, often of newspapers. During the 1930s radio was a money-making investment that was considered primarily as entertainment. There were newscasters, to be sure, but it would have been unthinkable to consider radio a primary source of news in the days prior to World War II.

After the war, television came on the scene —at first in small black-and-white boxes that didn't pick up many stations and were not effective more than a few miles from a transmitter. But in a relatively brief time the industry began to boom, and the sets became larger, the signals were carried further, the black and white (eventually) became color, and there was hardly a home without television.

The advertising dollar was stretched a little further and was split among magazines, newspapers, and radio and television stations, with the result that a number of newspapers and magazines went out of business.

As the world of broadcasting expanded and more and more people began watching and listening, broadcast news suddenly began to be an important means of communication.

At first, broadcast news personnel were recruited from newspapers and wire services. But

FIGURE 9–1. *A television crew covers the news. (Source: Courtesy of the Metropolitan Washington Council of Governments.)*

as journalism schools expanded their training, more and more of the new recruits came into the broadcast business with at least some idea of the workings of radio and television news.

It was during this period that reporting changed drastically as well. At first, stations would shoot only silent film of a news happening. Armed with a script or handout material, the anchorman would try to match what was being shown on the screen with what actually had happened.

Still later, sound equipment was being manufactured at a price that the larger stations could afford, and persons in their living rooms at night were treated to rather routine questions and often even more routine answers on the news events of the day.

It was all unprofessional, but at the same time all new, and the very newness of it made electronic journalism grow. The great response from the public brought the ultimate impor tance of electronic journalism into sharp focus at the networks and at the local station level in cities and towns from coast to coast.

Roving reporters were hired to cover the breaking events of the day—from ship sinkings to airplane crashes to murders, and even to the three-alarm fire that lent itself so well to spectacular motion picture film coverage.

Then came the investigative reporters, who were given the unheard-of luxury in the mid-sixties of digging into a story and not having to come up with it in minutes.

Out of this form of journalism came such events as the NBC "White Papers" and CBS "Reports," with exposés of the plight of migrant farm workers and the Berlin Wall. Just after the network efforts came local station investigations into the sorrier aspects of human behavior at all levels of society and in all areas of government. Some of the reporting was great, some of it was terrible, some was of benefit and some was ignored, but the growth of this type of reporting continued.

What was more, people watched, were intrigued by what they saw, and reacted enthusiastically. Newspapers had been doing the same thing for years and doing it more completely and probably even better, in most cases. But the new medium was attracting its following, too.

Out of the investigative fields came the consumer reporter, something else that was new and untried in broadcasting. The consumer reporter was the videotape newsfilm watchdog of the average citizen in his or her never-ending fight against rising prices, poor-quality commodities, and all who would take advantage of the unsuspecting householder.

Along the way, news departments quietly expanded and grew. Taking notes from their newspaper counterparts, news directors began assigning staff reporters to city halls, county buildings, and state government. The mission was more difficult in broadcasting because of the limitations of time, but the reporters were there each day, and each day their ranks grew. Armed with cameras and tape recorders, this new breed of reporter was more intent on having the newsmaker tell his or her own story than on reporting it second hand (Figures 9–2 and 9–4)

There were obstacles. Cameras were not allowed in many places where a print reporter could take paper and pencil. The courtrooms of the nation are still effectively closed to the tools of the electronic journalist. But many of the early barriers came down, and still more come down each year. Broadcast journalism has reached a higher level of acceptance now than ever before

THE REPORTER'S ROLE

The role of reporters is to dig, to verify, and to relate what is uncovered to the reader, viewer, or listener. Their sole purpose is to uncover what is going on in the public interest. Their job is always important to the people's right to know. It becomes even more important when what they are covering involves public funding, public trust, and public office. Reporters, then, have a tremendous burden of honesty placed upon them.

The Media and Local Government

PRESENTING THE NEWS

The first thought in presenting the day's news is given to the interest it evokes, the second to the purpose it is to serve, and the third to the way it can best be presented. In responsible

FIGURE 9–2. *Television reporters covering a council meeting.* (*Source: Courtesy of the Metropolitan Washington Council of Governments.*)

news operations the overriding rules governing this presentation are truth and fairness.

The debate over the responsibility of the press versus the responsiveness of government is a continuing one, covering all the years of the Republic. Few officeholders, from the selectmen of the post-Revolution New England towns to the highest elected officials of the land, have served their terms without at least one controversial encounter with the press.

Some of the cases are classic ones: Teapot Dome and Watergate were two of these. Some are known only to those who saw the events unfold. One of the latter, which appears immediately below, is a classic example of a case of political heavy-handedness and poorly managed local government public relations.

A CASE STUDY

Not too long ago, in one of the nation's larger cities, a crisis over police and firefighters' wages developed. The police and fire departments came under the jurisdiction of a public safety director. However, the city government was a closed group of one-party politicians controlled by a mayor who had inherited his power and political knowledge from an equally strong, if slightly wiser, old-line politician. The city had prospered and grown under the older politician's leadership and had attracted national attention because of its advanced programs in certain areas.

Its two main, protective agencies, the police and firefighters, were, however, among the lowest paid of all major metropolitan departments in either the United States or Canada. In fact, some members of its fire department with large families to support qualified for the food stamp program.

Repeatedly, the mayor and city council ignored pleas for relief, blaming their reluctance to raise salaries on the scarcity of tax money and the exodus of city residents to the booming metropolitan area in which this city was located.

There was intense pressure from the media and a year-long picket line around city hall by the firefighters (who continued to answer alarms during all this trouble).

The mayor of the city, during a long and relatively trouble-free career as state legislator and party professional, had never really had any difficulty with the media. He was clearly the choice of his predecessor, was an immensely popular politician, and was rarely called upon to explain any of his actions. His council was made up of members of his own party who rarely had competition for the seats they held.

On the coldest day of the winter, when the picket line was only a few months old, the mayor had to walk past shivering firefighters to get to his office. At a news conference shortly afterward he was asked what he had felt when he walked by them. He used a common street term to describe his reaction, referring continually to the firefighters as pinochle players who were hardly worth the same money that the police officers were. Shortly after his use of the term "pinochle players," a dramatic television news film was shown of a firefighter, face blackened and tears streaking both cheeks, attempting to breathe life into a dying four-year-old.

As the issue of better pay increased and the firemen continued their peaceful picketing and election day drew closer, the public relations department of the city all but collapsed. Tempers flared at news conferences, questions went unanswered, and the "How-dare-you-question-our-decisions?" attitude intensified while police and firefighter spokesmen carried their appeals to the city residents who were eventually going to pay the price of a salary increase anyway.

When the vote was taken the results were overwhelming; the two departments won their raises and the mayor was finished as a public official.

Aside from a moral issue of how much public safety is worth, the battle proved one thing: that media relations play a critical role in local government—sometimes a decisive one.

During the course of these events, the two newspapers in the city had been, if anything, pro-city hall. The television and radio stations hardly reacted at all at first, aside from covering the early days of the picket line and occasionally commenting on the fact that the police department was not actively participating in the picketing.

But the firefighters carried their battle to the public. By answering all alarms and doing their picket duty on their off-hours and off-days with no disruption to public convenience, they managed to win not only the vote they sought but a great deal of public goodwill in the bargain. Despite the fact that they had no paid public relations personnel and no budget for advertisements or broadcast commercials, they did have some solid spokesmen who decided to answer the questions rather than avoid them. This, in the long run, was what won them their battle. They got their space in the newspapers and on the air by utilizing all the positive information they could muster. Because all of them, by law, had to be city residents, they were the first to share their feelings of increased tax burdens because they had to pay them too. The news media eventually became strong advocates of their cause as a result of their efforts.

This case was a classic example of how not to conduct local government public relations, from the standpoint of the public, of the city employees, of the media and, in the end, of the officeholders themselves.

MEDIA RELATIONS: WHAT ARE THEY?

Because of the complex times in which we live and the tremendous growth of urban and suburban living, entire new generations of jobs and areas of expertise have come into being and, along with them, a key area: that of media relations.

No newspaper, no matter how large, can cover all of government—whether federal, state, or local. There is too much going on to assign reporters to each day's activities. Not everything that happens each day is a headline, but almost every item is of some news value in one way or another.

A new planned community, or the dedication of a multimillion-dollar bridge, or the groundbreaking for another leg of an interstate highway will almost surely get reams of copy, plenty of pictures, film on the principal newscasts on television that evening, and voice reports on most of the radio stations in the area. But this is the easy part of the job. The big stories, especially those that benefit the public, are easy to report. They almost tell themselves.

The little stories, however, are the ones that make up the bulk of the day's news and are the ones most easily lost in a newspaper's budget for the day. They are the ones generally discarded by a radio or television station's assignment editor or on-air reporter. More often than not, these are the stories that the public relations officer spends more time thinking about to find an interesting way of presenting them. There is nothing duller to a reader than the annual budget shown by the standard visual presentation of the pie effect, in which the year's funds appear as a circle—with a slice for salaries, another for sewers, another for schools, and so on. Because it is the old way of doing things and the standard method taught most reporters, it is the one most often used. Is there a better way? One way might be to use human interest stories in the press to attempt to bring home dramatically the need for increasing public funds. Television, which is constantly searching for better visual means of presenting its news and public affairs, would be all too happy to film the principal sources of the needed revenue as background for the percentages and the money being allocated.

A few years ago a television station in a large port city used a huge floor map of the city's metropolitan area, with county lines, rivers, and harbors marked out, to explain to the viewers the needs of a metropolitan form of government and what the costs of filling these needs are. It is one of the better examples of telling a story that is extremely hard to illustrate in an original way.

REACHING THE MEDIA:
NEWSPAPERS VERSUS BROADCASTING

What are the major differences between the needs of newspapers and those of broadcasting?

Until the mid-sixties or thereabouts, the job of a public relations specialist was a relatively easy one for the most part, because newspapers were the chief beneficiaries of public relations efforts. Releases were always marked either "Immediate," or "Hold for release." Many newspapers, daily and weekly, simply struck out the word "Immediate," added a headline, and sent the public relations person's deathless prose off to the composing room, where it was cast into type and appeared in the next edition.

Some newspapers were, of course, too professional for this sort of thing—or they had a number of rewrite people on the payroll. Such newspapers would generally rewrite the first paragraph to give it a "today" approach and to give the rewrite staff something to do; then it would be sent to the composing room. In those days (perhaps 1955–60) you could fire a cannon in the meeting halls of the American Society of Newspaper Editors and rarely hit one who would insist that press releases, or "handouts," as they were popularly called, be rewritten.

The handout has since become the standard method of communication between the public relations specialist and the public that person wishes to reach.

About 1960, broadcasting was just beginning to discover that news was something other than a part of the programming it was forced to carry to satisfy the demands of the Federal Communications Commission. Then, in the early sixties, broadcasters suddenly found that news would sell. Not only would it sell, but people would watch. Then came the boom days of broadcast news which have continued until today. News departments of television stations grew from three and four people to staffs of sixty and seventy, and in the big cities even to a hundred or more individuals reporting, writing, producing, filming, processing, editing, and anchoring half-hour, hour, and even two hour or more newscasts—these last in the early evening.

Although left behind because of the various attributes of television news (film, videotape, and numerous other details that go into video programming), radio was not to be outdone. It came up with the concept of all-news radio, news and talk formats, and news on the hour and the half hour. Today, comparatively few of the five thousand or more radio stations in the country—from the largest to the smallest—fail to devote more than a fourth of their time to news and public affairs.

What this has meant is more staffing of news events. Full-time correspondents are covering

FIGURE 9–3   *Newspaper reporters at work. (Source: Courtesy of the Metropolitan Washington Council of Governments.)*

the activities of city halls, county buildings, municipal governments, and state capitals, and full-time reporters are in Washington reporting on the activities of senators and congressmen.

If we are to believe the polls that are taken more or less regularly in this country, more and more people are getting their basic news of the day from television. Those who are getting all they learn each day about news events from television may never read a newspaper, may read one only occasionally or may read one every day but only superficially. (Some figures on this subject can be found in Chapter 2.)

This situation places great burdens on two specialists: the television broadcaster and the public relations specialist. It is one thing for a newspaper with forty or more pages to fill to print the name of a new appointee to the roads commission or the county finance committee.

Generally, an item of this nature, unless the individual is of great importance in the community, would pass unnoticed or, at least, unmentioned by the radio or television station.

Releases are still the main means of passing along information to the media. While newspapers may have several editors to read them over for story ideas and information, most radio and television stations have only one assignment editor. In addition to communications with two or three—or even as many as eight or nine—radio cars during the day, this editor must listen to police and fire scanners, answer innumerable calls from those who regularly have contact with a newsroom, and check two or more wires for information and ideas. The assignment editors, even on the largest stations, do not have time to carefully read the two to three hundred releases that arrive each day. It is physically

FIGURE 9–4. *Broadcast reporters interview Council Chairman Sterling Tucker. (Source: Courtesy of the Metropolitan Washington Council of Governments.)*

impossible for the editor, and financially unsound for a news director, to hire the necessary people to read these thousands of words.

There are other ways of handling important news that a public relations specialist can utilize to solve this problem. In many cities there is a leased wire that carries the important events of the following day for the information of assignment editors, both newspaper and broadcast. It is, of course, a luxury that not every community can afford.

But there is one way in which a public relations person can be heard, and it is probably the least expensive and simplest form of communication. Through personal contact with the editors the public relations person can become more than a written release. The individual is a familiar voice on the phone, and, if he or she wants to take it a step further, a face that goes with the voice. Nothing invented in the field of public relations has ever been more effective than personal contact.

KEY CONTACTS

There are certain individuals in any newsroom who are valuable contacts to have in the media. The city or metropolitan editors and their assistants on the newspapers are generally the key people to contact for newspaper coverage. In broadcasting, news directors and assignment editors generally are responsible for the daily news budgets of their operations. They are extremely valuable sources in a newsroom. In fact, the more members of a news staff who are known to the public relations person, the better it is. Reporters and others who are either business contacts or friends on a personal basis, can be extremely valuable—not only for the placement of material in a publication or a newscast, but also from the standpoint of advice.

These key people can also be valuable sources of advice on handling a difficult story. Most editors have had considerable experience with the hard-to-write, hard-to-illustrate story and will be happy to give advice to the public relations person in such a case.

For example, what might appear to be a simple one-part story for a major newscast or a newspaper's edition could, in many cases, turn out to be the basis for a series of reports or articles. The end result of such a series is, more often than not, better understanding on the part of the public.

Every editor or news director has especially close and dependable contacts in the field of public relations. It is to the public relations person's advantage to help this closeness grow and prosper. Despite what some may think, the best way to do this is not through free meals or personal gifts. This practice in fact is widely frowned on today.

The long-range standards by which all news contacts are gauged inevitably are believability, honesty, and clarity. The contact to be avoided is always the one who promises more than he or she can deliver, or who overplays what is basically a nonstory, or who puts pressure on an editor by going to someone higher up in the organization.

The highly pressurized story that a reporter or cameraman may be forced to cover even though it may be a nonnews item has various names. The pressure stories that come down from those in authority over editors and news directors were probably best named when someone complained about having to go out and cover a "hammer job." An assignment that is worse than a hammer job, for example, double coverage of an event of personal interest to someone highly placed in a newspaper or broadcast station, is sometimes called a "golden hammer." Most editors and reporters take great exception to having such an assignment. If it comes from a public relations source who has bypassed them for someone higher up, that public relations source usually pays the price of his or her indiscretion later on. It is important that the public relations person maintain his or her credibility with editors and other contacts.

APPROACH AND COVERAGE

The personal approach is obviously much easier to achieve in a smaller community. However, even in the largest cities the best job is often done by the person working alone. The initial contacts with the media may be time-consuming in the beginning, but the long-range benefits are strong personal relations with the editors, trust, and, most important of all, the results that will get the job done.

Public relations—good public relations—is knowing the problems of the editor and being able to cope with them. It is knowing the deadlines of the paper or the station, when to call a news conference for maximum coverage and when not to call one.

Generally, early in the day or right after lunch are the best times, especially for television news operations. Because of the pressures of processing and editing film and laying out a half-hour or hour newscast, it is best to avoid late afternoons. Broadcast news departments are geared to handle last minute or fast-breaking stories, but interviews and news conferences of only general interest are usually best scheduled early in the day.

In the larger cities the question of overtime and lunch penalties plays a heavy role in the assignment editor's decision to cover or not to cover. Because of the huge cost of operating a news department in the larger cities—in excess of $1 million or more each year—expenses are generally watched carefully. If the story the public relations officer wants to see covered is big enough and newsworthy enough, he or she could probably expect good response from the media. But it is always best to schedule events early.

It is beneficial to bear in mind the fact that even though the two principal news outlets, newspapers and broadcasting, are different in their concepts and missions, there is intense rivalry between the two. Fairness with both is the key to ultimate success or failure.

It is important for public relations people to learn all they can about television news and how it operates. It is a far more discerning outlet than newspapers. A newspaper reporter with a pad and pencil can write about a dull personality who has a good story and the story loses nothing because of the source. The television camera cannot do this. An individual with a monotonous voice or an odd appearance gets no break on film or tape, and what he or she has to say—no matter how important—can be lost because of his or her inability to tell it well. This is a lesson that has been learned by many politicians in recent years. Appearance and style are all-important, and (unfortunate as this may be in the case of highly qualified and dedicated people whose television performance is poor) this is an important consideration when a spokesman is being selected.

When planning campaigns, when trying to explain complicated issues, or when needing more than the normal minute and a half to two minutes afforded most broadcast news clips, it is good to remember that most radio and television stations schedule half-hour programs devoted to community issues and needs. Knowing the producers and hosts of these programs can be as important as knowing the station's news director or assignment editor. It is still another method of telling a story.

Another outlet usually available to public relations specialists these days is the broadcast editorial. Many stations—again, because of licensing obligations and more often because of a sense of community involvement—broadcast their own editorials. Some broadcast them more often than others. Some editorials have more to say than others. But when it comes to community needs and attracting public attention to problems, the editorial is an additional outlet.

It is important to have the basic contacts with the person who writes the station editorials. That person may not always be the one who delivers them, but the editorial director or station manager more often than not is the individual who formulates the position to be taken. When the public relations specialist can couple a campaign in the newspapers with one on the air, with editorial backing in both media, he or she is doing the job exceedingly well. But this requires planning.

It is always best to keep human interest stories in mind. Human interest and reader interest go hand-in-hand. If a story, print or broadcast, is dull, it will not be read, listened to, or watched with any great care.

People are generally interested in items that have some semblance of appeal—from either a humorous or a dramatic standpoint. Obviously, not everything a public relations specialist must deal with is going to have either of these elements. But there is always a better way to tell a story, or to present one to a reporter, than by simply presenting a list of facts.

People like to be entertained; they also want to be given reasons. It is one thing to call a news conference to announce next year's budget or a tax increase or a reduction in staff—but the all-important thing is to tell why this is happening. Giving the reasons for such decisions is a way of generating support from those who are most important—the public.

Most reporters and editors in the media are sticklers for clarity. With air time and newsprint as scarce as they have become in recent times, it is necessary that items of public interest and importance be presented as clearly and succinctly, and with as little confusion, as possible. When people feel they have been misled, it is invariably the public relations person or department that pays the penalty in man-hours and frustration.

HONESTY AND ETHICS

Honesty with newsmen is like honesty with anyone else—it may not be expected but it is appreciated, and, in the long run, it pays dividends.

People in the news business expect their public relations contacts to be honest with them. This does not mean, however, that the public relations department of a local government should adopt a tell-all policy. At times this can be as harmful to important plans as willfully withholding information after it has become a matter of public record. And matters involving personnel discussions, land acquisition, or litigation are recognized as subjects which need not be disclosed publicly until they are concluded.

The public relations specialist for a company or a union would be extremely inept if he relayed details of secret negotiations to the news media before both sides had agreed on a settlement. Reporters do not expect to be given such information. The same is true of city and county government.

By the same token, trying to hide legitimate

public information is equally foolish. Once such an attempt is uncovered it has a tendency to snowball. As the snowball grows, credibility disappears. This sort of thing has ruined careers.

THE FAIRNESS DOCTRINE

If newspaper publishers so wish, they can do almost anything they want short of libeling someone. The question of libel and what it constitutes becomes broad-based in dealing with government agencies, whether on the local, state, or federal level.

More than enough damage can be done by half-reporting stories and facts. Under the guarantees of the First Amendment, a publisher is almost exempt from telling more of a story than he or she wishes to tell.

The same is not true of broadcasting. There are rules that govern the conduct of broadcasters. One is the Fairness Doctrine, which is widely adhered to in the industry. That doctrine decrees that if there are two sides to an issue both sides must be told. For better or for worse, as far as broadcasters are concerned, the Fairness Doctrine works to the benefit of those singled out for adverse attention and of the public which the broadcaster serves. It is the public relations person's "ace in the hole" in dealing with broadcast news people.

While the Fairness Doctrine is not foolproof protection, it does come as close as anything to ensuring at least an answer to a broadcast story in which there is some measure of doubt as to accuracy or completeness. It is not a device to be abused or overplayed. But if information is broadcast that contains erroneous material, or if it is blatantly one-sided on an important issue, or if an editorial has been aired that leads the public to believe only one side of a story, it is time to raise the question of fairness. (Equal time is often considered an inalienable right. This, in fact, is not the case. The equal time provisions are aimed at giving political candidates the same amount of air time as their opponents.)

Where the Fairness Doctrine is concerned, most station owners or managers care enough about their obligations and responsibilities to provide the opposing view to responsible parties who take issue with broadcast material. It is important to know that this provision exists. It is equally important to know when it should be brought to bear.

CONSUMER AFFAIRS

Another major change in journalism in recent decades has been the commitment made to the consumer by the mass media. Consumer interest and consumer affairs have led to entire new departments in newspapers, magazines, and broadcast stations, all of which are geared toward coping with the problems of the readers, listeners, and viewers. Staffs of ten or more have been assigned to finding out why a vacuum cleaner purchaser received a machine that was faulty or how one should bring legal action to bear on those who have been cheating the consumer.

Government, too, is beginning to discover that the citizen has other recourse to complaints short of legal action. This has brought a new breed of reporter into being—the consumer affairs correspondent. The city hall reporter and courthouse reporter are still doing their jobs, but the consumer affairs correspondent receives considerable attention today.

IN CONCLUSION

It is well to remember that what matters in local government public relations is communications. What public relations does is, in its essence, what the reporter, photographer, and editor do—it keeps the public informed of what is going on, and where and when and why and who is doing it, and how. The successful public relations officer, then, should combine knowledge of available resources and how to use them, tact, a sense of timing, honesty, and credibility.

Media Relations[1]

The purpose of this section is to answer the perennial question of how to work with the media. The answer begins with the decision to in fact *work with* the media.

All too often an organization's inability to achieve the public reputation and stature it seeks is due in large measure to poor press relations stemming from an attitude of stand-offishness or distrust or dislike, or all three. In contrast, the organization which enjoys excellent media relations usually is in that happy position because it does work with the media.

This does not require a large and highly professional full-time public relations staff. In fact, it does not require any public relations staff at all. It requires only that those who do work on a government's staff, in whatever capacity, have a positive attitude toward the local media. Experience shows that good relations with the media stem, in large part, from such a positive attitude.

There are techniques and mechanical procedures which can be employed to aid in good relations with the news media. Or, if relations are already good, the same techniques can make them even better.

But techniques and procedures are only the tools of implementation. The attitude should be there first—an attitude which says that working with the mass media is worth the effort because it involves the improvement of one's government. It should be an attitude which acknowledges that working with the mass media is an essential undertaking and an investment that will earn dividends.

Working with the media is complex, involving writing and talking every day of the week about technically difficult subjects. The range may cover air pollution, crime, drugs, transportation, water pollution, housing, computerized data, and that elusive subject called planning.

Working with the mass media is sensitive, with interests sometimes conflicting between what public relations officers *should* say to a reporter and what they would *like* to say, or even whether they want to talk to the reporter at all.

And it is around-the-clock, with every reporter and editor in town having access to one's name and home phone number and some of them bent on displaying that knowledge at 6:00 A.M. or midnight.

Servicing the Press

Next to a positive attitude toward the news media, the most important requirement is service; this applies to all media. The importance of using all available media outlets cannot be stressed too strongly.

The media should be serviced through a variety of means. One obvious way is through press releases, which should be sent to reporters, editors and columnists, the wire services, and professional publications. A special effort should be made to allow for the unique timing problems of weekly newspapers, as well as for their special role in the community.

But press releases are only one part of the public relations service, one that will be covered in more detail. The local government public relations office can also service the media by advising them of meetings, with full agendas mailed to them well in advance.

During these meetings, service again becomes the byword. Reporters should be given copies of all reports and background papers to be considered at the meeting. The appropriate elected officials and key staff members who can speak intelligently on specific items should be lined up in advance for more detailed comments to the press when appropriate.

This kind of service should not be limited to these specific events, lest the effort become sporadic in its effectiveness because it is sporadic in its application. Servicing the media should be an everyday occupation. And it should be candid.

The same holds true for meetings and other events. If they ask whether a meeting looks routine and, in fact, it does, it is advisable to tell them. They will appreciate it and will be grateful. And when, at a later date, they are told that a meeting looks like a good story, they will know it is true and will probably cover that meeting.

Media contacts should hear from the public relations officer on ideas for features and on suggestions for editorials and pictures. In large metropolitan areas, reporters and editors cannot always keep up with developments in local government and may not really know of some of the good feature possibilities therein. Or some of these matters may be too complicated or unclear for the reporter to recognize them as good features. But if the public relations officer tells the reporter about an idea that the reporter did not know about, he or she may score with a good feature—and may be points ahead with that reporter or editor in the future.

This is especially true of the editorial writers —not just the ones for the newspapers, but those in the radio and television stations as well. They should hear frequently of possibilities for editorials on the local government. When they do, that government benefits. Beyond that, a priceless resource for editorial support is being developed.

A frequent complaint about the news media is that "we can never seem to get our story across, and even when we do, the articles somehow lose their meaning when printed or broadcast." Anyone in government public relations can identify with that problem.

Whether that problem can ever really be eliminated is doubtful, but it can be minimized through candor and communication. If the public relations person levels with reporters and editors, they will level with him or her. That is where candor comes in. Communications can help to minimize distortion of a story if it is kept simple, if the message is translated into the everyday language of a reporter and his readers. This can go a long way toward avoiding any accidental fracturing of facts.

On more complicated stories—budget submissions, new programs, referenda, or bond proposals—the reporters may be called in and given the story ahead of time on a hold-for-release basis. Then they have ample time to digest the complicated material, to ask questions before going back to their offices, and to telephone with questions which occur while they are writing their stories.

It sounds simple and obvious, and it is, but it is amazing how seldom people allow time for the reporter to read and understand and write a story about something which scores of other people have been preparing for months. This extra effort, simple and obvious though it is, will go miles toward ensuring complete and accurate reporting of a story.

Servicing Radio and Television

Radio news is nonwritten and brief. There is little reporter coverage of events, although a strong station may have some reporters on the street who attend meetings and cover breaking news events. Instead the station depends on wire service copy, press releases, and telephone tape interviews.

Consequently, radio stations need to know when something is taking place so they can cover it if they have reporters available. If radio is going to cover, it is important that an elected official or staff member be prepared to deliver a brief statement for taping by the reporter or over the telephone. This should be no more than two or three sentences that the official can read effectively. If a speech is part of the event or meeting, the most appropriate two or three sentences should be underlined for radio quoting. The underlined copy should be given to the radio reporter or station and the speaker should pause during the speech—before and after the underlined material—for the convenience of editing at the radio station.

Television can be one of the best allies in transmitting information. Where radio is obviously a verbal medium, television is just as obviously a visual medium. Consequently, much thinking about the use of television to tell a story should be geared to visual materials: original artwork, maps, charts, graphs, photographs, slides.

Again, public relations officers would be wise to approach television people with the emphasis on an opportunity to fill their needs, not a plea to have their own needs taken care of. Television people seek good news coverage and good public affairs programming and will respond to good available material to meet those needs.

Most television stations have at least one film crew, and usually more, working the street daily. They also have someone who spends all or most of his or her time assigning crew and reporters on a day-to-day basis. It is wise to find out who that person is, what his or her deadlines are, and how far ahead he or she must be told about a story in order to get a film crew there. Also, it is advisable to get to know the structure of the television newsroom—who decides which stories are given coverage, who actually writes the news, and what the deadlines are for getting on the air with either film or nonfilm stories.

The need to blend local stories, wire service

stories, film materials, and syndicated or off-the-network materials makes putting together a television news program far more complicated than a radio news program. This means there is a greater need to understand the process. A brief tour of the newsroom and a review of the news gathering process might provide a better understanding of what can be done to service the needs of the broadcast media. For a simplified presentation of the flow of radio and television news, see Figures 9–5a and 9–5b.

DAILIES AND WEEKLIES

Papers in each category have their own timing requirements. Morning papers begin processing the news in mid-morning and continue through the afternoon and evening. Afternoon papers start much earlier in the morning (around 6:00 A.M.) and continue until late afternoon.

Weekly papers generally are published on a Thursday or Friday and have a copy deadline of Tuesday. A story which in announced on Wednesday comes on the worst day for a Thursday or Friday weekly, immediately limiting its chances of success in the weekly paper.

Where the dailies are concerned, morning papers (A.M.'s) get the break on the bulk of the news by the nature of things. Most news except for crime and sports occurs during the day, and the A.M.'s are still in business beyond the close of the business day. But the earlier the better, even for the morning papers. Stories which are already in the city room stand a better chance of survival than those coming in just ahead of deadline.

A story intended for a morning paper stands its best chance if the paper receives it by noon. For the afternoon papers (P.M.'s) the chances are best if the story reaches them by 8:00 A.M. If the story reaches the afternoon papers in late afternoon or early evening of the day before, it is better still. For a simple presentation of the flow of news in a newspaper operation, see Figure 9–6.

Press releases which are marked "For immediate release" will break to the advantage of the morning papers. Such press releases, with no time restrictions, generally are mailed, and the mail arrives in the morning after at least one deadline of the afternoon paper has passed.

On major stories, it is a good practice to divide announcements as evenly as possible between morning and afternoon release times. The people on the afternoon paper are realistic enough to know they can never show an exact 50–50 split with their morning competitors in the major announcements from the government office, but they will hope for—and look for—an indication that that the government is making an honest attempt to give them the break on some of its stories. And in those regions where the morning and afternoon papers both have Sunday morning editions, it's a good practice to time some announcements for release to the Sunday morning papers, thus keeping everyone happy and increasing the chances of success.

RELEASES FOR RADIO AND TELEVISION

It is important to be familiar with the deadlines each station has for its various news shows. If there are a number of stations, it is a good idea to rate them as to importance in terms of coverage area and audience size and then to work down the list. It is essential to accommodate the reporters and news shows, meeting the deadlines of the most important ones first.

Releases aimed at the Sunday morning papers should be marked for release at 5:00 or 6:00 P.M. Saturday. In this way, a story may be used on the Saturday evening television news—with a good chance for success because the timing shown on the press release will tell the television news people that the story will be fresh when they use it on Saturday evening.

Stories intended for coverage on television as well as in the papers should be timed for early in the day, for noon, if at all possible. And stations should be alerted to the story early that morning at the latest—the day before, if possible. That tells the station's assignment editor that the story is coming up the next day, and he or she can put it down for a reporter and a camera crew.

Television news coverage requires advance notice, and it also requires that the announcement, when made, be made early enough in the day to allow time for film processing and editing back at the station in time for the reporter to be able to go on the air with it that evening. That is why announcements should be scheduled by midday. Any story that breaks after 2:00 P.M. will have to be good to make the evening news that same day.

PRESS KITS AND CONFERENCES

Even with advance notice, a release is not enough if a story about to be announced is complicated or could be misunderstood, or is one whose significance could be lost.

For this reason, many organizations have found that it pays to have background material on hand for briefing. If a major report is being announced, it is wise to have copies of the full report on hand. Equally important is a brief summary, written in simple English, in a brief, punchy format. It should answer the following questions, and can even be written in short paragraphs, with each paragraph headed this way:

What it is
What it means
Who did it
Findings
Recommendations
How much it cost
What happens next.

If television people are expected, necessary provision should be made; there should be something on which they can put their microphones (a lectern); an area in which they can set up their lights, near enough to a wall outlet to plug in; an area in which to set up the camera, out of the way because there will be a lot of trunks and carrying equipment scattered about.

When the crew arrives, they should be told about the arrangements and asked if they have any additional requirements. While the equipment is being set up, the reporter should be given a copy of what is going to happen—an agenda, a text of remarks, the report which is being released, etc. The public relations officer should point out the key parts and important points, and should offer to arrange a brief session with the reporter and the speaker in which

the speaker can say the things that are important for a film clip. Otherwise, the choice of what is covered will be left to a newsman back in the newsroom whose only knowledge of the story is the film running through the editing machine. Again, it is important to remember that the reporter and crew are trying their best to get the right coverage of the event—they will welcome any help.

Attractive, easy-to-read, large visuals should be on display at the press conference, preferably in more than one color and preferably on a light blue background to reduce the glare and washout which a white background creates for the television cameras. Horizontal slides picturing the display may also be helpful and may save time for television. (Vertical visuals are unsuitable for television needs.) If the same visuals can be made available in black-and-white, glossy, eight by ten inch prints for the newspapers, so much the better. Any story with good visual material stands a better chance of making television news than a comparable story that has nothing going for it but the anchorman reading copy.

And in all this advance preparation for the press conference, it is important to remember to brief the people presiding. The elected official or executive director should not only know the subject thoroughly, he or she should also have the benefit of the senior staff member most familiar with the subject. This staffer should be available in the room in case the person presiding needs to turn to him or her for elaboration, but the staff in most instances should not be a part of the press conference itself in front of the cameras. As further insurance, the official presiding should be told beforehand what questions to expect. Not all questions at a press conference are predictable, but many of them are. At a typical press conference, depending on what is being announced, some or all of the following questions may be asked:

1. What made this necessary?
2. What makes you think this will work when other efforts have failed?
3. How much did you say this cost, and where did the money come from?

FIGURE 9–5a. *The flow of news: radio and television. At 9:00 A.M., city manager schedules noon press conference; 12:00 noon, at press conference, manager's statement is recorded for radio and television, followed by interviews; 12:30 P.M., highlights of press conference begin appearing on radio newscasts.*

4. How will this directly benefit the people of our community?
5. Isn't it a fact that this problem is so big and so complex that no one really knows the answer?
6. What happens if what you're announcing today fails?
7. Doesn't this duplicate some work already going on here?
8. Are you doing this because you think it's a good idea, or just because the federal government says you have to do it?
9. What do you think will happen to your recommendations?
10. What are you asking the local governments to do now?
11. What can I, as an individual, do about this problem?
12. Were any citizens involved in these recommendations?

There is this added point about press conferences: the public relations officer should not call them unless he or she has a solid story. There are few experiences more disastrous and embarrassing than a press conference attended by one reporter—who then does not write a story because the press conference wasn't worth one.

WRITING PRESS RELEASES

Press releases should be written in simple, straightforward language, the way the story would read in the paper the next day. They should answer the same questions as those listed earlier, and any others which may be anticipated. A blanket release can be issued for all media. Most editors will edit to suit their style and length needs.

Most press releases can be marked "For immediate release." When there are particular time elements involved, the timing factors previously described should be remembered and applied to the greatest extent possible. A good story can be knocked down—or out—by a mistake in deciding when to release it.

Press releases should be short, preferably one page, and always double spaced on lively letterhead which both gives the necessary facts about the local government and carries some type of bold lettering which tells an editor that this is news. The necessary facts which should

FIGURE 9–5b. *At 1:00 P.M., television reporter and crew return to station to write story; 3:00 P.M., film is edited; 5:30 P.M., story appears on evening news.*

be found in the letterhead include the "name" of the government, the full address (including city, state, and ZIP code), and the telephone number (including area code).

It is not necessary to place a headline on the press release, although there is nothing wrong with this practice. Instead, it is better to use the release time as the heading, along with today's date. At the end of the story, the name, title, and telephone number of the official to contact for more information should be listed.

If the story is not for immediate release, specify at the top of the release when it can be used, for example: *Hold for release until 6 P.M. Saturday, September 30, 1976.*

Reporters and editors will honor this in line with established rules of their profession. The public relations officer should be sure, however, to have a *legitimate reason* for holding the release until a certain time. If not, newsmen will begin to wonder why the material cannot be used immediately on receipt and may feel that this news operation is not as professional in its execution as it should be.

If one paper or broadcasting station breaks a release date, the embargo is off. Others are then free to use the story immediately. This will happen occasionally but not often, and when it does, these are grounds for protesting vigorously to the senior officials of the paper or station involved. It should not occur more than once from the same source. If it does, again these are grounds for protest and for going as high as necessary until an editor is reached who will see to it that the condition is corrected immediately.

Two other points should be made about press releases. First, while press releases can be an excellent way of informing the media, they should not be overused. Governments should try to send out releases only when they have a legitimate reason and a potentially newsworthy story. There are always certain agencies that get a reputation with the media for sending out "daily" press releases which are of little news value. If this becomes a practice, the government's releases may be tossed in the circular file without being read.

This leads to the second point. On important stories, when it is important to have the media present at a certain meeting or press conference, press releases should be followed up with

FIGURE 9–6. *The flow of news: newspapers. At 9:00 A.M., city official and staff brief reporters on forthcoming budget; 10:00 A.M., budget is submitted to council; 11:00 A.M., reporter writes budget story; 1:00 P.M., story is edited; 2:30 P.M., the presses roll; 5:30 P.M., the public reads the story.*

a phone call a few days before to be sure the recipients are aware of time, place, and purpose and will be sending a reporter.

PUBLIC SERVICE BROADCASTING

Despite a tendency to dismiss public service broadcasting as "a waste of time," it can be a rich source of exposure in efforts to spotlight specific problems, and programs leading to their solution, or to generate public support and understanding on a more general basis for the work of a government. It all depends on the subject and how well it is presented.

Radio and television stations are required by regulations of the Federal Communications Commission to devote a certain percentage of their broadcast time to items in the public interest. This is one reason for those Sunday half-hour programs on public issues. The producers of these local programs are always looking for items and guests, but the items must be current and the guests should be prominent.

If public relations officers can convince the producer of a weekend interview show that they have a newsworthy subject coming in for major discussion in the community they have a chance at getting the story told on one of these programs. And the chances will be strengthened if public relations officers can assure producers that they can come up with a prominent local official to be interviewed. The radio news director or television producer should be approached with a clear idea of program content, for example:

Here are our ten most pressing problems. We have committees and task forces working on each of these problem areas, and we could provide you with the chairman of each of those groups, plus one of our professional staff members, to discuss each of the ten areas. We could review the problems, discuss possible alternative solutions, and discuss what specific work is being done toward solving the problems.

Public service programs often have spin-off benefits. The station will alert the daily press that a government representative will discuss this timely item, and the papers may cover the show and write a story for the following day on what the guest had to say. The station itself will frequently run excerpts from the interview on its Sunday evening television and radio news, and again Monday morning.

In this connection, educational television can also offer valuable opportunities for getting a story out to the community. It should never be assumed, however, that these stations, because they are noncommercial, will broadcast everything suggested. They have their own time requirements and their own financial problems. Despite these restrictions, educational television stations are completely responsive to the needs of the community and their opportunity to meet some of these needs by working with governments in focusing public attention on the issues. Both commercial television and educational television offer great opportunities in this respect, and both of these segments of the broadcast industry have shown that their ranks are rich in men of good public conscience who will listen to ideas and act on those which appeal to them.

All of the same things can be said about radio and the weekly radio interview programs. In many cases, the Sunday television interview is rebroadcast later that evening over the station's radio affiliate. Those radio stations which operate independent of any television connection broadcast their own public service programming, with the same concerns and standards. They should not be overlooked.

UNFAVORABLE STORIES

A question asked in every government office from time to time is, "What do we do about this story?" The answer generally is, "Nothing." Stories critical of a government or a specific project are usually passing things.

But what if the story could prove a disaster? Or what if it seems to be part of a deliberate pattern on the part of either the reporter or his or her paper or station? What courses of action are available?

Several avenues are open. In the case of a newspaper, there is always the letter to the editor. If choosing such a course, get the letter off immediately, keep it short (three or four brief paragraphs at the most), and show both the name and title of the official in whose name the letter is sent.

Several factors should be remembered about this approach. One is that letters to the editor do not always show up in the paper. The paper can ignore a letter if it chooses to. Or it can edit it to fit, without changing its substance. This latter fact should be kept in mind when the letter is being written. Another factor to keep in mind is that the paper, even though it may run the letter in full and unedited form, also has the entire editorial page left in which to fire back. This sobering fact accounts for the high casualty rate between the original idea for a letter to the editor and the decision to go through with it.

It is often even more effective—far more—to visit or talk with the offending reporter or his or her editor. If public relations officers have built a base of respect stemming from candor, they can approach the paper or the station with the knowledge that they will probably be listened to. One of the main purposes in calling attention to a bad story is to make sure it doesn't happen again. This is where the personal phone call or visit will pay far greater dividends than the letter to the editor.

It is possible that the editor will react by suggesting that the public relations officer write a "letter to the editor" which the editor will be sure to put into the paper, and, because of this call or visit, the editor will see the incident doesn't happen again.

OTHER STAFF MEMBERS AND THE PRESS

Any organization needs a written staff policy on who speaks to the news media and who doesn't and what is said and what is not. If the government's policy is an intelligent and objective one, the reporters will appreciate it because it will streamline their job of getting information. From the government's standpoint, it will help ensure that the information going out to the media goes from responsible senior staff members familiar with the subject and its policy implications. This will minimize the possibility of unfavorable stories.

Here are some guidelines which any staff can follow. These could be reissued from time to time.

1. Professional employees need not be required to clear every contact with the media, or any statements to them, in advance. If the practice has the chief administrator's approval, professionals can proceed under an arrangement in which they are free to answer questions on matters related to their own projects.
2. In granting this authorization, precaution is advisable. It is well to emphasize to professionals that they should be extremely careful that information which they give the media is 100 percent accurate. In every case, accuracy should be accompanied by complete discretion. This is essential not only because of the sensitivities frequently involved but also because a public comment, especially where radio and television are concerned, often cannot be corrected if it proves inaccurate or indiscreet.
3. Ground rules can also include the reminder to staff members that they should not answer questions of policy. Likewise, staff recommendations which have not yet been acted upon are usually treated as information not for release at the present time.

4. Chief administrators could also include an arrangement in the ground rules for media contacts allowing for some sort of reporting system so that they or their information officer can be kept informed of who on the staff is maintaining media contacts, what the subjects are, and what is being said. This is not a gag rule, especially since permission is not required before the contact is made or the statement given. This is simply asking to be kept abreast of what information is going out of the organization to the media, who is giving it out, and what the information is. This is reasonable and can be helpful knowledge, particularly when in-depth questions from the media indicate that the reporter is preparing an analysis either of the government or of one of its projects.

CONCLUSION

The media can be very useful tools. If brought into the development of a program from the beginning, the press can help bring government issues to the attention of the public, describe alternatives, obtain citizen contributions, and develop support for implementation once a plan or program has been developed.

When a government begins to receive any or all of these types of coverage, it is working with the media. This brings the discussion back to the beginning of this section and to the basis of the entire relationship with the news media: the decision to *work with* the media.

The media have been discussed in this chapter from two broad points of view. First, following a brief history of broadcast journalism, they have been considered as entities with which the local government public relations operation interacts. Aspects of this interaction that have been treated in detail are: presentation of news; media relations defined; newspapers versus broadcasting as media; public relations contacts in the media; approach and coverage needed for the media; honesty and ethics; the Fairness Doctrine; and consumer affairs.

The second part of the chapter has dealt with media relations from a "how to do it" viewpoint, encompassing: servicing the press and broadcasting; types of newspapers; press re-

leases; press kits and conferences; public service broadcasting; and the handling of unfavorable stories. A brief conclusion terminates this
section of the chapter.

The present chapter has introduced reporting and the media in some detail. Chapter 10
is concerned with the handling of a particular
aspect: special reports and events.

---

[1] This section of the present chapter is excerpted from
William H. Gilbert, "Media Relations," in REGIONAL COUN-
CIL COMMUNICATIONS: A GUIDE TO ISSUES AND TECHNIQUES
(Washington, D.C.: National Association of Regional
Councils, 1979), pp. 34–41.

10

Special Reports and Events

A KEY ELEMENT in any complete local or regional public relations program is the practice of issuing special publications as yet another means of conveying information to the citizens of the community. This function is both necessary and desirable. It is necessary because an informed citizenry is required if the people are to make intelligent decisions, through the electoral process, on such matters as bond questions, charter amendments, various other public policy issues, and the selection of their governing officials. The function of issuing special publications is desirable as well, because such publications can be instrumental in enhancing the prospect of a program reaching its objectives.

These same two characteristics apply to such special events as press conferences for major announcements, dedications of significant construction projects, visits by VIPs, and similar newsworthy occasions. These, too, can be said to be necessary as a means of informing the public of what a government is doing, and they can be said to be desirable as a means of increasing the chances that programs will accomplish what they were intended to accomplish.

In addition, the practice of repeatedly issuing relevant, substantive, attractive publications and conducting significant special events puts the public relations officer and his or her governmental organization clearly and indisputably on record as doing everything possible to ensure that information is getting out to the citizens often and through every possible vehicle.

This practice, obviously, is in addition to the public relations officer's work with the media

in disseminating as much news as possible about day-to-day activities through the daily press, the weekly papers, and the local radio and television stations. That extremely important responsibility and function has been covered in considerable depth in Chapter 9.

The present chapter opens with a detailed discussion of reports as publications of various kinds: after a definition of the audience for these materials, and of credibility and professionalism in the preparation of such materials, the following types of reports are discussed: annual reports; special reports; newsletters; and other reports.

Reporting in person is dealt with next, in terms of the importance of careful preparation, the correct use of visual aids, and the promotion of speaker engagements. The last part of the discussion is devoted to special events. The chapter ends with a brief conclusion and summary.

Publications

WHO IS THE AUDIENCE?

One of the first steps in producing any publication is a conscious decision on what the local government wants the publication to say. Not the words themselves: that is part of *how* to say it. But *what* to say? What story does the government want to relate? What message does it want to convey to the reader? Then the question to be answered is: What will the audience be for this particular publication? The general public, as in the case of an annual report? The New York bonding houses, as in the case of a supplemental publication to aid in a bond issue? The youth of the community, as with a feature publication prepared for distribution through the schools? This is a central question, because all too often what has seemed to the people who prepared it to be an outstanding publication is not really outstanding at all because it missed its mark. And it missed its mark because the people who produced it forgot one guiding rule: You are not your audience. Someone else is. Local government publications should be prepared with this and other such considerations in mind.

The preparation of publications is covered in considerable depth in Chapter 11, which deals with specifics on publications planning, development, and production and contains detailed discussions of such areas as: writing the publication, designing it, preparing the layout, drafting the specifications, producing the publication, and distributing it, and also describes types of publications, typography, composition methods, printing processes, etc.

CREDIBILITY

However, Chapter 11 will be only a reading exercise unless other factors are borne in mind. One is credibility. This has always been an essential ingredient in any government publication. Today, it is more so than ever, with the growing skepticism about government at all levels, and with opinion polls indicating that all too many Americans no longer believe what government, and not just national government, tells them. Any publication which strains this credibility further could be a disaster for a government and its programs.

Credibility in this case means giving an accurate impression. There is a world of difference, for example, between an annual report that says that the rate of increase in certain categories of crime decreased in the past year and a report that says (or comes close to saying) that last year the government solved the crime problem. If the publication says, or implies, that the air pollution problem is nearly solved, the government is in trouble with a reader who knows that yesterday his or her pollution-induced allergy was particularly troublesome.

Credibility as regards this type of problem takes on perhaps an even greater importance for councils of governments. The very reason for the existence of these organizations is to help local governments cope with those problems that cross the city limits and the county line. Thus, almost by definition, these organizations deal almost exclusively with complex issues. No such organization dares issue an annual report that implies that it is solving, for example, the traffic, air pollution, crime, or housing problems.

If, however, the annual report says that the organization is beginning a planning program aimed at producing solutions to these problems, or that it is *working toward* solutions, or that it has undertaken certain specific projects —such as an express bus experiment, or an air pollution monitoring network, or an allocation formula for distributing federal housing funds on a fair share basis, then that is another matter. In the latter case, the government is "telling it like it is." The government is also telling its readers that it is really doing something, that it is working on their behalf, and that it is beginning to make some progress. In this way, credibility remains intact and even grows.

PROFESSIONALISM

The quality of the writing in each of a government's publications is as vital as that in the daily newspaper. After all, the publication consists only of the writing, the layout, and the photographs and/or artwork. The quality of any affects the success of all. In writing, quantity—both in words and in syllables—is too often mistaken for quality.

The message need not be long, and neither need the words. The simplest writing is almost always the best writing. A famous boxing referee, in giving his last-minute instructions to two fighters in a nationally broadcast bout, deviated from the traditional final words, ". . . and may the best man win." Instead, he outdid himself, saying, ". . . and may the better participant emerge triumphant." That story is still told—and it's a true one. If a government's reports are written in a like manner, they, too, can become the subject of jokes.

The same insistence on professionalism should be applied to the layout, artwork, and photographs of every publication. This will occasionally pose dilemmas—especially when a government wants to produce a lively looking publication but must avoid the "slick, Madison Avenue" appearance that in turn creates the impression that too much of the taxpayers' money has been spent. This can be done—and is being done by many—with discretion and common sense. Avoiding the too-expensive look doesn't mean using poor photographs, or a layout that discourages the reader because it looks too heavy and, to quote a common complaint, because "it looks as if it will take too long to read."

The information officer for a county government was in Washington, D.C., several years ago, visiting a press secretary to one of the cabinet members. The press secretary, who was leafing through the county's annual report, looked up and said, "This is hard to believe. You're putting out publications that look as if you actually want people to read them."

That tells the whole story of design and makeup, as well as writing quality. Here was a top government official, himself a former newspaperman and public relations consultant, who was accustomed to being discouraged as everyone else when he picked up the average government publication. Specifics on preparing publications that are lively and attractive are given in considerable detail in Chapter 11.

THE ANNUAL REPORT

The annual report continues to be the mainstay publication of many local governments and regional organizations. In the case of local governments, publication of an annual report is frequently required by law. Annual reports have undergone vast changes in the last decade, with more emphasis on employing current practices followed in the private sector to enhance their readability and thus their effectiveness in what has come to be called "creating the right image." Tables and pie charts no longer dominate the annual report, and the detailed financial data are often transferred to a separate financial report.

This last item is worthy of amplification. The successful annual report—or any other type of publication, for that matter—avoids the potentially fatal flaw of mixing two different and sometimes even conflicting types of publications into one. There is, as mentioned earlier, a substantial difference between an annual report and a financial report—or between a county history and a bond prospectus. That difference should be kept in mind and should be reflected in the publication. The fact that it is borne in mind increasingly in most of today's governmental annual reports is the reason why graphs and pie charts and the like are going down in number and prominence. That, in turn, is why annual reports are better looking —and better received—today than ever before. Some examples of well-designed annual reports are given in Figures 10–1 to 10–7.

Those organizations and agencies that have made the change to the "new look" find it is worth many times the additional cost in dollars and manpower—if, in fact, there is any greater cost at all in either category. Whether there is or not, the greater difference is not so much in the cost as in whether the reader looks at the report or at least scans it. If a government's publications are still vintage 1950, with bar charts and graphs and pie slices showing how much money went for capital construction projects in the past year, chances are the reader will give them literally only a few seconds. However, if an annual report is modern and appealing the reader will at least leaf through its pages, stopping occasionally when attracted by an interesting subject, a dramatic photo, an unusual headline. And if it is really effective, the reader may even read it.

The move toward more attractive, more readable reports is reflected in the concerns of those people producing these reports. More and more attention is being given to questions of size, paper stock, inks, type of binding, use of colors, and kind and number of illustrations. In earlier years, many of these subjects never arose and texts were considerably longer and weightier, with the writer generally assuming that the reader was as intensely interested in the subject as he or she was.

The new reports are written with the reader more in mind, from the taxpayer's point of view rather than from the city's, county's, or regional council's. The rigidly departmentalized report,

KIPDA 1974 Kentuckiana Regional Planning and Development Agency
Annual Report

208 South Fifth Street, Suite 106
Louisville, Kentucky 40202

FIGURE 10–1. *Annual report cover in black, white, and silver.* (*Source: Kentuckiana Regional Planning and Development Agency,* ANNUAL REPORT 1974, *Louisville, Ky.: Kentuckiana Regional Planning and Development Agency, 1974, cover.*)

with information of interest only to the most avid follower of local government affairs, has given way to a *service-oriented* report. A central theme ties the subjects together into a concise, coherent whole, rather than a disjointed collection of reports from individual departments whose various activities are never clearly related to those of other departments.

Service-Oriented Reports. As is the case with the overall public relations program, the truly effective and convincing annual report is one based on the services which a local government or regional organization is providing to its citizens. If the report describes how the agency is

organized—in language suitable for the agency's budget document—and rattles off statistics like a stock market report, it will miss what should be its target: making people want to read the report so that they can understand and appreciate the value of the services the agency is giving them.

The report should outline the progress, during the past twelve-month period, in those activities that have made the community a better place in which to live and work. That is the point the annual report should drive home. It should concern itself with the issues and goals of its own community and the services and

TO SERVE THE REGION

Its People ...

Planning and providing services to the region's people is a responsibility of KIPDA that is administered through the divisions of human resources and aging, emergency medical service, and research and information. Many services are channeled through a variety of community-based organizations whose main functions are to provide direct service to any residents in the KIPDA region.

HUMAN RESOURCES. In the area of human resources, 1974 saw the reorganization of an advising committee composed of consumer representatives and service providers. The committee has established regional priorities against which A-95 review applications can be measured. In addition, human resource planning efforts in KIPDA were linked with efforts in the state and 9-county region through regular meetings of state human resource planners and an interagency council.

Efforts in the area of grantsmanship paid off with the awarding of a grant to Henry and Shelby counties for youth service bureaus and in Oldham and Shelby counties with a 50-50 state matching funds grant for tourism promotion.

The year also saw the completion of a comprehensive day care study conducted in Bullitt, Henry, Oldham, Shelby, Spencer, and Trimble counties through a grant from Title IVA of the Social Security Act. This study included an extensive inventory of all day care services and facilities and an assessment of need for these services.

Initial plans were formulated this year in the area of manpower services. It is anticipated that by early 1975 an ancillary manpower council

will be functioning and addressing needs and priorities in the planning of manpower programs for Bullitt, Henry, Oldham, Shelby, Spencer, and Trimble counties.

AGING. As of July 1, 1974, KIPDA became an area agency on aging and as such received a block grant of $295,065 for programs for the elderly under Title III of the Older Americans Act.

The first major function of the agency was to submit a plan of service for FY 75. This plan included an identification of funding priorities and program applications of those agencies selected to operate aging programs. The services extended under the programs include outreach, information and referral, counseling, escort and transportation, recreation, homemaker-home health, and preventative health. The programs are operated in Henry, Jefferson, Oldham, Shelby, Spencer, and Trimble counties.

The KIPDA staff provided ongoing technical assistance to the Metropolitan Social Services Department nutrition program. Through a coordination of

transportation and outreach services, many Jefferson County seniors were able to participate in the group meals.

As a result of the tornado disasters of April 1974, the staff was called on to plan for $36,152 in the Disaster Aging Program. Those persons over 60 who were victims of the tornadoes received transportation and escort services from the Red

10

FIGURE 10–2. *Double-page spread from an annual report, that is well designed and that shows an interesting use of photographs to back up the text. (Source: same as* FIGURE 10–1., *pp. 10–11.)*

11

FIGURE 10–2. (*continued.*)

Transportation

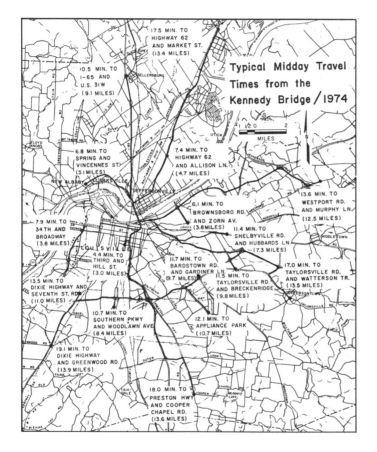

179 accidents in 1973 and I-264 and Newburg Road with 130 accidents.

COMPUTER MAPPING: Refinements during 1974 now allow KIPDA's computer to map any data that are collected and referenced to street address through use of a computerized geographic reference system called DIME (Dual Independent Map Encoding). A sample map may be found on the inside back cover of this report.

Short-range Programming.
During 1974 the Federal-aid Highway Act of 1973 gave KIPDA increased responsibility for promoting implementation of transportation plans through short-term programming. KIPDA's systems planning program will produce a short-term **Transportation Improvement Program** in addition to the previously required long-range transportation plan. Highway and other transportation improvements must be included in the short-term program in order to become eligible for federal aid.

Other procedural changes were proposed during 1974 by Kentucky and Indiana in state "action plans" that offer detailed descriptions of the steps necessary to carry a highway improvement from initial conception to actual construction. Following the systems planning phase, the stages in highway development are: 1. advance planning or project location study; 2. project planning or design; 3. right-of-way acquisition; and 4. contracts and actual construction.

These procedural changes are being implemented by KIPDA in its role of project review and provision of planning data necessary to agencies which implement specific

18

FIGURE 10–3. *Double-page spread from an annual report, showing an interesting and well-designed combination of text, photography, and line drawing. (Source: same as* FIGURE 10–1, *pp. 18–19.)*

improvements. The time required to carry a single improvement from start of advance studies to opening the improved facility to traffic may range from five to eleven years depending upon the complexity of the improvement.

Project Summary. Major highway projects entering the final stages of development or completed during

1974 include construction on Interstate 265 connecting Interstates 64 and 65 in southern Indiana; intersection improvements in New Albany including Daisy Lane and Green Valley Road, Silver and Elm Streets, and other locations in downtown New Albany; in Kentucky, Jefferson Freeway from LaGrange Road to Westport Road; New Cut Road from Kenwood Drive to Southern Parkway; and Cannons and Dutchmans Lane from Taylorsville Road north to I-64. In addition, $8 million was programmed for early acquisition of right-of-way for the Jefferson Freeway from I-65 to Preston Highway; and $2.8 million was approved by the TPC for upgrading of Hikes Lane from Bardstown Road to Taylorsville Road.

19

FIGURE 10–3. (*continued.*)

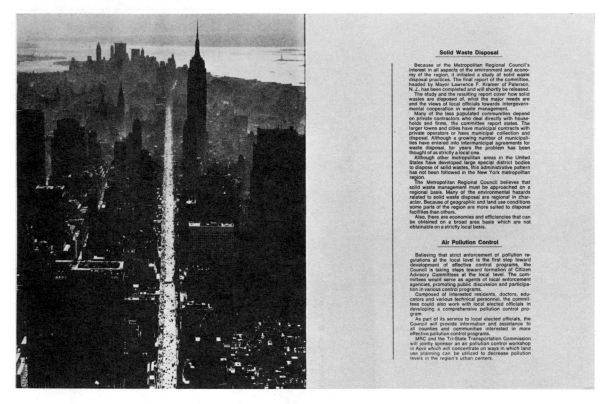

Solid Waste Disposal

Because of the Metropolitan Regional Council's interest in all aspects of the environment and economy of the region, it initiated a study of solid waste disposal practices. The final report of the committee, headed by Mayor Lawrence F. Kramer of Paterson, N. J., has been completed and will shortly be released.

The study and the resulting report cover how solid wastes are disposed of, what the major needs are and the views of local officials towards intergovernmental cooperation in waste management.

Many of the less populated communities depend on private contractors who deal directly with households and firms, the committee report states. The larger towns and cities have municipal contracts with private operators or have municipal collection and disposal. Although a growing number of municipalities have entered into intermunicipal agreements for waste disposal, for years the problem has been thought of as strictly a local one.

Although other metropolitan areas in the United States have developed large special district bodies to dispose of solid wastes, this administrative pattern has not been followed in the New York metropolitan region.

The Metropolitan Regional Council believes that solid waste management must be approached on a regional basis. Many of the environmental hazards related to solid waste disposal are regional in character. Because of geographic and land use conditions some parts of the region are more suited to disposal facilities than others.

Also, there are economies and efficiencies that can be obtained on a broad area basis which are not obtainable on a strictly local basis.

Air Pollution Control

Believing that strict enforcement of pollution regulations at the local level is the first step toward development of effective control programs, the Council is taking steps toward formation of Citizen Advisory Committees at the local level. The committees would serve as agents of local enforcement agencies, promoting public discussion and participation in various control programs.

Composed of interested residents, doctors, educators and various technical personnel, the committees could also work with local elected officials in developing a comprehensive pollution control program.

As part of its service to local elected officials, the Council will provide information and assistance to all counties and communities interested in more effective pollution control programs.

MRC and the Tri-State Transportation Commission will jointly sponsor an air pollution control workshop in April which will concentrate on ways in which land use planning can be utilized to decrease pollution levels in the region's urban centers.

FIGURE 10–4. *This double-page spread combines good photography and good text design on a gray paper with a matt finish. (Source: Metropolitan Regional Council, ANNUAL REPORT 1968, New York: Metropolitan Regional Council, 1968.)*

products which the citizens of the community look for from their local government, and should reflect the progress the government has made in achieving these goals, or the beginnings it has made in their direction. A mere recital of how many dog tags were issued, of the number of arrests made for serious crimes, and of how many books were borrowed from the library, while useful information, does not get this message across.

In the case of regional councils, the same point applies. Only the specifics are different. Telling the reader that the organization coordinates the efforts of the cities and counties in its region on those problems which cross jurisdictional boundaries is an essential point, but it is not the sole message of the annual report. The same can be said of the organization's regional planning responsibilities. While they are important and it is important for the reader to know of them, it is more important that the reader understand how that planning relates

(1) to the community and (2) to the reader individually. For example, to emphasize that the council is responsible for conducting a "continuing, comprehensive, cooperative transportation planning process" is to lose the reader in six words. But if the report opens with a story on the new express bus rush-hour experiment that the council started last year—or that was designed last year to start this year—the reader has something to relate to and will be interested enough to keep reading the report.

Variables in Preparing the Report. The straight annual report does not have to be published as a booklet in the conventional sense and distributed through the usual means. It can be published instead in the form of a special section of a local newspaper. The major advantage to this procedure is that it ensures virtual blanket distribution. The supplement will be delivered with this local newspaper to many times the number of homes the local government could afford to reach. Extra copies can be

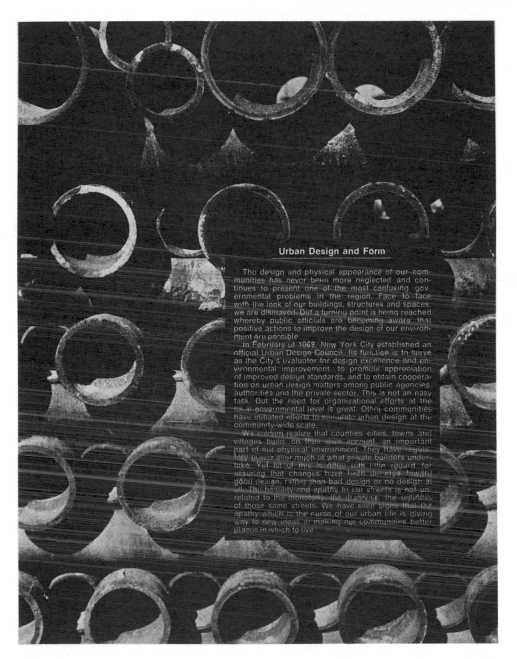

FIGURE 10–5. *A full page that is effective through a combination of an interesting photographic idea and an inset text which is white on black.* (*Source: same as* FIGURE 10–4.)

bought from the paper, which would simply run as many as the organization needed over its own normal requirements. These extras would serve throughout the balance of the year in answering mail requests, providing copies to visitors, and distributing copies at special events and at key locations.

There are disadvantages to this approach as well, however. Newspaper supplements, by their very nature, go only to subscribers, so extra copies would have to be obtained for the organization's mailing list.

A caveat is in order here, however, since some organizations and individuals will be get-

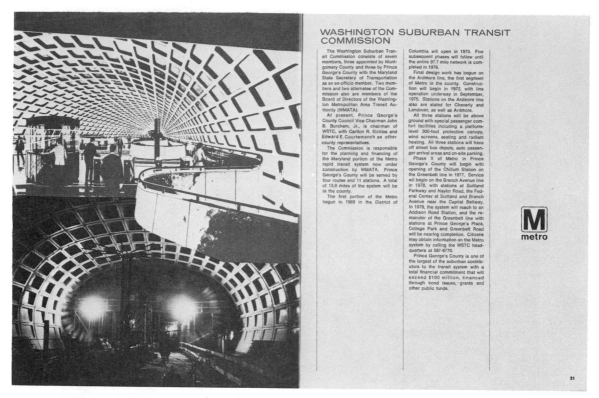

WASHINGTON SUBURBAN TRANSIT COMMISSION

The Washington Suburban Transit Commission consists of seven members, three appointed by Montgomery County and three by Prince George's County with the Maryland State Secretary of Transportation as an ex-officio member. Two members and two alternates of the Commission also are members of the Board of Directors of the Washington Metropolitan Area Transit Authority (WMATA).

At present, Prince George's County Council Vice Chairman John B. Burcham, Jr., is chairman of WSTC, with Carlton R. Sickles and Edward E. Courtemanch as other county representatives.

The Commission is responsible for the planning and financing of the Maryland portion of the Metro rapid transit system now under construction by WMATA. Prince George's County will be served by four routes and 11 stations. A total of 13.9 miles of the system will be in the county.

The first portion of the Metro begun in 1969 in the District of

Columbia will open in 1973. Five subsequent phases will follow until the entire 97.7 mile network is completed in 1979.

Final design work has begun on the Ardmore line, the first segment of Metro in the county. Construction will begin in 1972, with line operation underway in September, 1975. Stations on the Ardmore line also are slated for Cheverly and Landover, as well as Ardmore.

All three stations will be above ground with special passenger comfort facilities including a platform-level 300-foot protective canopy, wind screens, seating and radiant heating. All three stations will have off street bus depots, auto passenger arrival areas and on-site parking.

Phase II of Metro in Prince George's County will begin with opening of the Chillum Station on the Greenbelt line in 1977. Service will begin on the Branch Avenue line in 1978, with stations at Suitland Parkway and Naylor Road, the Federal Center at Suitland and Branch Avenue near the Capital Beltway. In 1979, the system will reach to an Addison Road Station, and the remainder of the Greenbelt line with stations at Prince George's Plaza, College Park and Greenbelt Road will be nearing completion. Citizens may obtain information on the Metro system by calling the WSTC headquarters at 587-8770.

Prince George's County is one of the largest of the suburban contributors to the transit system with a total financial commitment that will exceed $100 million, financed through bond issues, grants and other public funds.

M metro

31

FIGURE 10–6. *This double-page spread combines three colors in an effective design: a tan paper; text in black with a blue heading; and on the left an illustration combining a "black-and-white" photograph* (below) *with blue artwork* (above). (*Source: Prince George's County, Maryland, Office of Public Information,* PRINCE GEORGE'S COUNTY 1971, *Upper Marlboro, Md.: Office of Public Information, 1971, pp. 30–31.*)

ting their annual report twice, once in their paper and a second time from the government itself. Nothing annoys some people as much as getting two copies of something the government puts out. The classic reaction is: "No wonder our taxes are so high." On an equally practical level, going with one newspaper over another or others can cause certain feelings of resentment because of suspected favoritism, and that kind of damage to relations with another newspaper is seldom if ever worth the price. There is the additional drawback that, by going with one paper over another, the organization will miss that other paper's subscribers. The major advantage—reaching many thousands more citizens than with conventional means—must be weighed against these negative factors.

Some cities have experimented with a calendar-type annual report that not only shows im-

portant dates and related information on the calendar but also includes some information on each page about the progress achieved or aimed at by the government.

The disadvantage here is that the annual report and its appearance will be controlled by the calendar and its unique needs. For example, presumably the report would be only twelve pages long, although more could be added at the beginning and end. The design on each month's page would be dictated to a large extent by the need to show a whole month's calendar either on that page or next to it (on the facing page), or above it or below it. In addition, dates change, meetings are rescheduled, the council decides to cancel those meetings in the first two weeks of August, and the calendar may be as outdated as last year's the day it arrives in people's mail.

There are countless other variables in pre-

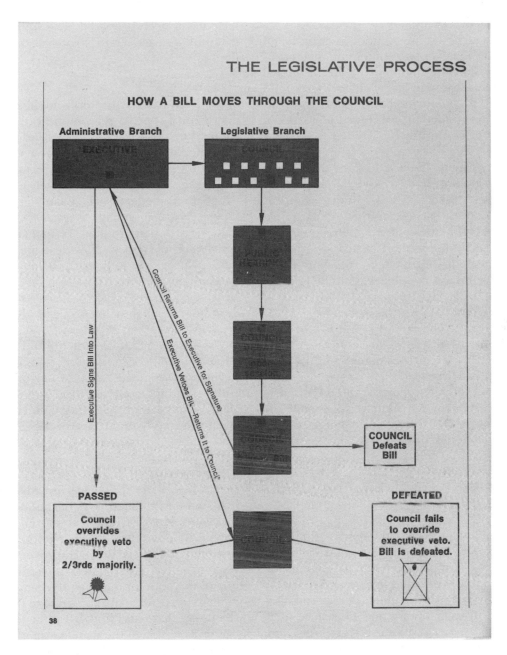

FIGURE 10–7. *Graphics can be handled with imagination, as is the case with this three-color (blue and black on tan) illustration of how a bill moves through the council. (Source: same as FIGURE 10–6.)*

paring reports, and many decisions to be made if the limited resources available—and they are always limited—arc to be used to the fullest. In addition to the detailed information in Chapter 11 of the present volume, the reader is referred to two chapters in a publication entitled *Re-gional Council Communications,* published in 1973 in Washington, D.C., by the National Association of Regional Councils. Chapter 7 of that publication covers "Making the Most of Your Publications." Chapter 8 describes "Making the Most of Your Printing Dollar."

Distribution. It should be mentioned here that the question of distribution is critical, and contains as many opportunities and dangers as other decisions on the report. Will the annual report be mailed to every residence? Or should it? Should the public relations officer try to interest a newspaper in carrying it as a special section, or should this be avoided for one or more of the reasons already mentioned? Should it be mailed second class or third class? and what would the difference be in price? If it goes other than first class, how long will it take to get to the people on the organization's mailing list? If it goes other than first class, will it look like junk mail and be tossed into the trash without being opened? And how much will it cost and will people feel that the government is wasting their money?

Perhaps it should not be mailed at all. Perhaps the Boy Scouts or Girl Scouts would want to distribute it on a home-to-home basis. This would give it wide distribution and would save on postage. However, such an arrangement needs considerable attention, and attention is needed to see that distribution is complete. In many cities there are companies that specialize in house-to-house distribution, and their fees for large quantity deliveries generally are lower than those of the mail.

Several other possibilities exist, for example, including the report in a utility company's monthly bill, which would go not only to virtually all homes but to all commercial establishments as well. The so-called secondary distribution is also important. An ample number of copies should be on hand in every office which deals directly with the public. Copies can also be placed in each library and in each branch library. High schools, junior high schools, and colleges and universities can also be given copies, either through the public relations office's standard distribution list or through special contacts made to notify these bodies that the new report is out and the office would be happy to supply them with copies.

Distribution can be a tedious and endless, and sometimes even confusing, matter, but there is this to be said about it: without good distribution, the publication might just as well have never been prepared. The subject of distribution is discussed in greater detail in Chapter 11.

SPECIAL REPORTS

Special reports, as the term implies, are produced for a specific reason and often are distributed to a specific audience, as opposed, for example, to something like an annual report or a newsletter, both of which are prepared in general terms for a general audience and distributed on a general scale. Examples of special reports are the familiar *Know Your City* pamphlets distributed to new residents and students in civics classes. They describe city facilities and programs and also provide telephone numbers to call for information on public services.

Some jurisdictions reproduce the budget message each year in booklet form (nothing fancy—it's a budget document) and distribute it to community organizations. This is the classic application of the need for thorough distribution. Nothing could be more unfortunate at budget time than distributing budget information to the most important organizations and then finding out that the League of Women Voters was missed.

A major change in any local service always carries with it the potential for adverse publicity, but an explanatory publication prepared in advance and distributed to citizens in those neighborhoods affected can minimize such a possibility. It can even turn the government action into a plus, with the local government winning praise both for making the change and for going to the trouble of explaining to the people why it was done and how it will benefit them.

Several years ago the manager of a county in Maryland gave a major speech before a federation of civic organizations in his county. He reported on the status of a broad range of both programs and problems. The county information officer told the press of the speech in advance, billing it as a major address on the "state of the county." The speech was reported prominently in the papers. The information officer then reproduced the text of the speech in question-and-answer form as a citizen's interview with the county manager on the status of things. At virtually no dollar expense the county was able to publish a popular booklet which told the taxpayers a great deal about the state of their county, and which proved useful for several years afterward.

Financial reports of special significance may be of interest to certain parts of the population. Certain members of the business community would be quite interested in financial reports, as would heads of appropriate committees in civic groups. Special reports on assessments, urban renewal projects, annexations, conservation, fire prevention, and countless other subjects may be worthy of preparation and distribution in simplified form.

The key questions raised earlier in this chapter about identifying the audience and deciding in advance on a method of distribution apply doubly here for obvious reasons. Any report which is a *special* report of necessity needs a pinpointed audience and a carefully designed distribution method.

NEWSLETTERS

Newsletters are not always feasible for large cities and counties because of the much greater expense involved in mailing something to every resident as often as twelve times a year (as opposed to only once a year for an annual report —if the annual report is even distributed to every home). Some larger cities are able to publish newsletters despite this, and many smaller cities and regional organizations use them to a great extent and with considerable effectiveness to tell their story on a regular basis to as many individuals and organizations as possible.

There are several differences between newsletters and annual reports, and they must be borne in mind if each type of publication is to be effective. Newsletters furnish information which is much more current than that in an annual report. Because they are published much more frequently, newsletters are a source of much greater direct contact with citizens, organizations, and the news media.

Their subject matter can be directed more precisely at specific problems and the events surrounding them. One city's newsletter carries articles on its canine police unit, street repair techniques, a new swimming pool, a new fire house, expansion of health clinics, and a dozen other subjects of genuine significance.

Newsletters can be used to trace current trends in building activity, crime, profit and loss on public transportation, library statistics, and similar newsworthy matters which frequently will appear again in the daily paper or the evening news because the story caught the eye of a reporter or editor.

Newsletter formats vary greatly. Many are mimeographed and limited to text only. Others are printed and include photographs and charts. Some are inserted in utility bills and must be of specified size, which dictates and limits their format. Some are extremely simple and are for limited distribution to a selected mailing list. Others are mailed to all residents and thus require—and justify—more work and expense in layout, typography, and other characteristics.

Their frequency of issue ranges from weekly to semiannually—if such a publication issued semiannually can really be called a newsletter. Monthly and quarterly newsletters are preferred by most. This regular and reasonably frequent publication schedule permits detailed descriptions of behind-the-scenes developments such as forthcoming recreation programs, training programs for employees of the local government, and dates for collection of leaves.

The periodic newsletter may also provide a vehicle for discussing matters of broad public concern which might resemble "propaganda" to some if issued as a single document. Instead, appearing in a recognized and respected newsletter whose readers have come to know of its value and restraint, the same stories become more acceptable to the citizen readers. Such subjects could include discussion of proposals for new tax measures, housing codes, capital improvement programs, and other matters which could be considered controversial at the time they are under consideration.

It is essential that such discussions be consistent with the policies and wishes of the policy officials. They should not be campaign material for one side of the issue. Impartial, factual reports on the status of major public issues are in the finest tradition of American government. They are essential to intelligent public discussions and represent what is certainly one of the highest—if not *the* highest—uses to which any public newsletter can be put.

Their primary function, despite the value of such discussions, still must be as *news*letters. They are the voice through which a government can tell its story in brief articles, and in attractive active pictures. This is the purpose and the value of the newsletter in its function as a month-to-month or quarter-to-quarter carrier of news of activities and projects—a complement to the annual report, with its yearly summary of results of a government's overall program.

OTHER "REPORTS"

It has been written that other types of documents not normally classified as reports nevertheless fall into that category in the practical sense. These would include reports from, for example, the city manager or the executive director to the governing body, or even letters or memoranda prepared on specific questions but released to the news media and other segments of the public. This suggestion to include such items as "publications" would seem valid when it is remembered that many characteristics apply to them that also apply to the more formalized publications: they contain public information, intended either for the general public or a specific target audience; they are intended either to disseminate information or generate support; and how they read and look has a definite impression on the citizens reading them. In short, like the more formal publications, these other items—such as letters and memos—can help a government's cause a great deal, or can hurt it just as much.

Reporting in Person

The other vehicle for reporting information on your local government is reporting in person. In one respect, this can have an even greater impact on the audience than reporting through

publications, because the chances are that more of it is done. Administrators and their fellow staff members may well be out speaking on a frequent schedule, so that their personal "reports" are appearing many times each month whereas the annual report comes out only once a year and the newsletter perhaps once a month. Administrators benefit their government considerably by using this opportunity in the right way.

There are several distinct advantages to the personal touch. It gives public officials the opportunity to appear before the citizens of their jurisdiction in flesh and blood. They can see that the official is not a sinister, scheming villain plotting against the public interest. To put it in positive terms, they can see that the official is experienced, knowledgeable, and sincerely interested in trying to serve them.

The credibility question is prominent in this function as it is and should be in all government functions. Government speakers who try to "slip one past" the civic association when answering a question from the floor or in their prepared remarks live at their own peril, and often die by their own words. It is important that such speakers be completely truthful in the presentation of information and in answering questions. For example, slides or films taken during atypical periods and then shown to illustrate typical improvement will be shouted down, and the word will get round that the speaker from the local government at last night's meeting tried to mislead the people.

Successful experiences have proved that complete candor is a strong ally when speakers stand before their fellow citizens representing their local government. When a question arises and a speaker does not know the answer and states this honestly, the audience will appreciate this honesty—and will appreciate, as well, an offer, on the part of the speaker, to "get the answer from the department head and call you first thing in the morning."

Assuming that the speaker's appearance is neat and clean, there are other features which the audience will notice. They will notice the speaker's delivery. They will notice whether the speaker stands up straight or slouches, whether he or she speaks in a clear, confident voice, enunciating clearly. They will notice whether the speaker looks relaxed and friendly and happy to be with them, and whether the speaker appears to feel he or she is one of them.

PREPARATION

There is a story about a young violinist, in his preteen years, who was on his way to Carnegie Hall to perform with his high school orchestra. He became lost, but he knew he was in the vicinity. He spotted an elderly man with a long beard, also carrying a violin case. Certain that the old man would know how to direct him, the young violinist stopped him and asked politely, "Excuse me, sir. Could you please tell me how to get to Carnegie Hall?"

The old man looked down at the boy and saw his violin case. He put his hand on his shoulder and said, "Practice, my son. Practice."

The same can be said of personal presentations before live audiences. While it is considered preparation rather than practice, the same point applies. The speaker needs to take the time and the trouble to prepare himself or herself for this performance.

The first step in preparation is deciding what to talk about, unless the organization inviting the speaker has already assigned the topic. In either case, one of the first decisions is on exactly what to cover and what not to, what is relevant and what is not, what is interesting and what is not, what is public information and what is still in negotiation. The speaker must also decide what information he or she already has on the subject—either through personal knowledge or through the facilities of his or her office —and what information must be requested from other officials in the speaker's government.

It is helpful to ask oneself several questions as part of this early stage of the process—to put oneself in the position of a member of the audience. If the audience is a neighborhood organization, the first question is, What are the issues in that neighborhood? Too much traffic at a particular intersection? Is there a fierce zoning battle going on? Is a freeway aimed at a park? Why did the city council just raise the property tax, and for the third year in a row? If our officials have been working so hard on the traffic

problem for so many years, why does it keep getting worse?

When the speaker knows what to cover and what to expect—as much as any speaker ever can—and has the needed information, the next step is to organize the material. It is one thing to *know* the information. It is quite another thing to *present* it. Some of the best informed speakers fail because their audience did not get the message. And they did not get the message because the speaker did not present it well. This goes beyond platform appearance and method of delivery, to organizing information ahead of time. Speakers who know what they are going to say and when it's coming, who build a logical sequence to the points they will make, and who build up to a convincing finish are the speakers who win the audience—for themselves and their government.

The advice of a speech teacher some years ago still applies: "Tell them what you're going to tell them. Tell them. Then tell them what you've told them." That is another way of urging the speaker to organize his or her thoughts into a logical order and then to present them in the three major parts outlined in the speech teacher's advice.

The desires of an audience are important. In a public hearing on the manager's proposed budget, for example, the audience is willing and prepared to sit through several hours of detailed and exhausting testimony on facts and figures and programs and proposals. Fifteen minutes after the Wednesday luncheon meeting of the Rotary Club is a very different situation. This sort of thing has a great influence on length of presentation, in addition to affecting coverage and amount of detail. Knowing when to stop is another formula for a successful performance.

VISUAL AIDS

Visual aids can be of immense help in making a presentation effective, but their use does not automatically ensure success. The wrong slide at the wrong time, a poor quality film, or a chart that used to have a white background but is gray now because of thumb prints help tell the audience a story, but not the one the speaker has in mind.

Slides. Slide shows have been used with increasing success in recent years by local governments and regional councils as well as by countless other segments of both the public and private sectors. They are extremely helpful when chosen well and used in the right spot.

Slides shows not only carry the obvious advantages of illustration, they also are highly flexible. If the speaker is in the Oak Hills section of the city tonight, he or she can use a slide at some point in the presentation showing that community's representative on the city council, Ms. Taylor, articulating a point before her colleagues on the council, clearly representing the interests of those people in the audience who are her neighbors in Oak Hills. If the speaker is speaking tomorrow night in Glenmont, he or she can remove the slide of the council member from Oak Hills and drop one in of the Glenmont member on the city council in action fighting in behalf of his neighbors in Glenmont.

When certain slides become outdated, they can be pulled out and more current slides added. Slides about a new project can be added even if they are not of a quality completely satisfactory, then replaced later when someone has had time to go out and take a better shot. In adding slides, however, one point should be remembered. Each additional slide requires additional talk. Additional talk makes the presentation longer. Most audiences requesting local government speakers are prepared for something between fifteen and thirty minutes in length, followed usually by a question-and-answer session. The closer the presentation is to fifteen minutes, the better. For this reason, as the speaker begins to add slides to his or her presentation, he or she should also begin to subtract, removing those that are not as good or not as timely as the newer ones. This will help the speaker stay closer to the fifteen minute mark and avoid running over the thirty minute mark—the point at which endurance begins to flag and speakers begin to lose their audience and their chances for success.

At the outset of the presentation, no visual material should be in view. Thus, even when showing movies or slides, before the communicator becomes only a voice in the dark, he

or she should first establish a meaningful context for the visual aid, telling the listeners precisely what to expect from the film or slide sequence, then proceeding with it in carefully rehearsed fashion, reemphasizing at the conclusion the particular message contained in the visual materials.

With films and slides, there is a fairly certain way of ensuring that the audiovisual portion of the evening will be a success. If a film is being used and it is of high quality technically, visually, and literally, the delivery is almost certain to be first-rate, because it will be the narrator's delivery on the film's sound track.

In the case of slides, many options are available. There is a recorded narration, much like the sound track on a film. That, however, offsets one of the advantages which slides have over films—the flexibility to change the presentation with a minimum of time, difficulty, and expense. A recorded narration locks the person showing the slides into those words, even if not into the pictures accompanying the words.

Unlike films, slides can be produced for virtually nothing, the only real expense being a slide projector costing less than $200. After that, the only dollar expenditures involved are the cost of slide film and development of the film. Speakers can do the narration themselves whenever they give the presentation, and here again preparation becomes vital. One successful practice is writing the narrative for the whole show as a unit, then keeping it in a notebook and training other members of the professional staff in its use. After that, the only real concern is keeping it current with new and better slides, and making certain that, as the content and the order of the slides are changed, the written narrative is changed accordingly.

Slides also help avoid the "slick Madison Avenue" approach, which can arise occasionally when a film is presented with beautiful shots, sophisticated "dissolves," and a professional narrator.

The narration to accompany slides can be simple yet almost foolproof as far as preparation is concerned if the notebook technique mentioned previously is used. The presentation should be smooth, precisely worded, and well structured, so that the narrator does not wander into irrelevancies and stretch out the presentation beyond the point of effectiveness. All that is required is that the narrator read what is there, flip the page to the narration for the next slide, then click the button to advance the projector to the next slide. The narrator can elaborate on anything he or she chooses, and can run as long as he or she likes, or as long as he or she thinks the audience is willing to listen; but if the narrator merely follows the script he or she can govern the total time literally to the minute. After presentation, of course, the narrator is free to—and should—answer questions for as long as listeners are willing to ask them.

Another flexibility with slides is that the narrator can edit the length of the show to fit the event. Occasionally, only a part of the overall show may be needed, perhaps as an introduction to another presentation, and only five minutes will be wanted instead of the overall fifteen. Some of the projects described in the slide show may have no relevance at all to a particular audience. The slides which are surplus for such occasions can be lifted and the others put together.

Films. This discussion should not be seen as a rejection of the film approach or as minimizing the value of a film. Films can be just as effective as slides—more so in some cases—but again there is a strong need to assess what the speaker wants to illustrate, who the audience generally will be, whether a film will be quickly outdated, and how much money a government is willing and able to spend. The cost factor heightens the need for a close and totally objective analysis of all other factors.

The cost factor involves production of the film itself and the purchase of the equipment with which to show it. Production costs can run to around $1,000 per minute, as a rule of thumb. Thus, if a government—perhaps a large government—would like to make a half-hour film, it should be prepared to spend something in the neighborhood of $30,000, and very possibly more than that, plus the cost of a sound projector and an amplifying system.

Producing films will require hiring a film company in virtually every case, to handle everything from writing the script to filming on location and editing the film into a cohesive presentation, with background music and all the other finishing touches required if the film is to be effective. It will also normally require several months to produce. With the much greater time and money involved, an important consideration to bear in mind throughout the production process is to make it adaptable for television. In this way it could be scheduled for broadcast as a public service film on a local station, which would greatly increase its exposure and its value.

Extra prints of films can be purchased at little additional cost compared to the initial cost of producing the master print. This, too, is something to bear in mind. One extra print means having one copy in the office at all times, when the other may be out in use. It also gives the added capability of having the show presented in two different locations on the same evening, something which is also possible with slide presentations if the slight extra time is taken to make a duplicate set of the slides and have a duplicate of the prepared narration typed.

PROMOTION OF SPEAKING ENGAGEMENTS

Having a first-rate slide presentation or film is only half the project. The other half is to let people know it is there. Its availability can be promoted through a variety of simple, inexpensive, and quick techniques. The government can advertise the show through its newsletter. It can issue a press release as soon as the show is completed and ready for the public. Flyers can be mailed to the various community organizations, such as local civic and service clubs, church groups, cultural groups, women's clubs, business and professional organizations, chambers of commerce, veterans' clubs, educational and fraternal groups, and organizations attending various celebrations and dedications. There are other opportunities in special events, including high school and college career days, conferences on public service careers, county fairs, trade exhibitions, and high school and college classes in civic affairs and planning. Those engaged in promotional efforts should also seek out organized minority groups, labor unions, and specialized professional and occupational organizations.

The contact with this wide range of community groups should not be limited to the promotional effort and to the speaking event itself. The appearance of someone from the government can be a valuable opportunity for "feedback," for bringing back to the government extremely helpful information on what is on the minds of citizens. Merely returning with information on the questions asked by citizens can serve as an indicator as to what the citizens of a community are thinking about or of "what's bothering them." Any additional indicators, such as the mood of the audience or extra emphasis on one particular subject in the question-and-answer session, or a particularly strong reaction to one part of the prepared presentation, are that much more help to those in the government who are shaping policies and outlining programs to implement those policies.

"Think Public!"

"Reporting" the plans and projects and achievements of a government need not be limited to the above techniques of the printed word and the public appearance. "Reporting" also includes the face-to-face and telephone-to-telephone contacts made by every employee in a government with the citizens of that government's community. This is "personal reporting," but it is reporting nevertheless, and this very specialized style of reporting often outweighs all others in impact on the public, and, if it is badly handled, usually will also offset any gains made through publications and public appearances.

Every time a caller is treated rudely, every time someone is transferred three times on the telephone because no one knows the answer to the question or even what office should handle it, every time a letter goes out with sloppy corrections on the typographical errors, every time a telephone rings too long before being picked up—all efforts in reporting to the public with effectiveness are undermined.

Great stress should be placed in any public organization on how to handle direct contact with citizens, and how not to. This concern led one organization, the Metropolitan Washington Council of Governments, to publish a booklet for its employees called *Think Public!* (Figure 10–8). It is intended to accomplish what its title implies, to condition the employees of that organization to remember the public relations aspect inherent in each of their daily phone calls, letters, or visits with any and every member of the public. Employees are reminded to minimize the number of calls to be transferred, to make sure citizens receive their information promptly and accurately, to make sure the correspondence which leaves the office reflects the highest professional standards in content and appearance, and to respond to calls from the news media in an open manner and with complete information.

On the subject of media inquiries, special emphasis is placed not only on the easy availability of members of the senior professional staff to the media but also on the corresponding obligation of those staff members to know their subjects, to get answers and return calls promptly on questions which they are unable to answer immediately, and to leave questions of policy to policy officials. It can be reported here that, coincidentally or otherwise, the Metropolitan Washington Council of Governments has enjoyed outstanding relations with the news media over the years and has also enjoyed great support from the media for COG programs.

Special Events

Another form of reporting is the special event —civic celebrations, visits by VIPs, publicity on special developments such as an improved bond rating, city government days for the youth of a community, adoption of a sister city or county overseas, or winning special recognition such as an "All-American City Award."

These occasions present an ideal situation for distribution of considerable factual information about a local government or regional organization. Special publications can be pre-

metropolitan washington
COUNCIL OF GOVERNMENTS
1225 Connecticut Avenue, N.W., Washington, D.C. 20036   223-6800

THINK PUBLIC!

Public relations is the art of making COG liked and respected.
Everyone from the Executive Director on down is a public relations
specialist for the Council of Governments. The activities of COG's
departments and offices hold more and more public relations and
political implications for COG, its members and the residents of
the Washington area. This booklet has been prepared to help all
COG employees recognize the public relations element in their
work -- from adding a new member to a technical committee to
signing a public safety agreement. It also spells out the
responsibilities which each employee has and how COG's Office of
Public Affairs can help you meet those responsibilities.

This booklet features a case study approach. Each item begins
with an example of things which happen every day in any office,
followed by a description of the appropriate public relations
steps to be taken.

All employees should remember that it's better to check with the
Public Affairs Office about the public relations potential --
good or bad -- of any activity or development than to ignore that
potential at your own risk.

No one -- the Executive Director, the Public Affairs staff or
anyone else -- knows everything about the important and sensitive
subject of public relations For this reason, we welcome
suggestions from any employee on any aspect of our mutual public
relations responsibilities.

Walt Scheiber

Walter A. Scheiber
Executive Director

May, 1975

District of Columbia ● Arlington County ● Fairfax County ● Loudoun County ● Montgomery County ● Prince George's County ● Prince William County
Alexandria ● Bowie ● College Park ● Fairfax City ● Falls Church ● Gaithersburg ● Greenbelt ● Rockville ● Takoma Park

FIGURE 10–8. *Introductory letter to the booklet* THINK PUBLIC! *which is a public relations guide for
employees of the Metropolitan Washington Council of Governments. (Source: Metropolitan Washington
Council of Governments,* THINK PUBLIC! *Washington, D.C.: Metropolitan Washington Council of
Governments, 1975.)*

pared, press releases issued, and displays built —depending on the nature of the event.

The Student Government Day is a highly successful special event during which tours are conducted through government facilities for students of the community, and students "substitute" for members of the governing body and the executive branch in conducting the community's affairs for one day. They even grapple with some of the specific controversial issues and decide how they should be resolved. By so doing, the students become exposed to what the agency is doing for them, and this information often is relayed home to their parents. Thus it has a spin-off value.

Town meetings are still appropriate and are used effectively in many communities as a means of taking the government to the people instead of the opposite. Programs are conducted as a series, with one session for each of the major neighborhoods selected. Meetings are held in school buildings or other public facilities, and representatives of the government staff and elected body are on hand to speak and answer questions—often with the help of films, slide shows, and other visual aids. Occasionally, the meeting is televised live to the rest of the community.

The program should be well organized and well conducted or the audience will be lost and a real opportunity will be converted into a real setback. It is important that the story be told well, and with sufficient advance publicity, or there will be no audience. This is an ideal opportunity for distributing printed information—something inexpensive but attractive which the audience can take home.

Distinguished visitors to the community are a source of rich potential and provide the vehicle for a special event or program which will draw attention to the government. The nature of the event to mark the visit will vary widely to ensure its appropriateness, but if the event is handled well the visitor will be impressed with the community and the citizens will be impressed with the visitor's recognition of their community's importance.

Conclusion

This chapter has pointed out the great importance of factual reports and events in the overall public relations program, through a variety of techniques and outlets. It has also discussed the need for building this program on the sound foundation of a high level of services to the public.

Three major techniques by means of which the public can be informed of government activities have been the subject of this chapter. The first of these, the area of published reports, discusses annual reports, special reports, newsletters, and other types of reports. The next section is concerned with reporting in person and gives considerable attention to the use of slide and film showings. The final section deals with special events and how to use them to promote better relations between government and the community.

These and other techniques can form the skeleton for an effective public relations program, but the organization itself must add meat to the skeleton by its own process of selection and adaptation of ideas. In developing its own public relations program, a government should search for the effective, the original, the means through which the government would like to convey its particular story to the audience of its choice to create the desired impression—all at a cost it can afford.

It must be remembered, however, that these techniques of reporting through every vehicle possible and at every opportunity possible constitute only parts of the multifaceted public relations program. And all parts, individually and combined, must contain the same basic virtues and characteristics: credibility, professionalism, and relevance to the public's interests and needs.

11

Publications Planning, Development, and Production

Every local government issues publications ranging from one-page flyers to multicolored books with elaborate charts, tables, and photographs. A small government may limit its efforts to a simple audit report, required by state law, plus notices posted on bulletin boards. A larger jurisdiction may issue an annual report, a newsletter, and a few information pieces. Still larger governments, including cities that are central to metropolitan areas, are likely to prepare elaborate promotional brochures, folders, and reports for a variety of purposes, including such purposes as tourism and industrial development.

In addition to these kinds of printed and duplicated pieces, governments also issue documents and reports of more limited circulation, including the annual budget, reports to citizen associations, explanatory booklets on specific local ordinances, and technical documents for land developers, building contractors, and others. In the planning, writing, design, production, and distribution of these materials, the city or county government is conveying information in visual form.

For purposes of this chapter, the term "publications" will be used to designate all printed and duplicated materials issued by the local government that are intended for general or specific publics, including the local government at large, various groups and associations within the jurisdiction, professional and trade associations, labor unions, the chamber of commerce, local government employees, and others.

Until now, the emphasis in this book as far as publications are concerned has tended to concern itself more with their place in the local government public relations program than with the actual details of writing, design, and production.

The present chapter carries these processes through the following stages: planning; writing; designing; drafting; production; and distribution. A number of special features pertaining to the chapter and encompassing such subjects as tables, charts and graphs, photography, and printing processes are included in this volume as Appendix D.

Planning the Publication

The process of designating *objectives, audience,* and *components* is a convenient way of assembling the facts, plus projections, for annual reports, newsletters, and various other publication materials.

Objectives

In dealing with publications, it is not necessary to set up an elaborate goals/objectives study as with long-range social, economic, and physical development objectives for the entire government. It is helpful, however, to have a planning process that is established and then reviewed every year. This can be done conveniently during the annual budget preparation process.

The first step is to review the publications

basic to the government's communications program. The National Association of Regional Councils calls three publications basic: a general descriptive brochure about the regional council, a newsletter, and an annual report. This could serve as a good starting point for any city or county government. Others could be added of course, including the budget, an employee handbook, news releases, and technical materials issued in standardized form, such as building regulations and reports of council or board actions.

The next step is to define the objectives for a specific publication. The annual report, issued by hundreds of cities, provides a good example.

The most common purpose of an annual report is to convey information on what the government actually did, department by department, during the preceding year. This might be termed the historical, for-the-record objective.

Another approach is to highlight accomplishments, to talk about major continuing activities, and even to set forth a few objectives for the future. The report in this case covers major points of interest and omits much of the routine activity. This might be called a progress approach.

A third objective would be to increase understanding about the government. While such a report might include a great deal about what was done during the past year, it would also give attention to how the local government fits in with both public and private organizations and with other governments in the area, how it contributes to the general betterment of community life, and the other contributions it makes for informed citizenry. This could be termed the "image" or public relations objective.

The definition of objectives may be much easier for other types of publications. In a report for the city or county council, for example, the objective ordinarily is limited to providing information for making a decision. The information may be presented quite elaborately, as is the case with consultant reports, or it may be a short memorandum, but the objective is usually the same—a straightforward presentation of information.

AUDIENCE

The most difficult audience to pin down is the intended readership for the annual report. It is probably impossible to design a "general" annual report to reach "the public." Both terms are so broad that they can't be brought together. On the other hand, an annual report that is written in the traditional department-by-department format, if well done, might get a good response in the public schools as a supplemental resource for social studies classes.

The city or county council is an audience that is besieged with publications, especially in medium-sized and larger cities. It is a mistake, however, to think that this is an easy audience to reach. Council members, like other busy people with many demands on their time, are not inclined to read any lengthy report, especially if it is badly written.

PUBLICATION COMPONENTS

The next time the reader gets a piece of direct mail advertising, he or she may look inside the envelope and find a two-page letter, a four-page descriptive folder, a one-page list of endorsements, an order card, and a business reply envelope. All of these pieces make up the components for an advertising publication that originated (probably) in New York, Chicago, Washington, or some other major city.

Local governments seldom need numerous components for publications, but nothing that is really necessary should be overlooked. When a city or county publication is mailed, two components may be used: a mailing envelope and the publication itself. Even this relatively simple process could include such additional components as a specially designed mailing label, a reader reply card, and a transmittal letter from the chief administrator or the council or board. By planning for components, consideration can be given to writing, design, and consistency in printing and packaging.

The importance of assembling and checking all components is, of course, that it prevents unpleasant surprises. A last-minute decision to print and mail an odd-sized publication may show that envelopes are unobtainable except on special order, which would mean a delay of several weeks.

GETTING STARTED

Most publications, especially the annual report, the annual budget and supporting documents, and the city hall newsletter, are the responsibility of the public affairs office or the chief executive of the local government.

A clear assignment of responsibility should be made for each publication. In those governments without a public affairs office, the annual report might be the job of the city manager or an assistant. A departmental report might be assigned to an assistant to the director of public works or to a staff member in the office of the city or county librarian. The importance of assigning clear responsibility should be obvious. This person has to take care of the steps set forth above (defining objectives, ascertaining the audience, and outlining components), check on money available, select somebody to write the publication, and set up a schedule.

Elements of Cost. Even small publications need a budget that includes all outside services and supplies. Such costs may include the services of a graphic designer, illustrators, and authors or copywriters; outside typing and duplicating services for the preparation of manuscripts and report drafts; all production costs, including composition, printing, and binding; and mailing or other methods of distribution.

Who Writes the Publication? The dilemma of most governmental report writing is balancing the need for clear transmittal of information, requiring journalistic and writing skills, with the need for accurate substantive information which comes from professional and technical background. Because of cost and other factors, many publications are written by city or county employees.

For some reports it may be helpful to use special talent in the community: a newspaper reporter or editorial writer with wide interests, a high school teacher who has written training guides, a minister with a feel for community needs and desires, or someone who has a background in creative writing through publication as a short story writer.

Schedule. Finally, a schedule should be drafted for all major steps in the production of a publication: preparation of first draft, review of draft, preparation of final copy, selection of printer, selection of photos and illustrations, preparation of specifications, etc.

Writing the Publication

This chapter provides some guidelines by which those engaged in writing government publications can organize their work the next time they are called on to draft anything more complicated than a relatively simple letter or memorandum.

STEPS IN WRITING

The writing needed for a city, county, or other government is usually expository writing (often loosely called report writing) rather than creative or scholarly writing. Much of expository writing is setting forth information in an organized factual way—also, it is hoped, in an interesting and verbally pleasing way. The major steps involved are set forth in the following paragraphs, with an annual report serving as the example.

Selecting the Subject. It should be easy enough in an annual report to decide on the subject: it is what the government did during the most recent fiscal or calendar year. But a broad statement like that is not very helpful. It should be narrowed down to more specific kinds of information that can be built into the publication. Many communities in recent years have turned away from the stereotyped *Report of the Activities of the City of _____ for the Year Ending _____* to such topics as *A Progress Report, A Look Ahead for the City of _____,* and *A Report to the People.* Annual reports of the mid-1970s for the Metropolitan Washington Council of Governments have been titled *Common Goals, Uncommon Progress, Where We Are One, Here Now and Tomorrow,* and *Beyond the Handshake.*

Palo Alto, California, for example, in its annual report for 1972–73 narrowed its subject to the theme of *People Serving People.* While the report followed conventional departmental organization, each agency highlighted a city employee and the way his or her work fitted in with the objectives of the agency and the contributions that the program made in providing services to the people.

Gathering Material. The material for writing the annual report will come largely from records, reports, and documents, but other sources should be explored. The librarian is often a good source for ideas. It is useful to check with the local newspaper editor and read some of the newspaper accounts of important government actions that took place during the year. The mayor and other informed persons should be interviewed for their ideas on recent significant events. The small bits of information that can be picked up from observation, interviews, reading, and systematic search in a few well-organized places can lead to a variety of material that can be sorted by subjects.

Evaluating and Selecting Material. Once the materials are sorted by subjects, the first runthrough will probably show that much of the information is of little value and can be set aside. The remaining information can then be reviewed analytically with further thought given to the overall theme or subject and the way the report can be organized.

At this stage, the writer need not worry about the personal and judgmental aspect of reviewing and screening the material and pulling out the best information. There is plenty of opportunity later for the city manager, department heads, and others to review the work for appropriateness and accuracy. This is the stage at which the writer should begin to blend the materials and the major subject and subsidiary subject areas so that he or she gets a feel for the entire report.

Drafting an Outline. Almost all annual reports are organized on a department-by-department basis, but they need not be. The departmental approach provides a complete review for a permanent record, but it inevitably leads to variation in levels of interest. By the mid-1970s, for example, people in many cities were more interested in the growth/no growth activities of the planning department than in the street maintenance program of the public works department.

The outline should clearly reflect the theme, should include primary and secondary headings, and should show the components of the report, including the front cover, the photos and illustrations that may be used, and the directory of officials and other kinds of reference information.

Writing the First Draft. The writing for the annual report or any other publication should be appropriate for the purpose. It is important not to lose sight of the fact that the annual report primarily conveys information to people in the community. It is not primarily a sales piece intended for the industrial development commission.

The report should also be appropriate for the reader. In other words, it should be based on an informed estimate of the educational and readership level of most people in the community. Generally speaking, the reading ability of people should not be underestimated; nor should their reading motivation be overestimated. If a technical term must be used, it can be defined unobtrusively in the text and the reader will not be offended. The general objective is to write for the nonspecialist.

Beyond these broad generalizations, three specific suggestions can be offered.

1. The writing should be clear. The writer should test it to make sure others understand it.
2. The writing should be simple—not simplistic. If long words are needed, they should be used. Generally, however, it is advisable to use the language of ordinary conversation, of the newspaper, and of radio and television.
3. The writing should be informal. This does not mean that writing should be unstructured. It means that the writer should avoid the notion that every paragraph must start out with a topical sentence; that no sentence can ever begin with the word "but"; and that a sentence can never end with a preposition. It is well to remember, however, that there is a fine line between informality and sloppiness; the latter should be avoided.

Revising the Manuscript. When the manuscript comes out of the typewriter, the writer should read it through and mark in the margins the places where he or she wants to make additions and deletions. The copy should always be typed double-spaced to leave room for the editing of the manuscript.

Now the writer will want to take a look at the first paragraph. Sometimes, surprisingly, a report or other document can be improved simply by dropping the first paragraph.

Next, the writer should look through for flow—that is, to see that paragraphs lead logically and smoothly from one idea to another within major subjects.

A check should be made for mechanics and consistent style (punctuation, spelling, and all of the other details that add up to a finished piece of work).

Finally, the writer should check for accuracy, particularly in the case of statistical or financial information. Most annual reports will draw heavily on this kind of information, and it needs to be checked carefully. The writer should also be sure that such material is up-to-date.

At this stage the report is ready for circulation to others in the city hall or county courthouse for commentary and for further checking for accuracy.

Final Preparation of Manuscript. After the report has been reviewed by department heads and other knowledgeable persons, the writer can begin the final preparation of the manuscript. This is the point once more to check for spelling, grammar, and other aspects of mechanics and style; to enter all factual corrections that have been pointed out by department heads and others who have reviewed the material; and to make any final editorial changes.

WRITING STYLES AND WHAT THEY MEAN

Most professional writers, especially the talented persons who produce our best fiction, poetry, drama, and criticism, would reject the idea that they have a writing style. This would imply, in their view, a rigidity and repetitiveness that inhibits creativity and originality. Nevertheless, students and teachers of writing, including most editors and publishers, agree that most kinds of writing, when viewed broadly, can be classified.

One useful approach, used by Porter G. Perrin in his *Writer's Guide and Index to English,* is a breakdown of English usage into nonstandard

and standard English.[1] His groupings include not only writing but also speech, conversation, and other oral usage, and the English that reaches our ears through radio, television, and the movies. His classification is shown as Figure 11–1.

Another classification, limited to writing style itself, is a three-way breakdown into creative, scholarly, and expository writing.

Creative writing is usually identified with poetry, novels, short stories, plays, biographies,

---

Nonstandard English. *Limited use.* Chiefly spoken. Language not much touched by school instruction; often conspicuously local; not appropriate for public affairs or for use by educated people.
Typical uses: conversations of many people at home, with friends, on the job. Representations of this speech in stories, plays, movies, comic strips, on radio and television.

Standard English: Informal English. *Limited use.* More often spoken than written. Speaking and writing of educated people in informal situations; includes shoptalk or slang and some localisms.
Typical uses: casual conversation. Letters between people who know each other well; diaries, personal writing; writing close to popular speech, as fiction and some newspaper columns.

Standard English: General English. *Unlimited use.* Both spoken and written. Speaking and writing of educated people in their private or public affairs.
Typical uses: conversation, talks to general audiences. Most business letters and advertising. News and feature stories, newspaper columns. Magazine articles and books on subjects of general interest. Most fiction and other literature for general circulation. Many college papers.

Standard English: Formal English. *Limited use.* More often written than spoken. Speaking and writing for somewhat restricted groups in formal situations.
Typical uses: addresses and lectures to special audiences. Some editorials and business writing. Literature of somewhat limited circulation: essays and criticisms, much poetry, some fiction. Academic writing: reference works, dissertations, most term papers, reference papers, some textbooks. Scientific and technical reports. Books and articles dealing with special subjects for professional groups and experts.

FIGURE 11–1. *Summary of the principal varieties of English. (Source: Porter G. Perrin,* WRITER'S GUIDE AND INDEX TO ENGLISH, *4th ed.,* Chicago: Scott, Foresman and Company, 1965, pp. 18–19.)

and literary criticism. It is the kind of writing often thought of as "literary" writing.

Scholarly writing can cover such areas as history, scientific works, a wide range of the social sciences, mathematics, the many branches of engineering, philosophy, theology, and other areas of learning. Scholarly writing is distinguished by original research, conceptualization and synthesis of information, formulation of hypotheses, attempts to generate theories, comparative analyses, application of the scientific method, and careful attention to documentation, reasoning, and argumentation. This sounds formidable, and it usually is.

Expository writing, the kind of writing dealt with in this chapter, is used primarily to transmit information. It includes reports, manuals, instruction books, newspaper stories, textbooks, advertising copy, and letters and memoranda of more than routine content. Expository writing stresses delineation of subject matter, organization of material, progression of subjects in some particular order, documentation, and various types of information needed to convey the message.

The purpose of outlining these three styles of writing is to show where most of the writing done for local governments fits in. Some expository writing is relatively easy in terms of content and development of complex and interrelated systems of ideas. On the other hand, expository writing may be difficult in the demands it makes to organize information in a logical and coherent manner. Expository writing often is disciplined writing. Even a letter, if it is fairly long and complicated, benefits from a short outline that is jotted down in longhand before it is dictated or written.

EXAMPLES OF WRITING

Since so much of writing depends on local circumstances, a person's interests and abilities, and other individual circumstances, the "how to write" portion of this chapter cannot be pushed much further. It might help, however, to provide a few examples of writing from city and county publications.

"Palo Alto's city government exists to provide services to its residents. Those services are provided by people—about 725 city em-

ployees." This is the way the Palo Alto annual report for 1972–73 leads off. The statement is simple and direct. It says what the city is and who services it. The report then goes on to explain its theme of providing information "on Palo Alto's day-to-day activities by acquainting the citizens of the city with some of the employees—your employees."[2]

Another example of a clear and direct opening is the city manager's transmittal letter for the Kansas City, Missouri, 1973–74 budget. The letter, dated March 9, 1973, and appearing at the beginning of the budget document, opens as follows:

Two special factors highlight this year's budget. They are federal programs cuts and budgeting by objective.

The proposed federal budget, the proposed community development revenue sharing, existing freezes and moratoria, combine to create what Washington calls the "New Federalism." Whether this is good or bad in the long run for Kansas City is a matter of debate. I think it will clearly result in a lower federal funding level for Kansas City. Certainly it will mean great problems in the coming year of transition.[3]

Here is an example of how to open up a publication and, so to speak, get it on its feet. This one is from a Management Information Service Report issued by the International City Management Association in December 1972:

A city, town, county, or other local government can be defined as sets of communication links. This report is about the development and management of one set of communication links—the city graphic identification program.[4]

In writing news releases the most important point should be made in the first sentence. Here is an example from a newsletter of the Association of Bay Area Governments which serves the San Francisco Bay Area:

If airports and residential communities . . . are not kept from encroaching on one another by local planning then the state will move into this planning area, according to Los Angeles assemblyman Robert E. Badham, author of AB1856 which established airport land use commissions.[5]

The final example is from a consultant's report prepared for the New York State Urban

Development Corporation. The report, a highly professional job in design, photographs, and typography, leads off as follows:

New York City is land hungry. The 1969 comprehensive plan prepared by the New York City Planning Commission calls it the "National Center," but to continue as such New York City must provide adequate housing for its people, and suitable space for their jobs.[6]

The report deals with proposed changes in land use for Sunnyside Yards, a storage area for freight and suburban passenger trains totaling 300 acres in the borough of Queens. The report summary sets forth the principal ideas as follows:

The proposed plan for Sunnyside Yards provides a framework for developing a new community on this site, given the limitations of high construction costs, continuing full use of the railroad yards, and the existing traffic patterns and public transit facilities. This proposal is an idea for a new urban community that recognizes both human needs and values and the technical and practical problems of building and maintaining such an unusual project.[7]

Designing the Publication

Design, even in its simplest form, is an analytical process somewhat like systems analysis. It involves: (1) definition and study of the problem, including consideration of objectives; (2) consideration of alternatives and solutions; and (3) selection of the best approach. This problem-solving process provides the framework within which creativity can flourish in the form of symbols, drawings, photographs, and other visual elements.

Most cities and counties will not be involved often in publication design, but the need will arise occasionally, especially for format or framework design for a newsletter, a press release, a budget, or reports to the council. When the time comes, it is worth putting considerable effort into the development of publications that will be readily identified by style, content, and format.

Ideally, the design process should be within the larger framework of a graphic identification program, which is "a plan for the development and management of an appropriate and standardized set of graphic elements which provide visual identification for all municipal activities."[8]

The elements of a graphic identification program include: (1) the symbol and the logotype, often identified as a logo or trademark in industrial usage; (2) specific colors to be used with the symbol and logotype; (3) rules for use of the symbol, logotype, and colors on reports, letterheads, and other materials; (4) models, including sketches, flow charts, and other representations; and (5) documentation, including copies of finished work and records of experience.

Graphic design is the term widely used for commercial and large institutional applications. One of the most easily observed examples is the corporate identity program for the American Telephone and Telegraph Company. Their familiar symbol of the bell inside the circle can be seen in almost every part of the United States. Their design manuals include specific and general uses of their logotype, graphic standards, trademark and service marks, office stationery, motor vehicle graphics, building identification, and business forms. No city or county is ready to embark on any program as ambitious as this one, but the AT&T objectives are valid: pleasing visibility and consistent identification.

DESIGN APPLICATIONS

If the publications department strives for simplicity, dignity, and consistent identification, it will have made a good start in publication design. If the city or county has a management commitment to graphic identification and design improvement, then the services of a graphic designer will be a good long-term investment, especially if he or she can develop a program and train city employees.

It is beyond the scope of this chapter to provide a design manual, but a few suggestions are offered in the following paragraphs for newsletters and other types of publications.

Newsletters. An unpretentious design usually serves the purpose best. A gaudy newsletter head, crowded with arrows, wheels, gears, and other devices, distracts the reader by promising more than it delivers. It looks like an advertising piece instead of what it really is—a framework for the conveyance of information. It might be termed the "periodical package fallacy" to assume that a newsletter heading that is a grabber is effective. The novelty wears off quickly, and the crudities and banalities of design soon are evident to even the casual reader.

It usually is a mistake to attempt to crowd in everything at the top: title, name of organization, slogan, symbol and logotype, volume and issue number, date, address, and phone number. A practical way to resolve the difficulty is to break up the information. Keep the newsletter masthead with name, organization, and symbol or logotype. Show other identifica-

tion—volume and issue number, date, address, etc.—elsewhere on the first page of the newsletter.

The method of composition should be inexpensive. Usually office composition will suffice. Just because a newsletter is typewritten, however, does not mean that it needs to look amateurish. Typing specifications can be established for page width, number of columns, paragraphing, and underlining or separation of copy to provide emphasis.

The masthead should be simple and straightforward. Three examples are shown in Figures 11–2a and 11–2b. Two are in use by Public Technology, Incorporated, and by the Institute of Public Service, University of Connecticut.

FIGURE 11–2a. *Newsletter mastheads for Public Technology, Incorporated, and the Institute of Public Service, University of Connecticut.*

CITY HALL City of Springfield
NEWSLETTER
September 1975

INNOVATION AWARD ENTRIES

In July 1975, the City of Springfield announced a management innovation program and awards. The management innovation program addressed the need for better information concerning innovative achievements in urban management.

The first applications for the innovation award have been submitted. They include the following:

Standard Procedures System. As a result of rapid city government growth, city officials found that communications with citizens and among departments were hampered by inaccurate information about city services. In response, city officials designed a standard procedures system to give management control over all procedures, operations and services. Great attention has been given to the ability of the system to cut across departmental lines and address basic city functions.

Service Request Program. This is a system established to verify that citizen requests for services have been fulfilled. Utilizing postcards, the city administrators have established a method of evaluating city responsiveness to citizen requests.

The Rainy Day Beautification Project Faced with sanitation crews unable to work on rainy days and unsightly dumpster containers, city officials initiated a program to use sanitation workers to paint the dumpster containers bright colors with the city name and seal on the sides.

The Corporate Image Program. City officials felt that there should be an imaginative symbol for the city and sponsored a contest to have such symbol designed. As a result, the city adopted a modernistic symbol and implemented a program to coordinate the graphics and design on all city stationary, publications and signs.

The VIC (Very Important Citizen) Program. The city started the VIC Program to encourage great citizen participation with the government. Before each meeting of the city legislative body, the city mails special invitations to a list of citizens who become the special guests of the city at the next meeting.

MUNICIPAL BOND BANK

A State Municipal Bond Bank would be established under a bill presented to the 1975 General Assembly with the support of the State Treasurer. The objective of the proposal, as stated in the draft bill, are to foster and promote adequate markets for borrowing by local governments, to reduce costs of local government indebtedness, and to encourage continued investor interest in the purchase of bonds or notes of governmental units.

FIGURE 11-2b. *Newsletter masthead and opening page for the hypothetical city of Springfield.*

The third example, Figure 11–2b, has been drawn as an example for this book. It can be adapted for any city or county by substituting the name of the jurisdiction. The identifying information (issue number, date, address, etc.) can be typed near the top on the left-hand side and placed in a box, or placed at the bottom right if a less conspicuous position is desired. Composition can be done by an ordinary office typewriter. An attractive color combination can be achieved at little additional cost by using a dark brown ink on an ivory paper, a dark green ink on a pale green paper, a deep blue ink on white paper, or other combinations that might be suggested by a graphic designer or printer.

News Releases. Adaptation of the newsletter probably will serve the purpose for most communities as a news release form. The news release form for the city of Phoenix, Arizona, is a good example (Figure 11–3). Identification is the essential point; symbols, drawings, and slogans will not impress newspaper reporters, editors, and other media people.

Annual Reports. Here is the best opportunity for a large-scale creative effort in publications writing, design, and production. Even if the report is relatively small, say sixteen pages in 6-by-9-inch format, there is still opportunity for developing an attractive and effective piece.

The annual report provides many options: in format, including booklets, folders, and newspaper supplements; in size, with 6 by 9 and 8½ by 11 inches the most common; in typography, with choices from contemporary sans serif faces to more traditional faces (see the heading "Type Classification," under "Typography," below); and in a very large range of photographs and drawings.

Most annual reports are issued as booklets, either 6 by 9 or 8½ by 11 inches in size. Most have separate covers, and many are quite attractive and imaginative in the use of drawings and photographs. Unfortunately, however, in too many cases the attractive cover could be dubbed "the annual report cover-up." The body of the report, poorly written, drab in appearance, and totally lacking in photos and illustrations, makes the cover look like a piece of false advertising.

Various aspects of report preparation are discussed elsewhere in this chapter, but one point will be stressed here—the use of drawings and photographs. Every jurisdiction can use photos. Almost every community has a competent photographer who, with a little coaching and imagination, can take some lively shots of the city government delivering services to citizens. Details on the use of photography are found in Appendix D of this book.

Line drawings can be an interesting variation if they are well done (often they are not). Usually, these drawings should be done by professionals: it is an underestimated skill. If the drawings are not of good quality, it is better to leave them out.

The design of an annual report should not attempt to do too much. The careful blending of suitable size, a few typographic elements, well-written text, and good quality photos and illustrations provides a pleasing overall effect. This effect cannot be achieved by borders, ornaments, random placement of irrelevant cartoons, and other stylistic devices. Further discussion of annual reports, and illustrations of such reports, are found in Chapter 10 of the present volume.

The Budget. Ordinarily, preparation of the annual budget and the capital budget would not seem to generate any design problems. This type of publication should be a straightforward job of presenting financial information for the council. Essentially this is correct, but the information still should be organized and in a clear, consistent, and readable format. Two examples are shown, from Kansas City, Missouri, and Dallas, Texas (Figures 11–4 and 11–5). Both use typewriter composition with careful, consistent layout.

Other Publications. Other publications cover a wide range of materials, including reports to the city council and to citizen boards and commissions, leaflets and flyers to announce new regulations or new city programs, posters announcing civic events, and legal documents. It is not possible within the limits of this chapter to provide design considerations for this wide variety of printed materials, but those preparing government publications should cultivate a healthy skepticism and curiosity about every publication proposal involving the govern-

CITY OF PHOENIX		NEWS
PUBLIC INFORMATION		

BILL HERMANN
PUBLIC INFORMATION OFFICER

LEO MOORE
PUBLIC INFORMATION SPECIALIST

DAVE KRIGBAUM
PUBLIC INFORMATION SPECIALIST

PRESS RELEASE

FOR IMMEDIATE RELEASE

MAY 6, 1975

FIGURE 11–3. *News release masthead, Phoenix, Arizona.*

ment. For example, there is no law that says that every line of a legal document *must* be printed in very small type in a line that is six inches wide on a piece of paper that measures fourteen inches from top to bottom. It just might be possible to have the type set in two columns in a larger size for better readability.

TYPOGRAPHY

Many discussions of typography are placed in a historic and artistic context, largely chronological, that is of little use to city or county employees who are planning a printing job. Their concerns are more practical and have to do with function and suitability.

Suitability is especially important: it means the appropriateness of the type for the job at hand. For example, an information folder for older persons probably should be printed in large type (11 or 12 point) because older persons often have vision problems. If you are selecting type for a folder welcoming citizens to council meetings, dignity should prevail. Type faces should not be mixed indiscriminately; they tend to distract attention from the information that is to be conveyed. Large initials, ornaments, and bizarre arrangements of type are best avoided.

Type Classification. For most purposes, the following functional classification of type will serve in planning printed materials: roman, abstract, cursive, and decorative.

Roman type shows letters with serifs (fine vertical and horizontal cross strokes) and graduated thick and thin strokes. Roman type is used for the bulk of the material—usually termed the "text" or "body"—in books, magazines, and other printed items.

Abstract type looks as if the letters are based on mechanical drawing. The letters have straight edges and lines of uniform thickness. Abstract letters are either without serifs (sans serif) or with square serifs of the same weight as the letter (block serifs). The sans serif versions of abstract type have been very popular in the late sixties and seventies. Many examples can be seen in specialized magazines, corporation annual reports, airline timetables, magazine ads, and school textbooks.

Cursive letters are slanted. Italic is the best-known form, but there are other variations.

Decorative type covers an enormous range of faces for advertising display, college diplomas, posters, public announcements, and many other specialized uses.

Each of these classifications contains many type faces (the primary unit of classification for type), and some of these type faces tend to cluster in groups. Figure 11–6 shows the four type classifications; an example for the Baskerville family (the face used in this book) in roman and other forms; and type measurement.

Type Measurement. Some familiarity with type measurement is needed in planning printed

Air Pollution Control
Environmental Protection

OBJECTIVES

Provide local Air Pollution Control programs that meet the standards and requirements of the Missouri Air Conservation Commission and the Environmental Protection Agency.

Prevent or reduce air pollution caused by vehicles, open burning and commercial and industrial activities.

Review and monitor plans and progress of industrial and commercial plants to install emission control equipment.

Maintain continuous air sampling and analysis activities.

Maintain an "air alert" mechanism to halt major sources of pollutants if critical levels accumulate during inversion periods.

MEASUREMENT DATA

	1971-72	1972-73	1973-74
Complaints investigated	780	736	600
Incinerators tested, permits issued	94	124	130
Major industries achieving compliance	12	17	15
Air samples collected and analyzed, and readings taken	3,623	47,700	68,000

COMMENTS

During the 1972-73 fiscal year a Trust Fund was established for this program. Thus, the budgeted amount is the City contribution or matching share. It is anticipated that the federal share will be $110,000 for a total of $245,481.

All personnel are budgeted in the Trust Fund. The cost of the thirteen positions will be $164,580.

Personnel Summary	1972-73	1973-74
Man Years	10.00	13.00
Man-Years-EEA	2.00	2.00
Man Years-TOTAL	12.00	15.00

Basic Program	1972-73	1973-74	% Change	1972 Revenue Sharing	1973 Revenue Sharing	1973 EEA Program
Non-Payroll Costs	$108,775	$135,481	24.6			
Payroll Costs	109,847	–	-100.0			
Subtotal	$218,622	$135,481	- 38.0	–	–	$19,854
Support Costs	21,239	9,113	- 57.1			
TOTAL	$239,861	$144,594	- 39.7			

41

FIGURE 11–4. *Sample budget page, Kansas City, Missouri. (Source: City of Kansas City, Missouri,* CITY OF KANSAS CITY, MISSOURI, BUDGET 1973–1974, *Kansas City, Mo.: City of Kansas City, Missouri, 1973, p. 41.)*

REVENUE SHARING BUDGET

PAGE NO. 20

PROGRAM   PUBLIC SAFETY

PROJECT   EAST DALLAS DEMONSTRATION PROGRAM

ACCOUNT NO.   024-9165

DESCRIPTION:

ALLOCATION PROPOSED

This program responds to the conclusions drawn by the recently completed Community Analysis Program. Principal emphasis would be placed upon the mobilization of resources from the private sector to address community development considerations related to the East Dallas area. Liaison would be established with the financial institutions in the community, with social services agencies in the community, with City agencies whose services affect the area, and with citizen groups actively engaged in the affairs of this community.

EXPENSE CLASSIFICATION

Salaries	$56,024
Supplies/Services	15,377
Maintenance/Equipment	250
Capital Outlay-Equipment	12,627
Total	$84,278

POSITION SUMMARY
PROPOSED
1973-74

5

CITY OF DALLAS

FIGURE 11-5. *Sample page from revenue sharing budget, Dallas, Texas. (Source: City of Dallas,* CITY OF DALLAS, TEXAS, REVENUE SHARING BUDGET FOR ENTITLEMENT PERIOD BEGINNING JULY 1, 1973, AND ENDING JUNE 30, 1974, *Dallas, Tex.: City of Dallas, 1973, p. 20.)*

materials, from the standpoint of both the usefulness of the completed work and the printing cost. The point system is used to measure type. It is as follows: 12 points to one pica; 6 picas to one inch; or 72 points to one inch.[9]

The size of each type face is measured by the depth of the metal block on which the character is cast. Thus, a letter cast in 18 point Times Roman is cast on a block 18 points high. The point size is only an approximate indication of the size of the type face itself. Usually the type size is somewhat larger than the type face.

Printers use a system of picas and points for expressing measurements of type itself, or the "type page," in their terminology. Printers use inches for measurement of paper, illustrations, and margins.

For example, in this book, the type is a 10 point VideoComp Baskerville on a 12 point spacing. Expressed vertically, there are 6 lines of 12 point type to the inch (that is, 6 picas or 72 points). Each column is 17½ picas in width, and the space between the two columns is 1½ picas. Expressed horizontally, the type page is 36½ picas wide, including both columns of type and the space between the columns. For a more detailed discussion of composition, including both traditional and new methods, see Appendix D of this book.

Selection of Type. The general character of the printed page has been treated exhaustively over the years by artists, designers, and typographers. Among them, there has been about as much disagreement as agreement on how to

The type selected should be appropriate

Civic Institutions

CIVIC INSTITUTIONS

The Baskerville family

ABCDEFGHIJKLMNOPQRSTUVWXYZ
Roman capitals

ABCDEFGHIJKLMNOPQRSTUVWXYZ
Roman small capitals

abcdefghijklmnopqrstuvwxyz
Roman lower case

ABCDEFGHIJKLMNOPQRSTUVWXYZ
Italic capitals

abcdefghijklmnopqrstuvwxyz
Italic lower case

ABCDEFGHIJKLMNOPQRSTUVWXYZ
Bold capitals

abcdefghijklmnopqrstuvwxyz
Bold lower case

A method of type classification

Roman
Abstract
Cursive
DECORATIVE

Type measurement

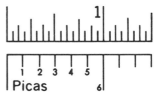

Picas

12 points = 1 pica
6 picas = 1 inch
72 points = 1 inch

FIGURE 11–6. *Type selection, classification, and measurement.*

achieve good typography. All agree, however, that *ease of reading* is the primary objective. To attain this, there are several generally accepted principles for selecting type.

The type face should be legible. Legibility has to do with type design. Because most of the contemporary type faces are of good legibility, this does not present a troublesome problem. It is a worthwhile practice to observe type faces used in various publications; if a particular type has personal appeal, it can be used as a sample in type selection specifications. The chances are that if the typesetter does not have that particular type, he or she will have one of similar design. The difference may be quite subtle and obvious only to the experienced typographer. Decorative faces are best avoided unless selected by a professional designer.

The type size and line length should ensure comforta-

ble reading. Type should be set to be read with little effort or eyestrain. The relationship between the size of type, length of line, and space between lines (leading) are factors of readability. A small type size set on a wide measure (line length) with no leading is difficult to read. However, there are few hard and fast rules. The requirements of the publication (space available and number of pages) may be determining factors in the type specifications. A type size and line length that cause excessive end-of-line word division or wide spacing between words should be avoided. If there is any doubt about the size, line length, and leading, it is advisable to have sample paragraphs set before committing the entire publication to type.

Different type faces and sizes should be combined sparingly. Many different type styles, sizes, and weights in one publication contribute to reader confusion. As a general practice, readability is enhanced if a single type family (all the variations of the same type face) is used. Some variations may be introduced in the choice of contrasting type for headlines and captions. Usually, italic and boldface styles are specified only for emphasis and not for setting large masses of type.

Paper and printing process should be considered. A perfectly smooth paper surface (coated as contrasted to noncoated) offers the greatest latitude in type selection. A finely designed type face (delicate serifs and thin strokes) will not print with the same definition on a rough-textured paper as on a smooth paper: the characteristics of the type design may be altered. This is less of a consideration in offset lithography than letterpress, but paper is a factor regardless of the printing process and should be given consideration when selecting a type face.

ILLUSTRATIONS

A convenient classification of illustrations is: (1) informative—generally those that explain or show facts, circumstances, characters, people, and places; (2) suggestive—drawings or photos that establish a mood or an atmosphere; (3) decorative—those that are strictly ornamental; and (4) representative—those that are shown as reproductions of works of art, including reproductions and prints in art books.[10] Government publications rely primarily on informative illustrations, with occasional use of suggestive or decorative illustrations.

Governments have excellent sources of illustrations in their own backyards. For many purposes, nothing is better than a photo of government activities and people against a backdrop of government buildings and equipment. If those preparing government publications wish to go further, the next step is to consult the reference desks of the public library, the historical society, and the photo files of the local newspapers.

An enormous amount of illustrative material, particularly photographs, is in the public domain and is obtainable without charge and without the need for copyright clearance. Libraries, historical societies, and museums are excellent sources. Curators usually are helpful

in providing assistance by subject area, geographic area, and time period.

Effective use of photography is discussed further in Appendix D of this book.

USE OF COLOR

The use of two colors (black usually being the first color) can often enhance a publication by giving it a certain style.

Of all the graphic elements, color has the most powerful psychological effect. . . . Color is almost entirely without intellectual content, it speaks directly to the subconscious. Tests have definitely established a connection between color and emotions. Color is thus one of the most effective tools of communication. . . . Because of its psychological powers, color is particularly valuable in creating atmosphere and mood.[11]

In local government it is easy to associate certain colors with certain activities: red for the fire department, blue for the police force, green and brown for parks and recreation areas. If your community has colors that are used with a symbol and logotype, these may be appropriate. Three guidelines on selection of colors may be helpful:

1. Limit the selection. Two colors, black and a second color, usually are enough.
2. Use restraint. The second color should provide emphasis and contrast rather than being a dominant element.
3. Use relatively standard colors that people are familiar with. Avoid offbeat shades of chartreuse, magenta, pink, and tangerine. Such colors are best left to the professionals.

Drafting Specifications

Once basic tasks of planning, writing, editing, and design are completed, the physical process of putting the publication in print can begin. The writing and design processes will indicate major decisions on size, number of pages, etc., and the next step is to draft printing specifications.

Clear specifications are essential for orderly production of the publication. The specifications must include all pertinent details and physical requirements of the publication and must be set forth in an organized style. The more comprehensive the specifications, the less likelihood there is of possible disappointment in the final appearance of the publication. Also, the process of selecting the printer dictates that each printing bidder have identical information on which to base his or her pricing. Otherwise, the quality of workmanship and service of different printers cannot be compared accurately, and the pricing differences between printers will be misleading.

The form shown in Figure 11–7 is used by the International City Management Association for ordering printing and might suggest a useful checklist for adaptation to the individual city or county. It covers most of the specifications described in the following paragraphs.

To be complete, the specifications should be organized in six principal sections: overall specification; prepress preparation; paper; printing process; binding; and distribution.

Overall Specification

The overall specification includes the publication name, quantity, trim size, number of pages (self-cover or plus cover), and identification of bleed pages (those pages with the printed image extending to the trim edge).

If the quantity has not been set, an estimate must be made and the cost of additional one hundreds or thousands of copies over the base quantity should be requested. The additional cost rate may then be applied (within limits) to the base quantity. This unit cost is useful information to have in reconciling overrun or underrun cost on the completion of the printing.

If it is likely that at some future time it will be necessary to reprint the publication, the back-to-press cost should be requested. This price will emphasize the need for carefully considering quantity on the initial printing. Ordering a few hundred extra copies in the beginning, with low incremental cost, is good printing insurance.

If little latitude is allowed in determining ordered quantity, it is important that specifications define an acceptable underrun or overrun. Rarely will the printer deliver the exact number of copies ordered, not by choice but because of spoilage variables in presswork and bindery operations. Unless otherwise specified in the printing order, the printing trade custom states that a 10 percent overrun or underrun of the quantity ordered is acceptable.

Prepress Preparation

After the overall specifications have been determined, the physical materials of the publication must be prepared for printing. These specifications should include details on composition and illustrations.

From the standpoint of printing, illustrations are of two types: line and continuous tone.

Line illustrations are formed by lines suitable for reproduction without using a halftone screen. Pen-and-ink drawings and cartoons are common examples.

Continuous tone illustrations consist of a broad range of tones requiring reproduction by the halftone screen process. Photographs almost always are reproduced in this way. The halftone screen makes the printing of continuous tones possible by converting the continuous tone image into a pattern of very small and clearly defined dots of varying size. The halftone principle is an optical illusion in which tones are represented by solid dots which all have equal spacing and ink density but vary in area.

The composition specifications include method of typesetting, size of type and type face, type page size, column width, and number of pages of composition. Manuscript or copy should be carefully prepared and clearly marked. The specification should also include reference to copy of a difficult nature, such as tables or varying line length requirements around illustrations and design elements.

The final step in prepress preparation is putting the illustration and copy elements together in pages ready for the printing process to follow. This is generally referred to as "ready-for-camera." Reproduction quality proofs of the type elements are pasted exactly in position on art boards, together with key lines or "windows" marked for the exact position and size of illustrations. The printer may do this work, or it may be done by one's own staff or by an art studio. Care and skill at this stage of prepa-

International
City
Management
Association

1140
Connecticut
Avenue
Northwest
Washington DC
20036

Area Code 202
293-2200

Printing Specifications

To:

Date: _____

ICMA Order No.: _____

Job Title: _____

_____

Quantity: _____

Delivery Date: _____

Trim Size: _____

No. of Pages _____

Self cover ☐ plus cover ☐

Paper: Cover _____

      Text _____

Colors: Cover _____

      Text _____

Illustrations:

  No. halftones _____

  No. line _____

Artwork: _____

Binding: Saddle stitch ☐; Smyth ☐; Side wire ☐; Perfect ☐

  Other _____

Folding: _____

  For No. 10 envelope ☐

Drill _____ holes on _____ inch side.

Perforate: _____

Delivery: ICMA ☐; mail _____ class ☐; date _____

  Envelopes _____

  Enclosures _____

  Labels _____

Ship ☐ via _____ date _____

Special Instructions

_____
          Signature

FIGURE 11–7. *Printing specifications checklist used by the International City Management Association.*

ration are critical to the overall quality of the printing.

PAPER

Specifying paper can be confusing, since it is made in unbelievable varieties. Considerations include: color, weight, bulk, opacity, surface (glossy, matt, ribbed, and other types of finish), availability, and—not least—cost. Often the difference in papers can be seen only by direct comparison. For example, papers of the same weight vary in bulk, opacity, and surface. If paper choice is important to the character of the publication, one can refer to sample books of the various papers available. Then the printer or paper dealer can make up sample blank dummies to the size and number of pages of the publication.

The nature of the publication will often suggest paper possibilities. An annual report with many photographs and illustrations might suggest a coated paper for fidelity of halftone reproduction. Or perhaps the detail of the illustrations is not as important as the tone and atmosphere of the publication. Then, perhaps, a softer paper is desired, a paper offering a textured surface with characteristics which will add another dimension to the publication. Or a colored paper may be desired. Colors are limited in coated papers, but are offered generally in a wide range in uncoated papers. They always cost more than white paper. It may be less expensive on long press runs to use ink to add an overall tint of color to the paper as part of the printing instead of using colored paper.

Depending on the number of pages and the quantity printed, paper represents a significant factor in overall cost. On long runs it may represent the greatest single cost (i.e., paper versus prepress preparation, presswork, binding). The paper specification must be exact as to manufacturer, color, finish, and weight. Otherwise, the printers' bids may not be comparable. See elsewhere in this chapter for additional information on paper.

PRINTING PROCESS

The printing requirements of the publication will usually dictate the process to use. Unless there are unusual requirements involving quantity, paper, and quality, the offset lithography process will usually be specified. This process offers the greatest flexibility, whether the publication is a typewritten report or a full-scale publication with color, text, and illustration elements. A closer look at printing processes is provided in Appendix D of this book.

If color is used in the printing process, the color specifications must be clearly stated. Color printing requires additional presswork (even if a single color other than black is used), and often different press equipment. Also, colored inks cost more than black. As a general practice, the color selection should be made from standard colors available from the printer. Otherwise, it will be necessary to formulate and mix the color.

The paper, its surface characteristics, and its color may influence color ink selection. An ink printed on a smooth, glossy paper appears purer and more brilliant than the same ink printed on a textured surface. And an ink printed on a white paper compared to that same ink printed on a colored paper may appear to be an entirely different color. The light source under which a color is observed and the proximity of other colors likewise influence color judgment.

The artist/designer and the printer should be consulted if color is critical to the publication. Elaborate procedures are available to minimize the chances for disappointment. If color is used merely for limited accent or for variety, it is best to pick standard colors. The printer will have an ink book of sample swatches identified by number. The color varieties are wide ranging. And if there are doubts about color choices for a particular paper, ask for flat proof swatches of the particular color on the specific paper selected.

BINDING

The next step in publication production is some form of bindery operation. The different types of folds and the limitations of mechanical folding equipment should be considered at the design and planning level. Otherwise, folding might become a costly hand operation.

Usually, if there are more than four or six pages one of several different binding styles may be used. The two most common styles are saddle-stitch and side-stitch binding. In saddle stitching, the staples are forced through the backbone (the back connecting the two covers) of the publication. This type of binding is the simplest and least expensive. The publication lies flat and stays open for ease of reading.

If the bulk of the number of pages of the publication is too thick for saddle stitching (the wire staples tend to tear through the binding edge), then side stitching is often specified. The pages are collated, by machine or hand, and placed flat under a stitcher. The stitches are inserted about a quarter of an inch from the binding edge. With this type of binding the inside margin must be wider than in a saddle-stitched publication to accommodate the stitches. Side-stitched publications cannot be completely opened flat, but the style does offer the characteristic of a square back which is sometimes preferred. A separate, glued-on cover may be used for a more finished appearance.

There are many other ways to bind a publication; the most frequently used styles are mechanical, perfect, and edition binding.

Mechanical Binding. The sheets of the publication are punched with a series of round or slotted holes on the binding edge. Then wire, plastic coils, or rings are inserted by special equipment through the holes. As with side-wire stitching, an allowance must be made in the inner margin for punching the holes.

Perfect Binding. An adhesive is applied to the backbone of the assembled sheets of the publication and a cover is glued into place. Most telephone books are bound in this manner, as are the millions of paperbacks sold in drug stores, supermarkets, bookstores, airline terminals, and other high-traffic areas. The style has the characteristic of a square back but does not require an allowance in the binding edge for staples or mechanical binding. With the advances made in adhesives today, this is a practical and long-lasting method of binding.

Edition Binding. This style is generally used only when permanence is required and is the traditional method of binding a hard-cover book. It is a more expensive method of binding. It involves sewing the signatures (multiple page

flat sheets folded in their proper page sequence) together by special sewing machines, coating the sewn edges with glue, rounding the backbone, gluing a strip of gauze onto the backbone, and, finally, putting the book into its cover (case) on a special machine which applies paste and fits the cover into place. The cover is made separately and usually is stamped in a metallic foil with the title.

DISTRIBUTION

The final part of the specification covers packaging and delivery. Although often overlooked in the first stages of production, these instructions should be incorporated in the original specifications. This enables the printer to order boxes or special packaging if necessary, and arrange for possible unusual delivery or mailing requirements. It also eliminates repackaging and extra handling. All too often, distribution specifications are an afterthought, creating confusion and sometimes disappointment in an otherwise well-executed production plan. The publication is not complete until it is delivered where it is wanted and in an acceptable manner.

Producing the Publication

The publication is now ready, in the terminology of publishing and printing, to go into production. For big jobs the process may be called manufacturing, which it surely is in the sense of assembling materials and labor to turn out a finished product. The critical first steps are scheduling and picking suppliers, which may be done concurrently. These steps will, of course, be discussed as part of the overall planning of the publication—probably even before writing has commenced.

SCHEDULING

Once the specifications have been drafted, setting deadlines for each step pinpoints responsibilities and provides control of the total production process. If the target date for delivery is to be met, each part must fall into place at predetermined times and in an orderly manner.

The schedule should include checkpoints for copy preparation, design and layout, typesetting, proofreading, artwork, illustrations, final okay, printing, and delivery. A good approach is to start with the completion date and work backward, allowing appropriate time intervals for each operation. Some steps may be accomplished concurrently; others must follow in sequence. It is important to show the time intervals in working days, and to be sure to allow for Saturdays, Sundays, and all holidays.

It is best to prepare a schedule in chart form with space to show planned start and finish times and actual completion times. The chart form offers a quick visual check of the progress of the publication and whether it is on schedule. Figure 11–8 suggests a simple scheduling format.

PICKING SUPPLIERS

Selecting the right supplier can be a perplexing problem, and unfortunately, in graphic arts services, whether the right decision was made is not known until the work is substantially completed. The objective is to pick suppliers who will provide service on time, provide acceptable workmanship, and set prices which can be forecast with accuracy and on a competitive basis. It is important to set standards for each depending on the total requirements of the publication. Price alone should not be the overriding consideration.

A worthwhile means of making the process easier is to build a supplier file. Every opportunity should be used to gather information on sources for artwork, photography, typesetting, printing, etc. Evaluations of each source can be made and noted by talking with printers' representatives, examining samples of work, checking references, and maintaining performance records. In time, the file becomes a valuable source of reliable information for buyer judgments.

Since printing usually represents the largest

Publication Production Schedule

Title:

Operation	Responsibility	Progress start/finish				Completion date	
						Scheduled	Actual
Publication plan and specifications							
Copy preparation							
Layout / design							
Illustrations							
Composition and proofing							
Artwork							
Printing							
Delivery							

NOTES

FIGURE 11–8. *Major elements of a printing production schedule.*

single cost in the publication budget, special care must be exercised in the buying decision. Narrow the choice to those printers with adequate facilities to perform within the time frame of the publication schedule and to serve on a regular basis other publications of the same general requirements.

Bid specifications should be carefully prepared and should cover all elements of the publication, so that each printer has the identical information for his estimates. Otherwise, prices will not be comparative, and a buying decision may be made which could create untold problems in the final production of the publication. Printing specifications similar to those shown in Figure 11–7 can be used to solicit bids, but the specifications must be precisely drafted. The phrase "or equivalent" is full of traps for the inexperienced buyer of printing.

Copy Preparation

The one basic principle to remember in preparing copy for printing is: *clean copy saves time, error, and cost.* The ground rules are simple, and if they are followed typesetting will move with a minimum of alterations, in the shortest time, and at the lowest cost.

Copy should be prepared on standard 8½-by-11-inch paper. The typing should be double-spaced, with wide margins, and *on one side of the sheet only.*

Corrections must be marked legibly, above the line wherever possible or in the right margin. If there are substantial alterations, the copy should be retyped. What may be clear to the editor may be confusing to the typesetter.

The sheets of copy should be numbered consecutively, and each sheet should be identified at the top with the name of the publication. On the last page of copy, the end should be indicated either with a hash mark (#) or the word "end."

The editor will often avoid additional type correction cost—no small factor in the case of modern photocomposition techniques—by knowing in advance how much space the copy will occupy on the printed page. Forecasting the space requirements also helps determine the size of type and length of line to specify. The character count method is the most widely used in estimating the copy length. Total characters and spaces of copy are counted; for greatest accuracy, the count should be made on a paragraph basis.

If the typed copy is of a uniform line length, the number of lines multiplied by the average character count per line will give the total count. Pica typewriters have ten characters and spaces to the inch; elite typewriters have twelve to the inch. If copy is typed on a nonstandard typewriter it will be necessary to count several lines of copy to arrive at the average number of characters to the inch. After the count is completed, the next step is to calculate the area into which the copy will fit in the selected type face.

Most type composition companies provide type specimens of the type faces they have available, and list with each type face the average number of characters per pica (6 picas equal 1 inch) of line length. Table 11–1 is a typical character count chart for the Times Roman type face. This table indicates, for example, that Times Roman set in 10 point in a line 26 picas wide (a common line length in novels) will have approximately 690 characters (10 × 69). It is a simple process to convert from typewritten manuscript to material in type by using this

Table 11–1. *Average character count for Times Roman type face by pica width and point size.*

Point size	Pica width											
	1	10	12	14	16	18	20	22	24	26	28	30
8	3.05	31	37	43	49	55	61	67	73	79	85	92
9	2.85	29	34	40	46	51	57	63	68	74	80	86
10	2.65	27	32	37	42	48	53	58	64	69	74	80
12	2.30	23	28	32	37	41	46	51	55	60	64	69

method and allowing for leading (space between lines), point sizes, and type faces (different type faces have different character counts in the same point sizes).

When the copy is ready to go, the printer's representative can help in the process—called copy fitting—so that copy can be adjusted in length before the composition begins. Also, most printers can provide explanatory booklets on copy fitting with detailed descriptions and examples.

The type specifications should be marked on the first page of the manuscript. The accepted style is to show size, leading, type face, and measure in that order. In marking the size, the leading should be specified in the form of a fraction, and the line length in picas. Thus, 10/11 Times Roman $\times$ 18 means 10 point type on 11 point body in Times Roman face to the line length of 18 picas.

Paragraph instructions should also be marked on the typed copy. Paragraphs may be indented or kept flush. Headings should be marked centered, flush left, or flush right. An indention is indicated in ems of the point size. An em is the square of the body type (i.e., a 10 point em is 10 points square). A single square box marked at the beginning of a paragraph indicates a 1 em indention. Clearly marking paragraph style and other indention styles in the copy is important. Otherwise, costly resetting may be necessary.

Other copy markings will indicate type style for word, phrase, or paragraph emphasis. One underscore means set in *italic;* two underscores, set in SMALL CAPITAL LETTERS; three underscores, set in ALL CAPS; and a wavy line underneath, set in **boldface.** Before the editor adopts one or more of these styles, he or she should check with the typesetter to be sure the variations are available in the particular type face selected.

Once the copy is in type, a careful proofreading must be made for possible typesetting errors and author's alterations. Most typesetting has had at least one reading before proofs are submitted, but the responsibility for error free work ultimately rests with the editor. Errors and/or changes should be marked with a colored pen or pencil so that the typesetter will see the corrections easily. Standard proofreaders' marks (shown in most dictionaries) should be used. The above discussion is concerned only with the traditional types of typesetting, and not with such techniques as computer typesetting. For a discussion of other techniques, and for material supplementary to the remainder of this section, see Appendix D.

ARTWORK

The preparation of artwork often poses many technical problems which should be left to the experienced commercial artist. The overriding considerations are neatness, accuracy, and a complete understanding of the printing process from camera and film layout, through platemaking, to presswork and binding. Once the artwork is released to the printer, nothing should be left to later change and adjustment if at all possible. Revisions after the publication has been photographically transferred to film for platemaking and printing may prove costly.

The art board represents the basic structure for the publication page. This is the final assembly of all art and copy elements into a unit for photomechanical reproduction. It is called a pasteup or mechanical. It should have all copy elements mounted in position. Continuous tone images, such as photographs, and other elements of a scale[12] different from the base art, are handled as separate pieces of art. Key lines or "knockouts" (carefully defined areas by exact shape and size) indicate on the base art where these elements are to be positioned. These separate elements must be coded, usually by letters or numbers, and cross-referenced to the base art board.

Care is the key to handling the pasteup. Smudged type and blurred lines cannot be corrected easily. A precautionary measure for the professional artist is to overlay each art board with a protective sheet of blank paper.

Unfortunately, photographs are often mishandled. Crop marks should be indicated with a grease pencil in the margins of the print outside the image area. Instructions should not be written on the back of photographs, as the writing may crack the emulsion of the print, causing the message to appear on the photograph. Clips should not be used, as they may scratch and damage the print. Coding and instructions should be written on a small piece of paper and taped to the back of the print, or hinged from the back at the top or bottom of the print.

The basic difference between artwork for letterpress printing, the second most available printing process, and that for offset lithography is that a base art board is not usually prepared for letterpress. The elements of the publication, illustrations and copy, are physically assembled in pages from metal type and plates. The illustrations are photomechanically etched on plates by the photoengraving process. The printer makes up the pages from a dummy (a preliminary layout showing the position of the elements as they are to appear in the final reproduction). Complete pages are proofed mechanically on a proof press. At this stage in production, corrections and minor space adjustments may be made at minimum cost.

WORKING WITH THE PRINTER

The key to a good working relationship between buyer and printer is communication. Once the printer's proposal has been accepted, instructions should be brought into sharp focus and loose ends tied down. What follows may make a difference in the degree of success of the publication.

All production requirements should be reviewed at the time the publication is turned over to the printer. Changes in number of pages, quantity, paper, etc., may cause a substantial change in the production plan, affecting cost and service. The printer is dependent on outside sources for paper and ink, and the control he or she can exercise over these sources is limited.

Ideally, all materials should be turned over to the printer at the same time. Since this is not always feasible, it is helpful to the printer to have in advance those elements requiring the most time (such as illustrations which can go into the camera department in advance of the rest of the publication).

Working together at every stage of the production will keep the publication moving through to completion. Many times, an experienced printer can suggest ways to improve the publication at no added cost. The printer may be able to suggest a more practical size by minor changes in dimensions, a better plan for use of color, a different reproduction technique for illustrations, or any number of other possibilities related to areas of expertise in his or her own operation.

OK TO PRESS

Opportunities are presented throughout the production process to check and approve the elements going into the publication. Type has been set, proofs have been submitted, corrections have been made. The final checkout is the release for printing: OK to print.

In offset lithography the artwork is photographically prepared on film with all elements of the pages in place and the pages imposed (arranged in a form so that they will be in the correct order after the printed sheet is folded). A contact print (a photographic positive) is then made on two-sided light-sensitive paper. This is the offset proof, usually a blueprint or brownprint. It is folded into pages and trimmed to conform to the final trim dimensions of the publication.

The offset proof, despite previous proofing of the type composition and the pasteup, should be checked out carefully. Elements of the pasteup may have come loose in handling, foreign matter may appear on the artwork or film, a photograph inadvertently may have flopped (reversed) or been placed upside down, or a headline may have been covered over. Errors of this type can be corrected easily prior to printing. Corrections in publication content, however, may require revising the original pasteup and repeating most of the operations of making the original set of blueprint proofs.

If color is being used in the publication, it is often difficult to distinguish in the blueprint those elements to be printed in color. The image to appear in color is of a lighter tone in the proof than the black. The printer should mark the color elements, but this may be overlooked. Also, it is difficult to visualize the effect of the color use.

At a nominal extra charge, if not covered in the original specifications, the printer can prepare color keys. These are proofs made by exposing the black negative and each color negative separately to light-sensitive dye-colored transparencies. The dye colors approximate standard printing ink colors. The transparencies are assembled one over the other and affixed to a white sheet of backing paper. This proof, although not color accurate, provides an excellent method of checking color elements in relation to the black elements, and the general appearance of the publication in print.

For critical color work demanding precise color reproduction, the artist and printer should be consulted. Work of this character usually demands press proofing on the same paper on which the publication is to be printed. Possibly extensive color corrections will have to be made to achieve the desired color effect. The preparation work and proofing are time-consuming and costly.

Releasing a letterpress-printed publication requires the same careful attention, but the preparation procedure is different and the proofs are of a different character. Each page is proofed separately on inexpensive proof paper. Rarely is a folded sample of all pages in printed sequence prepared. If folios (page numbers) are not used on the pages, the page sequence must be marked on each page proof. In reading the pages, attention should be given to the makeup of the pages and the carryover of the content from column to column and page to page. Once the full set of page proofs has been checked carefully, the publication is OK to release to print.

FOLLOW-UP AND DELIVERY

Although it is the printer's responsibility to keep the customer informed of the progress of the publication, it is small comfort to blame the printer for missing a critical delivery date. Knowing in advance of developing problem areas offers an opportunity to make adjustments and avoid disappointment. For example, if the OK to release to print is going to be delayed for one reason or another, notifying the printer immediately will offer the person concerned the chance to make adjustments in his or her production scheduling and possibly accommodate the delay without changing the delivery date. Telephone calls to the printer during the course of the production emphasize interest in the publication and keep the printer alert to possible problem areas.

Delivery instructions should be made a part of the original printing order. They should always be in writing and should be submitted well in advance of the delivery date. Packing requirements should be specified. For later handling, it may be advantageous to have the publication wrapped in units of a certain number and packed in cartons. Proper attention to delivery and packing instructions may save both time and effort.

Distributing the Publication

Mail delivery offers the opportunity to direct the publication to selected individuals by name or to saturate an area by mailing to all the households by selected ZIP codes. The latter is called "resident" or "occupant" mailing, and the publication is addressed accordingly, not by the name of the individual resident.

MAILING CLASSES

There are primarily two classes of service for mailing publications available to local governments: first class and third class. Each class has a different postage rate structure and service capability. The postal rates quoted in this section date from fall 1975. They are subject to change, but are given here as necessary for an understanding of how the various mailing classes work.

First Class. Other than special fee services, first class mail provides the best service. According to the United States Postal Service, delivery should be made within a radius of 600 miles by the second day. The rate is based on the weight of each piece at 10 cents per ounce. Although recommended and encouraged by the Postal Service, ZIP-coded addresses are not mandatory. Ordinarily, first class mail, because of its high cost, should be used only for priority mailings of limited appeal publications weighing less than one ounce.

Third Class. Because of the rate structure, third class mail should be the most popular publication mailing classification for municipalities. It is limited to printed matter weighing less than sixteen ounces per unit. Service in on a nonpriority basis, but delivery should be made within the local area within three to four days. The mailer has the option of two different postal rate classifications: (1) single piece rate and (2) bulk rate.

The only possible benefit of mailing at the single piece rate rather than first class would be when the publication weighs more than one ounce. The rate is 8 cents for each two ounces or fraction of two ounces, with a minimum rate of 10 cents per piece. ZIP-coded addresses are recommended but not mandatory.

Bulk rate mail is the most economical from the standpoint of postage expense, but it is far more complicated and requires close adherence to postal regulations in the preparation for mailing. To qualify for the special bulk postage rate, a single mailing must contain 200 or more identical pieces (or fifty pounds), and the mailing must be ZIP-coded and mailed according to ZIP code regulations. Also, an annual $30 bulk mailing fee is required. For trouble-free mailings in this rate classification, an experienced mailing service should be used.

The minimum postage rate for bulk third class mailings is 6.1 cents for the first 250,000 pieces mailed during each calendar year, and any piece in excess of this quantity is at the rate of 6.3 cents each. To complicate the rate structure, there is a pound rate of 32 cents per pound or fraction which applies if the number of copies per pound divided into the pound rate exceeds the minimum piece rate (for example, four copies per pound divided into 32 cents equals a single copy postage cost of 8 cents).

Other special mailing classes and privileges, such as second class, controlled circulation publication classification, and the nonprofit classification are not offered to local governments because of special qualifying postal requirements.

A Word of Caution. Postal rates are changed frequently. Mail classifications are likely to be changed. It is a worthwhile practice to keep informed on postal matters. There is a postal customer service representative in every area whose responsibility is to work with mailers. Consult the local postmaster for guidance. The United States Postal Service publishes a monthly newsletter, *Memo to Mailers,* which may be subscribed to at no cost by writing to: P.O. Box 6400, Arlington, Virginia 22206.

MAILING LISTS

The mailing list requires special attention. Maintenance of the list (corrections, additions, deletions) must be a continuing responsibility to avoid misdirected copies of the publication.

In addition to efforts within the organization, the Postal Service offers help. Generally upon payment of a 10 cent fee for each change, the service will send notification of an addressee's new address or reason for nondelivery. To merit this service, mail must bear the words "Address Correction Requested." There are options to this service, depending on class of mail and weight of publication. To gain full advantage of this service, it is recommended that the postal customer service representative be consulted.

There are sources of other lists which may prove valuable in the public relations publications program. Usually, within a geographic area there is at least one mailing service which maintains "occupant" lists for saturation mailings. Local merchants frequently use such lists for promotional mailings. The telephone directory is another important source for compiling a special list. The Postal Service will help in ZIP-coding the list.

There are companies that specialize in list rentals of many categories of names: lawyers, doctors, clergy, teachers, etc. Often these lists may be purchased outright; always they may be rented. Address selection by areas is usually offered. These companies service all types of business organizations and associations. If difficulty is experienced in locating sources, it is advisable to write to the Direct Mail and Marketing Association, 6 East 43rd Street, New York, New York 10017.

OTHER METHODS OF DISTRIBUTION

If the publication is of broad community interest and fits easily into an ordinary mailing envelope, cooperative mailing with a civic or community organization is often possible. Sharing the mailing expense enables both parties to benefit.

Any regular or special occasion involving a gathering of people presents an excellent opportunity for distributing the publication. Organizations catering to the public (banks, savings and loan offices, utility offices, stores, etc.) usually cooperate by permitting counter or rack displays. Also, community centers, libraries, and schools offer distribution opportunities to the public. Civic and club meetings are other possibilities for handing out copies of the publication. The opportunities are limited only by the restrictions placed on the distribution.

Summary

This chapter is intended as a practical guide to the mechanics of preparing, producing, and distributing local government publications.

First, a discussion of publications planning has detailed ways of handling different types of government publications. What special requirements are basic to the way a government publication is written? This is made clear in the next section of the chapter. A discussion of design follows, with considerable emphasis on selecting type. Following this, the subjects of printer's specifications and producing the publication are treated in detail. A section on distributing publications concludes the chapter.

With this final chapter of Part Three of this book, the subject of reaching the public through the media and through publications comes to an end. The next chapter, which constitutes Part Four, draws the subjects in the first three parts together into an integrated whole.

---

[1] Porter G. Perrin, WRITER'S GUIDE AND INDEX TO ENGLISH, 4th ed. (Chicago: Scott, Foresman and Company, 1965), pp. 18–19.

[2] City of Palo Alto, PEOPLE SERVING PEOPLE: A REPORT TO THE CITIZENS OF PALO ALTO (Palo Alto, Calif.: City of Palo Alto, 1973), p. 1.

[3] City of Kansas City, Missouri, CITY OF KANSAS CITY, MISSOURI, BUDGET 1973–1974 (Kansas City, Mo.: City of Kansas City, Missouri, 1973), p. iii.

[4] David S. Arnold and Herbert Slobin, CITY GRAPHIC IDENTIFICATION PROGRAMS, Management Information Service Reports, vol. 4 no. 12 (Washington, D.C.: International City Management Association, 1972), p. 1.

[5] Association of Bay Area Governments, BAY VIEW, April 1972, p. 3.

[6] Gruzen & Partners and The Lefrak Organization, SUNNYSIDE YARDS: A FEASIBILITY STUDY FOR THE MULTIPLE USE OF AIR RIGHTS OVER THE SUNNYSIDE YARDS (New York: New York State Urban Development Corporation, 1971), p. 5.

[7] Ibid., p. 7.

[8] Arnold and Slobin, CITY GRAPHIC IDENTIFICATION PROGRAMS, p. 1.

[9] The typewriter measurements of elite (twelve typewriter characters to the inch) and pica (ten typewriter characters to the inch) have no connection with the point system used in printing.

[10] This classification is based on Marshall Lee, BOOKMAKING: THE ILLUSTRATED GUIDE TO DESIGN AND PRODUCTION (New York: R. R. Bowker Co., 1965), pp. 144–45.

[11] Ibid., p. 235.

[12] Scale means changing the size of the original to the size of the reproduction with no change in the *ratio* of the dimensions. It is usually expressed as a percentage of the original. Cropping is a term meaning to eliminate certain areas from the original. The original may be marked for both scale and cropping.

Part Four

Integrating the Whole

12

Organizing and Training for Public Relations

THE PRECEDING CHAPTERS have developed in some detail the philosophy, relationships, techniques, and methods of the modern public relations program. To the local official seeking to improve his or her government's public relations, the question then becomes one of how to organize to produce the desired results in the most efficient manner possible. How large should a city or county be before a public relations department is necessary? What about professional public relations counsel? What type of organization is appropriate if professional counsel is not employed? How much will a solid program cost? What results can be expected from the program?

Obviously, no single answer can be given for every community in every circumstance. No single "package" can be applied to every situation and yield the same type of results. In fact, the highly successful program of one city may prove to be of little value in another city. There are, however, certain guidelines which can be observed by the public administrator, and the final determination as to the precise type of organization that is best in a given situation must be made by the administrator, in consultation, of course, with the members of the elected governing body.

Developments of recent years, moreover, have placed an even higher premium on an effective approach to a local government's relations with its publics and have required some modifications in organizational structure and programs. The rise of consumerism, for exam-

ple, has greatly increased citizen awareness and concern, resulting in more widespread belief that "you *can* fight city hall" (or major corporations), and that it is incumbent upon individuals to do so when they feel they did not get a "fair shake." Increased citizen involvement has also been fostered by certain federal programs designed around participation by the citizen groups being served. Another influence of recent years has been increased concern for environmental matters; this has brought about broad citizen participation in areas that previously concerned a few special interest groups. Another factor has been an increasing interest on the part of governmental agencies in the scientific sampling of citizen opinion as a means of relating policies more closely to the interests and concerns of the people being served. Each of these influences merits consideration as organizational plans are developed, and each is discussed briefly in the course of this chapter.

The chapter first discusses a "basic organization" for a government public relations operation, then becomes more specific, detailing the various ways in which a government can organize for a public relations program. After outlining and evaluating the trends of recent years (the rise of consumerism; federal programs encouraging citizen participation; environmental concerns; opinion surveys), the chapter turns to the subject of training for effective public relations.

This second part of the chapter initially treats its subject under the following headings: management and employee relations; the importance of communication; employee opinion and public opinion. The latter portion of the discussion deals with training itself. A brief summary concludes the chapter.

Basic Organization

Among the basic considerations in developing an effective organization for public relations is the generalization that the city or county with 185 employees should have 185 public relations representatives. And the city or county with 2,050 employees should have 2,050 representatives. Setting aside for the moment other facets of the public relations program, it is clear that no organization and no program is likely to be successful without the basic underlying understanding that *every* employee has, in addition to his or her primary job assignment, a collateral public relations duty.

The government's image as seen by the taxpayer is an extremely delicate and volatile thing which may be dramatically affected—for better or for worse—by the acts of the government's employees. Only when it is considered in this light does the great importance of sound public relations training for employees become fully apparent. The latter part of this chapter concerns itself with methods of promoting effective public relations through the training of employees.

Another generalization that may be made is that a public relations program of any type must enjoy the full understanding and cooperation of the legislative body—the city council or the county board. As the source of all policy, the governing body should not only watch its own public relations (of critical importance to itself) but should also insist upon sound public relations throughout the governmental organization.

Regardless of the community, certain public relations measures can always be taken, many without incurring any additional expense. The most obvious and important of these is the training of public-relations-conscious employees. Many such measures or elements are not necessarily thought of as part of a public

relations program, although they are, in fact, an integral part of the program. Clean, well-organized offices, for example, convey a feeling of efficiency. Modern office machines and field equipment also build a favorable image, as does the courteous driver of a government vehicle. The examples are virtually endless, as has been suggested in the preceding chapters.

In brief, it is the responsibility of the governing body to take the lead in policy establishment in public relations, just as it does in all other areas of local government concern. It should establish clear guidelines for the professional staff to follow, and should then give the chief administrator sufficient authority to match his or her responsibility in carrying out public relations policies.

Another generalization is that chief administrators should not only be "sold" on the importance of the public relations program but should be in the vanguard, assisting the council or board to develop public relations policy and setting the example themselves. Administrators should also impress upon department heads both the importance and the philosophy of the public relations program, developing their awareness of the fact that every act of departments or individuals, from refuse collection to plan checking, has its public relations aspects. Administrators should motivate department heads, so that they, in turn, may motivate employees under their supervision.

It is important that administrators instigate training for employees in all areas of public relations and see that training programs are properly staffed, equipped, supported, and attended. It is important, too, that administrators see to the development of sound press relations, observing the guidelines set forth in earlier chapters. In other words, the administrator should constantly seek to improve the public's image of the government through all means at his or her disposal.

The chief administrator's commitment to sound public relations, then, is no less compelling than his or her commitment should be to sound public finance or effective personnel systems, for example.

The basic organization for conducting an effective public relations program is the entire organization of the city or county government or regional council. No amount of "frosting," frills, or fancy salesmanship is going to develop a good public relations program if services are not sound and the organization is not aware of and actively working on its public relations responsibilities.

Beyond the Basic Organization

Once the development of the basic organization is accomplished (that is, once every employee and official knows his or her job and public relations responsibilities), decisions should be made regarding refinements and additions. There are several ways to organize, and the extent to which a city elaborates on its program in adopting any particular choice is largely a question of its size, available funds, local citizen attitudes, goals, and desires regarding the range of public relations activities. The options range from what might be termed the "one-man or one-woman show," through decentralization and the use of consultants, to what might be called the "staff pro."

THE "ONE-MAN SHOW"

The "one-man show" is used primarily by smaller jurisdictions, for example, cities of 50,000 and under population. As the name suggests, the public relations program is the responsibility of one person, generally the chief administrator, who is also responsible for preparing whatever formal reports or events constitute the bulk of the public relations program.

The fact that the responsibility for the entire program rests with one person does not mean that the end product need be inferior or in any way less effective than other approaches. Many highly imaginative and effective ideas have come out of the offices of administrators who have little or no formal assistance in carrying out the program. Under this arrangement, it is important that the chief administrator take full advantage of the talents of department heads and others, not only to lighten his or her personal burden but also to furnish the diversity of opinions, approaches, and language that results from cross-fertilization of ideas.

The "do-it-yourself" approach is an extension of the "one-man show." Under this approach the chief administrator has staff assistance or a particularly well-qualified department head who can assume the burden of detail that is inherent in the public relations program. The responsibility still rests with the chief administrator, but he or she is relieved of the task of conceiving, writing, rewriting, and following through to completion every public relations project. In general, this approach is feasible for the jurisdiction of roughly 50,000 to 200,000 population.

This approach permits the chief administrator to retain control over the public relations function and to act as the prime motivating force in the program. The hazards of departmentalization are avoided, and costs inherent in the use of consultants (discussed below) are also avoided.

DECENTRALIZATION TO DEPARTMENTS

In some cities or counties the emphasis is primarily on the departmental public relations program, sometimes to the exclusion or detriment of any overall approach for the local government. This is particularly true in two widely divergent types: first, the extremely large city or county, of perhaps one million population and over, and second, the smaller community in which the chief administrator does not have the time or possibly the skills required to develop a truly effective public relations program.

Some large cities feel that individual departments are large and complex enough to justify public information or public relations units of their own. Such units can (presumably) present the individual department's case more effectively than a centralized department assigned to serve the entire organization. It is also possible, however, for such a unit to become engrossed in "empire building" and the development of public relations materials which may run counter to the total organization's best interests. The unit can also be too isolated from the rest of the city government, and may thereby operate with greatly reduced effectiveness.

Virtually the opposite is true in many smaller governments. The chief administrator is faced with the responsibility for the operation of the entire organization, often with a staff too small to perform all the management functions generally considered necessary. He or she may therefore elect to delegate the responsibility for public relations activities, along with a number of other responsibilities, to department heads, with only slight guidance to coordinate the efforts of all departments.

Thus, it may be concluded that in the smaller jurisdictions, at least, decentralization to departments and the "one-man show" are actually extremes of a single continuum, with many shades of difference in between. Both may exist in a single organization, and both may make important contributions to the overall public relations effort.

The Collaborating Consultant

At some point—and no generalization is possible here—a government may find itself in need of outside professional assistance. This depends not so much on the size of the jurisdiction as on the talents of the chief administrator's staff and the complexity of the public relations job to be done.

A competent, qualified consultant can bring a fresh approach to the public relations job and can save considerable time and prevent many "false starts." In some instances he or she can actually save the government money through the techniques of his or her profession. As a practical matter, however, the employment of a consultant must be viewed as representing a net outlay in dollars which must be weighed against the final product and its probable effect on the public.

Nor is the consultant a cure-all. Balanced against the advantages of his or her fresh approach is the fact that the person concerned probably has little or no knowledge about the governmental organization and has much to learn before any productive work can be performed for the organization. Depending upon their degree of sophistication, such consultants may be able to develop a program or a single report with considerable "punch" and attractiveness—or they may come up with a proposal that is quite naive in terms of the organization's real problems, progress, and expectations. It

may require considerable orientation and close cooperation on the part of the chief administrator or that officer's representative to bring the consultant's talents and ideas into harmony with the public relations needs of the organization.

The Staff Pro

A department of public relations with a full-time director is often created principally in larger areas, although communities with under 100,000 population have been known to have such a department. This department may be established as a potential answer to a specific problem, or it may simply be intended to develop a continuing program of improved public relations. This stage of development is generally reached when the occasional services of a consultant become inadequate for the program desired. Often, a professional staff is established for the primary purpose of spearheading some specific program, such as attracting industry, or promoting a harbor, airport, or other major proprietary facility.

Specific Trends

How do the several basic types of local government public relations organizations described above square with *actual* organizations? What have the trends in the field been, and what general guidelines can a government adopt to help it arrive at a successful program? The latest available data, taken from a field study conducted by the International City Management Association, show the following:[1]

1. In actual practice, nearly half (48 percent) of the 839 cities reporting utilized some variation of the decentralized approach to organizing for public relations. Only in the 250,000 to 500,000 population group was the centralized approach predominant. A total of 38 percent of the cities centralized their public relations function, while 14 percent used some type of combined approach.
2. The same cities, in evaluating the "ideal" type of public relations organization, tended to favor centralization over decentralization

(58 percent majority); from this it was concluded that there might be more support for centralization than one would think from studying the existing organizations only. Perhaps this was a reflection of the old saying that "everyone's business is no one's business," and that in order to get the job done some degree of centralization of responsibility and authority is desirable if not essential.

3. Expenditures for staffing and operating a public relations function varied dramatically among cities, often depending upon the type of city and its public relations objectives, but 92 percent of those reporting spent less than 1 percent of their total budget on public relations. Fully one-third of the reporting cities did not know how much they spent on public relations, which suggested that the public relations function is often less than clearly defined in the organization, perhaps because of the assumption that people do not want their tax funds spent in telling them how well their government is performing on their behalf.

4. Contrary to this assumption, data contained in a Management Information Service Report (based on the same field study) suggested that the creation of public relations offices in city hall did not result in the flood of criticism often expected.[2]

5. Whatever the number of staff members, and whatever the organizational structure, the city manager (or mayor, depending on municipal organization) had the final responsibility for public relations activities in the predominant majority of cities responding.

6. Functions of public relations units included press relations, publications, various services (complaint bureau, speakers' bureau, etc.), public relations training, and a variety of other services, in that order.

7. Public relations problems encountered by the cities surveyed included inadequate time for public relations activities (59 percent), inadequately trained personnel (50 percent), and insufficient money to conduct the program (49 percent).

8. Major emphasis was needed on the defining of a city's public relations *goals*, at an early stage, so that resources and efforts could be properly directed. If a city's goal were primarily promotional, its efforts would differ from those of a city whose goal was primarily informational.[3]

Harnessing Trends

What, if anything, can be drawn from trends that will be useful to governments in meeting public relations challenges in the future? Sometimes the private sector provides a useful indicator of the shape of things to come in the public sector.

If the experience of the private sector *is* any kind of preview for the public sector, it would be appropriate to forecast much greater local government involvement in public relations in the near future, not necessarily in the traditional sense of annual reports and press releases, but in a much more sophisticated sense. Canfield and Moore report that while only 2 percent of the top 300 companies in the United States had public relations departments in 1936, 75 percent had such departments in 1973.[4] They note that responsibility for public relations is lodged with the top management level,[5] with public relations departments enjoying the same status as other major corporate functions, and headed by an individual of vice-presidential rank.[6]

There is widespread use of outside public relations consultants, particularly in research functions such as the conducting of public opinion studies.[7] If the private sector model were grafted onto the governmental organization, there would be in many governments a public relations policy committee composed of the mayor, chief administrator, and all top department heads, and every critical decision having public relations implications would come before this policy committee.[8] Whether this trend is truly applicable to local governmental organizations or not, it does suggest a *level of importance* that public relations has assumed in many leading corporations that perhaps has not yet been widely appreciated or emulated on the governmental scene. A mitigating factor in the application of such techniques from the private sector may be the rather unique political features of, for example, city government, which demand that certain roles be played by mayors and city councils, and which relegate the equivalent of the private sector's vice-president for public relations to a secondary role.

Whether the context is public or private, Canfield and Moore present a few axioms of public relations that bear repeating as organizational problems are contemplated. These include the reminder that public relations cannot be expected to serve as a substitute for good management, nor is it a panacea for poor policies, products, or services. It requires a long-term effort, and it should never be used in a "remedial" sense, for example, as a means of hiding mistakes.[9]

Near the beginning of this chapter it was suggested that at least four current trends or developments are having and will continue to have an impact on the way in which local governments organize for public relations, and that these point to greater citizen participation in government. A brief discussion of these major trends treats them in the following order: the rise of consumerism; citizen participation owing to federal fiat; environmental concerns; and public opinion sampling.

The Rise of Consumerism

In recent years organized consumer–voter–citizen reaction to shoddy merchandise, corporate abuse, and governmental lack of responsiveness has become a major thrust in American life. It has gained in influence through the efforts of a wide range of individuals and groups. Major corporations which in the past might have been thought of as less than sensitive to the problems of the consumer have been brought around to new policies through class action suits, manipulation of proxies, public exposure of product failure, and other techniques. Ralph Nader, Common Cause, and hundreds of other individuals and groups concerned with broad or narrow bands of the consumerism spectrum have made their impact on public affairs, and it is most unlikely that the trend will reverse. This phenomenon has presented a method of achieving certain types of

goals through concerted, organized citizen action.

One 1970s publication in the field (actually a "how-to-do-it" handbook) gives some indication of what local government officials should expect in citizen involvement in the near future, if not in the present.[10] In a chapter entitled "Making Government Responsive," the author notes that governments that shield themselves from their citizens have a tendency to stagnate and to become lazy and insensitive toward their citizens,[11] and outlines guidelines on how to form a citizens' lobby.[12] In another section the author notes that "local and state agencies are at least as susceptible to the stimulus of a citizen probe" as federal agencies, and can be studied more easily.[13] All in all, this manual is basically a text with which officials should be familiar.

The message is clear: consumerism is on the rise, and public officials who ignore this trend do so at their peril.

An interesting variation on this theme—unrelated to consumerism as such, but a facet of citizen involvement that should not be overlooked by local governments—is an increasing corporate social conscience and involvement. Publications such as the *Harvard Business Review* carry articles advocating that business groups become more directly involved in the affairs of their communities in leadership roles;[14] today, also, major corporations are giving their executives leave for public service. Such executive talent should be sought out and welcomed to the government organization, both for the obvious capability that can be utilized for the public good, and for purposes of extending the government contacts with the private sector.

Citizen Participation by Federal Fiat

Although they tend to have an uneven success, federal programs of various types have thrust citizen participation upon local governments. Community Action Programs, Model Cities, and other federal programs have mandated greater citizen participation as inherent features of community development. In some quarters there is the belief that such programs have tended to weaken local government through the cultivation of parallel power structures. Nor have such programs yielded un-mixed blessings for the citizens they were de-signed to bring into the decision-making proc-ess: many such programs have built unrealisti-cally high levels of expectation on the part of the people only to have those hopes dashed when performance has fallen short of expecta-tions.

In 1972 a special issue of *Public Administration Review*[15] featured articles on this subject which summarized experiences under these pro-grams. One problem that was pointed up by various articles in the issue was that such pro-grams were often characterized by great ineffi-ciency of participation (in terms of getting the basic job done).

If, as one author indicated, the loss of ability to participate in local affairs is traceable to the growth of jurisdictions and the relative anonymity that arises from greater size,[16] the charge to local government is clear: citizen in-volvement is an essential and integral part of the process of governing, and governments need to organize services for the citizen in such a way as to bring the citizens more fully into the decision-making (or at least the decision-influencing) process.

Indeed, as the New Federalism and revenue sharing have emerged to take the place of categorical grants for local government, so has a new form of citizen involvement been sug-gested. On the basis of the theory that "local government has been weakened by a decade of federal program emphasis and now the trend is being reversed to an emphasis on local gov-ernment . . . [and that] . . . citizens will shift their attention from federal programs and offi-cials to local program administrators," the for-mation of "citizen councils" is advocated.[17] Such councils are visualized as nonprofit corpo-rations, geographical in orientation (paralleling local and state government organizations), and financed from revenue sharing funds. Presuma-bly, such councils would supplant the special purpose organizations characteristic of earlier federal programs, and as such may have great merit. If a citizen council is established to represent the interests of the people on a broad base, however, fundamental questions regard-ing its relationship to the local governing body arise—a situation that suggests that extreme caution is needed in approaching such experi-ments.

THE RESPONSE TO ENVIRONMENTAL CONCERNS

The phenomenal growth of environmental concern has mobilized vast numbers of people on a broad front. Environmental problems that once seemed to worry only a few specialized groups have come to concern average citizens in increasing numbers. While this swing of the pendulum may have been modified by the con-flicting demands arising from the energy short-age, a significant point remains: when the peo-ple become aware of a problem that directly concerns them, they can mobilize or be mobil-ized into a force of considerable strength. *Early citizen involvement is the key to successful en-vironmental planning*, city managers were told at a national conference on managing the envi-ronment (cosponsored by the Environmental Protection Agency and the International City Management Association),[18] and certainly this advice can be applied with equal validity to many other areas in which governments serve people.

SAMPLING PUBLIC OPINION

Although public opinion surveys have been utilized by commercial and political interests for decades, their widespread administrative use by local governments for the purpose of gearing services to public needs and interests is still in the embryonic stage.

Kenneth Webb and Harry P. Hatry provide an excellent introductory handbook for local governments that may wish to consider meth-ods of sampling public opinion.[19] The authors suggest that the full potential of citizen surveys is far from realized. They outline methods of organizing and conducting surveys and of util-izing data, and even suggest that as a "possibil-ity for the future" regional citizen survey or-ganizations might be set up to serve many government agencies in a particular region.[20]

Opinion surveys can be broadly based, cover-ing a number of issues, or narrowly drawn to meet a particular need, such as neighborhood attitudes toward a new local facility. And they can (and should, according to Webb and Hatry) be conducted periodically rather than as a "one-shot" effort.

Effective use of this approach requires extreme care by a government, as adverse results can flow from a well-meaning effort just as readily as positive ones. Careful consideration and thorough deliberation of goals and objectives should precede any action. For fuller details on this subject, see Chapter 2 of the present volume.

Which Method Is Best?

Of the several alternatives discussed in this chapter (and considering the pressures of current trends), which is the best way to organize for effective public relations? As mentioned earlier in this chapter, no single, infallible model for a public relations organization is feasible. The public relations program needs to be tailored to the population it is to serve. A successful arrangement for one jurisdiction may be inadequate or inappropriate for another. The limited guidelines and examples suggested in this chapter should provide a reasonable starting point for officials contemplating building up the public relations function, but the needs of the individual community always remain paramount.[21]

Characteristically, citizens tend to harbor the belief that no one needs to tell them what they ought to know about their government, that the important facts will be self-evident, and that the presence of a specialist in public relations or public information is immediately suspect. This fact is less true today than it was, for example, in the 1940s. With the passage of time and the concurrent increasing complexity of urban activities, the public information function will be more widely accepted as a necessary operation of local government.

In the final analysis, *every* local government has public relations, whether formalized or not. Whether its public relations are good or bad, however, depends largely on the degree of sophistication employed in approaching public

relations problems. A government in general pays the cost of a good public relations program in one way or another: it may adopt a well-conceived program and pay in dollars and effort, or it may tend to ignore this critical area of responsibility and, because of this, pay in loss of goodwill, of community pride, and of more tangible goals.

This is not to say that a good public relations program necessarily means the expenditure of thousands of dollars. A truly good public relations program is more basic than that. It is, as suggested above, inherent in the very services the government provides its citizens. A good public relations program begins in the minds and attitudes of the public officials and employees concerned: the particular form of organization and the specific type of approach are secondary matters.

Training for Effective Public Relations

Assuming that a government has developed an organizational structure that meets its specific public relations needs, one of the most useful tools for implementing the public relations program is readily available (or at least latent) in every organization: the employee work force. The critical question then becomes how to mobilize that force most effectively, and the answer lies largely in one technique: training, together with the development of sound employee relations.

MANAGEMENT AND EMPLOYEE RELATIONS

The top management of an organization sets the tone of the organization, as regards both internal relations and external public relations. In a local government the chief administrator and the department heads and their staffs determine the character of the administrative environment through their actions, attitudes, and policies. If they demonstrate genuine concern for good human relations, this concern will be found throughout the organization.

Effective employee relations—as all local government administrators will recognize— need to be based on a team approach. Management should practice, as well as advocate, good personnel policies and procedures.

Often an employee's relation to the team will determine the use he or she makes of his or her abilities and capacities. One very effective method of promoting the team approach is to recognize the value of employee participation in program planning and to invite and use suggestions submitted by employees. A democratic approach to management is the key to good human relations in an organization. Such an approach on the part of management and supervisory personnel can build understanding and cooperation among employees and can in turn serve to promote loyalty and efficiency.

PEOPLE HAVE MANY NEEDS

The essence of the human relations approach to management is the recognition of each employee as a unique person with varying desires, needs, and capacities. In order to achieve satisfaction among employees, management must consider the social as well as the economic needs of the individuals comprising the organization. Although the importance of salaries and other means of compensation should not be unduly minimized, the pay check serves to meet only one of the many needs of employees.

Howard Wilson identifies the following as additional social and psychological needs of people in organizations:

1. *The need to belong.* People want to identify themselves with other people; they want to be part of a group.
2. *The need for accomplishment.* People want to feel that they are making progress toward worthy goals.
3. *The need for self-esteem.* Each person develops his or her own sense of worth, and of pride and dignity.
4. *The need for acceptance.* People want to feel that they are accepted by the groups with which they identify themselves.
5. *The need for security.* The interdependence of modern life has sapped the quality of self-reliance. Today, people are insecure and thus need greater assurance of security.
6. *The need for creativity.* Too often in modern life the skill function has been taken from

people and given to machines. When people lack the chance to be creative, their egos suffer.[22]

If healthy internal relations are to be maintained in an organization, these sociopsychological needs should be recognized by management. It is important that supervisors at all levels should not only be aware of these needs but should demonstrate by their actions that they have a positive interest in the well-being of employees.

An awareness of management's concern for *physiological* needs alone may produce beneficial reactions in employees. For example, management should show an interest in employee health standards by providing adequate sanitation, rest facilities, and medical services.

If a proper attitude is to be instilled in the personnel of an organization—an attitude evidenced by pride in work, motivated effort, and effective performance—then management must demonstrate a genuine interest in employee affairs. If management does not, then employee organizations will—as the experience of the 1960s and 1970s indicated.

THE IMPORTANCE OF COMMUNICATIONS

The most effective administrative method by which management can substantiate its interest in employee relations is in maintenance of a free and open flow of information among all levels of the organization.

Two-way Communication. The importance of two-way communication cannot be overemphasized, for it is only by this type of communications network that an effective interchange of information and ideas can occur in an organization. In practice such a system requires the exchange of differing viewpoints between supervisors and staff. It may require substantial effort on the part of all concerned to reconcile their differences for the best interests of all the individuals and groups within the total organization.

By practicing two-way communication, management can show a true interest in employee relations. Through such a system an employee can learn what is really expected of him or her, and how his or her work fits into total organizational goals.

Two-way communication means, for example, that management informs employees of events throughout the organization by means of newsletters, conferences, and the like; that employees are encouraged to participate in programs for system improvement; that grievance committees are recognized and employee problems resolved; and that employee incentive is recognized and superior performance rewarded.

Particularly important is management recognition of and attention to "feedback" from employees. Sometimes information reported on the grapevine is more revealing than the more formal kinds of information that come to the attention of management through employee grievances and suggestions. Administrators should give continuing and careful attention to information that they pick up informally. Often, this information can alert administrators to a serious situation with respect to employee attitudes and morale, and the effectiveness of management policies. Communications within the organization are discussed in some detail in Chapter 6 of the present volume.

Employee Opinion Affects Public Opinion. Attitudes and opinions of municipal employees toward the government are determined largely by their work experience. If employees feel that they are recognized as individuals and not merely as "parts of the machine," if they are respected by their associates, and if working conditions are satisfactory, they will ordinarily have a favorable attitude toward the local government. In addition, they will tend to be more dedicated in their work and more imbued with the spirit of public service.

Quite the opposite type of attitude may develop, however, if they do not feel that they or their work are of some worth in the organization. If their experience with associates and supervisors is not pleasant, and if they do not feel that they are truly accepted as members of their work groups and of the total organization, their attitude will probably be negative.

If negative attitudes develop and continue to grow, it is likely that they will soon not only find

expression in an employee organization but also take the form of opinions which are then expressed and passed on to other persons, both inside and outside the organization. It is only natural that city employees should discuss their work with associates, families, and friends. And when such opinions are multiplied hundreds and sometimes thousands of times, it is easy to see how the public can be influenced in its opinion of a government.

THE KEY TO EFFECTIVE PUBLIC RELATIONS

No local government is administered so effectively that it can remain immune from public relations problems. There is always room for improvement in relations with the public.

With effective public relations predicated upon the quality of services, the basic objective of any training program should be improvement of performance. A public relations training program raises false and undesirable aspirations if its goal is the acceptance of the government regardless of whether it "deserves" acceptance. Much more appropriate and rewarding twofold objectives for a public relations training program are the continuing improvement of (1) internal procedures for greater effectiveness, and (2) employees' ability to empathize with the external publics. A normal consequence of such a training program will be better acceptance of the organization by its publics.

Training for better public relations is really a matter of increasing the social awareness of employees. A local government's employees should not be taught to "be nice" to the public because the government will gain a better public image; rather, the training should be *goal-oriented,* so that employees understand typical citizen actions and reactions and can thus more easily and effectively perform the services for which they are employed.

A local public relations training program, then, should be a mutually rewarding relationship in which:

1. An orientation program facilitates the efforts of employees to provide help to the public

2. Continuing attention is given to maintaining high morale among employees who take pride in their work

3. Participation of employees at all levels is obtained in spotting and correcting service problems and in auditing public relations programs for strengths and weaknesses

4. Key people are trained to lead group meetings and to speak effectively in public

5. There is developed and maintained in employees a high interest in: (*a*) operating motor vehicles courteously; (*b*) responding courteously on the telephone; (*c*) maintaining attitudes of attention, fairness, and helpfulness in all contacts: (*d*) preparing clearly written and courteous letters; and (*e*) minimizing delays experienced by citizens.

To be most effective, public relations training programs should be part of a larger overall training program for the government. The following guidelines are suggested in the establishment of such a training program:

1. Establish a written training policy
2. Assign qualified personnel
3. Develop a training plan
4. Insist on quality support—facilities, materials, and procedures
5. Demand results and require evidence of results
6. Appoint an advisory committee.

Who Should Be Trained? Since almost all government employees have direct or indirect contacts with the public during their employment, all personnel should be brought into the public relations training program. Some personnel will require more extensive or specialized training than others, since their duties involve more contact with the public. And since operating personnel tend to emulate the behavior and attitudes of their supervisors toward the public, managerial personnel should participate actively in public relations training programs.

Whether training classes should involve the personnel from one or more departments will depend largely upon the size and organizational pattern of the government, the relevance of topics to be considered, and training facilities available. There may be economical advantages in establishing training classes that involve more than one department. Such an arrangement can help persons from different departments to understand each other's problems and also help to prevent interoffice rivalries.

What Should Be Taught? In addition to improvement of communication skills, the subject matter of municipal public relations training courses frequently includes materials on (1) organization and operation of the government; (2) safety and courtesy; (3) increasing social awareness; (4) effective correspondence; (5) telephone manners; and (6) municipal reports and publicity.

1. Organization and Operation of Government. A fundamental part of a public relations training program should involve the history, organization, and operations of the city or county itself. If employees are to be effective in explaining and interpreting the policies, procedures, and activities of their government, they must first have a good understanding of these factors. If employees understand the past achievements of the government, they are more likely to take pride in its heritage and to be motivated to maintain high standards of public service.

2. Safety. Care and safety in personal behavior and in relations with others often have far-reaching consequences. In the field and in offices, the well-being of both individuals and the government is improved with safety in personal conduct and care in orderly arrangement and use of space, equipment, and materials. Courtesy and safety in the use of motor vehicles is especially significant. With the advent of the U.S. Occupational Safety and Health Administration, safety is not only good business but is mandated under the law.

3. Increasing Social Awareness. Training should be geared to increasing employee sensitivity to the citizen's viewpoint. Whether a particular service or inquiry seems important to the employee or not, it *is* significant to the citizen and should be handled accordingly. It is important that employees assume that their

contact with a citizen may be the only one between the government and that particular citizen for a year, or perhaps a decade—as indeed may well be the case. Therefore, the manner in which the matter is handled is of paramount importance to the government as well as the citizen.

4. Correspondence. While correspondence is an indirect method of contacting the public, a city or county is often judged upon the basis of the appearance and tone of letters. Instructions should be given on letter writing, including clarity, accuracy, conciseness, style, punctuation, grammar, and tone. Actual practice should be provided to enable employees to evaluate their own letters, so they can improve their letter-writing skill. This subject has been discussed in greater detail in Chapter 5 of the present volume.

5. Telephone Manners. Proper use of the telephone is a valuable and important subject for public relations training, as the telephone is used so extensively for communicating with the public. This subject has been covered in more detail in Chapter 5.

6. Public Information Techniques. Employees responsible for public information functions should be given special training if they do not already have it. This should include the development of skills in writing news releases, magazine articles, radio and television scripts, and spot announcements. If they are responsible for the preparation of municipal reports, they should be given special training in typography, layout, design of reports, and possibly photography. If personnel or facilities for such specialized training are not available in the city organization, an opportunity should be made available for employees to obtain this training at outside educational or other institutions. Chapters 9, 10, and 11 have covered the above subjects in considerable detail.

Responsibility for Training. Although training, in the larger view, is the responsibility of each supervisor, responsibility must be assigned for organizing and implementing it. In a larger city or county, overall responsibility for coordinating the training program may be placed in the personnel office. In smaller jurisdictions, the chief administrator may delegate this duty to one of his or her assistants. In any event, it should be emphasized that the training function should be integrated into the overall management process.

In public relations training it is usually advisable to decentralize much of the actual training function to the departmental level, since specific aspects of public relations will need special emphasis in the different organizational units. This will usually mean that the supervisors will be given the actual responsibility for carrying out the program. This is a logical assignment for supervisors at the lower levels, since they ordinarily are in the best position to observe the behavior of employees who have problems in dealing with the public. It is the first-line supervisor who must make constructive suggestions to prevent poor contacts with the public.

It is usually advisable to use government personnel as training instructors, since they are familiar with the pattern of local operations and potential problem areas. It may be advisable from time to time, however, to obtain outside instructors if a subject is highly specialized.

Although the ability to teach others is natural to some persons, it is not a trait that is common to all. Some supervisors may have the responsibility for training and yet lack the skill. If this is the case, special training sessions should be set up for these supervisors.

Methods of Training. The broad scope of topics that need to be included in a government public relations training program requires a variety of training techniques and approaches; among these are the following:

1. Case Method. Specific incidents that have actually occurred can be analyzed by the group as a form of case study. It is important that such discussions be conducted in an objective manner so that personal criticism of employees is not implied. If members of the group are reluctant to contribute their own cases, the instructor may supply cases—either real or fictional.

The basic procedure in the case method is to first define the problem, second, determine the facts, and third, have the group suggest as many solutions as possible. Ultimately, the group can determine the "best" solution.

Case discussion of this type is thought by many to be therapeutic as well as instructional, because employees will tend to compare their own actions with the standards of behavior agreed upon by the group. As Pfiffner has stated:

When each employee has shortcomings pointed out by his own colleagues without the finger of criticism being pointed directly at him, it is thought by some that he will be motivated to follow a more correct behavior pattern in the future.[23]

It is usually helpful to supplement oral group discussion with written materials such as training guides or manuals. It is important that such documents contain materials that are directly related to the organization, however, and it is best if the materials can be developed within the organization itself.

2. Role Playing. The technique of role playing involves members of the group in acting out roles in real-life situations involving problems of human behavior. This technique can be useful in public relations training if it is used in an objective, open-minded manner. It can be used effectively with the case method by having members of the group act out the various situations. The atmosphere should be permissive, and the objective is to obtain group involvement and participation.

The basic purpose of the role playing technique is to help persons see themselves as others see them, usually vicariously. This experience may point up some of their problems and help motivate them to modify mannerisms and attitudes.

3. Lecture Approach. More or less formal lectures can be useful in certain phases of training. In orientation sessions for new employees they may be the only feasible method for reaching large numbers of employees. Even in these situations, however, most lectures are more effective if supplemented by demonstrations or by visual aids, such as films and charts. There should always be an opportunity for questions from the group.

4. Conference Method. One of the most effective techniques for public relations training is the conference method. This technique involves group discussion under the direction of a training leader.

Although formal presentations may be made by the leader as a part of the session, the basic purpose is to involve the members of the group in the analysis of the subject matter under discussion. In most conference-type training sessions, the leader should function primarily as a moderator. He or she should present the problem or subjects and then stimulate discussion and suggestions from the members of the group. The discussion should be kept on the main subject.

In this technique the employees are expected to supply a substantial part of the actual training themselves, by suggesting solutions to problems and by self-analysis and comparison of their experiences with those of other employees.

If, for example, the topic under discussion involves the handling of citizen complaints, the first step might be to determine what types of complaints are most common. The leader should list these on a blackboard so that they can remain in view of the participants throughout the discussion. After there is general agreement on the types of complaints, the leader may ask for suggestions as to the best procedure for handling such complaints. There will undoubtedly be disagreements or modifications, but the net result will probably be a solution that is better than that which has been used by any single employee.

INTERPERSONAL EFFECTIVENESS

Regardless of the technique that may be used in public relations training, the key to the program's success will depend basically on the interpersonal effectiveness of the personnel involved. A basic requirement in the learning process is that the persons who are being instructed must understand the instructor and the information being presented before effective learning can take place.

The responsibility lies with the instructor to see that he or she is sensitive to the reactions of the group. This means that the trainees must not only receive the message but must also understand the information that is transmitted. Moreover, in order for the instructor to determine whether he or she is successfully communicating, he or she must also receive information back from the members of the group.

This feedback can be in the form of opinions, comments, or questions on subject matter being discussed.

After he or she has identified the topic for discussion at the session and perhaps made some introductory comments, the experienced training leader will usually solicit comments and questions from the group. If the response is not adequate to induce general discussion, the instructor may then pose some questions to the group and initiate discussion in this way.

The point is that training instructors should not inject themselves into the discussion to such an extent that they discourage or inhibit individuals in the group from participating freely. The leader's basic function in a training session is to introduce the subject, to guide the discussion, and to bring about some measure of consensus. Leaders should, of course, control the discussion and keep it on the subject. It may be advisable or necessary for them to overrule the opinion of the group from time to time, particularly when a leader is responsible for the results of procedures or actions, or when he or she has more experience or knowledge relating to a particular activity.

Free interchange of ideas encourages common understanding. Cooperation can evolve, and this constitutes the fundamental requirement for good public relations in governments as elsewhere in human organizations.

GUIDELINES FOR TRAINING

As has been noted above, each training program in public relations should be structured to fit the specific needs of the agency or jurisdiction involved. There are certain basic factors or guidelines, however, that should be kept in mind in the development of any public relations training program. These are listed immediately below.

1. Establish training objectives, taking into consideration both the needs and resources available.
2. The scope and content of the training program should be prepared well in advance of the actual training session.
3. All personnel who will be involved in the program should be encouraged to participate in the development of its scope and content.
4. Training classes should be held frequently, but they should be relatively brief so as not to require an unreasonable amount of time away from regular duties.
5. Training sessions should be held during working hours.
6. Responsibility for specific training topics and sessions should be assigned to individuals, and they should be given sufficient time to prepare for sessions.
7. Visual aids, such as films, slides, and charts, should be used frequently to supplement lectures and discussions.
8. Occasional "ventilation sessions" should be held to enable individual employees to discuss their specific problems and "gripes." This enables employees to get things off their chest; also, group discussion may help to solve such problems.
9. Training assignments should be rotated among all those persons who are capable of conducting sessions. Special sessions for training trainers should be set up as well.
10. Results of training sessions should be summarized and condensed in the form of training guides or manuals for future classes. Such documents should list the subject areas, include examples of pertinent situations, and set forth some guidelines. Care should be taken that such guidelines are not stereotyped or stilted and that they relate to the particular department or unit involved.
11. Training sessions should generally be conducted on a rather informal basis so as to encourage free discussion and interchange of ideas. The training leader should coordinate and guide the session rather than attempt to dominate it, but he or she should summarize the conclusions for the benefit of all, and he or she should be sure that general agreement exists on the various conclusions reached.
12. Provision should be made for continuing evaluation of both needs and the adopted training program itself.

Summary

This chapter, which constitutes Part Four of the present volume, is intended to tie together the previous discussions of the public relations perspective (Part One), the public and the programs (Part Two), and informational reporting (Part Three).

The chapter opens with a generalized discussion of a basic organization for public relations operations. A more specific section follows, in which ways to organize for public relations are outlined.

The next section is concerned with four important factors which, in recent years, have come to have an impact on government public relations: consumerism; federal programs requiring citizen participation; environmental concerns; and opinion surveys.

The second half of the chapter is devoted to public relations training. First, the importance of good management–employee relations is stressed. The effect of employee opinion on public opinion is treated next. Certain factors essential to good government public relations (the awareness of one's own government operation; safety; social awareness; good procedures in public contacts) are then emphasized and are followed by discussions of responsibility for and methods of training. Some important "guidelines for training" are listed. The chapter closes with a brief summary.

[1] Marion C. Tureck, "Municipal Public Relations in 1966," THE MUNICIPAL YEAR BOOK 1967 (Chicago: International City Managers' Association, 1967), pp. 242–75.

[2] Marion Tureck, ORGANIZATION AND OPERATION OF PUBLIC RELATIONS PROGRAMS, Management Information Service Reports, no. 282 (Chicago: International City Managers' Association, July 1967), p. 2.

[3] Ibid., pp. 1–5.

[4] Bertrand R. Canfield and H. Frazier Moore, PUBLIC RELATIONS: PRINCIPLES, CASES AND PROBLEMS, 6th ed. (Homewood, Ill.: Richard D. Irwin, Inc., 1973), p. 92.

[5] Ibid., p. 100.

[6] Ibid., p. 106.

[7] Ibid., p. 77.

[8] Ibid., p. 94.

[9] Ibid., pp. 7–10.

[10] Donald K. Ross, A PUBLIC CITIZEN'S ACTION MANUAL (New York: Grossman Publishers, 1973).

[11] Ibid., p. 169.

[12] Ibid., pp. 174–78.

[13] Ibid., p. 199.

[14] Dan H. Fenn, Jr., "Executives as Community Volunteers," HARVARD BUSINESS REVIEW 71 (March–April 1971): 4.

[15] John H. Strange, ed., "Citizens Action in Model Cities and CAP Programs: Case Studies and Evaluations," PUBLIC ADMINISTRATION REVIEW 32 (September 1972): entire issue.

[16] John H. Strange, "The Impact of Citizen Participation on Public Administration," in ibid.: 457–70.

[17] Morris L. Lewis, "New Citizen Roles in Local Government," NATIONAL CIVIC REVIEW 62 (July 1973): 390–93.

[18] Harold Semling, "Early Citizen Involvement Key to Successful Environmental Planning," THE AMERICAN CITY, July 1973, p. 18.

[19] Kenneth Webb and Harry P. Hatry, OBTAINING CITIZEN FEEDBACK: THE APPLICATION OF CITIZEN SURVEYS TO LOCAL GOVERNMENTS (Washington, D.C.: The Urban Institute, 1973).

[20] Ibid., p. 63.

[21] In addition to sources cited elsewhere in this chapter, specific assistance in tailoring a government's public relations organization to fit its own needs can be obtained from a variety of publications available from: the International City Management Association, 1140 Connecticut Avenue, N.W., Washington, D.C. 20036; the National Association of Counties, 1735 New York Avenue, N.W., Washington, D.C. 20006; and the National Association of Regional Councils, 1700 K Street, N.W., Washington, D.C. 20037.

[22] Howard Wilson, "The Psychological Needs of Man," PUBLIC RELATIONS, October 1955, p. 146.

[23] John M. Pfiffner, THE SUPERVISION OF PERSONNEL (Englewood Cliffs, N.J.: Prentice-Hall, Inc., 1958), p. 483.

Appendix A

Suggested Code of Ethics and Creeds
for Municipal Officials and Employees

In February 1962 the International City Managers' Association disseminated widely this suggested code of ethics and creeds for municipal officials and employees, together with a suggested creed for council members. The texts of these appear below.

Be it resolved [enacted] by the Council of the City of ———————————— that the following be a "Code of Ethics for the Public Service of the City of ————————————."

1. DECLARATION OF POLICY

The proper operation of democratic government requires that public officials and employees be independent, impartial, and responsible to the people; that governmental decisions and policy be made in the proper channels of the governmental structure; that public office not be used for personal gain; and that the public have confidence in the integrity of its government. In recognition of these goals there is hereby established a Code of Ethics for all officials and employees, whether elected or appointed, paid or unpaid. The purpose of this Code is to establish ethical standards of conduct for all such officials and employees by setting forth those acts or actions that are incompatible with the best interests of the city and by directing disclosure by such officials and employees of private financial or other interests in matters affecting the city. The provisions and purpose of this Code and such rules and regulations as may be established are hereby declared to be in the best interests of the City of ————————————.

2. RESPONSIBILITIES OF PUBLIC OFFICE

Public officials and employees are agents of public purpose and hold office for the benefit of the public. They are bound to uphold the Constitution of the United States and the Constitution of this State and to carry out impartially the laws of the nation, state, and municipality and thus to foster respect for all government. They are bound to observe in their official acts the highest standards of morality and to discharge faithfully the duties of their office regardless of personal considerations, recognizing that the public interest must be their primary concern. Their conduct in both their official and private affairs should be above reproach.

3. DEDICATED SERVICE

All officials and employees of the municipality should be loyal to the political objectives expressed by the electorate and the programs developed to attain those objectives. Appointive officials and employees should adhere to the rules of work and performance established as the standard for their positions by the appropriate authority.

Officials and employees should not exceed their authority or breach the law or ask others to do so, and they should work in full cooperation with other public officials and employees unless prohibited from so doing by law or by officially recognized confidentiality of their work.

4. FAIR AND EQUAL TREATMENT

a. *Interest in Appointments.* Canvassing of members of the council, directly or indirectly, in order to obtain preferential consideration in connection with any appointment to the municipal service shall disqualify the candidate for appointment except with reference to positions filled by appointment by the council.

b. *Use of Public Property.* No official or employee shall request or permit the use of city-owned vehicles, equipment, materials, or property for personal convenience or profit, except when such services are available to the public generally or are provided as municipal policy for the use of such official or employee in the conduct of official business.

c. *Obligations to Citizens.* No official or employee shall grant any special consideration, treatment, or advantage to any citizen beyond that which is available to every other citizen.

5. CONFLICT OF INTEREST

No council member or other official or employee, whether paid or unpaid, shall engage in any business or transaction or shall have a financial or other personal interest, direct or indirect, which is incompatible with the proper discharge of his or her official duties in the public interest or would tend to impair his or her independence of judgment or action in the performance of his or her official duties. Personal as distinguished from financial interest includes an interest arising from blood or marriage relationships or close business or political association.

Specific conflicts of interest are enumerated below for the guidance of officials and employees:

a. *Incompatible Employment.* No council member or other official or employee shall engage in or accept private employment or render services for private interests when such employment or service is incompatible with the proper discharge of his or her official duties or would tend to impair his or her independence of judgment or action in the performance of his or her official duties.

b. *Disclosure of Confidential Information.* No council member or other official or employee shall, without proper legal authorization, disclose confidential information concerning the property, government, or affairs of the city. Nor shall they use such information to advance the financial or other private interest of themselves or others.

c. *Gifts and Favors.* No council member or other official or employee shall accept any valuable gift, whether in the form of service, loan, thing, or promise, from any person, firm, or corporation which to his or her knowledge is interested directly or indirectly in any manner whatsoever in business dealings with the city; nor shall any such officials or employees (1) accept any gift, favor, or thing of value that may tend to influence them in the discharge of their duties, or (2) grant in the discharge of their duties any improper favor, service, or thing of value.

d. *Representing Private Interests before City Agencies or Courts.* No council member or other official or employee whose salary is paid in whole or in part by the city shall appear in behalf of private interests before any agency of the city. He or she shall not represent private interests in any action or proceeding against the interests of the city in any litigation to which the city is a party.

A council member may appear before city agencies on behalf of constituents in the course of his or her duties as a representative of the electorate or in the performance of public or civic obligations. However, no council member or other official or employee shall accept a retainer or compensation that is contingent upon a specific action by a city agency.

e. *Contracts with the City.* Any council member or other official or employee who has a substantial or controlling financial interest in any business entity, transaction, or contract with the city, or in the sale of real estate, materials, supplies, or services to the city, shall make known to the proper authority such interest in any matter on which he or she may be called to act in his official capacity. He or she shall refrain from voting upon or otherwise participating in the transaction or the making of such contract or sale.

A council member or other official or employee shall not be deemed interested in any contract or purchase or sale of land or other thing of value unless such contract or sale is approved, awarded, entered into, or authorized by him or her in his or her official capacity.

f. *Disclosure of Interest in Legislation.* A council member who has a financial or other private interest in any legislation shall disclose on the records of the council or other appropriate authority the nature and extent of such interest. This provision shall not apply if the council member disqualifies himself or herself from voting.

Any other official or employee who has a financial or other private interest, and who participates in discussion with or gives an official opinion to the council, shall disclose on the records of the council or other appropriate authority the nature and extent of such interest.

6. POLITICAL ACTIVITY

No appointive official or employee in the administrative service shall use the prestige of his or her position in behalf of any political party.

No appointive official or employee in the administrative service shall orally, by letter, or otherwise, solicit or be in any manner concerned in soliciting any assessment, subscription, or contribution to any political party; nor shall he or she be a party to such solicitation by others. Such appointed officials and employees shall not take an active part in political campaigns for candidates.

No official or employee, whether elected or appointed, shall promise an appointment to any municipal position as a reward for any political activity.

7. APPLICABILITY OF CODE

When a council member or other official or employee has doubt as to the applicability of a provision of this Code to a particular situation, he or she should apply to the authority on ethical conduct constituted for the implementation of this Code for an advisory opinion and be guided by that opinion when given. The council member or other official or employee shall have the opportunity to present his or her interpretation of the facts at issue and of the applicable provision(s) of the Code before such advisory decision is made. This Code shall be operative in all instances covered by its provisions except when superseded by an applicable statutory or charter provision and statutory or charter action is mandatory, or when the application of a statutory or charter provision is discretionary but determined to be more appropriate or desirable.

8. SANCTIONS

Violation of any provisions of this Code should raise conscientious questions for the council member or other official or employee concerned as to whether voluntary resignation or other action is indicated to promote the best interests of the city. Violation may constitute a cause for suspension, removal from office or employment, or other disciplinary action.

Suggested Creed for Council Members

As a City Council member I believe:

That the proper operation of democratic government requires that public officials be independent and impartial in their judgment and actions; that government decisions and policy be made in the proper channels of the governmental structure; that public office not be used for personal gain; and that the public have confidence in the integrity of its government and public officials.

And that the realization of these ends is impaired whenever there exists, or appears to exist, an actual or potential conflict between the private interests of a governmental official and his or her public duties. The public interest requires ethical standards with respect to official conduct.

Therefore, as a City Council member of the City of _____ I assert my solemn belief that the primary responsibility for maintaining a high level of ethics among city officials and employees falls upon the Council as the governing body elected by the people:

Consequently, as a Council member, I believe it is my duty to:

1. Respect the importance of American ideals of government, of the rule of law, of the principles of public administration, and of ethical conduct in the performance of my public duties.

2. Represent and work for the common good of the people of my city and not for private interest, assuring fair and equal treatment of all persons, claims, and transactions coming before me in my official capacity.

3. Refrain from accepting gifts or favors or promises of future benefit which might compromise or tend to impair my independence of judgment or action as a Council member.

4. Learn the background and purposes of major ordinances before voting.

5. Faithfully perform my duties as a Council member by attending all sessions of the Council and of its committees of which I am a member, unless unable to do so for some compelling reason or disability.

6. Help the Council maintain the highest standards of ethical conduct by refusing to approve breaches of public trust or improper attempts to influence legislation and by being willing to vote to censure or otherwise discipline any Council member who willfully violates the duly established rules of conduct for Council members.

7. Disclose all sources of income which may represent a substantial conflict of interest with my duties as a Council member and to disclose the nature and extent of my interest as an officer, agent, member, or owner of any business entity or other association which is subject to regulation by the city, such disclosure to be made to the proper authority established for that purpose.

8. Refuse to represent private interests before city agencies or in the courts, except as may be my duty toward constituents, such service to be rendered without compensation, and refuse to accept or engage in any employment incompatible with my public duties.

9. Disclose any private interest I may have in legislation before the Council or to refrain from voting when such interest is in substantial conflict with my public duties.

10. Refrain from disclosing confidential information concerning the city government.

Suggested Creed for Administrative Officials and Employees

As a municipal official or employee I believe:

That the proper operation of democratic government requires that public officials be independent and impartial in their judgment and actions; that government decisions and policy be made in the proper channels of the governmental structure; that public office not be used for personal gain; and that the public have confidence in the integrity of its government and officials.

And that the realization of these ends is impaired whenever there exists, or appears to exist, an actual or potential conflict between the private interests of a governmental official and his or her public duties and that the public interest requires ethical standards with respect to official conduct.

Therefore, as a public official or employee of the City of _____ I assert my solemn belief that I have a responsibility to the people of _____ to do all in my power to maintain the integrity of their government.

Consequently, I believe it is my duty to:

1. Respect the importance of American ideals of government, the rule of law, the principles of public administration, and ethical conduct in the performance of my public duties; and to be efficient, courteous, and impartial in the performance of those du-

ties, assuring fair and equal treatment of all persons, claims, and transactions coming before me in my official capacity.

2. Work in full cooperation with other public employees in promoting the public welfare, recognizing that my private interest must always be subordinate to the public interest.

3. Make decisions conscientiously in compliance with public law and policies of the City Council, and subordinate my personal views to the requirements of law, my oath of office, and the regulations of the agency in which I perform my public duties.

4. Be scrupulously honest in handling public funds and in the conservation of public property, never using any funds or property under my care for private benefit of myself or others.

5. Never accept or engage in employment incompatible with my public duties.

6. Refuse to represent private interests before city agencies or in the courts in any matter involving the interests of the city as a party or in which my official position is a consideration.

7. Disclose all sources of income which may represent a substantial conflict of interest with my official duties and to disclose the nature and extent of any personal interest in a business entity engaging in any transaction with the city in which I may be involved in my official capacity as a public official or employee.

8. Refrain from disclosing confidential information concerning the city government.

9. Refrain from accepting gifts or favors or promise of future benefit which might compromise my independence of judgment or action as a public official or employee.

Appendix B

Public Relations Society of America

Code

This Code, adopted in November, 1959, by the PRSA Board of Directors and ratified by the 1960 PRSA Assembly, was amended in 1963 by the 1963 Board of Directors and 1963 Assembly. It replaces and strengthens a similar Code of Professional Standards for the Practice of Public Relations previously in force since 1954.

DECLARATION OF PRINCIPLES

Members of the Public Relations Society of America acknowledge and publicly declare that the public relations profession in serving the legitimate interests of clients or employers is dedicated fundamentally to the goals of better mutual understanding and cooperation among the diverse individuals, groups, institutions, and elements of our modern society.

In the performance of this mission, we pledge ourselves:

1. To conduct ourselves both privately and professionally in accord with the public welfare.
2. To be guided in all our activities by the generally accepted standards of truth, accuracy, fair dealing, and good taste.
3. To support efforts designed to increase the proficiency of the profession by encouraging the continuous development of sound training and resourceful education in the practice of public relations.
4. To adhere faithfully to provisions of the duly adopted Code of Professional Standards for the Practice of Public Relations, a copy of which is in the possession of every member.

CODE OF PROFESSIONAL STANDARDS
FOR THE PRACTICE OF PUBLIC RELATIONS

This Code of Professional Standards for the Practice of Public Relations is adopted by the Public Relations Society of America to promote and maintain high standards of public service and conduct among its members in order that membership in the Society may be deemed a badge of ethical conduct; that Public Relations justly may be regarded as a profession; that the public may have increasing confidence in its integrity; and that the practice of Public Relations may best serve the public interest.

1. A member has a general duty of fair dealing towards his clients or employers, past and present, his fellow members, and the general public.

2. A member shall conduct his professional life in accord with the public welfare.

3. A member has the affirmative duty of adhering to generally accepted standards of accuracy, truth, and good taste.

4. A member shall not represent conflicting or competing interests without the express consent of those concerned, given after a full disclosure of the facts; nor shall he place himself in a position where his interest is or may be in conflict with his duty to his client, employer, another member, or the public, without a full disclosure of such interests to all concerned.

5. A member shall safeguard the confidences of both present and former clients or employers and shall not accept retainers or employment which may involve the disclosure or use of these confidences to the disadvantage or prejudice of such clients or employers.

6. A member shall not engage in any practice which tends to corrupt the integrity of channels of public communication.

7. A member shall not intentionally disseminate false or misleading information and is obligated to use ordinary care to avoid dissemination of false or misleading information.

8. A member shall be prepared to identify to the public the source of any communication for which he is responsible, including the name of the client or employer on whose behalf the communication is made.

9. A member shall not make use of any individual or organization purporting to serve or represent some announced cause, or purporting to be independent or unbiased, but actually serving an undisclosed special or private interest of a member or his client or his employer.

10. A member shall not intentionally injure the professional reputation or practice of another member. However, if a member has evidence that another member has been guilty of unethical, illegal, or unfair practices, including practices in violation of this Code, he should present the information to the proper authorities of the Society for action in accor-

dance with the procedure set forth in Article XIII of the Bylaws.

11. A member shall not employ methods tending to be derogatory of another member's client or employer or of the products, business, or services of such client or employer.

12. In performing services for a client or employer a member shall not accept fees, commissions, or any other valuable consideration in connection with those services from anyone other than his client or employer without the express consent of his client or employer, given after a full disclosure of the facts.

13. A member shall not propose to a prospective client or employer that the amount of his fee or other compensation be contingent on or measured by the achievement of specified results; nor shall he enter into any fee agreement to the same effect.

14. A member shall not encroach upon the professional employment of another member. Where there are two engagements, both must be assured that there is no conflict between them.

15. A member shall, as soon as possible, sever his relations with any organization when he knows or should know that his continued employment would require him to conduct himself contrary to the principles of this Code.

16. A member called as a witness in a proceeding for the enforcement of this Code shall be bound to appear unless, for sufficient reason, he shall be excused by the panel hearing the same.

17. A member shall co-operate with fellow members in upholding and enforcing this Code.

Official Interpretations of the Code

The following interpretations of Code paragraphs 6, 13, and 14 were adopted by the PRSA Board of Directors on November 6, 1966, and became effective that date.

Interpretation of Code Paragraph 6 which reads, "A member shall not engage in any practice which tends to corrupt the integrity of the channels of public communication."

1. Practices prohibited by this Code paragraph are those which tend to place representatives of media under obligation to the member or his company or his client, such as—

(a.) any form of payment or compensation to a media representative in order to obtain, and in exchange for which, preferential or guaranteed news or editorial coverage in the medium is promised, implied, or delivered.

(b.) any retainer of a media employee which involves the use of his position as a media employee for the private purposes of the member or his client or employer where the circumstances of such retainer are not fully disclosed to and accepted by the media employer.

(c.) an agreement between a member and a media employee when such agreement includes a provision that the media employee will secure preferential or guaranteed coverage in the medium for the member, his firm, or his client, or utilization by a member of such an agreement between his employer, his firm, or his client and a media employee.

(d.) providing vacation trips to media representatives where no news assignment is involved.

(e.) any attempt by a member to lead his employer or client to believe that a member has obtained independent coverage for the employer or client in a medium over which the member has financial or editorial influence or control.

(f.) the use by a member of an investment made by the member, his firm, or his client in a medium to obtain preferential or guaranteed coverage in the medium.

(g.) the use by a member of a loan of money made to a medium by the member, his firm, or his client to obtain preferential or guaranteed coverage in the medium.

2. This Code paragraph does not prohibit entertaining media representatives at meals, cocktails, or press parties, nor does it prohibit the bona fide press junket where media representatives are given an opportunity for on-the-spot viewing of a news event or product or service in which the media representative has a legitimate news interest, provided that independence of action is left to the media representative.

3. This Code paragraph does not prohibit the gift or loan of sample products or services to media representatives whose assignments indicate an interest in such products or services, if the sample products or services are manufactured, sold, or rendered by the member's company or client and the sampling is a reasonable method of demonstrating the product or service.

4. This Code paragraph does not prohibit the giving of souvenirs or holiday gifts of nominal value as goodwill gestures to media representatives.

Interpretation of Code Paragraph 13 which reads, "A member shall not propose to a prospective client or employer that the amount of his fee or other compensation be contingent on or measured by the achievement of specified results; nor shall he enter into any fee agreement to the same effect."

1. This Code paragraph means that a member may take into consideration the following factors in determining compensation for his services:

(a.) the experience, judgment, and skills required to handle the matter properly.

(b.) the characteristics and difficulty of the problems involved.

(c.) the time and labor required.

(d.) the effect on the member's employment by other clients or potential clients.

(e.) the customary or prevailing compensation for similar services.

(f.) the values involved in the matter and the benefits resulting to the client or employer from the services.

(g.) the duration and character of the employment, whether casual or for a continuing period.

(h.) the equipment or personnel investment required in order to perform the function.

2. This Code paragraph prohibits a member from entering into any agreement whereby the member's rate of compensation is determined or conditioned by the amount of newspaper or magazine lineage obtained for the member's company or client. This applies equally to radio and television coverage, or any form of exposure to a client's message. It applies further to any contingency fee based on increase in sales volume, increase in profit margins, increase in stock value, or the attainment of specified political or legislative results. . . .

3. This Code paragraph means that a member may guarantee to produce certain materials, such as films, feature articles, scripts, news releases, etc., and promise that these will be of high quality or specific type; but any guarantee that such materials, once produced, shall achieve a specified minimum use by media outlets, in other than paid time or space, and failing which use the fee or compensation will be reduced, is a practice prohibited by this Code paragraph.

Interpretation of Code Paragraph 14 which reads, "A member shall not encroach upon the professional employment of another member. Where there are two engagements, both must be assured that there is no conflict between them."

1. This Code paragraph is not designed to curb the freedom of a member to seek employment or business for his counseling firm by all approved and legitimate means. However, it is interpreted to mean that a member shall not invade or infringe upon the counselor–client or employee–employer relationship of another member.

2. A member would not violate this Code paragraph by—

(a.) sending copies of his resume and examples of his work to potential employers even if the employers currently employ members of the Society.

(b.) advertising his or his firm's qualifications in any publication he deems suitable.

(c.) mailing copies of advertisements, circulars, or booklets describing his or his firm's services, or copies of speeches or articles to potential clients, provided any such mailing is not one of solicitation and provided the mailing contains no derogatory comment about another member.

(d.) furnishing, upon specific request, factual information about his firm, its principals, personnel, and types of services rendered, including names of clients, provided such information contains no proposals to a client of another member.

3. This Code paragraph prohibits a member from seeking individual professional employment by deprecating the character, ability, or performance of another member.

4. This Code paragraph requires that a counselor member—

(a.) before soliciting a prospective client, make all reasonable attempts to determine whether the prospective client has an existing relationship with another counselor member who would be replaced, and, if so, make no contact until the incumbent has been notified that his replacement is being considered or that the employment of the incumbent has been terminated.

(b.) after making an initial contact with a prospective client and subsequently learning that a counselor member–client relationship exists of which he was unaware, shall at that point make no further overtures nor conduct any negotiations with the prospective client until the incumbent has been notified that his replacement is being considered or that the employment of the incumbent has been terminated.

5. Where a member is solicited by a prospective client to take over the functions currently performed by another member, he shall decline to consider the offer until the incumbent member has been advised that a replacement of his services is being considered. Upon specific request, the member may provide information of a factual nature about his firm and its services but shall make no proposals to the client of another member until he has determined that the incumbent has been notified of a possible change.

6. Where a member is solicited by a prospective

client to perform functions separate from those currently performed for the same client by another member, it is the responsibility of the solicited member to determine that the incumbent member has been informed, since both must be assured that there is no conflict between the two functions.

An Official Interpretation of the PRSA Code of Professional Standards for the Practice of Public Relations as It Applies to Political Public Relations

Adopted by the PRSA Board of Directors, April 3, 1974

PREAMBLE

It is understood that in the practice of political public relations, the PRSA member will have something professional and substantial to offer his employer or client quite apart from the political dynamics of the client circumstance, and that he may serve his employer or client without having attributed to him the character, reputation, or beliefs of those he serves.

DEFINITION

"Political Public Relations" is defined as those areas of public relations which relate to:

(a.) the counseling of political organizations, committees, candidates, or potential candidates for public office; and groups constituted for the purpose of influencing the vote on any ballot issue;

(b.) the counseling of holders of public office;

(c.) the management, or direction, of a political campaign for or against a candidate for political office; or for or against a ballot issue to be determined by voter approval or rejection;

(d.) the practice of public relations on behalf of a client or an employer in connection with that client's or employer's relationships with any candidates or holders of public office with the purpose of influencing legislation or government regulation or treatment of a client or employer, regardless of whether the PRSA member is a recognized lobbyist;

(e.) the counseling of government bodies, or segments thereof, either domestic or foreign.

PRECEPTS

1. It is the responsibility of a PRSA member practicing political public relations, as defined above, to be conversant with the various statutes, local, state, and federal, governing such activities and to adhere to them strictly. This includes, but is not limited to, the various local, state, and federal laws, court decisions, and official interpretations governing lobbying, political contributions, elections, libel, slander, and the like. In carrying out this responsibility, the member shall seek appropriate counseling whenever necessary.

2. It is also the responsibility of a member to abide by PRSA's Code of Professional Standards and to heed especially articles 4, 5, 6, 8, 9, 13, and 15.

3. A member shall represent his client or employer in good faith, and while partisan advocacy on behalf of a candidate or public issue may be expected, the member shall act in the public interest and exercise care in adhering to accepted standards of accuracy, truth, and good taste.

4. A member shall not issue descriptive material or any advertising or publicity information or participate in the preparation or use thereof which is not signed by responsible persons or is false, misleading, or unlabeled as to its source, and is obligated to use care to avoid dissemination of any such material.

5. A member has an obligation to his client to disclose what remuneration beyond his fee he expects to receive as a result of their relationship, such as commissions for media advertising, printing, and the like, and should not accept such extra payment without his client's consent.

6. A member's compensation shall not be contingent on, or measured by, the achievement of specified results, nor shall the member improperly use his position to encourage additional future employment or compensation.

7. A member shall voluntarily disclose to his employer or client the identity of other employers or clients with whom he is currently associated and whose interests might be affected favorably or unfavorably by his political representation.

8. A member shall respect the confidentiality of information pertaining to his employer or client even after their relationship ceases.

Appendix C

City of La Habra, California
Use of the Service Request Form

USE

Use a Service Request for an external matter originating from a citizen, requiring attention by a City department. This request serves as:

A work order to the department responsible for the proper handling of the matter.

A record of the volume and intensity of requests for services.

A record of the volume of the work load in comparison with the capacity of the department under the current budget.

All requests for service are referred to by the name. Never call such a request a "complaint."

PAPER

Use printed Service Request forms.

Use the white sheet for the original, and the pink and yellow sheets for the second and third copies.

NUMBER OF COPIES

Prepare each Service Request in triplicate.

FILL IN PRINTED FORM COMPLETELY

Be sure to get the name, address, and telephone number of the person making the request. Place this information at the top of the form.

Fill in your name and department, and the date.

Give a short summary of the request.

After "Details" list any further information given by the person making the Request.

After "Referred to" type the name of the department to which the request is to be referred for action.

DISTRIBUTION

Send the white (original) copy to the office of the City Administrator.

Send the pink and yellow copies to the department which is to handle the request.

ACTION TAKEN

As soon as the appropriate department has completed the action, the pink and yellow copies of the Service Requests are to be filled in.

Be sure that a description of the action taken is given after "Report."

The Service Request should be dated and signed by the person fulfilling the request.

DISPOSITION OF COPIES

As soon as the pink and yellow copies have been filled in, indicating completion of the request, the pink copy should be forwarded to the Office of the City Administrator. The yellow copy is to be retained in the files of the department which acted upon the request as a record of work performed.

Appendix D

Publications Planning, Development, and Production: Special Features

The following Special Features, which supplement Chapter 11 of this book, deal with certain aspects of development and production which should prove helpful to those wishing to pursue these subjects in more detail. The length of Chapter 11, and the complexity of the subject matter, have suggested placing these features in this appendix.

TABULAR INFORMATION

Certain kinds of information, especially revenues and expenditures, budget estimates, land use data, and population characteristics, should be set up in tables. This is the organized and concise way of showing information and is indispensable for handling large amounts of data. Most tables need not be complicated, but they should include basic elements of: a table title; box heads or column heads (the terms are interchangeable); a stub (the entries that go down the left-hand side of the table); the body of the table; and the footnotes. A complex table may also require a headnote to explain the information shown, but this usually can be better handled by accompanying text.

Examples of straightforward presentation of data can be found in *The Municipal Year Book,* published by the International City Management Association. More elegant visual presentations can be found in the annual reports issued by many large corporations, foundations, and universities. The many reports and other documents issued by most governmental bodies in the United States, unfortunately, are not a good source to draw on.

CHARTS AND GRAPHS

Charts and graphs that highlight points in the text strengthen some publications, especially the annual report and reports to the city council. The common varieties are bar charts, line graphs, and pie charts. Several variations are possible, depending on time, money available, and ingenuity. Most charts and graphs can be prepared by the local government staff with simple drafting instruments and a variety of commercial products (alphabets, lines, screens, templates, symbols, and patterns) that can be mounted for photographic reproduction. The Selected Bibliography to this book lists basic references.

COMPOSITION METHODS

Strike-on Composition. Usually called "cold type," strike-on composition is type set by direct impression on paper. At the heart of the method is a typewriter. Composition units range from the ordinary office typewriter with uniform character widths to typewriters with proportionally designed type faces and line justification. The more sophisticated equipment produces composition approaching the quality of so-called "printer's type." Many of the more popular type faces are available in several sizes. This method of composition is generally the least expensive and it is well suited for tabular and straight matter typesetting. Type size changes and changes between roman, bold face, and italic type must be kept to a minimum, however, because of limitations in the method.

Several different machines are widely used: the VariTyper, the Friden Justowriter, the IBM Selectric Composer, and the IBM Magnetic Tape/Selectric Composer (MT/SC) system.

Metal Composition. Metal composition is type cast in metal by machine from matrices (metal type molds). Proofs of the composition are prepared separately on a proof press. This method is popularly known as "hot type."

Metal composition can be produced on any of four different machines: the Linotype and Intertype (essentially the same equipment but from different manufacturers) machines cast a line of type at a time from matrices assembled automatically by keyboard operation; the Monotype machine casts individual type characters in lines from matrices assembled automatically by a separate keyboard operation; and the Ludlow machine casts a line of type at a time from hand-assembled matrices. The Ludlow is used only for headlines and display composition.

Hand composition is the only other method of metal composition. The individual metal characters and spaces are assembled by hand, line for line, in a composing stick. It is slow and is used only for small amounts of type, primarily the larger sizes. It is by far the most expensive method of composition.

Photocomposition. Phototypesetting machines use the photographic process to produce type. The resulting product is a sharply defined image on paper or film. Optical systems permit adjustment of type size and, in some instances, modification of proportion of the type. Systems available today are wide ranging and offer a variety of typesetting capabilities for composing words, lines, or full-page layouts (text type, display heads, captions, and folios made up in pages). The systems with the greatest capabilities are tied in with computers for handling any number of different functions, such as line justification, word hyphenation, storage for retrieval and later updating, etc.

Speed, versatility, and reduction of the number of production steps leading up to the final printed page are a few of the benefits of phototypesetting. Most of the type faces are adaptations from metal type, but there are a growing number of photo faces of exclusive design.

New equipment and system developments are constantly being offered. There are many different manufacturers with equipment of varying capabilities: display phototypesetters to text phototypesetters, and manual systems to cathode-ray-tube systems. A few of the systems include names such as Fototronic, Photon, Monophoto, Linofilm, Compugraphic, Alphatype, CompStar, PhotoTypositor, Headliner, Protype, Linotron, and VideoComp.

PRINTING PROCESSES

There are basically four different printing processes: letterpress printing (relief), offset printing (planograph), gravure printing (intaglio), and screen printing (stencil). Each process offers certain benefits and advantages depending on the printing requirements, but offset has become the most available and widely used process, having replaced letterpress printing as the number one process. Offset offers great flexibility in design, lower cost, and exceptional latitude in printing on a variety of paper surfaces.

In addition to printing processes, brief consideration is given below to office duplicating and copying.

Letterpress. The image is printed from a raised (relief) surface above the nonprinting areas. The raised areas are inked and the image transferred by pressure to the paper surface. There are three types of letterpress presses. In the *platen press,* the bed of the press holds the type form, the platen holds the paper, and the two surfaces come together much like a clamp pressing the inked type against the paper. In the *cylinder press,* a moving flat bed holds the inked form and a fixed rotating cylinder carrying the paper impresses it against the type. In the *rotary press,* both the impression and printing surfaces are cylinders: one holds the curved type form and the other provides the pressure against the paper. Paper is fed to platen presses and cylinder presses in precut sheets and usually in roll form for rotary presses. Because of the high cost of making a rotary press ready for printing, publication work is primarily restricted for press runs of hundreds of thousands.

Offset. The printing image and nonprinting area in offset are on the same level plane (planograph). The thin, photomechanically prepared printing plate is chemically sensitized to accept ink and repel water in the printing areas. The nonprinting areas accept water and repel ink. It is based on the principle that grease (ink) and water do not mix. A film of water is passed over the printing plate followed by a film of ink. The image is transferred from the printing plate by minimal pressure onto a rubber blanket cylinder and then *offset* onto the paper. The resilience of the rubber blanket permits printing on a wide range of paper surfaces and textures.

There are two basic types of offset presses: sheet-fed and web. On both types of presses there are three separate cylinders: the plate, the blanket, and the impression cylinders. The sheet-fed press prints single sheets of paper; the web press prints a continuous sheet of paper from rolls. Some sheet-fed presses will feed from roll paper, but the paper is cut automatically in single sheets as it enters the printing unit. Paper on a web press is always fed from rolls and it is cut automatically into sheets as it is delivered from the press. Most web presses have folding capabilities in line with the press to reduce paper handling.

Gravure. This process is the opposite of letterpress (relief) printing. The image areas are recessed into a metal plate to form uniform wells of equal dimension for holding ink. The depth of the wells controls the amount of ink transferred to the paper. In the process of printing, the plate is inked (filling the wells), then a blade passes over the plate wiping all ink from the nonrecessed, nonimage areas. The image is then transferred directly from the plate onto paper by the impression cylinder.

Presses used for gravure printing are sheet-fed and rotogravure. Both types operate on the rotary principle. Because of the high cost of plate preparation, sheet-fed gravure is usually limited to prestige printing demanding exceptional quality. Rotogravure, on the other hand, because of the high operating speeds and exceptionally long plate life, is used for all classes of long-run printing. Technical advances now being made in gravure, particularly in the cost reduction of plate preparation, indicate that the process will become more widely used in the future.

Screen Printing. Stencil printing has limited applications for publications work. The process is accomplished by forcing ink through a fabric screen onto the printing surface. It is possible to reproduce continuous tone artwork or photos by photomechanically cut stencils, but normally the process is confined to reproduction of line work or flat masses. The amount of ink applied is far greater than in letterpress, offset, or gravure; thus unusual effects may be achieved. It is primarily a hand operation on slow, cumbersome equipment. Equipment advances are being made, but the very nature of the process limits its usage. For runs over a few hundred the advantage is soon lost.

Office Duplicating and Copying. For limited size and quantity, the offset duplicator is a useful, versatile machine. It uses the same printing process as larger commercial offset presses, and faithful reproduction is obtained from handwritten or typewritten copy prepared directly on paper plates. Presensitized metal plates may also be used to reproduce line and halftone copy. These plates are made photomechanically by direct image or separately prepared film. The duplicators (among them the widely used Multilith and Davidson duplicators) are made by about a dozen different manufacturers for printing sheet sizes up to 10 by 14 inches.

Office copiers, as distinguished from office duplicators, have a more limited application. They are grouped into two classes: wet copiers that use some variation of photography to create a copy, and dry copiers that use electrostatic, thermographic, or some other patented process to do the work. Some copiers require special papers; others use ordinary paper. They are compact, easy to use, and in offices today are about as common as the typewriter. Xerox and 3-M are two of the many manufacturers offering this type of equipment.

PAPER

There are several classes of paper, and each class has its own standard of measurement known as basis weight. This is the weight in pounds of a ream (500 sheets) of paper, cut to a given standard size (known as the basic size) of that class of paper. Since paper is made and sold by the pound, the language of paper weights should be understood to select and specify paper.

Book papers and *cover* papers are the two classes most often used in publications. Book papers are offered in a vast variety of finishes (both coated and uncoated), colors, and weights. The basic size for determining book paper weight is 25 by 38 inches. This means that 500 sheets of 25 by 38 book paper will have a weight of X number of pounds. The most commonly used basis weights for *uncoated* book papers are 40, 50, 60, 70, and 80 pounds. The most commonly used basis weights of *coated* paper are 50, 60, 70, 80, 90, 100, and 120 pounds.

While basis weights are normally given in terms of ream weights, the weight of any particular size of paper is often referred to in terms of M weight. This weight is just double the ream weight.

Comparative weights of *coated* and *uncoated* book papers do not have the same bulk because of the character of the paper. The clay coating process makes a *coated* paper more compact; hence it has less bulk than the equivalent weight of an uncoated paper.

The other class of paper most commonly used in publications is *cover* paper. To add to the confusion of understanding paper weights, the basic size for cover papers is 20 by 26 inches. This is determined by weighing a ream of the size 20 by 26 rather than 25 by 38 inches for book papers. Comparatively, a 50-pound cover paper is roughly twice as heavy as a 50-pound book paper.

Cover papers are available both in coated and uncoated surfaces. The most commonly used basis weights for *uncoated* cover papers are 50, 65, 80, 90, and 100 pounds. For *coated:* 50, 60, 65, 80, and 90

pounds. As with book papers, the coating process makes the coated cover papers less bulky.

Another class of paper which is used particularly for report-type publications is *writing* or *bond* paper. The basic size is different from either book or cover paper. It is 17 by 22 inches, which is four times the size of a standard letterhead. Basis weight (called substance weight in writing papers) is determined by the same method of weighing 500 sheets. Commonly used weights are 16, 20, 24, and 28 pounds. A 20-pound bond paper corresponds roughly to a 50-pound book paper.

In addition to the basic sizes used in calculating weight, each class of paper is offered in a number of other standard sheet sizes to accommodate various printing requirements.

The most economical use of paper is achieved by planning the trim size of the publication to cut out of standard paper sizes. Otherwise paper is wasted, which adds to the cost of the publication. If an odd-size publication is planned, the printer or paper dealer should be consulted before specifications are set in final form.

PHOTOGRAPHY

The effective use of photography in a local government's public affairs efforts is similar in several ways to effectiveness in writing: The photos, like the writing, must be simple, clear and concise—and they must say something—if they are to be effective. And even if they are all these things, they won't work if they are displayed in the wrong way.

Photographs should show something. That sounds like a cynical remark, but not all photographs do. They should show people doing things. A new library should not be shown by a picture that shows only the building. If it is an inside picture, people should be shown *using* the library. If it is an outside shot, people should be shown going in or out of the new building.

A street improvement project should show workers and equipment in operation. If the project is finished, the picture should show cars driving over the improved portion.

If the mayor and the city council are presiding at a ceremony, they should be shown talking in animated conversation, or, better still, actually doing something. They should not simply stand, hands at their sides, looking at the camera. It is better not to crowd more than three or four people into the picture; and they should be close to each other.

Photographs must be processed with care, so that they are developed in sharp tones with high contrast. Gray, dull photos hurt one's cause. They look bad in a publication; or, if they are sent out, they won't be used.

In using photographs in publications, care should be taken to do them justice. They should not be so small that people have to squint to see them. A good action picture which is run large in a publication is tremendously effective in creating the impression of a dynamic local government, up-to-date and doing things the right way.

Pictures should be cropped effectively (the blank space or the irrelevant material in the photo should be marked out with a grease pencil so that the printer will run only the portion inside the crop marks). Pictures being sent to the papers or other publications must be left uncropped, because the recipients will have their own preferences about how they want to run these pictures—what they want to crop out and what they want to leave in. An important consideration here is to make certain that the pictures a public relations department releases to others do not have a lot of dead space. If they do, they are not good publicity pictures and should not be released.

For pictures being released to the news media, it is essential to include a caption explaining the picture and identifying everyone, from left to right, by full name and title. The caption should be attached to the bottom of the picture, with the top of the caption paper taped to the back of the photo. Paper clips should not be used: they can damage the print. It is inadvisable to write on a piece of paper over the picture because the weight of the pencil or pen will often come through onto the picture. In mailing photographs, cardboard backing should be used to prevent the picture from being twisted or torn in the mail, and "Photographs: Do Not Bend" should be written on the envelope. When mailing first class, one should make sure the envelope says so on both front and back.

Selected Bibliography

This bibliography is highly selective and is based primarily on recommendations of the chapter authors for this book. It represents informed judgments about basic materials in the area of public relations, particularly public relations as it applies to local government operations.

In addition to the books and other references listed, certain basic periodicals are recommended for keeping up-to-date on developments in the field. These are listed immediately below.

Jack O'Dwyer's Newsletter. Weekly. Jack O'Dwyer, Publisher, 271 Madison Avenue, New York, New York 10016. (212) OR 9–2471. Broad coverage of public relations field and public relations firms. Subjects featured in the newsletter include consumer affairs and environmental concerns.

PR Aids' Party Line. Weekly. Richard Toohey, Publishers, 221 Park Avenue South, New York, New York 10003. (212) 673–6363. Covers feature and story material needed by editors in the various media. Considerable interest in public affairs. A good source reference for placement of local government news stories.

PR Reporter. Weekly. PR Publishing Company, Inc., Meriden, New Hampshire 03770. (603) 469–3266. Gives an upper echelon perspective on what's happening today in public relations. Has a "how-to" and special report supplement each week. Twice yearly statistical issues. Each year publishes a statistical table that covers government information and public relations people.

Practical Public Relations. Semimonthly. Currents Information Services, Inc., 31 Gibbs Street, Rochester, New York 14604. (716) 454–4553. The *how* and *why* newsletter for public relations practitioners. Emphasizes the tools and techniques of publicity and public relations. Much "how-to" material.

Public Relations Journal. Monthly. Public Relations Society of America, 845 Third Avenue, New York, New York 10022. (212) 826–1757. Serves public relations practitioners, educators, and management. The approach is both practical and theoretical. Features of interest to local government practitioners are: case studies covering a variety of points of view; "how-to" articles; material of consumer and environmental interest; and a regular feature on working with the "new media" (for example, cable television, videodiscs, videocassettes). The Public Relations Society of America operates an information center and has chapters in many parts of the United States.

Public Relations News. Weekly. Denny Griswold, Publisher, 127 East 80th Street, New York, New York 10021. (212) 879–7090. Provides a clearinghouse for ideas and techniques in public relations. Presents statistics, trends, case studies. Is interested in the need for a more informed public and for better public relations in government.

Public Relations Quarterly. Howard Hudson, Publishers, 44 West Market Street, Rhinebeck, New York 12572. (914) 876–2081. The only quarterly in the field. Works toward the improvement and upgrading of the practice of the profession. The approach tends to be long-term; trends are predicted in the field. The publication is oriented toward the professional practitioner and is international in character.

1. Public Relations in Society

BAILEY, STEPHEN K. "Ethics and the Public Service." *Public Administration Review* 24 (December 1964): 234–43.

BERNAYS, EDWARD L. *Public Relations.* Rev. ed. Norman: University of Oklahoma Press, 1970.

BISHOP, ROBERT L. *Public Relations: A Comprehensive Bibliography, 1964–72.* New York: Foundation for Public Relations Research and Education, 1974.

CONWAY, ANNE; HOLBROOK, DAVID; BRADLEY, ROBERT; BEZOLD, CLEMENT; and MILLS, JON L. "Florida's 'Government in the Sunshine' Law: A Summary Report." Gainesville: University of Florida, Center for Governmental Responsibility, 1975. (Mimeographed.)

CUTLIP, SCOTT M. *A Public Relations Bibliography.* 2nd ed. Madison: University of Wisconsin Press, 1965.

CUTLIP, SCOTT M., and CENTER, ALLEN H. *Effective Public Relations.* 4th ed. Englewood Cliffs, N.J.: Prentice-Hall, Inc., 1971.

ETZIONI, AMITAI. *A Comparative Analysis of Complex Organizations.* New York: Free Press of Glencoe, 1961. Available in paperback.

GRISWOLD, DENNY. *Public Relations Comes of Age.* Boston: Boston University School of Public Relations, 1947.

INTERNATIONAL CITY MANAGEMENT ASSOCIATION. *City Management Code of Ethics.* Washington, D.C.: International City Management Association, 1972.

KEY, V. O., JR. *Politics, Parties, and Pressure Groups.* 5th ed. New York: Thomas Y. Crowell, 1964.

———. *Public Opinion and American Democracy.* New York: Alfred A. Knopf, Inc., 1961.

LEYS, WAYNE A. *Ethics for Policy Decisions: The Art of Asking Deliberate Questions.* Englewood Cliffs, N.J.: Prentice-Hall, Inc., 1952. Reprinted 1968 by Greenwood Press, Inc., Westport, Conn.

MCKAY, GERALD. "The Public's Right To Know." *Minnesota Municipalities,* June 1972, pp. 172–78.

NATIONAL ASSOCIATION OF REGIONAL COUNCILS. *Regional Council Communications: A Guide to Issues and Techniques.* Washington, D.C.: National Association of Regional Councils, 1973.

NOLTE, L. W. *Fundamentals of Public Relations.* Elmsford, N.Y.: Pergamon Press, Inc., 1974.

SCAMMON, RICHARD M., and WATTENBERG, BEN J. *The Real Majority: How the Silent Center of the American Electorate Chooses Its President.*

New York: Coward, McCann & Geoghegan, 1970.

SIMON, RAYMOND, ed. *Perspectives in Public Relations.* Norman: University of Oklahoma Press, 1966.

WHYTE, WILLIAM H., JR., and the editors of FORTUNE. *Is Anybody Listening? How and Why U.S. Business Fumbles When It Talks with Human Beings.* New York: Simon & Schuster, Inc., 1952.

WRIGHT, J. HANDLY, and CHRISTIAN, BYRON H. *Public Relations in Management.* New York: McGraw-Hill Book Company, 1949.

2. Research and the Public Relations Process

BACKSTROM, CHARLES H., and HURSH, GERALD D. *Survey Research.* Evanston, Ill.: Northwestern University Press, 1963.

BUDD, RICHARD W.; THORP, ROBERT L.; and DONOHEW, LEWIS. *Content Analysis of Communication.* New York: The Macmillan Company, 1967.

COCHRAN, WILLIAM G. *Sampling Techniques.* 2nd ed. New York: John Wiley & Sons, Inc., 1963.

ERDOS, PAUL L. *Professional Mail Surveys.* New York: McGraw-Hill Book Company, 1968.

LERBINGER, OTTO. *Designs for Persuasive Communication,* Englewood Cliffs, N.J.: Prentice-Hall, Inc., 1972. Available in paperback.

MILLER, DELBERT C. *Handbook of Research Design and Social Measurement.* New York: David McKay Co., Inc., 1964.

NORTH, ROBERT C.; HOLSTI, OLE R.; ZANINOVICH, M. GEORGE; and ZINNES, DINA A. *Content Analysis.* Evanston, Ill.: Northwestern University Press, 1963.

ROBINSON, EDWARD J. *Communication and Public Relations.* Columbus, Ohio: Charles E. Merrill Publishing Co., 1966.

———. *Public Relations and Survey Research.* New York: Irvington Books, 1969.

ROLL, CHARLES W., JR., and CANTRIL, ALBERT H. *Polls: Their Use and Misuse in Politics.* New York: Basic Books, Inc., 1972.

WEBB, KENNETH, and HATRY, HARRY P. *Obtaining Citizen Feedback: The Application of Citizen*

Surveys to Local Governments. Washington, D.C.: The Urban Institute, 1973.

WILLIAMS, FREDERICK. *Reasoning with Statistics: Simplified Examples in Communications Research.* New York: Holt, Rinehart & Winston, Inc., 1968.

3. The Council: Focal Point of Interests

BANFIELD, EDWARD C., and WILSON, JAMES Q. *City Politics.* New York: Vintage Books, 1966.

HILL, JOHN W. *The Function of Public Relations in Helping To Restore Confidence in American Institutions.* New York: Foundation for Public Relations Research and Education, 1974.

INTERNATIONAL CITY MANAGERS' ASSOCIATION. *Handbook for Councilmen in Council-Manager Cities.* 2nd ed. Chicago: International City Managers' Association, 1964. Reissued by the National Municipal League, New York, 1973.

LIPPMANN, WALTER. *Public Opinion.* New York: Harcourt & Brace, 1922. Reissued in paperback by The Free Press, New York, 1965.

PIMLOTT, J. A. *Public Relations and American Democracy.* Princeton, N.J.: Princeton University Press, 1951. Reissued by Kennikat Press Inc., Port Washington, N.Y., 1971.

RIDLEY, CLARENCE E. *The Role of the City Manager in Policy Formulation.* Chicago: International City Managers' Association, 1958.

SCAMMON, RICHARD M., and WATTENBERG, BEN J. *The Real Majority: How the Silent Center of the American Electorate Chooses Its President.* New York: Coward, McCann & Geoghegan, 1970.

4. The Multitudinous Publics

BANFIELD, EDWARD C., and WILSON, JAMES Q. *City Politics.* New York: Vintage Books, 1966.

BERELSON, BERNARD, and JANOWITZ, MORRIS, eds. *Reader in Public Opinion and Communication.* Rev. ed. New York: The Free Press, 1966.

BERELSON, BERNARD, and STEINER, GARY A. *Human Behavior: An Inventory of Scientific Findings.* Shorter ed. New York: Harcourt, Brace & World, Inc., 1967. Paperback.

BLACK, MAX, ed. *The Social Theories of Talcott Parsons.* Englewood Cliffs, N.J.: Prentice-Hall, Inc., 1961.

BOGART, LEO. *Silent Politics: Polls and the Awareness of Public Opinion.* New York: John Wiley & Sons, Inc., 1972.

BOULDING, KENNETH E. *Conflict and Defense: A General Theory.* New York: Harper Torchbooks, 1962.

CUTLIP, SCOTT M., and CENTER, ALLEN H. *Effective Public Relations.* 4th ed. Englewood Cliffs, N.J.: Prentice-Hall, Inc., 1971.

FISHBEIN, M., ed. *Readings in Attitude Theory and Measurement.* New York: John Wiley & Sons, Inc., 1967.

GORDON, GEORGE. *Persuasion: Theory and Practice of Manipulative Communication.* New York: Hastings House, Publishers, 1971.

HARLOW, REX F. *Social Science in Public Relations.* New York: Harper & Brothers, Publishers, 1957.

HARLOW, REX F., and BLACK, MARVIN M. *Practical Public Relations.* Rev. ed. New York: Harper & Row, Publishers, 1962.

HENNESSY, BERNARD C. *Public Opinion.* 2nd ed. Belmont, Calif.: Duxbury Press, 1971.

JONES, GARTH N. "Integration of Political Ethos and Local Government Systems." *Human Organization* 23 (Fall 1964): 210–22.

————. *Planned Organizational Change: A Study in Change Dynamics.* New York: Praeger Publishers, Inc., 1969.

JONES, GARTH N., and others. *Planning, Development, and Change: A Bibliography on Development Administration.* Honolulu: East–West Center, 1970.

LIPPMANN, WALTER. *Public Opinion.* New York: Harcourt & Brace, 1922. Reissued in paperback by The Free Press, New York, 1965.

MAYER, KURT B., and BUCKLEY, WALTER. *Class and Society.* 3rd ed. New York: Random House, 1970.

PARSONS, TALCOTT. *The Social System.* New York: The Free Press, 1951.

ROGERS, EVERETT M. *Diffusion of Innovations.* New York: The Free Press, 1962.

ROPER, ELMO. "Who Tells the Story Teller?" *Saturday Review,* July 31, 1954, pp. 25–26.

ROSENAU, JAMES N. *Public Opinion and Foreign Policy.* New York: Random House, 1961.

SCHRAMM, WILBUR, and ROBERTS, DONALD F. *The Process and Effects of Mass Communications.* Rev. ed. Urbana: University of Illinois Press, 1971.

TRIANDIS, HARRY C. *Attitude and Attitude Change.* New York: John Wiley & Sons, Inc., 1971.

ZIMBARDO, PHILIP G., and EBBESEN, EBBE B. *Influencing Attitudes and Changing Behavior.* Reading, Mass.: Addison-Wesley Publishing Co., 1969.

5. Serving the Public

BUDD, JOHN F., JR. *An Executive's Primer on Public Relations.* Philadelphia: Chilton Book Company, 1969.

CANFIELD, BERTRAND R., and MOORE, H. FRAZIER. *Public Relations: Principles, Cases and Problems.* 6th ed. Homewood, Ill.: Richard D. Irwin, Inc., 1973.

CITY OF BEVERLY HILLS, CALIFORNIA. *Public Relations Training Manual.* Rev. ed. Beverly Hills, Calif.: City of Beverly Hills, 1962.

CITY OF LA HABRA, CALIFORNIA. "Training in Public Relations." La Habra, 1962. (Mimeographed.)

CUTLIP, SCOTT M., and CENTER, ALLEN H. *Effective Public Relations.* 4th ed. Englewood Cliffs, N.J.: Prentice-Hall, Inc., 1971.

LESLY, PHILIP. *Lesly's Public Relations Handbook.* Englewood Cliffs, N.J.: Prentice-Hall, Inc., 1971.

RIESELBACH, LEROY N. *People vs. Government: The Responsiveness of American Institutions.* Bloomington: Indiana University Press, 1975.

SCHMIDT, FRANCES, and WEINER, HAROLD M. *Public Relations in Health and Welfare.* New York: Columbia University Press, 1966.

6. The Employee–Citizen Team

ALESHIRE, ROBERT A. "Organizing for Neighborhood Management: Drawing on the Federal Experience." *Public Management,* January 1971, pp. 7–9.

ARNOLD, JOHN E. "People Involvement: Participation To Restore Confidence." *Public Management,* September 1971, p. 11.

ARNSTEIN, SHERRY R. "Eight Rungs on the Ladder of Citizen Participation." In *Citizen Participation: Effecting Community Change,* pp. 69–91. Edited by Edgar S. Cahn and Barry A. Passett. New York: Praeger Publishers, Inc., 1971.

CASSELLA, WILLIAM N., JR. "The Role of the Charter Commission." *Public Management,* July 1971, pp. 19–21.

FORRESTER, JAY W. *Urban Dynamics.* Cambridge, Mass.: The M.I.T. Press, 1969.

HANEY, WILLIAM V. *Communication and Organizational Behavior: Text and Cases.* Homewood, Ill.: Richard D. Irwin, Inc., 1973.

JOYNER, CONRAD. "Marketing City Services: Overlooked Opportunity." *Public Management,* February 1970, pp. 7–9.

POWELL, ORVILLE. *Compass.* Winston-Salem: City of Winston-Salem, January–February 1973, pp. 1–2.

SHIRLEY, FRANKLIN R. "What Is Government Public Relations?" *Public Relations Journal* 29 (June 1973): 2.

SLIPY, DAVID. "Community Service: A Look at Who Does the Work." *Nation's Cities,* August 1973, pp. 25–27.

TOWNSEND, LYNN A. "A Corporate President's View of the Internal Communication Function." In *Readings in Interpersonal and Organizational Communication,* pp. 70–77. Edited by Richard C. Huseman, Cal M. Logue, and Dwight L. Freshley. Boston: Holbrook Press, Inc., 1973.

WILCOX, ROBERT F. "Have Things Really Changed That Much?" *Public Management,* March 1971, pp. 4–7.

7. Community Group Relations

ADRIAN, CHARLES R. *State and Local Government.* New York: McGraw-Hill Book Company, 1950.

ADRIAN, CHARLES R., and PRESS, CHARLES. *Governing Urban America.* 4th ed. New York: McGraw-Hill Book Company, 1972.

ADRIAN, CHARLES R., ed. *Social Science and Community Action.* East Lansing: Michigan State University, 1960.

ADULT EDUCATION ASSOCIATION OF THE U.S.A. *Better Boards and Committees.* Leadership Pamphlet no. 14. Washington, D.C.: Adult Education Association of the U.S.A., 1957.

ALTSHULER, ALAN A. *Community Control: The Black Demand for Participation in Large American Cities.* New York: Pegasus, 1970.

BANFIELD, EDWARD C., and BANFIELD, LAURA. *The Moral Basis for Backward Society.* New York: The Free Press, 1958.

BENELLO, C. GEORGE, and ROUSSOUPOULOUS, DIMITRIOS, eds. *The Case for Participatory Democracy.* New York: Viking Press, 1971.

BOBBITT, H. RANDOLPH, JR., and others. *Organizational Behavior, Understanding, and Prediction.* Englewood Cliffs, N.J.: Prentice-Hall, Inc., 1974.

COX, FRED M., and others, eds. *Strategies of Community Organization.* Itasca, Ill.: F. F. Publishers, 1970.

DAHL, ROBERT A., and LINDBLOM, CHARLES E. *Politics, Economics, and Welfare.* New York: Harper & Brothers, Publishers, 1953. Available in paperback.

EULAU, HEINZ. *The Behavioral Persuasion in Politics.* New York: Random House, 1963.

FINKEL, C. *How To Plan Meetings.* New York: Bill Communications, 1973.

GILMORE, DONALD R. *Developing the Little Economies.* New York: Committee for Economic Development, 1959.

GODSCHALK, DAVID R. *Participation, Planning, and Exchange in Old and New Communities: A Collaborative Paradigm.* Chapel Hill: University of North Carolina, Center for Urban and Regional Studies, 1971.

JONES, GARTH N. *Planned Organizational Change: A Study in Change Dynamics.* New York: Praeger Publishers, Inc., 1969.

KOTLER, MILTON. *Neighborhood Government: The Local Foundations of Political Life.* New York: Bobbs-Merrill Co., Inc., 1969.

LUNDBORG, LOUIS B. *Public Relations in the Local Community.* New York: Harper & Brothers, Publishers, 1950.

OLMSTEAD, DONALD W. *Social Groups: Roles and Leadership.* East Lansing: Michigan State University, 1961.

POLSKY, NELSON W. *Community Power and Political Theory.* New Haven, Conn.: Yale University Press, 1963.

RICCI, DAVID. *Community Power and Democratic Theory: The Logic of Political Analysis.* New York: Random House, 1971.

SPIEGEL, HANS B. C., ed. *Citizen Participation in Urban Development.* Vol. 1: *Concepts and Issues.* Washington, D.C.: National Training Laboratories Institute for Applied Behavioral Science, 1968.

STEDMAN, MURRAY S., JR. *Urban Politics.* Cambridge, Mass.: Winthrop Publishers, Inc., 1972.

THOMAS, MRS. HARRY HARVEY, comp. *Simplified Parliamentary Procedure: Based on Robert's Rules of Order.* Washington, D.C.: League of Women Voters of the United States, 1971. Reprint.

U.S. ADVISORY COMMISSION ON INTERGOVERNMENTAL RELATIONS. *The New Grass Roots Government?* Washington, D.C.: Government Printing Office, 1972.

WARREN, ROLAND I. *The Community in American Life.* 2nd ed. Chicago: Rand McNally & Company, 1971.

WHITE, ORION, JR., and GATES, BRUCE L. "Statistical Theory and Equity in the Delivery of Social Services." *Public Administration Review* 34 (January/February 1974): 43–51.

WILLIAMS, ROBIN M., JR. *American Society: A Sociological Interpretation.* New York: Alfred A. Knopf, Inc., 1951.

8. Police Public Relations

ADAMS, THOMAS F., ed. *Criminal Justice Readings.* Pacific Palisades, Calif.: Goodyear Publishing Co., Inc., 1972.

AMERICAN BAR ASSOCIATION. *Standards for Criminal Justice: Standards in Relation to the Urban Police Function.* Chicago: American Bar Association, 1974.

BANTON, MICHAEL P. "Police." In *The New Encyclopedia Britannica.* 15th ed. Chicago: Encyclopedia Britannica, Inc., Helen Hemingway Benton, Publisher, 1974.

CUTLIP, SCOTT M., and CENTER, ALLEN H. *Effective Public Relations.* 4th ed. Englewood Cliffs, N.J.: Prentice-Hall, Inc., 1971.

DERNING, DON R., "The True Measures of Police/Public Relations." *The Police Chief,* March 1973, p. 8.

DIXON, SAMUEL, and TROJANOWICZ, ROBERT C. *Criminal Justice and the Community.* Englewood Cliffs, N.J.: Prentice-Hall, Inc., 1974.

GOLDSMITH, JACK, and GOLDSMITH, SHARON S., eds. *The Police Community: Dimensions of an Occupational Subculture.* Pacific Palisades, Calif.: Palisades Publishers, 1974.

MORE, HARRY W., ed. *Critical Issues in Law Enforcement.* Cincinnati: The W. H. Anderson Company, 1972.

PLATT, ROBERT M., ed. *The Concept of Police–Community Relations.* Kennedale, Tex.: The Criminal Justice Press, 1973.

RADELET, LOUIS A. "Public Information and Community Relations." In *Municipal Police Administration,* pp. 217–43. Edited by George D. Eastman and Esther M. Eastman. 7th ed. Washington, D.C.: International City Management Association, 1971.

WILSON, ORLANDO W., and MCLAREN, ROY C. *Police Administration.* 3rd ed. New York: McGraw-Hill Book Company, 1972.

9. The Role of Reporters and the Mass Media

BARBOUR, ROBERT L. *PR Blue Book.* 4th ed. Meriden, N.H.: PR Publishing Company, Inc., 1973.

COLE, JAMES K., ed. *Non-Verbal Communications: Nebraska Symposium on Motivation 1971.* Vol. 19. Lincoln: University of Nebraska Press, 1972.

COMMITTEE FOR ECONOMIC DEVELOPMENT. *Broadcasting and Cable Television: Policies for Diversity and Change.* New York: Committee for Economic Development, 1975.

"Communicating with the Communicators." *Public Management,* December 1970, entire issue.

DE SOLA POOL, ITHIEL, and SCHRAMM, WILBUR, eds. *Handbook of Communications.* Chicago: Rand McNally & Company, 1973.

ELLSWORTH, P. C., and LUDWIG, L. M. "Visual Behavior in Social Interaction." *Journal of Communication* 22 (December 1972): 375–403.

Hudson's Washington News Media Contacts Directory. Washington, D.C.: Hudson's Directory. Annual.

ISAACS, HAROLD. *Scratches on Our Minds.* New York: The John Day Company, Inc., 1958.

JACOB, PHILIP E., and TOSCANO, JAMES P. *Integration of Political Communities.* Philadelphia: J. B. Lippincott, Co., 1964.

JACOBS, HERBERT. *Practical Publicity: A Handbook for Public and Private Workers.* New York: McGraw-Hill Book Company, 1964.

KINTNER, R. E. "TV and the World of Politics." *Harper's,* May 1965, pp. 121–23.

KLEIN, TED, and DANZIG, FRED. *How To Be Heard: Making the Media Work for You.* New York: The Macmillan Company, 1974.

KLENSIN, JOHN C., and NAGLE, JOHN D. *Mass Media Stimulation Program: User's Manual.* Cambridge, Mass.: Massachusetts Institute of Technology, Center for International Studies, 1969.

MCLUHAN, MARSHALL. *Understanding the Media.* New York: McGraw-Hill Book Company, 1964.

NORTON, ALICE. *Public Relations: Guide to Information Sources.* Detroit: Gale Research, 1970.

O'Dwyer's Directory of Public Relations Firms. New York: Jack O'Dwyer, Publisher. Annual.

"Public Relations in Local Government." Speech by William H. Gilbert, Director of Public Affairs, Metropolitan Washington Council of Governments, at the Middle Atlantic Institute for Executive Training, University of Delaware, March 9, 1970.

"A Public Relations Program for a Regional Council." Speech by William H. Gilbert, Director of Public Affairs, Metropolitan Washington Council of Governments, to the National Association of Regional Councils, at New Orleans, Louisiana, March 10, 1971.

SCANDLYN, SAMMIE LYNN. *101 Ways to Better Municipal Public Relations.* Washington, D.C.: National League of Cities, 1967.

STAHR, JOHN. *Write to the Point: The Byoir Style Book for Press Material.* New York: The Macmillan Company, 1969.

STARRETT, PETER. *Communication for Local Officials*. Tempe: Arizona State University Institute of Public Administration, 1970.

WALL, NED L. *Municipal Reporting to the Public*. Chicago: International City Managers' Association, 1963.

WEINER, RICHARD. *News Bureaus in the U.S.* New York: Richard Weiner, Inc., 1974.

———. *Professional's Guide to Publicity*. New York: Richard Weiner, Inc., 1975.

Who's Who in Public Relations. 4th ed. Meriden, N.H.: PR Publishing Company, Inc., 1972.

10. Special Reports and Events

FOWLER, FLOYD J., JR. *Citizen Attitudes toward Local Government Services and Taxes*. Cambridge, Mass.: Ballinger Publishing Company, 1974.

GOLDEN, H., and HANSON, K. *How To Plan, Produce, and Publicize Special Events*. Dobbs Ferry, N.Y.: Oceana Publications, Inc., 1960.

HENRY, ALBERT C., and WEBER, EDWIN W. *Handbook for the Preparation of an Annual Progress Report*. Kingston: University of Rhode Island, Bureau of Government Research, 1963.

LIEBERT, E., and SHELDON, B. *Handbook of Special Events for Nonprofit Organizations*. New York: Association Press, 1972.

MATTHEWS, LEMPI K. *Making the Most of Your Annual Report*. Chicago: Public Personnel Association, 1963.

METROPOLITAN WASHINGTON COUNCIL OF GOVERNMENTS. *Think Public!* Washington, D.C.: Metropolitan Washington Council of Governments, 1975.

NATIONAL ASSOCIATION OF REGIONAL COUNCILS. *Regional Council Communications: A Guide to Issues and Techniques*. Washington, D.C.: National Association of Regional Councils, 1973.

11. Publications Planning, Development, and Production

AMERICAN SOCIETY OF MECHANICAL ENGINEERS. *American Standard Time Series Charts*. New York: American Society of Mechanical Engineers, 1960. ASA Y15.2–1960. Authoritative technical guide.

ARNOLD, DAVID S., and SLOBIN, HERBERT. *City Graphic Identification Programs*. Management Information Service Reports, vol. 4 no. 12 (December 1972). Washington, D.C.: International City Management Association, 1972. Shows how to develop and manage standard graphic elements for consistent visual identification of publications and other municipal activities. Specific, practical, well illustrated.

BERNSTEIN, THEODORE M. *The Careful Writer: A Modern Guide to English Usage*. New York: Atheneum Publishers, 1966. Discussion of word usages, in alphabetical order, with examples and descriptions. Clear, direct, unpretentious.

FOWLER, H. W. *A Dictionary of Modern English Usage*. 2nd ed., revised by Sir Ernest Gowers. New York: Oxford University Press, 1965. The classic work on English usage. Helpful on precise use of words and on difficult questions involving that–which, split infinitives, shall–will, etc.

HUFF, DARRELL, and GEIS, IRVING. *How To Lie with Statistics*. New York: W. W. Norton and Company, 1954. A primer on the traps and pitfalls in presenting statistics both in tabular and graphic form. The text, by Huff, and the drawings, by Geis, blend into an enjoyable and informative book.

INTERNATIONAL PAPER COMPANY. *paper'n graphics*. New York: International Paper Company, 1974. Unpaged booklet with useful information on paper and envelope sizes, paper weights and grades, and copy fitting.

———. *Pocket Pal: A Graphic Arts Digest for Printers and Advertising Production Managers*. 10th ed. New York: International Paper Company, 1970. Excellent introduction to printing processes, copy preparation, photography, plates, printing, binding, and ink. Glossary.

LEE, MARSHALL. *Bookmaking: The Illustrated Guide to Design and Production*. New York: R. R. Bowker Co., 1965. The best book for learning about all aspects of composition, printing, and binding. Also an excellent reference on publication design, whether you are going to do it yourself or work with a professional designer.

NATIONAL ASSOCIATION OF REGIONAL COUNCILS. *Regional Council Communications: A Guide to Issues and Techniques.* Washington, D.C.: National Association of Regional Councils, 1973. Chapters on communications programs, working with the media, audiovisuals, and other subjects. Includes useful chapter on "Making the Most of Your Publications." Especially helpful on newsletter writing and layout.

O'HAYRE, JOHN. *Gobbledygook Has Gotta Go.* Washington, D.C.: Government Printing Office, n.d. Written with commitment and wit by an employee of the Bureau of Land Management, U.S. Department of the Interior. Helpful in writing clear news releases on complex, technical subjects that have public impact.

PERRIN, PORTER G. *Writer's Guide and Index to English.* 4th ed. Chicago: Scott, Foresman and Company, 1965. Textbook for the beginning writer. Covers grammar, punctuation, spelling, paragraph construction, sentence form, etc. Also includes detailed index with entries on grammar, word usage, and manuscript preparation.

SCHMID, CALVIN F. *Handbook of Graphic Presentation.* New York: The Ronald Press Company, 1954. Chapters on line, bar, and ratio charts; frequency graphs; pie charts and other forms; maps; pictorial charts; and drafting techniques and equipment. Well written and amply illustrated.

SPEAR, MARY ELEANOR. *Practical Charting Techniques.* New York: McGraw-Hill Book Company, 1969. Practical manual covering line, surface, column, and bar charts; pie charts, flow charts, and other special forms; maps; and pictorial symbols and diagrams. Guides for planning, layout, and equipment. Profusely illustrated. Highly recommended.

SPENCER, HERBERT. *The Visible Word.* 2nd ed., rev. New York: Hastings House, Publishers, 1969. Review and analysis of extensive legibility research carried out in many countries during the past century to improve the efficiency of typographic communication. Clear-cut findings are few but helpful.

STRAUSS, VICTOR. *The Printing Industry: An Introduction to Its Many Branches, Processes, and Products.* Washington, D.C.: Printing Industries of America, Inc., 1967. A printing manual that explains the complexities of modern graphic arts methods and offers a comprehensive definition of their relationships to each other. Well illustrated.

TURABIAN, KATE L. *A Manual for Writers of Term Papers, Theses, and Dissertations.* 4th ed. Chicago: University of Chicago Press, 1973. A simplified version of much of the material found in the University of Chicago's *A Manual of Style.* Ideal for students and for those new to the publications field.

STRUNK, WILLIAM, JR., and WHITE, E. B. *The Elements of Style.* New York: The Macmillan Company, 1959. A small book, elegantly written, with factual advice on developing a clear expository style.

U.S. National Institutes of Health. Division of Research Grants. Statistics and Analysis Branch. Statistical Analysis and Surveys Section. *Manual of Statistical Presentation.* Statistical DRG Items, no. 10. Washington, D.C.: Government Printing Office, 1970. Section on "Presentation of Tables," pages 25–47, is a good brief guide to techniques of table construction.

U.S. Postal Service. *Mailer's Guide.* Washington, D.C.: U.S. Postal Service, 1974. A practical guide to services and rates offered by the Postal Service.

UNIVERSITY OF CHICAGO PRESS. *A Manual of Style.* 12th ed., rev. Chicago: University of Chicago Press, 1969. The most widely used reference of its kind. Authoritative treatment of punctuation, capitalization, use of quotations, abbreviations, and documentation. Although it is intended primarily for book work, much of the information is useful for any kind of publication.

VANCE, JOHN E. *Information Communication Handbook: Policies for Working with the Media.*

Minneapolis: Viking Press, Inc., 1973. Useful information on newsletters and other publications; intended primarily for quick release of information to news media.

WALL, NED L. *Municipal Reporting to the Public.* Chicago: International City Managers' Association, 1963. Excellent information on all aspects of the annual municipal report, including illustrations, typography, and layout. 88 illustrations.

WEBB, WALTER L. *Presenting the Budget Document.* Management Information Service Reports, no. 232 (May 1963). Chicago: International City Managers' Association, 1963. Good suggestions on format, illustrations, and writing an effective budget message.

Webster's New Collegiate Dictionary. Springfield, Mass.: G. & C. Merriam Company, 1973. Widely used desk-top dictionary. Especially good on synonyms and cross references to help pin down the precise meaning of words. Eighth in the Collegiate series.

12. Organizing and Training for Public Relations

CANFIELD, BERTRAND R., and MOORE, H. FRAZIER. *Public Relations: Principles, Cases and Problems.* 6th ed. Homewood, Ill.: Richard D. Irwin, Inc., 1973.

FENN, DAN H., JR. "Executives as Community Volunteers." *Harvard Business Review* 71 (March–April 1971): 4–16, 156–57.

HIEBERT, RAY ELDON. *Trends in Public Relations Education, 1964–70.* New York: Foundation for Public Relations Research and Education, 1971.

LEWIS, MORRIS L. "New Citizen Roles in Local Government." *National Civic Review* 62 (July 1973): 390–93.

PFIFFNER, JOHN M. *The Supervision of Personnel.* Englewood Cliffs, N.J.: Prentice-Hall, Inc., 1958.

ROSS, DONALD K. *A Public Citizen's Action Manual.* New York: Grossman Publishers, 1973.

STRANGE, JOHN H., ed. "Citizens Action in Model Cities and CAP Programs: Case Studies and Evaluations." *Public Administration Review* 32 (September 1972): entire issue.

TURECK, MARION C. "Municipal Public Relations in 1966." In *The Municipal Year Book 1967*, pp. 242–75. Chicago: International City Managers' Association, 1967.

———. *Organization and Operation of Public Relations Programs.* Management Information Service Reports, no. 282 (July 1967). Chicago: International City Managers' Association, 1967.

WEBB, KENNETH, and HATRY, HARRY P. *Obtaining Citizen Feedback: The Application of Citizen Surveys to Local Governments.* Washington, D.C.: The Urban Institute, 1973.

List of Contributors

Persons who have contributed to this book are listed below with the editor first and the authors following in alphabetical order. A brief review of experience, training, and major points of interest in each person's background is presented. Since most of the contributors have published extensively, books, monographs, articles, or other publications are listed for the editor only, but are omitted for the other contributors.

WILLIAM H. GILBERT (Editor, and Chapters 1, 3, 9, and 10) is Director of Public Affairs for the Metropolitan Washington Council of Governments, a position he has held since 1965. Mr. Gilbert began his career in 1947 as a copy boy on the sports staff of the *Washington Post*. He became a sports writer and later a news room reporter for the same paper. During the Korean War he spent four years in the Air Force as an information specialist. He has held positions as Director of Information for the Montgomery County, Maryland, government, Promotion Director for the Washington Senators baseball team, and Public Affairs Officer for the U.S. Department of Defense. He is co-author of *Keep Off My Turf*, with Mike Curtis of the Baltimore Colts, and co-author of *All These Mornings*, with columnist Shirley Povich.

DESMOND L. ANDERSON (Chapter 1) is Mayor of Logan, Utah. Before that, he was Academic Adviser, National Institute of Administration of Vietnam (U.S. Department of State, Agency for Internal Development). From 1962 to 1966 he was Associate Dean, School of Public Administration, University of Southern California. He was with the University of Southern California in a number of teaching, research, and administrative capacities. For many years he served as a training and management consultant to the state of California and to a number of local governments in that state. He has served on the National Council of the American Society for Public Administration. Dr. Anderson holds bachelor's and master's degrees from Utah State University and a doctorate in public administration from the University of Southern California.

DAVID S. ARNOLD (Chapter 11) is Director, Publications Center, the International City Management Association. He has been with ICMA since 1949 with a variety of responsibilities in research, editing, writing, and publications production. From 1943 to 1949 he was on the field staff of Public Administration Service. He has been President, the Chicago Chapter, American Society for Public Administration. He holds a bachelor's degree from Lafayette College and a master's in public administration from the Maxwell Graduate School, Syracuse University.

ROBERT B. CALLAHAN (Chapters 5 and 12) is currently Professor of Political Science and Public Administration at California State College at Los Angeles, where he has also held various administrative positions since coming there in 1960, including Director of Peace Corps Programs and Director of Admissions. From 1950 to 1958 he was an administrator with the U.S. Department of Health, Education, and Welfare, and also served as public relations consultant to federal, state, and local agencies. From 1958 to 1960 he was Assistant Director of the Civic Center Campus, University of Southern California. He also has taught in public administration. He holds two bachelor's degrees, a master's degree, and a doctorate in public administration—all from the University of Southern California.

ROBERT M. CHRISTOFFERSON (Chapter 12) is City Manager of Salinas, California. He was City Administrator of Covina, California, from

1968 to 1972, and of San Dimas, California, from 1965 to 1968. From 1956 to 1965 he was Assistant to the City Manager of Glendale, California. He holds a bachelor's degree from the University of California at Santa Barbara and a master's in public administration from the University of Southern California. In 1955 he held a Coro Foundation Internship in Public Affairs in San Francisco. Mr. Christofferson has lectured in public administration at the University of Southern California and is currently a lecturer in the graduate school of public administration at Golden Gate University.

RAY ELDON HIEBERT (Chapter 2) has been Dean of the College of Journalism at the University of Maryland since January 1973. From 1968 through 1972 he served as Chairman and Professor of the Department of Journalism at the University of Maryland, during which time it became a college. He was founding Director of the Washington Journalism Center and is a former Professor and Chairman of the Department of Journalism, Public Relations, and Broadcasting at the American University, Washington, D.C. He also taught English and journalism at the University of Minnesota, Duluth. He is vice chairman of the Montgomery County Citizens' Commission on Cable Television and a trustee of the Foundation for Public Relations Research and Education. Dean Hiebert received his B.A. from Stanford University, an M.S. from Columbia University's Graduate School of Journalism, and an M.A. and a Ph.D. in American Studies from the University of Maryland.

ROBERT J. HUNTLEY (Chapter 3) is City Administrator of the city of Westminster, California. He was formerly Director of Real Estate Development for Alpha Beta Acme Markets, Inc., San Leandro, California. He was Administrative Officer (city manager) for La Habra, California, from 1959 to 1964, and prior to that had served as city administrator of Santa Paula, administrative assistant in Beverly Hills, and research technician in Los Angeles. He holds a master's degree and a doctorate in public administration from the University of Southern California and has taught courses in public ad-

ministration at several colleges and universities.

RALPH N. IVES (Chapter 11) is Vice-President, McArdle Printing Company, Inc., in Washington, D.C. He was formerly Vice-President, Boyce Morgan Associates, consultants in publishing and direct mail, and has been assistant to a publisher of business magazines. He has taught typography at the Chicago campus of Northwestern University. He is a past President of the Mail Advertising Club of Washington, D.C., and is currently Vice Chairman of the Washington Metropolitan Postal Customer Council. He holds a bachelor's degree from Carnegie Institute of Technology (now Carnegie Mellon University). In 1965 he received the Direct Mail Man of the Year Award of the Mail Advertising Club of Washington.

GARTH N. JONES (Chapters 4 and 7) is Professor of Public Policy and Administration, and also Head, Division of Business, Economics, and Public Administration, University of Alaska at Anchorage. From 1972 to 1973 he was Population Specialist, Public Administration Division, United Nations, New York; from 1970 to 1972 he was Professor of Political Science at Colorado State University. He was Senior Scholar, East–West Center, Hawaii, in 1969–70, and Chief of the Public Administration Division, AID, in Pakistan, 1967–69. Before that, he was Associate Professor, School of Public Administration, University of Southern California. He has held other university teaching posts and various research and consulting assignments with such agencies as the U.S. Department of Agriculture and the Trust Territory of the Pacific Islands. He holds a bachelor's degree from Utah State University and master's and doctor's degrees in political science from the University of Utah.

DAVID J. KELLY (chapter 9) is a commentator and investigative reporter for Station WIIC–TV in Pittsburgh. A veteran of over twenty-five years in the news and writing professions, he began as a reporter for the *Washington Post* and later the *Pittsburgh Press*. He has been radio news director and television news director for Station KDKA in Pittsburgh, and news director for Station WIIC, in Pittsburgh, and has been news director of Station WWJ–TV in Detroit. Before taking his present post, he was news director for Station WMAL–TV in Washington, D.C. A graduate of the University of Maryland, Mr. Kelly has won numerous awards both for his writing and as a news director: he was twice given the National Headliners Club Award for directing the nation's "best news operation."

NORMAN E. POMRENKE (Chapter 8) is Director of Public Safety for the city of Winston-Salem, North Carolina. He received his B.S. from Michigan State University, and his master's from Florida State University. His law enforcement operational experience has been with the cities of Oakland, California, and Baltimore, Maryland, and with Florida State University and the University of North Carolina. He is the author of numerous law-enforcement-related publications, and has served as consultant to several federal programs, including the President's Crime Commission. Mr. Pomrenke has also lectured at several universities and at the F.B.I. Academy.

THOMAS A. SURRATT (chapter 8) is now Vice Chairman of the North Carolina Criminal Justice Training and Standards Council and serves on several of its committees. He is past President of the North Carolina Police Executive Association and serves on the Board of Directors. He has received training at the Institute of Government, University of North Carolina, Chapel Hill; Northwestern Traffic Institute, Evanston, Illinois; Wake Forest University, Winston-Salem; and the University of Georgia at Athens. Chief Surratt is a member of the Exchange Club and has served as past President of that organization.

NANCY J. WOLFE (chapters 6 and 8) is Director of Public Relations for the City of Winston-Salem. She received her B.S. degree from the University of Vermont and her M.S. from Southern Illinois University. She was Director of Information for High Schools in Vermont and Colorado, and has been active in the United Fund, the Winston-Salem Arts Council, the Altrusa Club, the Forsyth Extension Advisory Board, and the Forsyth Community Development. She is President of the Public Relations Roundtable of Winston-Salem, is Chairman of the Government Section of the Public Relations Society of America, and has recently received the George C. Franklin award in municipal administration.

Index

MUNICIPAL MANAGEMENT SERIES
Public Relations in
Local Government

TEXT TYPE:
VideoComp Baskerville

COMPOSITION, PRINTING, AND BINDING:
Kingsport Press, Kingsport, Tennessee

PAPER:
P&S White Offset A–69

PRODUCTION:
Emily Evershed

DESIGN:
Herbert Slobin